Low-carbon, Sustainable Future in East Asia

T0295570

East Asia is a key region in the global economy, containing both the second and third largest global economies and, led by China, continuing to expand at a rapid rate. This economic growth has led to unprecedented gains in prosperity in the region, but it has also led to increasing environmental pressures and energy issues.

This book assesses ways in which East Asia can continue or even increase existing rates of economic growth while at the same time reducing greenhouse gas emissions and other environmental degradation. Using advanced modeling approaches, future scenarios for four East Asian countries are assessed in detail, including analysis of particular challenges in each country (e.g., coal power in China, nuclear power in Japan). Prospects for each country's energy system are assessed in detail, and the potential effects of various types of environmental tax reform in the four countries are also considered carefully. The final section of the book explores the interaction between trade liberalization, a key driver of growth, and emission levels in the East Asia region.

Soocheol Lee is a professor in the faculty of economics at Meijo University, Japan. He graduated from Seoul National University and received his PhD at the Graduate School of Kyoto University. He has published many books and papers on sustainable low carbon economy in East Asia.

Hector Pollitt is a director and head of international modeling at Cambridge Econometrics. He has extensive expertise in the development and application of macroeconomic modeling approaches for policy assessment.

Park Seung-Joon is a professor in the School of Policy Studies at Kwansei Gakuin University, Japan. He specializes in environmental economics and policies, especially in the field of the environmental tax reform and energy policies, and has published several books and papers in this field.

Routledge Studies in the Modern World Economy

Low-carbon, Sustainable Future in East Asia

Improving energy systems, taxation and policy cooperation

Edited by Soocheol Lee,
Hector Pollitt and Park Seung-Joon

Routledge
Taylor & Francis Group

LONDON AND NEW YORK

First published 2016
Routledge
2 Park Square, Milton Park, Abingdon, Oxon OX14 4RN

and Routledge
711 Third Avenue, New York, NY 10017

First issued in paperback 2017

*Routledge is an imprint of the Taylor & Francis Group,
an informa business*

British Library Cataloguing in Publication Data
A catalogue record for this book is available from the British
Library

Library of Congress Cataloging-in-Publication Data
Low-carbon, sustainable future in East Asia : improving energy
   systems, taxation and policy cooperation / edited by Soocheol
   Lee, Hector Pollitt and Park Seung-Joon.
      pages cm
   1. Energy policy—East Asia.   2. Environmental policy—East
Asia.   3. Sustainable development—East Asia.   4. Environmental
impact charges—East Asia.   I. Lee, Soocheol.
   HD9502.E182L69 2015
      338.95′07—dc23
      2015011522

ISBN 13: 978-0-8153-5072-9 (pbk)
ISBN 13: 978-1-138-78209-9 (hbk)

Typeset in Galliard
by Apex CoVantage, LLC

Contents

Figures

Tables

Notes on contributors

Eva Alexandri is a senior researcher at Cambridge Econometrics, United Kingdom.

Hikari Ban is a professor at Kobe Gakuin University, Japan.

Terry Barker is the chairman of Cambridge Econometrics, United Kingdom.

Li-Chun Chen is a professor at Yamaguchi University, Japan.

Unnada Chewpreecha is a manager at Cambridge Econometrics, United Kingdom.

Akihiro Chiashi is a researcher at Kyoto University, Japan.

Yongsung Cho is a professor at Korea University, South Korea.

Paul Ekins is a professor at University College London, United Kingdom.

Kiyoshi Fujikawa is a professor at Nagoya University, Japan.

Alicia Higson is a senior macro-economist based in London, United Kingdom.

Emiko Inoue is a senior lecturer at Kyoto University, Japan.

Yoshifumi Ishikawa is a professor at Nanzan University, Japan.

Takeshi Kawakatsu is an associate professor at Kyoto Prefectural University, Japan.

Seonghee Kim is a senior researcher at the Institute of Energy Economics, Japan.

Soocheol Lee is a professor at Meijo University, Japan.

Tae-Yeoun Lee is a professor at Ryukoku University, Japan.

Shih-Mo Lin is a professor at Chung Yuan Christian University, Taiwan.

Xianbing Liu is a senior researcher at the Institute for Global Environmental Strategies, Japan.

Ken'ichi Matsumoto is an assistant professor at The University of Shiga Prefecture, Japan.

Jean-François Mercure is a senior research associate at Cambridge University, United Kingdom.

Sung-in Na is a professor at Hiroshima Shudo University, Japan.

Yuki Ogawa is a graduate student at Kyoto University, Japan.

Jun Pang is an associate professor at Renmin University of China, China.

Jiro Sakurai is an associate professor at Kobe City University of Foreign Studies, Japan.

Park Seung-Joon is a professor at Kwansei Gakuin University, Japan.

Hector Pollitt is a director at Cambridge Econometrics, United Kingdom.

Lisa Ryan is a researcher at University College Dublin, Ireland.

Yuri Sadoi is a professor at Meijo University, Japan.

Sunhee Suk is a policy researcher at the Institute for Global Environmental Strategies, Japan.

Kazuhiro Ueta is a professor at Kyoto University, Japan.

Hiroshi Yoshida is an associate professor at Tokyo University of Agriculture and Technology, Japan.

Foreword

This book provides a very welcome addition to the literature on policies affecting energy and environmental futures in East Asia.

All countries now have very difficult choices to be made about how to develop their energy systems. What is now widely called the 'trilemma' of energy requires decisions to be made on the sometimes competing policy priorities of energy security, energy affordability, and the reduction of emissions of greenhouse gases, especially of the main greenhouse gas – carbon dioxide – from the use of fossil energy.

It is no exaggeration to say that East Asia is the part of the world where the effort to mitigate climate change – and in particular to keep open the option of limiting average global warming to 2°C – will be won or lost. All countries, obviously, have their role to play and, being at different stages of development, these roles will be different. It goes without saying that the choices that China makes, as the world's largest greenhouse gas emitter and largest economy in purchasing power parity terms, will be key. It is already making some of these choices in terms of the huge development and deployment of renewable energy technologies that it has implemented. China is making ambitious commitments in respect of its intended nationally determined contributions (INDCs) to the global climate change mitigation effort under the UN Framework Convention on Climate Change. The government intends to ensure that national carbon dioxide emissions will peak by 2030, if not before, implying early adoption of strong abatement policies. And it is clear that the co-benefits of China moving away from coal in power generation, in terms of improved local air quality, would be immense, and provide an additional incentive for it to go down this route.

Japan faces its own challenges following the Fukushima tragedy of 2011. Many less resilient countries would have buckled completely under the impact of such a shock. It is greatly to Japan's credit that it continues to sustain a disciplined and democratic discussion about the best way to recover from the disaster, and to be committed to a low-carbon development pathway. The compatibility of the low-carbon society with a nuclear reduction policy is examined in this book. Less traumatically, Korea, too, has difficult decisions to take about the desirable balance between different sources of energy but, again, in a context of determination to pursue green growth leading to a low-carbon economy.

The analyses in the book are mainly concerned with economy-wide implications of policies and measures, using models of the economies and their energy systems and emissions. The book includes analyses using both simulation models of the economies, including input-output models, as well as optimizing equilibrium models. The book will be helpful to those interested in the different approaches of simulation and optimization because it gives insights as to their different results and capabilities. The differences become especially significant when the low-carbon policies are a mixture of regulation and carbon taxation or emission trading, since equilibrium models normally include the assumption that markets are efficient so that regulation is costly and reduces output, whereas simulation models recognize that economies operate in conditions of uncertainty, incomplete information and ongoing technological change, so that regulation can improve performance.

This book generates great insights into all these issues, and its publication in a critical year in the process of global climate change is especially important. We hope and believe that it will prove a very useful source of evidence and knowledge for scholars, national policy makers in the region, and all those interested in how the world will address the issue of climate change, both in this year and thereafter.

Paul Ekins, Kazuhiro Ueta, and Terry Barker
February 2015

Introduction

This book describes and assesses the current situation and policies that are aimed at the development of sustainable, low-carbon economies in East Asia. We consider how existing policies, including carbon and energy taxes and regulations on nuclear power, compare with those of the rest of the world, and how they could be improved upon. Our analysis is carried out in the context of the region's growing economic and environmental interdependence, which is likely to increase in the future, for example due to international free-trade agreements for finance and services, the Trans-Pacific Partnership, and the China-Japan-Korea Free Trade Agreements.

In recent decades, East Asia has become established as a key part of the global economy. The region now includes both the second and third largest global economies at market exchange rates, and it seems only a matter of time before China passes the US to become the world's largest economy.

The rapid growth in living standards in China and the number of people removed from poverty is almost unprecedented in history and has undoubtedly improved the lives of hundreds of millions of people. Such rapid growth has brought new social and environmental challenges that are increasingly becoming the focus of new policies in China. At the same time, the other major economy in the region, Japan, has gone through a period of economic stagnation that is, in part, due to a declining and ageing population. Although there have been some signs of recovery as a result of 'Abenomics,' Japan faces its own unique challenges that, after the nuclear disaster in 2011, include determining its future energy supply.

In this book we focus on four countries or regions[1] in East Asia, including Korea[2] and Taiwan, as well as China and Japan (Korea and Taiwan were the world's 15th and 25th largest economies in 2013, respectively, according to IMF statistics). Current estimates show that, in total, the four countries are home to 21–22 percent of the world's population and economic production.

Less positively, the East Asia region now accounts for almost one-third of global CO_2 emissions (excluding emissions from land-use change). As described in Chapter 1 of this book, the majority of this share originates in China, where coal-fired electricity generation has grown rapidly to fuel the manufacturing sector. However, if Japan replaces its nuclear fleet with fossil-fuel-based plants then it, too, could see its share of global emissions rise. The other countries in the region are also facing decisions on how to develop their energy systems, particularly relating to electricity generation and transport.

In our assessments in this book, we employ a variety of analytical approaches, including the application of advanced energy–environment–economy (E3) models so as to get scientific answers for our three main research issues. Two distinct types of modeling are introduced in Chapter 2, and used throughout this book:

- A macro-econometric approach
- Computable general equilibrium (CGE) modeling

We use the E3ME-Asia[3] model for a macro-econometric approach and, in some chapters, employ CGE models. The E3ME-Asia model, which is based on the E3ME model developed by Cambridge Econometrics,[4] was built to analyze the subjects of this book as part of a two-year collaboration between the Research Group for East Asia Environmental Policy Studies (REEPS) and Cambridge Econometrics.

A key feature of this book is the comparison of results from two models with different structures and backgrounds. However, the scope of the analysis is not limited to macroeconomic modeling. Throughout the book, other quantitative approaches are applied, including data analysis, input–output techniques, and a separate simulation of the energy system. And not all impacts may be quantified; at various points we also consider in detail the qualitative effects of policies that are designed to promote low-carbon development and 'green' growth. This book is written for both readers who are familiar with the modeling techniques and those who are not familiar with them – an effort has been made to explain the approaches so that the non-expert can understand what the book describes easily.

The book identifies three major questions concerning the pathway to a future in East Asia that is environmentally sustainable; each is allocated its own section.

The first question is 'how should East Asia choose its energy and power sources?' Thus, in Part 1 of the book we discuss the energy system, as overall decarbonization will not be possible without a substantial reduction in emissions from the energy supply sector. As we shall explore, at present there are a range of policy measures in place to promote the use of renewables in East Asia that could be expanded (Chapters 3–4), but the possible role for nuclear power and renewable energies (Chapter 5) remains controversial. In the first part of the book we also discuss the often-neglected issue of energy efficiency (Chapter 6) and cover the related issue of energy security (Chapter 7).

The second question is 'how could East Asian countries design energy/carbon taxes or other carbon-pricing instruments?' In Part 2 of the book, we assess the potential for Environmental Tax Reform (ETR) and carbon pricing in East Asia. The use of market-based instruments in climate policy is becoming more common worldwide but is still in its development phase in East Asia. Several different scenarios of possible designs of ETR considering the possibility of 'double dividend' are explored in Chapter 8, and they are compared to previous analyses in Chapter 9. This second section of the book also considers related issues, such as fiscal deficits (Chapter 10), social distributional impacts (Chapter 11), and the effects of human capital investment (Chapter 12). In the final two chapters of this section we discuss the difficult question of competitiveness (Chapter 13) and look at one of the potential instruments, border tax adjustments, which could address the issue of carbon leakage (Chapter 14).

The third question is 'how should East Asia choose and coordinate low-carbon policies in the tide of free trade?' Thus, Part 3 of the book considers the relationship between energy/climate policy and international trade. Recent growth in prosperity in East Asia has, in part, been due to increases in trade between countries within the region, and several new deals are currently on the table. As we shall see in this section, the interactions through trade are both complex and growing in importance, with the urgent need for a new view on the 'national responsibility for emissions' and for coordination of policy between countries. In Part 3, we then move on to the issue of who is responsible for current emissions and demonstrate the calculation of consumption-based CO_2 emissions instead of the conventional production-based emissions (Chapters 15–16) and CO_2 emissions from the international maritime sector (Chapter 17). Finally, we show that increased trade presents both opportunities and challenges in the development of sustainable and prosperous economies in East Asia (Chapter 18–19).

Whereas each of the three issues has been allocated its own section in the book, readers will find that the interactions between them are strong, and that they cannot be addressed in isolation. The concluding chapter, therefore, considers possible future policy options for East Asia across all three areas. The ultimate aim of the book is to improve the fundamental understanding of possible future energy and environmental initiatives and, thus, to facilitate improved policy coordination between the countries in East Asia.

We believe that our collection of analyses will provide valuable insight to our three key research issues, and that we have opened the door to further detailed analyses of possible policies and pathways – including assessments using E3 models – leading to a sustainable low-carbon future in East Asia. We view our contribution as work-in-progress and are very much looking forward to feedback from our readers.

This book is the synthesis of a collaborative study by the members of REEPS and the staff at Cambridge Econometrics during the last two-and-a-half years. The discussions included six intensive workshops (four in Japan and two in Cambridge) and countless electronic discussions. The book is financially supported by Grants-in-Aid for Scientific Research of the Japanese Society for the xxvi*Soocheol Lee et al.*

Promotion of Science. We would like to take this opportunity to thank the Society for this support deeply.

On the behalf of authors of this book,
September 2015
Soocheol Lee, Hector Pollitt,
and Park Seung-Joon

Notes

1 The terms 'countries' and 'regions' are used here to accommodate the China–Taiwan issue, which makes it problematic to simply call Taiwan a country. Throughout this book, 'countries and regions' will be abbreviated to just 'countries' for the sake of simplicity. The authors and editors would like to state clearly that they understand the complexity of the issue, and are by no means making any statement about the statehood of Taiwan by use of the word 'countries.'
2 In this book, when we say Korea, we are referring to South Korea.
3 E3ME stands for energy-environment-economy model that is econometric in design.
4 See http://www.camecon.com.

1 Energy systems and environmental policy in East Asia

Soocheol Lee, Xianbing Liu, Ken'ichi Matsumoto, Sung-in Na, and Li-Chun Chen

1.1 Overview

In recent years, East Asian countries have pushed for environmental and energy policy reforms, moving towards sustainable low-carbon economies and 'green growth' models.[1] Policies have been planned or introduced both to price carbon and to support the generation of electricity from renewable technologies. In 2012, Japan introduced feed-in tariffs (FITs) and the first carbon tax in the region; Korea introduced a renewable portfolio standard (RPS) in 2012 and started an emission trading scheme (ETS) in 2015; China held discussions in 2012 for introducing a carbon tax, reforming the resource tax, and introducing ETS; and Taiwan has current plans for a renewable energy policy reform.

However, at 289 yen per ton CO_2, the carbon tax rate in Japan is extremely low and far-off from environmental tax reforms (ETR) realized in some European countries. It is even below the price set by the EU ETS (€5–10/tCO2). Although an introduction of ETS in Japan has been discussed within the government, it has not yet been implemented because of strong resistance from business circles, such as Keidanren. ETS in Korea – the first one at national level in East Asia – has been watered down considerably and is very lenient toward industries (which will receive 100 percent free allowances from 2015–2017). A carbon tax is still under discussion and its introduction remains uncertain.

Carbon taxes in China and Taiwan are faced with political resistance and are not likely to be introduced in the near future. These situations show that barriers to policy and institutional reform to achieve a low-carbon economy are very difficult to overcome, in particular because of the political resistance from business circles that relate to international competitiveness issues. In summary, almost none of the societal cost of carbon in East Asia is currently reflected in market prices. Subsidization of low-carbon technologies, appliances, and so on are still the main incentive-based system in East Asia.

There are also other factors that contribute to the challenge for policy makers. In particular, the Fukushima Daiichi Nuclear Power Plant accident in 2011 had a large impact on the National Energy Plan of Japan. The accident significantly shook people's faith in nuclear power, and the previous Japanese government came under pressure to introduce a zero-nuclear plan by 2030. But the – in December 2012 newly elected – Abe government later declared nuclear power to be an essential energy source and, therefore, one that should be kept. Other East Asian countries were also affected by the Fukushima accident; public opinion led to the Korean government forming a New National Energy Plan in 2014 to reduce the share of nuclear power generation from originally 55 percent to 29 percent in 2030. By contrast, the Chinese government has not changed its current plan to expand nuclear power (see Table 1.1), and the Taiwanese government is trying to keep the current share of nuclear power, although it is faced with strong popular opposition.

If nuclear power is reduced, decarbonization of the electricity sector is dependent on renewables.[2] East Asian countries have introduced policies to develop and support renewable technologies and to promote low-carbon energy sources and green technology innovation. Japan changed its renewables policy from RPS to FIT in 2012 in an attempt to dramatically speed up the adoption of renewables. Korea changed back its renewable supporting policy from FIT to RPS to meet the 2022 renewable target of a 10 percent share in electricity generation (currently it is 3–4 percent, including conventional hydropower). After the policy changes, both countries experienced a sharp increase in the use of renewables – mainly solar photovoltaic panels (solar PV panels). But in Japan, the FIT has led to unpopular increases in electricity prices (i.e., a monthly 225 JPY 'renewable charge' per household that consumed 300 kWh per month in 2014), whereas Korea has seen a decline of small- and medium-sized renewable energy companies under the RPS (Jeong and Lee, 2014).

China also has an ambitious renewable energy target, with primary energy supply comprising a 15 percent share of renewable energy in 2020 and 10,000 MW from PV by 2030. Taiwan also has a very high target regarding renewable energy supply, a 15 percent share of renewable energy for its total power generation, 1,000 MW from PV and 3,000 MW from wind power by 2025.

Therefore, over the next decade there are likely to be quite profound changes to the ways in which energy is consumed in East Asia. Due to 'lock-in' effects, the decisions made in the coming years could result in lasting consequences; therefore, it is important for East Asian countries to create an institutional system that properly assesses the social costs and benefits of different power sources in addition to conventional economic gains. For example, the cost of nuclear power generation with improved safety standards, the risks associated with nuclear power generation, and a reexamination of relevant damage-compensation laws should be adequately evaluated. However, it is also essential to evaluate the social benefits of renewable energy, which include safety, sustainability and environmental friendliness, promotion of green innovation, and development of local common property. And, of course, renewables have also economic and social costs that must be considered, including land requirements, grid improvements, intermittency and back-up capacity. These assessments should then form the basis of decisions on energy policies.

Table 1.1 GDP, GHG targets, energy, and low-carbon policy in East Asia

		China (year)	Japan (year)	Korea (year)	Taiwan (year)
GDP	GDP (bn US$)	390 (1990), 9,181 (2013)	3,104 (1990), 4,902 (2013)	270 (1990), 1,222 (2013)	165 (1990), 489 (2013)
	GDP (per capita US$)	341 (1990), 6,747 (2013)	25,140 (1990), 38,491 (2013)	6,308 (1990), 24,329 (2013)	8,087 (1990), 20,930 (2013)
CO_2 emission and GHG targets	CO_2 emission (M CO_2ton)	2,461 (1990), 9,860 (2012)	1,095 (1990), 1,320 (2012)	247 (1990), 640 (2012)	137 (1990), 271 (2012)
	2030 GHG target	60–65% reduction per unit of GDP compared to 2005	25.4% reduction compared to 2005 (18% reduction compared to 1990)	37% reduction compared to BAU scenario	Return to 2005 emission levels by 2020
Renewable energy and nuclear power target	Renewable (% of total electricity)	19.2% (2012), 15% of primary energy (2020)	10.7% (2013), 13.5% (2020), 22~24% (2030)	3.7% (2012), 10% (2022), 15% (2035)	5.2% (2012), 15% (2025)
	Nuclear (% of total electricity)	1.8% (2010), 2.1% (2013), 11 GW (2012), 200 GW (2030)	29.2% (2010), 1.7% (2013), 20~22% (2030)	32.2% (2010), 27.6% (2013), 27.8% (2024), 29% (2035)	19.3% (2010), 19.1% (2013)
Low-carbon policy	Carbon tax	Not yet; under discussion	289 yen/tCO_2 from 2012	Not yet; under discussion	Not yet; tried but failed
	ETS	Nationally from 2016 (not fixed yet), piloting regional ETS from 2011	Not yet nationally but municipally from 2010 (Tokyo City), 2011 (Saitama Prefecture)	Nationally from 2015	Not yet
	Renewable energy policy	FIT	RPS (~2012), FIT(2012)	FIT (~2012), RPS (2012)	FIT

Sources: Websites of the World Bank, IEA, IAEA, World Nuclear Association.

Note: The Japanese government aims to introduce a higher share of renewable energy than the one indicated in the previous National Basic Energy Plan. But these targets were not clarified in the new National Basic Energy Plan in 2014. Conventional hydropower is excluded from Korea's renewable targets for 2020 and 2022.

If East Asia is to move toward a low-carbon and sustainable future, it is necessary to transform the current fossil fuel and nuclear-centered energy system to one based on renewables. The remainder of this chapter provides a brief description of the energy system in each of the four countries, as well as current and recent environmental and energy policies.

1.2   China

Energy resources and the energy system

Energy resources

During the 11th Five-Year Plan (FPY) period (2006–2010), China's energy industry developed rapidly. As shown in Table 1.2, primary energy production reached 2.97 billion tons of coal equivalent (tce)[3] in 2010 (State Council, 2013). It further increased to 3.32 billion tce in 2012 (NBS, 2013).

Coal is the dominant source of energy in China. China is almost self-sufficient in coal, with a supply of 1.806 billion tce and a consumption of 1.839 billion tce

Table 1.2 Energy development during the 11th FYP and in the 12th FYP's targets

Indicator	Unit	2005	2010	2015	Annual growth rate (%)
Production of primary energy	100 mtce	21.6	29.7	36.6	4.3
Of which:					
Coal	100 mt	23.5	32.4	41	4.8
Crude oil	100 mt	1.8	2.0	2.0	0
Natural gas	100 m m³	493	948	1,565	10.5
Non-fossil energy	100 mtce	1.6	2.8	4.7	10.9
Consumption of primary energy	100 mtce	23.6	32.5	40	4.3
Power installed capacity	100 m kW	5.2	9.7	14.9	9.0
Of which:					
Hydro power	100 m kW	1.2	2.2	2.9	5.7
Thermal power	100 m kW	3.9	7.1		
Coal-fired power	100 m kW		6.6	9.6	7.8
Natural gas power	10,000 kW		2,642	5,600	16.2
Nuclear power	10,000 kW	685	1,082	4,000	29.9
Wind power	10,000 kW	126	3,100	10,000	26.4
Solar power	10,000 kW		86	2,100	89.5

Source: the 12th Five-year Plan of Energy Development.

Note: mtce: million tons of coal equivalent; mt: million tons; m m³: million m³; m kW: million kW in 2006. China's coal supply increased to 2.123 billion tce in 2009, accounting for 47 percent of the world's total supply. In 2012, China's coal production reached 2.539 billion tce (NBS, 2013).

China's oil production was 271.87 million tce in 2009, around 10 percent of the world's total production, and increased to 295.34 million tce in 2012 (NBS, 2013). However, China has been an oil importer since the 1990s. In 2002, production of crude petroleum was 1.30 billion barrels, whereas consumption was 1.67 billion barrels. In 2006, China imported 145 million tons of crude oil, accounting for 47 percent of the country's total oil consumption (AFX News Limited, 2007). The three largest companies, Sinopec (China Petrochemical Corporation), CNPC (China National Petroleum Corporation), and CNOOC (China National Offshore Oil Corporation), are state-owned and dominate the domestic oil market.

China's natural gas production was 112.59 million tce in 2009, around 3 percent of the world's total production, which increased to 142.69 million tce in 2012 (NBS, 2013). China has been one of the top seven global gas producers since 2010 (IEA, 2011).

The energy system

In 2011, China's total electricity generation was 4,713 TWh and consumption was 4,700 TWh. In the same year, the installed electricity generation capacity was 874 GW (NBS, 2013). China is undertaking substantial long-distance transmission projects and has the goal of achieving an integrated nationwide grid between 2015 and 2020. Around 80 percent of the country's electricity is currently generated by coal-fired power plants. Coal-based electricity nearly doubled from 1,713 TWh in 2004 to 3,814 TWh in 2011 (IEA, 2012).

China is the world's leading producer of renewable energy, with an installed capacity of 152 GW in 2008 (Jha, 2008). The main renewable energy in China is hydropower. Total output of hydropower in 2012 was 860.85 TWh, constituting 17.43 percent of the total electricity generated (NBS, 2013). China has invested heavily in renewable energy in recent years. In 2007, total investment for renewable energy was 12 bn US$, second only to Germany. Investment then grew rapidly and, of the total 51 bn US$ invested in renewable energy in 2011, 87.7 percent was devoted to wind power and solar PV. State-owned enterprises are the main developers in wind and solar PV markets. They shared 79.9 percent of the total installed wind power capacity and 61.0 percent of total installed solar PV capacity in 2011. Also in 2011, four of the world's top ten producers of wind turbines were in China, and nine of the top 15 solar PV manufacturers were located in China. The latter accounted for 30 percent of sales globally (Climate Policy Initiative, 2012). In 2012, China invested 65.1 bn US$ in clean energy, an increase of 20 percent from the previous year. Accordingly, 23 GW of clean power capacity was installed in 2012 (Pew Charitable Trusts, 2012).

In 2012, China had 15 nuclear power stations with a capacity of 11 GW and output of 54.8 billion kWh, around 1.9 percent of the country's total electricity generation. As of January 2014, China has 20 nuclear power reactors in operation, 28 under construction and more planned. Additional reactors are planned to give a four-fold increase of nuclear capacity, to at least 58 GW by 2020 followed by, possibly, 200 GW by 2030 and 400 GW by 2050. China has become largely self-sufficient in reactor design and construction but is still making full use of Western technology (WNA, 2014).

Energy development targets during the 12th FYP

Table 1.2 lists the targets for energy consumption during the 12th FYP period (2011–2015). Targets for total energy consumption and energy intensity are under implementation simultaneously. Under the plan, by 2015 total energy consumption will not exceed 4 billion tce, and total electricity use will be below 6,150 TWh.

Also under the plan, the capacity of primary energy supply will increase to 4.3 billion tce, of which 3.66 billion tce is from the domestic market. The foreign dependence ratio of oil will be held at under 61 percent. The share of non-fossil energy will be increased to 11.4 percent, and the share of installed power capacity from non-fossil sources will reach 30 percent. The share of natural gas in primary energy will increase to 7.5 percent, and the share of coal consumption will decrease to around 65 percent. The installed capacity of conventional hydropower and pumped storage hydropower will respectively reach 260 GW and 30 GW by 2015. The capacity of nuclear power in operation will be 40 GW and the scale under construction will be 18 GW. The installed capacity of wind power will reach 100 GW and the capacity of solar power will be 21 GW. The installed capacity of power generation from biomass will reach 13 GW.

Climate targets and policy

Climate policy in China took center stage with the finalization of the 12th FYP in March 2011. The plan is significant in its commitment to energy efficiency and emissions reduction and is the first one to address climate change as a key issue. With regard to energy and climate change, the plan has four targets that are all designated as binding (see Table 1.3). They specify to decrease the energy intensity (energy consumption per unit of GDP) and CO_2 intensity (carbon emissions per unit of GDP) by 16 percent and 17 percent, respectively, and to increase the share of non-fossil energy in primary energy consumption to 11.4 percent from the current level of 8.3 percent over the period 2010–2015.

The current 16 percent energy intensity target was chosen after assessing the progress as well as the energy-saving potential in previous plans, with the Copenhagen commitment of China as another factor. The dual targets in energy and carbon intensity are transitional. A carbon intensity target is likely to replace the

Table 1.3 Energy and climate targets in the 12th FYP of China

Items	2010	2015	Change over 5 years (%)	Forecast or binding
Increase of non-fossil in primary energy consumption (%)	8.3	11.4	3.1	Binding
Decrease in energy consumption per unit of GDP (%)			16	Binding
Decrease in CO_2 emissions per unit of GDP (%)			17	Binding
Forest coverage rate (%)	20.36	21.66	1.3	Binding

Source: 12th Five-Year Plan (2011–2015), China.

energy intensity target after the 13th FYP (2016–2020), as the former is more comprehensive and comparable internationally (Yuan and Feng, 2011). More demanding targets regarding energy and carbon emission intensities were set for the most developed regions and those with the most heavy industry.

Under the Copenhagen Accord, China committed to reduce its carbon emissions per unit of GDP by 40 percent to 45 percent by 2020, from 2005 levels. Correspondingly, China has been making great efforts to suppress its carbon emissions through improvements in energy efficiency, increase of its use of non-fossil energies, and increased implementation of low-carbon technologies. During the 11th FYP period, energy consumption per unit of GDP was reduced by 19.1 percent (State Council, 2013). For further energy efficiency improvement, China expanded its Top 1,000 Enterprises Energy Conservation Project to the top 10,000 enterprises. This administrative program includes energy audits, retirement of inefficient plants, and reporting and management requirements for energy efficiency.

China was the largest recipient of clean development mechanism (CDM) projects under the Kyoto Protocol. As of August 2012, 2,271 projects in China were successfully registered as CDM projects, accounting for 50 percent of the global total. The accumulated certified emissions reductions are equivalent to 597 mt CO_2.

In November 2011, the National Development Reform Commission announced pilot programs for Greenhouse Gas (GHG) emission trading schemes (GHG ETS) in seven municipalities and provinces (Beijing, Chongqing, Guangdong, Hubei, Shanghai, Shenzhen, and Tianjin). These regions hosting the pilot programs have a population of 200 million, account for 30 percent of the country's GDP and produce more than 20 percent of China's CO_2 emissions. The regional pilot scheme GHG ETS is ongoing, with a goal to establish a national scheme during the 13th FYP period (2016–2020). The mitigation targets vary across the areas. On June 18, 2013, Shenzhen became the first pilot region with a GHG ETS in operation, covering 635 companies and aiming to achieve a 30 percent reduction in carbon emissions per unit of output (*Economist*, 2013a).

Together with the pilot carbon markets, there will be a national cap on energy consumption. The next step is to turn the energy cap into a national carbon emission target over the period of 2016–2020, with a fully national GHG ETS in 2021–2025 (*Economist*, 2013b).

In China, taxes related to the environment and to resources include a resource tax, the consumption tax, vehicle and vessel-usage taxes and a vehicle purchase tax. Some of these taxes are related to energy use. In recent years, experts at research institutes under the Ministry of Environmental Protection, the Ministry of Finance, and the State Administration of Taxation actively discussed how to develop carbon taxes in China. A carbon tax in China would be limited to fossil fuels, including coal, oil, and natural gas. The setting of the carbon tax rates would be a gradual process. The tax rate proposed by the experts starts from 10 Yuan/tCO_2 (approximately 1.6 US\$/tCO_2 in 2014) for the initial phase, and then increases to 40 Yuan/tCO_2 (approximately 6.5 US\$/tCO_2 in 2014) some years later (Liu et al., 2011).

Challenges for energy and climate policy in China

One challenge for China's energy sector is to bridge the gap between its natural resource endowments and the level of actual demand. Energy resource constraints in China are increasing, and energy security is a growing issue. There is a shortage of energy resources in China, and the supply of conventional fossil fuels is currently insufficient. At the same time, China's energy demand continues to grow rapidly due to rapid economic growth. The rate of dependence on foreign oil increased from 26 percent at the beginning of this century to 57 percent in 2011.

The second challenge for China is that its energy consumption is dominated by coal. The current energy structure is very carbon intensive, and air pollution is a major problem in many areas.

The four energy-intensive sectors, iron and steel, non-ferrous metals, building materials (including cement), and chemical industries, account for around half of the country's total energy consumption. This level, unsurprisingly, is much higher than the global average ratio of energy used by industry. For example, China produces almost 50 percent of the world's steel, and it is the largest producer of cement, accounting for 58 percent of global production in 2011 (EIA, 2013).

China has made great efforts in the development of renewable energy in recent years. The lack of investment in grid connections is the biggest problem faced by the renewable energy industry in China, although it over-invested in PV and many large solar PV firms currently face considerable losses. Rooftop solar PV panels, however, remain undeveloped. Chinese authorities need to establish a strong support for grid construction, and clear policies supporting renewable energy should be continued in order to improve China's energy supply structure.

China needs to build a capacity for innovation in the energy sector, as it typically relies on core technologies and large equipment that are developed and produced abroad. Energy pricing could be much improved, and further reform needs to be embraced. It is necessary for China to speed up the reform of energy system management in order to remove institutional limitations, and more incentives should be provided for companies to invest in R&D to enable China to converse from energy technology follower to technology leader.

Traditionally, energy efficiency and climate policies in China have relied on regulatory and administrative approaches. China needs to learn to also introduce and implement market-based instruments in order to reach the country's climate target in a cost-efficient manner. In recent years, China has heavily subsidized energy efficiency improvements and carbon mitigation. With fiscal constraints, it is questionable how far China can progress solely on this basis. Progress in the pricing of carbon emissions in China lags behind other countries, and the design and introduction of a carbon tax is still under discussion. Furthermore, as a developing country, it is hard for China to set a quantitative ceiling for its carbon emissions, which hinders the establishment of a domestic GHG ETS at the national level (Liu et al., 2014). In addition, the business awareness of GHG ETS in China is currently very low. Many companies lack the capacity for accurate monitoring, reporting, and verification of GHG emissions. These factors may limit the practical implementation of GHG ETS in China in the near future.

1.3 Japan

Energy resources and the energy system

Energy resources

The energy self-sufficiency rate in Japan was 4.8 percent in 2010; this included the use of hydro, geothermal, solar, and biomass power[4] (METI, 2012b). Like other major industrialized countries, Japan is highly dependent on fossil fuels; they accounted for more than 80 percent of energy supply before the Fukushima nuclear accident and are now more than 90 percent. However, because much fossil fuel is imported from the politically unstable Middle East,[5] and because the energy demands of emerging countries are increasing and these countries are trying to secure their energy supply, it is becoming more difficult for Japan to rely on importing most of its energy as fossil fuel. Therefore, Japan needs to develop its own energy sources.

One of the energy sources Japan has focused on to reduce fossil fuel dependence has been nuclear power. The Law Concerning the Promotion of Measures to Cope with Global Warming was adopted in 1998, and nuclear power gained attention as one of the important energy sources that reduces GHG emissions. In February 2011, 54 commercial nuclear power plants were operating. However, the Fukushima nuclear accident highlighted the safety issues of using nuclear power and, as of December 2014, all nuclear power plants are offline (Japan Nuclear Technology Institute, 2014).

The Democratic Party of Japan (DPJ) has contributed to increasing renewable electricity by providing policy targets on renewable energy, such as the Bill of the Basic Act on Global Warming Countermeasures, which included a target of raising the share of renewables to 10 percent by 2020, and the decision made by the Energy and Environmental Council of the Government of Japan in September 2012, which aims for zero nuclear power generation by the 2030s. However, these were scrapped after the dissolution of the lower house in November 2012.

As an alternative energy source, renewables will be one of the most important elements in securing Japan's national energy supply and solving climate change issues. Although multiple national renewables-related policies and institutions were introduced to diffuse the generation of renewables in Japan after the oil crisis in the 1970s, renewables (excluding hydropower) accounted for only 3.7 percent of total primary energy supply in 2010 (Meritas, 2012). The key barriers to increasing energy generation through renewables in Japan include geographical restrictions high costs, and instability in supply.

Energy policy

The RPS scheme was promulgated in 2002 and enacted in 2003 to further the use of renewables. In 2009, the net-metering scheme for photovoltaic power was launched. Under the scheme, electricity companies are required to purchase any surplus electricity generated by customers' PV facilities. The cost of buying back surplus electricity is borne by electricity customers in the form of a PV promotion surcharge (METI, 2012a). This scheme has evolved into the FIT scheme, which launched in 2012.

The RPS and net-metering schemes had some effects in increasing the use of renewable electricity. In particular, there was a large increase in PV after the Net-metering scheme was introduced (Figure 1.1). However, the share of renewables was still small when the RPS and net-metering schemes came to an end in 2012, suggesting that the multiple renewables-related schemes, including RPS and

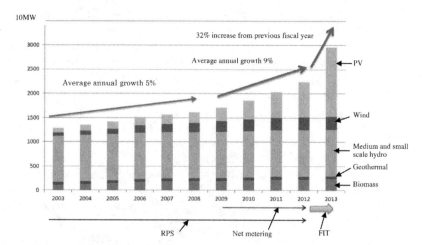

Figure 1.1 Capacity of renewable electricity.
Source: ANRE (2014), translated by the authors.

net metering were not successful in significantly increasing the generation of renewable electricity.

Although net metering has contributed to increasing PV power generation, it does not support other forms of renewable electricity, and excess electricity is purchased only from residential and non-residential PV installations, not from power generators. Furthermore, after the Great East Japan Earthquake, the situation relating to energy has changed substantially. Following the Fukushima accident, a large part of the Japanese population wished to abandon nuclear power generation due to safety concerns, and to increase the share of generation from renewables. Then-Prime Minister Naoto Kan and his cabinet decided that the share of renewables should be expanded. Consequently, in 2012, the net-metering scheme evolved into the FIT scheme.

The FIT scheme in Japan requires that electricity companies accept electricity supply contracts requested by producers of renewable electricity at a long-term fixed purchase price that is guaranteed by the Japanese government (see Chapter 3 for more information about the FIT scheme in Japan). The scheme regulates the procedures followed by the government in deciding purchase prices and periods, certification of facilities, collection and adjustment of surcharges related to purchase costs, and the terms by which companies can reject the contracts. It covers PV, wind, small- and medium-scale hydro, geothermal, and biomass power. The FIT is expected to reduce uncertainty in investment recovery for renewable electricity facilities, and to encourage investment in order to increase the generation of renewable electricity (Kitamura, 2013).

The introduction of renewable electricity was greatly promoted after the FIT was introduced. From July 2012 to February 2015, the total capacity of renewable energy facilities that started to operate under the scheme was approximately 17,610 MW and that of certified renewable energy facilities was approximately 78,680 MW (ANRE, 2015) (cumulative capacity of renewable energy facilities before the FIT was 20,600 MW).

National energy plan

On April 11, 2014, the Basic Energy Plan was endorsed by the cabinet in Japan.[6] The purpose of the plan was to completely revise Japan's energy strategy, especially reducing dependency on nuclear power as much as possible followed by the Fukushima accident. The policy prioritizes energy security, but also includes economic efficiency and the conservation of the environment, all with a strong focus on safety (3E+S). However, to tackle energy-related issues (e.g. costs, stable energy supply, and energy security) and concerns regarding climate change, many different factors need to be taken into account, including both supply-side and demand-side technologies, energy storage, securing resources, the environment, and economic cost.

Under the Basic Energy Plan, coal-fired thermal, nuclear, conventional hydro, and geothermal power generation are considered as the baseload power sources. In particular, coal-fired thermal power is considered to be a very important power source because of its low geopolitical risk among fossil fuels and because of its low cost. Nuclear power is also seen as an important part of the energy mix because of its low operational costs and low CO_2 emissions. For the so-called middle power sources, gas-fired thermal power (natural gas and liquefied petroleum gas) is considered to fall into this category. It is expected that the proportion of natural gas-fired thermal power will be increased because of its low CO_2 emissions compared with other fossil fuels. Finally, for peak-load power, oil-fired thermal, pumped hydro, and other renewable power generation methods will play important roles. Although the Basic Energy Plan emphasizes the importance of renewables and stresses that the introduction of renewables should be accelerated, no targets for renewable energy are given.[7]

The Bill of the Basic Act on Global Warming Countermeasures included the target of raising the share of renewables to 10 percent of total primary energy supply by 2020. In addition, since the Fukushima accident and the resultant shutdown of nuclear power plants across Japan, there has been a growing demand to increase the generation of renewable electricity. Furthermore, the Energy and Environmental Council of the Government of Japan decided in September 2012 to aim for zero nuclear power generation by the 2030s. Although the Basic Act and the decision by the council were scrapped after the dissolution of the lower house, the DPJ has contributed to raising public awareness of the need for renewable electricity.

In addition to the above main policies to enhance renewables, there are other schemes, such as tax reductions, subsidies, and loans (ANRE, 2013). Furthermore, there are several voluntary schemes that are designed to enhance the use of renewables, such as the Green Power Certificate, which is a system that enhances the use of renewables by introducing tradable certificates based on environmental added value from renewable electricity (Ministry of the Environment, 2013). Since the FIT scheme was launched in 2012, the Japanese government has been trying to unite renewables-related institutions under it.

Carbon target

In parallel with the development of energy-related policies and institutions, there has been a growing interest in environmental integrity and climate change issues. As already noted, the Act on Promotion of Global Warming Countermeasures was adopted in 1998. It calls for the national government to implement the Kyoto Protocol Target Achievement plan.

In 2009, the cabinet under then-Prime Minister Taro Aso announced the mid-term target of reducing GHG emissions to 15 percent below the 2005 level by 2020. On March 12, 2010, the bill of the Basic Act on Global Warming Countermeasures was approved by Prime Minister Yukio Hatoyama and his cabinet and submitted to the Diet. The bill included mid- and long-term targets of GHG emission reduction, to 25 percent below the 1990 level by 2020 and 80 percent below the 1990 level by 2050, respectively. The bill also included the target of raising the share of renewables to 10 percent by 2020 and, although the bill was scrapped after the dissolution of the lower house on November 16, 2012, discussion on the bill contributed to raising the public awareness of the promotion of renewables.

Before the Fukushima accident, one of the key forms of energy used to address climate change was nuclear power. Since the accident, however, there has been a call to use renewables instead. Furthermore, after the accident, Japan's GHG reduction target was affected. That is, the situation has changed after the change of government from the DPJ to the Liberal Democratic Party (and also after the Fukushima nuclear accident). The Abe cabinet in 2013 announced a GHG emission reduction target to 3.8 percent below the 2005 level by 2020 and in 2015 announced 25.4 percent below the 2005 by 2030.

Challenges for energy and climate policy

Japan faces many challenges during the transition to a sustainable low-carbon society. The three main challenges for energy and environmental policies can be summarized as follows.

Energy structure

In the new Basic Energy Plan, there is no 'best mix' of energy. To establish a sustainable low-carbon society, the plan sets out that the share of renewables should be increased. However, no numerical targets on renewables exist, and the position of the government regarding nuclear power is unclear. The Basic Energy Plan indicates that nuclear is an 'important' baseload power source and, at the same time, that dependency on it should be reduced as soon as possible, which is why it is difficult for producers of electricity to develop investment plans. The energy structure also relates to energy security. Since Japan imports most energy resources, energy costs and a stable energy supply may be at risk if Japan continues to rely on fossil fuels.

Renewable energy policy

The most recent renewables policy in Japan, the FIT scheme, has successfully increased the share of electricity from renewables already, and aims to accelerate the deployment of renewables further over 2013–2016. However, it has also had negative impacts, such as large cost burdens to electricity consumers due to the high purchasing prices, a biased introduction of renewable energy,[8] and unstable power system connection (see Morita and Matsumoto, 2014 for further information on the challenges of the scheme). To solve these issues, measures such as technological development, introduction of large-scale storage technologies, and improvements of power grid connections should be promoted promptly.

Climate policy

The new GHG emission reduction target set by the Abe cabinet is not sufficient to combat climate change issues and was criticized by non-governmental organizations and other countries when it was announced at the 19th Conference of the Parties to the United Nations Framework Convention on Climate Change (UNFCCC/COP19) in 2013. Like other countries, Japan is required to create the framework for GHG emission reductions after 2020 by March 2015. This issue is related to the Basic Energy Plan, and the government is required to clarify its stance on energy – that is, what share of renewables is necessary to meet the target, and how is the government going to treat nuclear power plants for the newly set target and beyond. It seems very unlikely that the carbon target will be met if the existing carbon tax is not increased.

1.4   Korea

Energy consumption in Korea

Energy consumption is increasing at a fast rate in Korea. Between 1990 and 2000, primary energy consumption increased remarkably, from 93.2 million tons of oil equivalent (toe) to 192.9 million toe. By 2011, primary consumption was 275.7 million toe.[9] Per capita energy consumption also more than doubled from 2.17 toe in 1990 to 5.54 toe in 2011 (Korea Energy Economic Institute, KEEI, 2013). Petroleum makes up the largest share, followed by coal and liquefied natural gas (LNG). The share of renewable energy has been rising since 2000, but it still remains very low (see Table 1.4).

Table 1.4 Primary energy consumption by source in Korea (unit: 1,000 toe)

	1990	1995	2000	2005	2010	2011
Coal	24,385	28,091	42,911	54,788	77,092	83,640
	26.2%	18.7%	22.2%	24.0%	29.2%	30.3%
Oil	50,175	93,955	100,279	101,526	104,301	105,146
	53.8%	62.5%	52.0%	44.4%	39.5%	38.1%
LNG	3,023	9,213	18,924	30,335	43,008	46,284
	3.2%	6.1%	9.8%	13.3%	16.3%	16.8%
Hydro	1,590	1,369	1,402	1,297	1,392	1,715
	1.7%	0.9%	0.7%	0.6%	0.5%	0.6%
Nuclear	13,222	16,757	27,241	36,695	31,948	32,285
	14.2%	11.1%	14.1%	16.1%	12.1%	11.7%
Non-hydro renewable energy	797	1,051	2,130	3,961	6,064	6,618
	0.9%	0.7%	1.1%	1.7%	2.3%	2.4%
Total	93,192	150,436	192,887	228,602	263,805	275,688

Source: KEEI (2013).

Table 1.5 Recovery rate of electricity cost by sector in 2010

	Average	General	Residential	Industrial	Educational	Agriculture
Unit price (KRW/kWh)	86.8	98.9	119.9	76.6	87.2	42.5
Total unit cost (KRW/kWh)	96.3	102.7	127.2	85.7	103.1	116
Recovery rate in 2010 (%)	90.2	96.3	94.2	89.4	84.6	36.7

Source: KEPCO (2013).

Korea's energy consumption per unit of GDP (toe/1,000 US$) improved from 0.29 in 1990 to 0.25 in 2010. However, given the fact that the Organization for Economic Co-operation and Development (OECD) average was 0.14 in 2010, the rate of energy consumption per unit of GDP leaves some room for improvement.[10] In addition, the elasticity of primary energy consumption with respect to GDP was 1.3 in the early 1990s, meaning that the rate of increase in energy consumption outweighed the increase in GDP. However, the ratio improved in the late 1990s as a result of the Asian currency crisis in 1997 and has stabilized at less than 1.0 since 2000.

Korea's consumption of electricity has increased in line with primary energy consumption. Higher electricity consumption has been driven by increasing national income and growing demand from industrial sectors. Since 1990, electricity has replaced petroleum as a source for heating because it is cheaper than other energy sources in Korea. In addition, demand has been greater from electricity-intensive industrial sectors, such as the petrochemical, primary metal, and automobile industries. As a result, the country's per-capita electricity consumption increased from 2,200 kWh in 1990 to 9,142 kWh in 2011. At a high rate of 1.5, the elasticity of electricity consumption with respect to GDP has been stable since 1990, and has shown a different trend from the elasticity for other energy. That is, the rate of electricity consumption has risen 1.5 times faster than the rate of GDP since 1990.

In general, Korea's increase in energy consumption is attributed to its heavy dependence on industrial sectors that consume large amounts of energy, as well as its trade structure. The country's increase in electricity consumption is attributed to increased incomes and low electricity prices that are controlled by the government so that the price of electricity cannot be set so as to recover the cost (see Table 1.5).

Energy policy and the National Basic Energy Plan

Korea conducted a dramatic shift in energy policy after 1990 because of global climate change. Specifically, the country first shifted its focus from fossil fuels to the promotion of nuclear power and renewable energy.

Second, Korea adjusted its industrial energy structure from a monopoly system to a competition-based model. After undergoing two oil crises in the 1970s, Korea's energy policy was centered on maintaining a stable supply of energy, and the market was heavily regulated. In response to criticism of these regulations, Korea's heavy dependence on oil, low rates of efficiency, and a decline in the competitiveness of energy industries, the country carried out a major policy shift to rationalize the coal industry, liberalize the petroleum industry, and establish a market for electricity.

Third, Korea shifted its policy from energy supply management to energy demand management. Since the 1990s, the country has introduced a range of measures for saving energy and increasing energy efficiency, such as the expansion of ESCO (Energy Service Company) projects and the introduction of financial and tax-incentive measures for energy-saving investments.

The Korean government formulated the First Basic Energy Plan in 2008. The plan set goals of expanding nuclear power and renewable energy sources, improving energy independence by developing energy resources, reducing dependence on petroleum, improving basic units for energy, and developing energy technologies. However, the 2012 data show that these goals were only marginally achieved, and it can be said that the plan overall ended in failure.

More recently, the government reviewed its energy policy in response to the Fukushima accident and analyzed the setting of the midterm plan for reducing GHG emissions. The following paragraphs examine the focal points of shifts in Korea's energy policy, with a focus on the Second Basic Energy Plan formulated in January 2014.

The Second Basic Energy Plan is based on the following six policies: (1) a shift to an energy policy focusing on demand management, (2) the establishment of dispersive power generation systems, (3) the establishment of energy supply systems focusing on the environment and safety, (4) the establishment of safe energy supply structures, (5) energy security (through the development of overseas resources and the expansion of the renewable energy supply), and (6) the promotion of a consumer-friendly energy policy. Based on these basic policies, the Korean government set quantitative targets to achieve by 2035, such as, for example, reducing final energy consumption by 13.3 percent by 2035 compared with the business as usual (BAU) scenario (see Table 1.6 and Figure 1.2) and establishing a nuclear share of 29 percent.

Turning to emissions, Korea's GHG emissions increased broadly in line with energy consumption, from 2.957 billion tons CO_2-eq in 1990 to 6.977 billion tons CO_2-eq in 2011. In accordance with the Second Basic Energy Plan, formulated in January 2014, the government formulated the National Greenhouse Gas Emissions Reduction Roadmap. For the emissions reduction goal, the government maintained a target of 30 percent reduction by 2020 (compared to a BAU scenario).[11] In June 2015 Korea submitted GHG reduction target by 37% below BAU emissions of 850.6 $MtCO_2e$ by 2030 to UNFCCC.

Table 1.6 Final energy consumption in the basic and target scenarios (unit: million toe, %)

Sectors	2011	2025	2030	2035	Average rate of increase per year (%)
Basic scenario	205.9	248.7	254.3	254.1	0.88%
Target scenario	205.9	226.7	226.0	220.5	0.29%
Rate of reduction	–	Δ8.9%	Δ11.1%	Δ13.3%	–
Final energy consumption for sources					
Coal	33.5 (16.3)	34.7 (15.3)	35.3 (15.6)	34.4 (15.6)	0.10%
Petroleum	102.0 (49.5)	96.2 (42.4)	88.8 (39.3)	80.3 (36.4)	−0.99%
LNG	23.7 (11.5)	31.4 (13.8)	33.0 (14.6)	33.8 (15.4)	1.50%
Electricity	39.1 (19.0)	53.3 (23.5)	57.1 (25.3)	59.9 (27.2)	1.79%
Heat	1.7 (0.8)	2.8 (1.2)	3.0 (1.3)	3.2 (1.5)	2.72%
Renewables (in final demand)	5.8 (2.8)	8.3 (3.7)	8.7 (3.8)	8.8 (4.0)	1.71%

Source: Ministry of Industry, Trade and Energy (2014).

Note: Target scenario reached by demand control, price mechanism, and technological innovation.

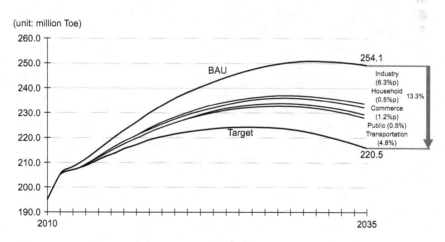

Figure 1.2 Final energy reduction rate by sector.

Source: Ministry of Industry, Trade a Resource (2014).

Each sector has been given an objective as part of the overall 2020 target. Transportation must cut emissions by 34.3 percent, construction by 26.9 percent, power generation by 26.7 percent, the public sector by 25.0 percent, industry by 18.5 percent, the waste management sector by 12.3 percent, and agriculture and fisheries by 5.2 percent. Together, this is equivalent to 233 million toe of GHG reduction at national level.

The Korean Ministry of Environment (MOE) laid out the following strategies for effective and efficient CO_2 reduction: (1) operate a market-oriented reduction scheme, (2) develop scientific technologies, (3) create jobs and new markets through GHG reduction, and (4) carry out public awareness campaigns. The principal market-oriented reduction schemes include the surcharge system that was enforced in 2014 (surcharges levied on automobile companies that fail to meet the criteria for GHG emissions and fuel efficiency), the emissions trading system that was introduced in 2015, a special system for promoting low-carbon vehicles,[12] and a system for expanding renewable energy (RPS) in 2012.

Challenges for energy and environmental policy

Korea still faces many challenges in developing a sustainable, low-carbon society. The three main challenges for energy and environmental policies can be summarized as follows.

Governance for the Basic Energy Plans

The First Basic Energy Plan was formulated by the combined deliberations of the Energy Committee, the Green Growth National Committee, and cabinet meetings. A government bill on the First Basic Energy Plan was compiled through public hearings. Related specialists and the representatives of civil society and industrial circles participated in the Energy Committee and the Green Growth National Committee, and public hearings were held, although they were mere formalities. Through these measures, civil opinions were reflected in the formulation of the First Basic Energy Plan. However, there were criticisms that the governance process failed to pay adequate attention to the opinions of civil society, especially non-governmental organizations, at the initial stage of draft planning.

Learning lessons from this experience, the formulation of the Second Basic Energy Plan involved 60 stakeholders, including related specialists and representatives of civil and industrial circles, at the initial stage of planning. The participants had discussions at the Private-Public Working Group for five categories and finally provided policy recommendations.

This governance method turned out to be epoch-making, as it actively facilitated the reflection of the stakeholders' opinions in the planning process before the initial draft was drawn up by the government. In fact, the Second Basic Energy Plan received less criticism from stakeholders than the previous one. A main reason for establishing such governance was that the Fukushima accident and setting the midterm plan for reducing GHG emissions greatly raised public awareness of the basic energy plan.

One point of criticism was the lack of necessary basic information (on economy, population, energy prices, and so on) among private-sector research institutes in formulating the basic energy plan; information provided by government research institutes was used instead. This is why the Basic Energy Plan and the National Greenhouse Gas Emissions Reduction Roadmap are inconsistent; that is, the Basic Energy Plan says that new power stations should be constructed to meet the growing demand for electric power – a statement that is not reinforced in the National Greenhouse Gas Emissions Reduction Roadmap.

What became clear from the latest governance method for the formulated Basic Energy Plan was that the opinions of industrial circles were less reflected than previously, whereas opinions of civil society were more reflected than previously. For example, with regard to the share of nuclear power, the First Basic Energy Plan set a goal of 41 percent by 2035. However, the Private-Public Working Group proposed that the goal would be 22–29 percent, and the final target was set at 29 percent. In response, many in industrial circles criticized the 29 percent goal as being rather low given the growing demand for electric power and the goal for reducing GHG emissions.

The National Greenhouse Gas Emissions Reduction Roadmap was drawn up by the MOE and was announced after careful consideration by the Green Growth National Committee. This process shows that the MOE plays a central role in promoting measures to combat global warming.

Renewable energy policy

In 2012, Korea introduced a dramatic change in renewable energy policy. The government replaced the FIT with the RPS on the grounds that the FIT had not promoted the distribution of renewable energy technology as expected and that it had placed a heavy financial burden on the government (because the policy cost of FIT in Korea was supported by central government). The RPS applies to the six publicly owned power generators of 500 MW capacity or more, Korea Water Resources Corporation, and Korea District Heating Corporation, covering 13 power generators in all. The renewable share to be supplied by target generators starts at 2 percent of all power generated in 2012, increasing by 0.5 percent each year up to 2016. Thereafter, it will rise by 1 percent per annum until 2022, by which time the portfolio will amount to 10 percent.

Generators under the obligation have to meet their target and submit a Renewable Energy Certificate (REC). There are three different ways for a company to get a REC, either by the company generating the energy from their own renewable facilities, by purchasing long-term contracts with other renewable developers, or through the REC market.

Climate policy

On January 1, 2015, Korea launched its national emission trading scheme (KETS), the first nation-wide cap-and-trade program operating in Asia. The Korean government aims to reduce its GHG emissions by 30 percent compared with a BAU scenario by 2020. Another key objective of KETS is to achieve a substantial reduction of GHG emissions through technology innovation. KETS covers over 65 percent of the country's total emissions. Participating companies will be given 100 percent of their emission allowances for free during the scheme's first phase (2015–2017), and 97 percent during the second phase (2018–2020). From the third phase onward (2021–2025), more than 10 percent of allowances will be auctioned and less than 90 percent of allowances freely allocated.

In addition, the Korean government is currently discussing the introduction of carbon taxes, but nothing has yet been decided.

1.5   Taiwan

Energy resources and the energy system

Energy resources

Taiwan has achieved sustained economic growth and corresponding improvements in living standards during the past two decades. Energy consumption has increased over this period to meet the higher demand. However, Taiwanese growth has slowed down recently. The dip in growth has partly been due to the rapid rise of the economies of China and other developing countries, but by taking advantage of more attractive business conditions on the Chinese mainland, Taiwanese manufacturers have accelerated the shift of their production footholds to China to regain international competitiveness.

This section outlines Taiwan's energy profile, before reviewing the evolution of energy policy in Taiwan and major issues presented by this policy, as well the energy challenges and opportunities that Taiwan's economy will face in the future.

According to the Bureau of Energy, Ministry of Economic Affairs (2013), Taiwan's total final energy consumption has doubled over the past two decades, going from 55.9 million kiloliters of oil equivalent (KLOE) in 1992 to 111.5 million KLOE in 2012, which is an average annual growth of 3.5 percent. Approximately 80 percent of this consumption was for energy use, whereas non-energy uses consumed the other 20 percent. When classified by consumer, the consumption of energy for each sector in 2012 was as follows: energy and industrial sectors consumed 45.3 percent; transportation 11.9 percent; agriculture, forestry, and fisheries 0.9 percent; services 11 percent; and the residential sector 10.9 percent. Sorted by form of energy, coal and coal products contributed 8.3 percent of consumption in 2012, petroleum products 38.4 percent, natural gas 3.4 percent, biomass and waste 0.2 percent, electricity 49.4 percent, solar thermal 0.1 percent, and heat 0.3 percent.

Taiwan's energy supply increased from 62.9 million KLOE in 1992 to 140.8 million KLOE in 2012, an average annual growth of 4.1 percent. Of this total in 2012, indigenous energy contributed 2.2 percent, and the remaining 97.8 percent was imported. Sorted by form of energy, coal contributed 29.7 percent; oil 48 percent; natural gas 12.1 percent; biomass and waste 1.3 percent; hydro power 0.4 percent; nuclear power 8.3 percent; geothermal, solar, and wind power 0.1 percent; and solar thermal 0.1 percent.

The total supply of coal in Taiwan grew from 22.5 million metric tons in 1992 to 64.6 million metric tons in 2012, an average annual increase of 5.4 percent. However, coal is no longer produced domestically, and all supplies have been imported since 2001. Coal consumption continues to grow, from 21.8 million metric tons in 1992 to 64.2 million metric tons in the same period, an annual growth rate of 5.5 percent. Petroleum product consumption grew from 30.2 million KLOE in 1992 to 45.3 million KLOE in 2012, an average annual growth of 2 percent. Of this total in 2012, 5.5 percent was used to produce electricity, 49 percent was consumed for non-energy uses, and 45.6 percent was used for fuel.

In 2012, imports of LNG were 16,694 million m^3, compared to 2,163 million m^3 in 1992, an average annual increase of 10.8 percent. In 2012, the consumption of LNG was 15,314 million m^3, whereas in 1992 it was only 1,521 million m^3, an average annual increase of 12.2 percent. Of the total gas consumed in 2012, power generation comprised 84.3 percent, industrial uses 13.4 percent, services 1.9 percent, and residential use 0.4 percent.

Electricity production grew from 105.5 TWh in 1992 to 250.4 TWh in 2012, an average annual increase of 4.4 percent. Of the total electricity production in 2012, hydro power by Taiwan Power Company (Taipower) comprised 3.4 percent, thermal power 49.2 percent (coal 27 percent, oil 2.3 percent, LNG 20 percent), nuclear power 16.1 percent, wind power 0.3 percent, cogeneration 15 percent, and independent power producers (IPPs) 16.1 percent. The peak load in 2011 reached a record 33,081 MW. Electricity consumption went from 99.6 TWh in 1992 to 241.3 TWh in 2012, an average annual increase of 4.5 percent. Sorted by sector, energy and industrial use consumed 61 percent of electricity in 2012, transportation 0.5 percent, agriculture 1.1 percent, residential use 18 percent, and services 19.5 percent.

Energy pricing and energy policy

Energy pricing

Energy pricing in Taiwan has long been subject to government intervention so that, in recent years, there has been a great deal of price rigidity for both electricity and petroleum products despite the volatility in global markets. Previously, both the electricity and petroleum-refining industries were state-owned monopolies. In 2000, a second petroleum-refining company, the Formosa Petrochemical Corporation, entered the market. The electricity market opened up with the entrance of IPPs in 1995. Currently, Taipower remains the only state-owned integrated utility, with eight IPPs and producers of renewable energy also in the market.

Under such a market structure, government control of domestic energy prices in Taiwan has long been a policy tool to maintain export competitiveness and a low-cost domestic energy supply. However, underpricing of electricity and petroleum products has greatly distorted the behavior of industrial and household consumers of energy. The true cost of imported energy is, therefore, hidden from the Taiwanese consumer, and there has been little incentive to implement clean energy projects and to establish low-carbon structures in both energy demand and supply.

Attempts to reform the system have not improved this situation. Although the Ministry of Economic Affairs (MOEA) authorized the Chinese Petroleum Corporation to adopt a floating fuel-pricing mechanism at the beginning of 2007, an unofficial mandate for the price of gasoline and diesel to remain at a level lower than Taiwan's neighbors is still in effect. Meanwhile, the pricing mechanism for electricity is controlled by the government rather than based on the generation cost. Currently, Taipower's proposal for electricity price adjustments is designated to be reviewed by a price advisory committee formed by MOEA.

The CO_2 emission factor and nuclear policy

As international pressure to lower CO_2 emissions keeps mounting, Taiwan has developed various climate change mitigation strategies aimed at reducing GHGs and building a low-carbon society. Consumers throughout the world have demanded detailed information on CO_2 emitted during the life cycle of various products and their journey through the supply chain. Since electricity is an essential input factor in the production process, emissions from electricity generation are often deemed to be a crucial factor in calculating the carbon footprint of a particular product. Realizing that Taiwan's competitive advantage is at risk due to its higher electricity emissions per kilowatt hour (kWh) compared to its foreign competitors, there is an urgent demand for Taipower to significantly lower emissions from electricity.

However, this is not an easy task (Liang, 2012). As previously mentioned, all possible alternative energy resources other than fossil fuels have known limitations for large-scale application in Taiwan. Some Taiwanese are now arguing that the nation's nuclear policy should be revised, because nuclear generation can be treated as a zero-carbon energy source. Demands for exceptions and even reversal of the existing 'nuclear-free homeland' policy have been rising. However, due to the political sensitivity of the issue, there is little consensus yet.

Challenges in the energy profile

Indeed, the challenges that confront Taiwan are especially difficult given the unique features that define its energy profile – the island's high import dependency, its isolated electricity supply system, a high concentration of fossil fuels deposits, currently limited use of renewable energy, and its rapid increase of CO_2 emissions (Huang and Wu, 2009; Chang, 2012).

High import dependency

Taiwan imports almost all of its energy for both direct use and energy transformation. In 2012, it was dependent on imports for 97.8 percent of its fuel needs (energy supply). Oil contributed the largest import share (48 percent) of Taiwan's energy profile, followed by coal (29.7 percent), natural gas (11.7 percent), and nuclear fuel (8.3 percent). Taiwan's fuel imports are also highly concentrated in a few source countries.

Isolated electricity supply systems

Power grids in many countries or regions are interconnected so that electricity costs can be lowered by reducing the need for generating capacity and by substituting expensive fuel for cheaper fuel, as well as by diversifying generation methods to minimize risks of supply and price volatilities. However, Taiwan's insular geography means its power supply is isolated. Because of the lack of interconnectedness with other regions, the island requires much higher power generation reserve margins than elsewhere to ensure reliability in the case of a transmission grid outage, to protect system safety, and to ensure continuous operation. Furthermore, with a mandatory renewable electricity target of 15 percent by 2025, and with 50 percent of total renewables expected to come from wind power, which is dependent on favorable weather conditions, there is likely to be more uncertainty in the operation of the power system.

High reliance on fossil fuel supply

As previously indicated, Taiwan's supply of primary energy is also highly reliant on traditional fossil fuels, of which oil, natural gas, and coal continue to be the dominant sources. Owing to the decline of nuclear energy from 15.5 percent of Taiwan's total energy supply in 1999 to 8.4 percent in 2013, fossil fuels contributed 89.7 percent of total primary energy supply in 2012, which is significantly higher than the equivalent share of 85.4 percent in 1994. As Chang (2012) indicated, there is little reason to see a significant change in this trend in the future. Nuclear power remains a very sensitive subject that the former governing party (the Democratic Progressive Party) invoked with its 'nuclear-free homeland' policy in 2002. This policy, which seeks to eliminate all nuclear generation on the island, is still binding and, as indicated by previous protests, any attempt to alter it may provoke economic as well as political disputes, seriously affecting internal political stability. Taiwan's carbon-intensive energy profile thus poses a large obstacle to efforts to separate economic development from CO_2 emissions. Energy diversification and the de-carbonization of energy supplies have topped the list on both public and private sector energy priorities, but nuclear power remains highly contentious.

Rapid increase of CO_2 emissions

Taiwan's CO_2 emissions totaled 109.5 million metric tons in 1990, which is equivalent to a per capita CO_2 emission of 5.4 tons. CO_2 emissions in 2012 reached 248.7 million metric tons, 127.1 percent more than that in 1990, corresponding to a per capita CO_2 emission of 10.7 tons. The annual growth rate was 5.8 percent from 1990 to 2012. As a consequence of worsening energy security and GHG emissions, and to encourage diversification of energy sources, improve energy intensity, and reduce CO_2 emissions, the current energy policy was formulated with the goal of enhancing sustainability, stability, efficiency, and cleanness. It is hoped that the policy will effectively balance Taiwan's energy security, environmental protection, and industrial competitiveness. However, in order to reduce CO_2 emissions, economic development must take place, with attention being paid to energy and environment, continuing a no-regrets policy, and increasing the share of independent energy, strengthening regional cooperation, enhancing market mechanisms, increasing energy efficiency, expanding technological capacity, and developing green industry.

The challenges for energy and climate policies in Taiwan

In response to global climate change issues, the government formally launched the energy-conservation/carbon-reduction policy with the publication of the 'Framework of Taiwan's Sustainable Energy Policy' in 2008, whose objective is to return to the emission level of 2005 by 2020, and to the emission level of 2000 by 2025. A further objective, to meet the world standard of a 50 percent reduction in emission levels by 2050 (compared to 2000), is not presented in the current framework obtained in May 2012, but is presented in its earlier version (Hwang and Chang, 2011; Liou, 2011; Chiun, 2013). The 'Framework of Taiwan's Sustainable Energy Policy' also aims to develop four GHG reduction laws, including the Energy Management Act (Amendment) and the Renewable Energy Development Act, both of which were implemented in 2011. Two other laws, the Energy Tax Act and the Greenhouse Gas Reduction Act, are still under legislative review to date (2015). A detailed comparison of the four laws can be found in Liou (2011).

A closer look at these regulations reveals that, at the present rate of development, three lines of related measures must be undertaken in order to achieve a low-carbon society in Taiwan. The first line focuses on action by the government to influence actions of all government-funded institutions through the use of decrees and punishments. The second line focuses on private companies with the use of subsidies and slight penalties when management regulations are violated. Subsidies are used to support the development of renewable energy industries according to the Renewable Energy Development Act. Penalties are provided if companies import, export, and produce energy products without permission from the government (Energy Management Act), lack air pollution control equipment, burn substances harmful to health (Air Pollution Control Act), or fail to reuse or recycle items specified by the government (Resource Recycling Act). The third line focuses on the general public with the use of campaigns and incentives. Related campaigns, such as the 'Green Hotel Competition, 'I love green-label products,' and 'Sign energy-conservation/carbon-reduction declarations' are carried out to educate and encourage the general public and private industries to use and create green products (Chiun, 2013).

The energy policy of Taiwan is thus at a crossroads. Compromises need to be made when assessing the economy, environment, and energy objectives, and two particular but contentious positions – that is, to rationalize energy prices and to reconsider nuclear policy – may be the only viable options to reach the goal of the framework. By removing governmental intervention in pricing, distortions in energy demand and industrial structure will be removed, thereby creating new incentives for the development of clean technologies and the shift to cleaner fuels. As well as supply issues, the price for each type of energy should convey the full cost that the energy imposes on society.

Notes

1 The concept of green growth has its origins in the Asia and Pacific region; it came out of the Fifth Ministerial Conference on Environment and Development (MCED) held in Seoul, in March 2005. The green growth approach adopted by the MCED sought to harmonize economic growth with environmental sustainability, while improving the eco-efficiency of economic growth and enhancing the synergies between environment and economy.
2 In the longer term, carbon capture and storage (CCS) may be another possibility. However, in the time line considered here (up to 2030), significant development of CCS seems unlikely.
3 The unit used for primary energy statistics in China is tce; 1 tce equals 0.7 toe (ton of oil equivalent).
4 Here, nuclear power is not considered domestic energy.
5 Oil dependence on the Middle East in 2013 was about 73 percent in Japan (BP, 2014).
6 The Basic Energy Plan was first developed in October 2003 and then updated in March 2007 and June 2010. The latest one is the fourth version.
7 Consequently, the government of Japan, in June 2015, showed the target of renewables in 2030 as 22–24% of total power generation.
8 The share of PV in total renewable energy certified under the FIT scheme (as of October 2014) is approximately 96 percent (ANRE, 2015).
9 Korea's primary energy consumption in 1998 decreased by 8.1 percent from 1997 in the wake of the Asian currency crisis of 1997.
10 This figure is based on IEA, 2013.
11 In July 2011, the Korean government submitted a bill to Parliament with the aim of cutting carbon emissions by 30 percent below expected levels in 2020, following approval by the Korean cabinet.

12 Under the special system for promoting low-carbon vehicles, car purchasers are given grants (below 130g/km) or are required to pay a certain amount (above 151g/km) according to their GHG emissions. It was originally planned to start in January 2015 but postponed to 2020 due to strong resistance from the motor industry in Korea. See Ministry of Environment (2014a, 2014b) for further details.

References

AFX News Limited (2007, January 11). 'China's 2006 crude oil imports 145 mln tons, up 14.5 pct – customs.' http://english.cri.cn/3130/2007/01/11/262@184135. htm (accessed March 22, 2014).

Agency for Natural Resources and Energy (ANRE) (2013). 'Support system for renewable energy introduction.' http://www.enecho.meti.go.jp/saiene/support/ (accessed June 28, 2013; in Japanese).

Agency for Natural Resources and Energy (ANRE) (2014). 'Current situation and challenges of renewable energy.' http://www.meti.go.jp/committee/ sougouenergy/shoene_shinene/shin_ene/pdf/001_03_00.pdf (accessed February 17, 2015; in Japanese).

Agency for Natural Resources and Energy (ANRE) (2015). 'Feed-in tariff: Website for public disclosure of information.' http://www.fit.go.jp/statistics/public_sp.html (accessed February 20, 2015; in Japanese).

BP (2014). 'Statistical review of world energy 2014.' http://www.bp.com/en/ global/corporate/about-bp/energy-economics/statistical-review-of-world-energy. html (accessed December 28, 2014).

Bureau of Energy, Ministry of Economic Affairs (2013). *Energy Statistics Handbook 2012.* http://web3.moeaboe.gov.tw/ECW/populace/content/SubMenu. aspx?menu_id=141 (accessed May 22, 2014).

Chang, Ssu-Li (2012). 'An overview of energy policy in Taiwan.' In Bryce Wakefield (Ed.), *Taiwan's Energy Conundrum—Asia Program Special Report*, no. 146. Woodrow Wilson International Center for Scholars, pp. 4–13.

Chiun, Mei-Shiu (2013). 'Tensions in implementing the energy-conservation/carbon-reduction policy in Taiwanese culture.' *Energy Policy*, 55, pp. 415–425.

Climate Policy Initiative (2012). 'Annual review of low-carbon development in China (2011–2012): Chapter summaries.' Beijing, Tsinghua University: Climate Policy Initiative.   http://climatepolicyinitiative.org/wp-content/uploads/2011/11/ China-Country-Study-Chapter-Summaries-Updated.pdf (accessed April 9, 2014).

Economist (2013a, June 19). 'Carbon emissions: The cap doesn't fit.' http://www. economist.com/blogs/analects/2013/06/carbon-emissions?fsrc=rss (accessed April 9, 2014).

Economist (2013b, August 10). 'China and the environment: The East is grey'. http:// www.economist.com/news/briefing/21583245-china-worlds-worst-polluter-largest-investor-green-energy-its-rise-will-have (accessed April 9, 2014).

Energy Information Administration (EIA) (2013, July 25). 'International energy outlook 2013.' http://www.eia.gov/forecasts/ieo/pdf/0484(2013).pdf (accessed April 9, 2014).

Huang, Yun-Hsun, and Wu, Jung-Hua (2009). 'Energy policy in Taiwan: Historical developments, current status and potential improvements.' *Energies*, 2(3), pp. 623–645.

Hwang, J.J., and Chang, W.R. (2011). 'Policy progress in mitigation of climate change in Taiwan.' *Energy Policy*, 39, pp. 1113–1122.

International Energy Agency (IEA) (2011). 'Key world energy statistics 2011.' Paris: International Energy Agency. https://www.iea.org/publications/freepublications/publication/key-world-energy-statistics-2011.html.

International Energy Agency (IEA) (2012). 'Key world energy statistics 2012.' Paris: International Energy Agency. https://www.iea.org/publications/freepublications/publication/key-world-energy-statistics-2012.html.

International Energy Agency (IEA) (2013). *Energy Balances of OECD/Non-OECD Countries*, 2013.

Japan Nuclear Technology Institute (2014). 'Operation of nuclear power plant.' http://www.gengikyo.jp/db/fm/plantstatus.php?x=d (accessed December 1, 2014; in Japanese).

Jeong, Seung-Yeon, and Lee, Soocheol (2014). 'Feature and challenges of policy changes on renewable energy in Japan and Korea.' *Meijo Review*, *14*(4), pp. 61–76.

Jha, A. (2008, August 1). 'China 'leads the world' in renewable energy.' *Guardian*, http://www.theguardian.com/environment/2008/aug/01/renewableenergy.climatechange (accessed April 9, 2014).

Kitamura, T. (2013). 'Situation of the FIT scheme and challenge toward substantial expansion of renewable energy.' *Energy and Resources*, *34*(3), pp. 129–133. (In Japanese).

Korea Electric Power Corporation (KEPCO) (2013). 'Electricity price in Korea.' http://home.kepco.co.kr/kepco/CO/ntcob/ntcobView.do?pageIndex (accessed December 3, 2014; in Korean).

Korea Energy Economic Institute (KEEI) (2013). 'Energy statistics yearbook 2013.' http://www.keei.re.kr/main.nsf/index_en.html?open&p=%2Fmain (accessed December 5, 2014; in Korean).

Liang, Chi-Yuan (2012). 'Energy security and policy in Taiwan.' In Wakefield, Bryce (Ed.), *Taiwan's Energy Conundrum – Asia Program Special Report*, No. 146, May 2012, pp. 21–28.

Liou, H. M. (2011). 'A comparison of the legislative framework and policies in Taiwan's four GHG reduction acts.' *Renewable and Sustainable Energy Reviews*, 15, pp. 1723–1747.

Liu, X. B., Ogisu, K., Suk, S. H., and Shishime, T. (2011). 'Carbon tax policy progress in north-east Asia.' In Kreiser, L., Sirisom, J., Ashiabor, H., and Milne, J. E. (Eds.), *Environmental Taxation in China and Asia-Pacific: Achieving Environmental Sustainability through Fiscal Policy*. Northampton, MA: Edward Elgar Publishing. pp. 103–118.

Liu, X. B., Suk, S. H., and Yamamoto, R. (2014, April). 'The feasibility of pricing of carbon emissions in the three Northeast Asian countries: Japan, China and the Republic of Korea.' *Policy Brief*, No. 29, Institute for Global Environmental Strategies (IGES).

Meritas (2012). *On the Horizon – Renewable Energy in Asia*. Meritas Report. http://www.jdsupra.com/legalnews/on-the-horizon-renewable-energy-in-asi-20913/

Ministry of Economy, Trade and Industry (METI) (2012a). 'Approval of electricity charges followed by the fixing of FY 2012 photovoltaic power promotion surcharge rates.' http://www.meti.go.jp/english/press/2012/0125_02.html (accessed June 28, 2013).

Ministry of Economy, Trade and Industry (METI) (2012b). *Energy White Paper 2012*. Tokyo: Energy Forum (in Japanese).

Ministry of Economy, Trade and Industry (METI) (2014). *The Basic Energy Plan*. Tokyo (In Japanese).

Ministry of the Environment (2013). 'What is a green electricity certificate?' http://www.env.go.jp/earth/ondanka/greenenergy/ (accessed June 28, 2013; in Japanese).

Ministry of Environment (2014a). *National Allocation Plan for 2015–2017.* Seoul: Ministry of Environment. (In Korean).

Ministry of Environment (2014b). *National Greenhouse Gas Emissions Reduction Roadmap.* Seoul: Ministry of Environment. (In Korean).

Ministry of Trade, Industry and Energy (2014). *The Second Basic Energy Plan.* Seoul: Ministry of Trade, Industry and Energy.(In Korean).

Morita, K., and Matsumoto, K. (2014). 'Renewable energy-related policies and institutions in Japan: Before and after the Fukushima nuclear accident and the feed-in tariff introduction.' In Gao, A.M.Z. and Fan, C. T. (Eds.), *Legal Issues of Renewable Electricity in Asia Region: Recent Development at a Post-Fukushima and Post-Kyoto Protocol Era.* Alphen aan den Rijn: Kluwer Law International. pp. 3–28.

National Bureau of Statistics (NBS) (2013). 'China energy statistical yearbook 2013.' Beijing: China Statistics Press (in Chinese).

Pew Charitable Trusts (2012). 'Who's winning the clean energy race? 2012 edition.' Pew Charitable Trusts. http://www.pewtrusts.org/en/research-and-analysis/reports/2013/04/17/whos-winning-the-clean-energy-race-2012-edition (accessed April 9, 2014).

State Council (2013). 'Circular of State Council on issuing the 12th Five-Year Plan of energy development.' (In Chinese). http://www.gov.cn/zwgk/2013-01/23/content_2318554.htm (accessed April 9, 2014).

World Nuclear Association (WNA) (2014). 'Nuclear power in China.' http://www.world-nuclear.org/info/Country-Profiles/Countries-A-F/China—Nuclear-Power (accessed January 28, 2014).

Yuan, D. D., and Feng, J. (2011). 'Behind China's green goals.' *Southern Weekend.* (In Chinese). https://www.chinadialogue.net/article/show/single/ch/4181-Behind-China-s-green-goals (accessed May 20, 2014).

2 Introduction to the modeling in this book

Hector Pollitt, Soocheol Lee, and Park Seung-Joon

2.1 The role of macroeconomic modeling in forming public policy

Introduction

Over the past two decades, computer-based macroeconomic modeling has become one of the key analytical tools for carrying out the assessment of public policy, with a particularly strong role in assessment of environmental policy. Models of varying degrees of complexity are now used in most areas of policy, and their role in determining policy formation has increased markedly in recent years.

Macroeconomic modeling provides two key inputs to policy analysis:

- A conceptual framework for understanding the problem – a key part of the policy process is understanding the problem at hand and the main determining factors (Probst and Bassi, 2014). Within the bounds of the economy, but sometimes extended into other areas, macroeconomic models provide this framework. They are also able to provide an assessment of the main feedback loops and can highlight possible unintended consequences of the introduction of new policies.
- Quantitative analysis – the second important input that macroeconomic modeling provides is a quantitative estimate of the costs and benefits. These are usually expressed in currency units (e.g. dollars, or proportion of GDP), but, as we shall discuss in this book, many models also provide estimates of physical costs and benefits. Quantitative assessment is now a key part of the process of formulating policy and is a requirement (where possible) for justifying many different types of policies, including environmental policies, in some countries (European Commission, 2009).

However, it is important for the user to be aware of the limitations of modeling.

1 There are policy issues that cannot be quantified or for which the necessary data do not exist. This of course does not mean that they are not important, but they can get left out of the assessment if the policy maker focuses exclusively on modeling results.

2   When developing policy scenarios, each modeling exercise makes certain assumptions so that real-world policies can be translated into a format that is compatible with the modeling approach. In some cases the nature of these assumptions can have a bearing on the model results.

3   There are subtle but important differences between models that rely on an optimisation approach based on a theory about rational choice and those that attempt to simulate actual behavior. We discuss these differences in our account of two different types of macroeconomic models: computable general equilibrium (CGE) models (optimisation) and macro-econometric models (simulation).

4   Because of the nature of the economic data that are fed into models, macroeconomic models cannot account for contexts and institutional structures that are important for the implementation of policies. Modeling should, therefore, be only one part of the policy analysis and should be combined with other sources of information drawn from such activities as interviews with stakeholders and case studies (Swann, 2008).

There is also anecdotal evidence that the training of policy makers does not acquaint them with the increasingly prominent role of quantitative modeling in policy analysis. If this is true, it implies that those who are using the results of modeling may not have a good grasp of the nature and limitations of the models and of the need to combine them with other methods of assessment. They would then be at risk of drawing misleading conclusions. One of the aims of this book is therefore to educate readers about the different modeling approaches that are used for the assessment of environmental policy.

A brief history of macroeconomic modeling

Changes in economic theory and increases in computing power have led to considerable developments in modeling approaches in recent decades. It is disputed just which was the first macroeconomic model, but several basic econometric forecasting tools were developed in the 1940s. Up until the mid-1970s, the models were further developed and became more complex, but the basic approach remained the same. Most were demand-oriented (Keynesian) macroeconomic models with no disaggregation into sectors. However, teams at the University of Cambridge were already incorporating sectoral detail into a model of the whole economy, forming an early macro-econometric model.

In the 1970s, the focus shifted to computable general equilibrium (CGE) models. Several reasons have been suggested for this shift, including the rise of supply-side economics, the importance of 'microeconomic foundations' (Hoover, 2012), and the 'Lucas critique' (Lucas, 1976) that it may not be appropriate to use past data to determine future behavior under different economic or policy conditions.

The central feature of CGE models is that they rely on neoclassical general equilibrium theory, which emphasizes effective market adjustment, the importance of the supply side, and a theory of human behavior based on rational choice. These features of CGE models are discussed further later in the present chapter.

In their early years, CGE models had quite limited empirical content. Subsequent increases in computing power have made it possible to expand the content and to introduce larger and more complex tools, including detailed differentiation between sectors and geographical regions. Today, CGE models are normally used for policy assessment rather than forecasting. Notable examples with a global scope include GTAP (Global Trade Analysis Project, Hertel, 1999), AIM (Asian Pacific Integrated Model, e.g. Matsuoka, Kainuma, and Morita, 1995) and the Monash model (Dixon and Rimmer, 2002).

The previous macro-econometric approach has also been developed further over the same period. Macro-econometric models too are now commonly applied for policy assessment. The most advanced macro-econometric models, including the E3ME-Asia model that is described later in this chapter, can offer a robust and highly empirical means of assessing a range of different policies, including policies relating to energy consumption and emissions.

More recently, other modeling approaches based on evolutionary economics have emerged and started to contribute to the academic debate. Many of these are referred to as 'agent-based' models, and they assess the emergent properties of the interactions of large numbers of individual agents. Agent-based modeling is described and compared to more common approaches in Beinhocker (2007) and is a rapidly developing area of research that is likely to make many important contributions to scientific debate in the coming years. However, as of yet, there is no solid representation of the whole economy using an agent-based model.

The two most common approaches to macroeconomic modeling, therefore, remain macro-econometric and CGE. In this book, we use both approaches and compare and contrast the results from the two types of models for sets of identical scenarios. The ultimate aim of the modeling in this book is to provide methods for the economic assessment of policies that are not dependent on a single set of modeling assumptions. In doing so, we also explain some of the key differences between the models.

2.2 The development of E3 models and IAMs

A natural extension of macroeconomic modeling is 'E3' modeling (see Figure 2.1). The three Es are economy, energy, and environment (mainly emissions), and both macro-econometric and CGE models may be extended to include these factors. Energy is a factor of the economic production process that may be measured in either economic or physical units. Emissions from energy consumption may be calculated from the carbon content of the fuels that are used. At the same time, there is feedback in the other direction, as changes in energy consumption will affect the output of the energy supply and extraction sectors.

It is important to make the distinction between E3 modeling and energy systems models like TIMES (Loulou et al., 2005). Energy systems models typically use assumptions about energy demand as an input and assess the different ways in

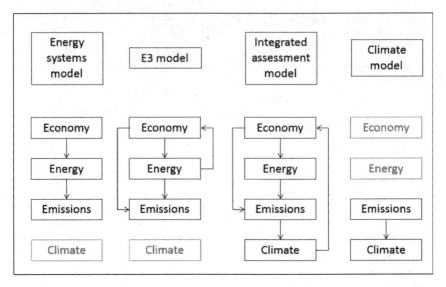

Figure 2.1 Different types of modeling systems.
Source: Cambridge Econometrics, SERI, and Wuppertal Institute, 2011.

which this demand may be met. While they do not generally model the economy, they are able to provide a great level of detail about the energy system, for example with specific technologies and grid linkages defined. Similarly to macroeconomic models, the choice of underlying assumptions is important. As we shall discuss in Chapter 3, most energy systems models assume optimizing behavior, but this is of limited use for simulation purposes.

As energy policy and environmental policy have moved up the political agenda, energy models and macroeconomic modeling approaches have been adapted to address the key issues that policy makers have faced. The macroeconomic models have done this by combining economic and physical data, for the main part linking economic national accounts data with physical energy balances and prices. This method also forms the basis for extending input–output analysis to the environment (see Chapters 15–16), but the modeling framework is generally more flexible, for example allowing certain economic relationships to change over time and vary in response to changes in other factors. One example is a fall in demand for a product when its price rises.

The analysis carried out by E3 models has made important contributions to recent policy debates. It has been particularly important in promoting the use of 'market-based instruments', including emissions trading schemes and environmental tax reform (see Chapter 8), as means of achieving economic growth without increased damage to the environment. Some models are also able to assess the impacts of particular regulations and other types of environmental policy. The coverage of these models is evolving constantly, both in terms of level of detail and geographical scope, and it can be difficult to keep up with all the most recent developments in the field.

Another recent trend has been to include climate change effects within the macroeconomic modeling framework. Such models are often referred to as integrated assessment models (IAMs). There are many types of IAMs, ranging from quite simplistic tools to the coupling of highly complex economic, energy and climate (and other) models.

IAMs have been severely criticized recently for their use of often arbitrary assumptions, including choice of discount rates and climate feedbacks (Pindyck, 2013; Stern, 2013). However, the criticism has been directed mainly at the simpler models that rely on rational choice theory and are typically used to determine 'optimal' carbon prices. The more complex modeling frameworks remain central to the analysis that is carried out by the Intergovernmental Panel on Climate Change (IPCC, 2014). Nevertheless, there is still a 'missing link' in the framework of the model, because it is difficult to identify and quantify the economic costs of climate change and extreme weather events. This is an area that is now being researched quite intensively, and we expect to see progress in the coming decade.

As the focus of this book is on East Asia and not the world as a whole, we do not include climate feedbacks in our modeling, because climate change is dependent on global GHG concentrations. The analysis in this book therefore draws heavily on a combination of macroeconomic modeling and energy systems modeling. In many of the chapters we make use of the E3ME-Asia macro-econometric model and several chapters also apply CGE models.

As outlined above, when interpreting the results of any modeling exercise, it is important to be aware of the strengths and limitations of the model and of the underlying assumptions that it uses. In this chapter, we discuss the key strengths, limitations, and assumptions that are most relevant for the following chapters. We first provide details about the E3ME model and then present the standard CGE modeling approach. The final section of this chapter outlines some of the key differences between the different modeling approaches.

2.3   The E3ME-Asia model

E3ME is a global E3 model, covering the world's economic and energy systems and the environment. The acronym stands for 'energy-environment-economy model that is econometric in design'. It was originally developed through the European Commission's research framework programmes and is now widely used for policy assessment, forecasting and other research purposes. A brief description is provided here; for further details the reader should refer to the model website[1], which includes an electronic version of the full manual (Cambridge Econometrics, 2014).

The current version, E3ME-Asia, was finalized in early 2014, following a two-year collaboration between Cambridge Econometrics and the Research Group for East Asia Environmental Policy Studies (REEPS). This version of the model was extended to include explicit coverage of the following East Asian countries:

- China
- Japan
- Korea
- Taiwan

The ASEAN countries are included as a single region in the model, with the exception of Indonesia, which is modelled separately. Other major economies are covered explicitly, and the remaining countries are grouped into regions to give complete global coverage.

The model includes a complete historical database with annual data going back to 1970 and can project forward annually to 2050, although a shorter time horizon is usually more relevant for policy makers. Within each country, the economy is split into 43 sectors to represent the different characteristics (e.g. cost patterns, energy usage, trade ratios) of different parts of the economy. The main data sources for the East Asian countries are:

- Asian Development Bank (ADB; main economic variables)
- Organisation for Economic Co-operation and Development (OECD; statistics – economic data, sectoral breakdowns)
- World Input–Output Database (WIOD; economic data, sectoral breakdowns, IO tables)
- National Statistics Offices (economic data, sectoral breakdowns)
- International Labour Organization (ILO; labor force)
- World Bank (WB; population, macroeconomic data)
- United Nations (UN; exchange rates, macroeconomic data)
- International Energy Agency (IEA; energy balances and prices)
- Emissions Database for Global Atmospheric Research (EDGAR; emissions data)

Figure 2.2 shows the basic structure of the model and the linkages between the three Es. The economic structure of E3ME is based on the system of national accounts (see Figure 2.3), as defined by European Communities et al. (2009), with further linkages to labor markets. There are econometric equations for the components of GDP (consumption, investment, and international trade), prices, and labor demand and supply. Each equation set is disaggregated by country/ region and by sector. Formal definitions of the equations are provided in the model manual (Cambridge Econometrics, 2014). The sectors are linked by using input-output tables and the countries are linked through the model's trade equations. The approach for modeling international trade is discussed in Chapter 19.

Energy demand is determined in the model as a function of economic activity, prices and the state of technology. The model solves first for aggregate energy demand and then for individual fuels. This sequence makes it possible to

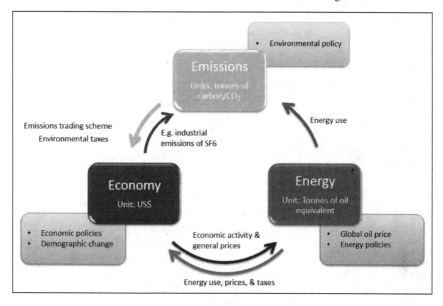

Figure 2.2 The basic structure of the E3ME model.

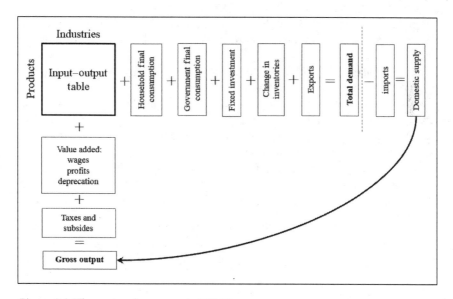

Figure 2.3 The national accounts in E3ME.

incorporate in the model changes of fuel type within a sector. Fuel demands feed back to the economy via the energy supplying and extraction sectors.

The model's representation of the power sector includes a detailed coverage of specific conventional and renewable technologies. As the power sector is an important source of emissions in East Asia (and most other parts of the world), this is a very important part of the model. It is described in much more detail and applied in Chapters 3–4 of this book.

CO_2 emissions from fuel consumption are determined by using fixed coefficients. The model outputs also include CO_2 emissions from industrial processes and calculations of other GHG emissions resulting from fuel consumption. However, other GHG emissions from agriculture, waste, or changes in land use lie beyond the scope of E3ME and so are not covered by the model.

E3ME includes measures of technological progress that are defined at the sectoral and national/regional level. There are various different ways of measuring technology in macroeconomic models (see Bosetti and Galeotti, 2009 for a discussion); in E3ME the formulation is based on accumulated capital, with an adjustment for R&D expenditure. Advances in technology may lead to improvements in efficiency (price competitiveness) or a higher quality of output (non-price competitiveness). Other modeling approaches also measure technological progress, because the consequences of new technologies can have a considerable influence on the overall costs and benefits of climate policy (Barker and Jenkins, 2007).

Behavioral relationships in E3ME (e.g., price elasticities) are estimated by econometric equations. The techniques used to specify the functional form of the equations are the concepts of cointegration and error-correction methodology, particularly as promoted by Engle and Granger (1987) and Hendry, Pagan, and Sargan (1984). Essentially, this method allows the model to assess both the initial response to a shock and the gradual transition to a long-term outcome. Further information about the model equations is provided in Chapter 8 of the model manual (Cambridge Econometrics, 2014).

E3ME is used to assess policy through a scenario-based approach, which can either be forward-looking (*ex ante*) or a representation of a past that might have been, but was not (*ex post*). The analysis in this book is mostly *ex ante*, and the starting point is a baseline case (often called 'business as usual') that is based on current policy. Additional policy inputs are then entered for each scenario and the model outputs from the scenario are compared to those from the baseline. In this way, the effects of the policy are identified. Typical model outputs include:

- GDP and the aggregate components of GDP (household expenditure, investment, government expenditure and international trade)
- Sectoral output and gross value added, prices, trade and competitiveness effects
- International trade by sector, origin, and destination
- Consumer prices and expenditures
- Sectoral employment, unemployment, sectoral wage rates, and labor supply
- Real incomes by socio-economic group (where data are available)
- Energy demand by sector and by fuel, energy prices
- CO_2 emissions by sector and by fuel
- Other GHG and air-borne emissions

2.4   CGE models

Computable General Equilibrium (CGE) models have been the cornerstone of quantitative macroeconomic analysis over the past two decades. Their use is particularly common in analysis of trade agreements and, more recently, energy and climate policy. In the last round of the Energy Modeling Forum (round 28, see Knopf et al., 2013), all six of the economic models that were included in the comparative assessment were either CGE or optimal growth in design. This is consistent with previous rounds of the forum.

The basic structure of CGE models is similar to that of the E3ME model described above. The core of the model is an accounting framework (namely the input–output tables or the social accounting matrices) that ensures consistency between the various economic flows in the model. As with the E3ME model, this core is extended to incorporate physical energy demands and greenhouse gas emissions. The outputs from CGE models are, therefore, also very similar to those described for E3ME in the previous section and they are usually produced by using the same scenario-based approach.

CGE models cover the whole economy within a single framework and are based on neoclassical economic theory. They assume that markets always return to an equilibrium position, meaning that prices adjust so that demand matches supply. An attractive feature of their coverage of the whole economy is that it is built up from 'microeconomic foundations'. This means that the models relate behavior at the individual level to the whole economy by aggregating the behavior of individuals across the whole economy, although to do this it is necessary to assume that all the individuals are identical.[2] Furthermore, in accord with neoclassical economic theory, it is assumed that each of these identical individuals acts rationally to optimize his/her economic welfare. Consequently, summing across individuals optimizes outcomes (usually measured as a utility or welfare function) across the whole economy.

In this book, we focus on this key assumption that individuals optimize outcomes for themselves, and we show that this assumption creates and explains many of the differences between CGE models and the E3ME model. Underlying assumptions about optimization lead to many further assumptions in the CGE modeling framework, including that individuals act rationally in their own self-interest to maximize profits (firms) or welfare (individuals), or that individuals have 'perfect knowledge' with which to make decisions. The optimizing behavior of individuals and firms is the basis for achieving market-clearing equilibrium in which demand and supply are equal and maximized.

For example, in a standard CGE modeling framework, there will never be any unemployed workers. This is because an unemployed worker could improve his/her utility by offering to accept a lower wage than someone currently employed, and a profit-maximizing firm would replace more expensive labor. The process would continue until there are no unemployed workers left and all workers reduce their wages to the rate that 'clears' the market.

It is important to note that there are also differences between CGE models, both in terms of theoretical construction and geographical/sectoral coverage.

The term CGE has increasingly been used to mean macroeconomic modeling more generally, as the more advanced models have gradually relaxed assumptions about market clearing (e.g., to allow for unemployment in labor markets) to allow for non-equilibrium outcomes.

There is a global community of CGE modellers and a set of standard resources available, notably the GTAP database[3], the GAMS programming system[4] and the training courses offered by Monash University. Groups such as the Energy Modeling Forum allow international researchers to meet and exchange ideas relating to the modeling approach.

Aside from the restrictive nature of the assumptions in CGE models, criticisms of the approach often relate to a lack of understanding and documentation of the models (Mitra-Khan, 2008) and some of their other key assumptions, for example the trade equations (McDaniel and Balistreri, 2003). Following the global financial and economic crisis, some of the underlying assumptions about quick and perfect market adjustments have also been questioned, including in the popular media, and the freedom that model builders have to choose their sometimes arbitrary parameters remains a key issue (Mitra-Khan, 2008). Nevertheless, the CGE model remains an important standard tool for macroeconomic analysis.

2.5   Comparison of approaches

The differences between the two modeling approaches which will be explored throughout this book are subtle but profound. It is important to note that, on the surface at least, the two approaches share many common features. Both are based on the national accounting system and are used for similar types of policy analysis. The model inputs and outputs are broadly comparable.

The main differences in approach arise from the assumptions that the models make about human and organizational behavior and about how the economy fits in with the wider social/environmental system. The assumptions about human and organizational behavior can be traced back to the different economic theories that underlie the models (see Table 2.1).

On the one hand, we have CGE models, based on mainstream neoclassical economic theory and its extension environmental economics. In these approaches, all economic agents (e.g., individuals and companies) act rationally in their own

Table 2.1 Summary of the underlying economic theories of the models

	Economic theory	*Environmental linkages*
E3ME	Post-Keynesian economics	Ecological economics (i.e., the economy is a sub-system of the environment)
CGE model	Neoclassical economics	Environmental economics (i.e., the environment is external to the economy)

self-interest. These models find 'optimal' solutions; for example, they find ways to maximize economic output under given market prices and various policy constraints. The models produce insights into how the economic system as a whole interacts and responds to policy stimuli. Impacts on the environment are treated as 'externalities', that is, as by-products of the economic system.

On the other hand we have E3ME, in which it is assumed that behavior in the future will be very similar to what it has been in the recent past (for most countries the last 40 years; that is what is meant by calling E3ME a simulation tool). While this model also gives important insights into interactions across the economic and energy systems, it is not designed to produce optimal outcomes for the individual or for society. Instead of doing that, it assesses the impacts of a predetermined set of policies. The model draws on theories of ecological economics, in which the economy is treated as a sub-system of the environment and is subject to natural constraints. Environmental impacts are measured in physical units and, where possible, compared with estimated natural carrying capacities.

The theoretical differences have important practical implications. If the firms and individuals in a model optimize their behavior, then imposing a policy constraint on them will by definition worsen the outcomes for them. This means that the use of CGE models for assessing 'green growth' strategies is limited because the possibility of higher growth rates as a result of policy is usually ruled out by assumption. In contrast, the E3ME framework allows that there are unused resources which could be put to use under the right policy conditions, leading to higher output and employment.

As policy makers become aware of these distinctions between modeling approaches, it is becoming increasingly common to assess policies using a combination of methods (e.g., European Commission, 2014). Not only does this add a degree of robustness to results, it engages policy makers with the key modeling concepts and differences between the various modeling approaches. It is one of the objectives of this book to increase such awareness and engagement.

Notes

1 http://www.e3me.com.
2 This is referred to as the 'representative agent' assumption; see Kirman (1992).
3 See the web page https://www.gtap.agecon.purdue.edu/databases/default.asp.
4 General Algebraic Modeling System; see http://www.gams.com/.

References

Barker, T., and Jenkins, K. (2007). 'The costs of avoiding dangerous climate change: Estimates derived from a meta-analysis of the literature.' A Briefing Paper for the United Nations Human Development Report 2007/2008, No. 2007/2. http://hdr.undp.org/sites/default/files/barker_terry_and_jenkins_katie.pdf (accessed May 17, 2015).

Beinhocker, E. (2007). *The Origin of Wealth: Evolution, Complexity, and the Radical Remaking of Economics*. London: Random House Business.

Bosetti, V., and Galeotti, M. (2009). 'Technical progress in TranSust models.' In Bosetti, V., Gerlagh, R., and Schleicher, S. P. (Eds.), *Modelling Sustainable Development: Transitions to a Sustainable Future*. Cheltenham, UK and Northamption, MA: Edward Elgar.

Cambridge Econometrics (2014). *E3ME Version 6 Model Manual*. http://www.e3me.com (accessed May 17, 2015).

Cambridge Econometrics, Sustainable Europe Research Institute (SERI), and Wuppertal Institute (2011). *Sustainability Scenarios for a Resource Efficient Europe*. Report submitted to the European Commission, DG Environment. http://ec.europa.eu/environment/enveco/studies_modelling/pdf/SustScen_Report_Final.pdf (accessed May 17, 2015).

Dixon, P. B., and Rimmer, M. T. (2002). *Dynamic General Equilibrium Modelling for Forecasting and Policy: A Practical Guide and Documentation of MONASH*. Amsterdam: North-Holland.

Engle, R. F., and Granger, C.W.J. (1987). 'Cointegration and error correction: Representation, estimation and testing.' *Econometrica*, 55, pp. 251–276.

European Commission (2009). *Impact Assessment Guidelines*. European Commission SEC(2009) 92. http://ec.europa.eu/smart-regulation/impact/commission_guidelines/docs/iag_2009_en.pdf (accessed May 17, 2015).

European Commission (2014). *A Policy Framework for Climate and Energy in the Period from 2020 up to 2030*. Impact Assessment, SWD(2014) 15 final. http://ec.europa.eu/clima/policies/2030/documentation_en.htm (accessed May 17, 2015).

European Communities, International Monetary Fund, Organisation for Economic Co-operation and Development, United Nations, and World Bank (2009). *System of National Accounts 2008*. New York: European Communities, International Monetary Fund, Organization for Economic Co-operation and Development, United Nations, and World Bank. http://unstats.un.org/unsd/nationalaccount/docs/SNA2008.pdf (accessed May 17, 2015)

Hendry, D. F., Pagan, A., and Sargan, J. D. (1984) 'Dynamic specification.' In Griliches, Z., and Intriligator, M. D. (Eds.), *Handbook of Econometrics*, Vol II. Amsterdam: North-Holland. Pp. 1023–1100.

Hertel, T. (1999). *Global Trade Analysis: Modelling and Applications*. Cambridge: Cambridge University Press.

Hoover, K. D. (2012). 'Microfoundational programs.' In Duarte, P.G., and Lima, G. T. (Eds.), *Microfoundations Reconsidered*. Cheltenham, UK; Northampton, MA: Edward Elgar. Pp. 19–61.

Intergovernmental Panel on Climate Change (IPCC) (2014). *Fifth Assessment Report*. Cambridge, UK; New York: Cambridge University Press.

Kirman, A. P. (1992, Spring). 'Whom or what does the representative individual represent?' *Journal of Economic Perspectives*, 6(2), pp. 117–136.

Knopf, B., Chen, Y.H.H., De Cian, E., Förster, H., Kanudia, A., Karkatsouli, I., Keppo, I., Koljonen, T., Schumacher, K., and Van Vuuren, D. P. (2013). 'Beyond 2020—strategies and costs for transforming the European energy system.' *Climate Change Economics*, 4(supplement 1), http://globalchange.mit.edu/files/document/MITJPSPGC_Reprint_13-35.pdf (accessed May 17, 2015).

Loulou, R., Remne, U., Kanudia, A., Lehtila, A., and Goldstein, G. (2005). *Documentation for the TIMES Model*. http://www.etsap.org/Docs/TIMESDoc-Intro.pdf (accessed May 17, 2015).

Lucas, R. (1976). 'Econometric policy evaluation: A critique.' In Brunner, K., and Meltzer, A. (Eds.), *The Phillips Curve and Labor Markets*. Amsterdam: North-Holland. Pp. 19–46.

Matsuoka, Y., Kainuma, M., and Morita, T. (1995). 'Scenario analysis of global warming using the Asian Pacific Integrated Model (AIM).' *Energy Policy*, 23(4/5), pp. 357–371.

McDaniel, C. A., and Balistreri, E. J. (2003). 'A review of Armington trade substitution elasticities.' *Integration and Trade*, 7(18), pp 161–173.

Mitra-Khan, B. M. (2008). 'Debunking the myths of computable general equilibrium models.' SCEPA Working Paper 2008–1, Schwarz Center for Economic Policy Analysis, The New School for Social Research, New York. http://www.economic policyresearch.org/images/docs/research/economic_growth/SCEPA%20 Working%20Paper%202008-1_Kahn.pdf (accessed May 17, 2015)

Pindyck, R. (2013, July). 'Climate change policy: What do the models tell us?' NBER Working Paper No. 19244. MIT Sloan School of Management, Cambridge, MA.

Probst, G., and Bassi, A. M. (2014). *Tackling Complexity: A Systemic Approach for Decision Makers*. Sheffield, UK: Greenleaf Publishing.

Stern, N. (2013). 'The structure of economic modelling of the potential impacts of climate change: Grafting gross underestimation of risk onto already narrow science models.' *Journal of Economic Literature*, 51(3), pp. 838–859.

Swann, G.M.P. (2008). *Putting Econometrics in Its Place: A New Direction in Applied Economics*. Cheltenham, UK; Northampton, MA: Edward Elgar.

Introduction to Part 1

The power choices and the sustainability of energy usage in East Asia

In relation to the sustainability of energy supply in East Asia, the use of nuclear power and renewable energy sources that do not emit CO_2 during power generation remain important issues.

Before 2011, Japan had set a goal of reducing greenhouse gas emissions to 75 percent of 1990 levels by 2020, and further expansion of nuclear power remained the primary means for doing so. The 2011 accident at the Fukushima Daiichi Nuclear Power Plant hampered such policies, however, causing the Japanese government to significantly ease its greenhouse gas reduction targets. In contrast, China and Korea still position nuclear power as the centerpieces of their respective low-carbon policies and have maintained their plans for nuclear power expansion. Nonetheless, increased use of nuclear power will not necessarily be sufficient for greenhouse gas emission reduction in the face of increased energy demands, and nuclear power poses significant potential risks to neighboring countries.

Interest in the widespread use of renewable energy is increasing worldwide, and East Asia is no exception. In Chapter 3, we consider ways in which the East Asian countries could reduce CO2 emissions without relying on nuclear power. The economic implications of these measures are discussed in Chapter 4. Chapter 5 expands on this analysis in the specific case of Japan, where the government has put forward future options for the power mix in response to the Fukushima accident.

In Chapter 6 we then turn attention to the often-neglected potential of energy efficiency and the so-called 'nega-watts' that offer possible low-cost solutions to reducing emissions. Finally, we discuss the related issue of energy security and how it might be affected by decarbonization within the energy system in Chapter 7.

3 Modeling the power sectors in East Asia

The choice of power sources

Yuki Ogawa, Jean-François Mercure,
Soocheol Lee, and Hector Pollitt

3.1 Introduction

East Asia currently faces choices regarding the use of power sources for the future. As discussed in Chapter 1, the choices made during the next few years are likely to affect and determine the directions of energy sector developments for the next few decades. This is particularly relevant after the Fukushima accident. However, such choices will also affect the regional economy and the environment. In this chapter, we explore possible scenarios of power sector development for four East Asian countries (China, Japan, Korea, and Taiwan), all of which have specific targets for changing the composition of their technology mix in order to generate power. We use a method that is based on technology diffusion, in which pathways of technology result from energy policy choices. We explore the feasibility of current aspirations and targets by evaluating the effectiveness of putative electricity policies in chosen scenarios.

After the Fukushima accident, public concern about the safety of nuclear power plants has become widespread in East Asia. Governments across the region have tried to emphasize the low-cost and low-CO_2 characteristics of nuclear power, and stated that existing nuclear plants are safe enough to continue operating. The risk of economic loss that might occur from reducing nuclear power generation has clearly factored in this position. On the environmental side, nuclear power does not emit CO_2 when generating electricity but, as revealed by the Fukushima accident, it can seriously damage human and environmental welfare.

In this chapter, the first scenario analyzes how reducing nuclear power affects the power mixes. In recent years, the reduction of carbon emissions has also become an important issue in East Asia and our second scenario (i.e., limiting the share of coal-fired power plants) focuses on this policy goal. Japan, Korea and Taiwan are heavily dependent on imported fossil fuel and China mainly relies on domestic coal production as an energy source. The second scenario analyses the restriction on both nuclear and coal-fired power. The economic impacts of these same scenarios are explored in Chapter 4.

Within this chapter, Section 3.2 provides an outline of the power sectors and related policies in each of the four countries; Section 3.3 describes the modeling methodology that was applied. Sections 3.4 and 3.5 describe the scenarios that were assessed, and show the corresponding energy mixes in each case. Section 3.6 concludes by outlining policy implications of the analysis.

3.2. Overview of the power sector in East Asia

China

Energy demand continues to grow rapidly in China, and coal has been the main source of energy supply, supported by massive domestic production. Concern over local air pollution and increasing greenhouse gas (GHG) emissions from coal combustion has become a great concern. While making efforts to build more-efficient coal-fired power plants, developing other energy sources has drawn great interest as well. Nuclear power is regarded as an important energy source, even after the Fukushima Accident. Renewable energy, including large-scale generation of hydroelectricity, is also strongly supported to meet the growing demand and reduce GHG emissions.

In 2012, 78.0 percent of electricity was provided by fossil fuels in China (IEA, 2014d). Coal was and remains the main source, providing 75.9 percent of electricity and accounting for 49.1 percent of energy-related CO_2 emissions in the country in its power generating capacity (IEA, 2014d). Hydropower was the largest among non-fossil fuel energy sources, accounting for 17.2 percent of electricity supply. China had the largest capacity of wind-powered electricity generation in the world (75 GW) and the fourth largest capacity of solar panel electricity systems (i.e., photovoltaics, PV, which produce 7 GW; REN21, 2013), but the share of these technologies in domestic energy supply is still low given China's very high total energy demand.

In its 12th five-year plan (FYP, 2010–2015) China outlines the target that 9.5 percent of total primary energy consumption should come from renewable energy, with different aims for different types of renewable energy, as summarized in Table 3.1.

Nuclear capacity is anticipated to reach 40 GW by 2015 in the 12th FYP and 58 GW by 2020; 150 GW of nuclear capacity is expected by 2030 (World Nuclear Association, 2014).

Table 3.1 Targets of different renewable technology in China's 12th FYP

Technology	Installed capacity target for 2015 (GW)
Conventional hydro	260
Pumped storage hydro	30
Wind, onshore	100
Wind, offshore	5
PV	21
Ocean energy	0.05

Source: IEA (2014c).

Japan

Before the Fukushima accident on 11 March 2011, caused by the Great East Japan Earthquake, nuclear power was regarded as the main source for generating electricity, contributing to reducing both GHG emissions and fossil-fuel imports. However, the Fukushima accident has led to acute concern over the safety of nuclear power. As of July 2014, no nuclear power plant in Japan was operating again to supply electricity (Japan Nuclear Technology Institute, 2014).

In 2012, fossil fuels provided 85.6 percent of electricity supply in Japan (IEA, 2014a). Renewable energy, excluding conventional hydro energy, accounted for only 1.7 percent of the electricity supply. Ninety-nine point five percent of fossil fuels consumed in Japan are imported in terms of tons of oil equivalent (IEA, 2014b), and the import bill for fossil fuels went up by 2.4 trillion JPY from 2010 to 2013 (Japan Renewable Energy Foundation, 2014). This has increased recently because electricity supplied by nuclear power is now substituted by energy from fossil fuels, and also because of the low exchange rate of the yen and increases in fossil fuel prices. This situation reveals the economic risk of relying more on imported fuel as an energy source. At the same time, CO_2 emissions from the power sector have increased by 12.0 percent in 2013 compared to 2010.

Renewable energy will be one of the most important energy sources to tackle the security of the national energy supply and to promote climate change mitigation by substituting and reducing fossil fuel consumption. In 2012, the feed-in tariff scheme (FIT) was introduced to replace the renewable portfolio standard scheme (RPS) and net-metering scheme for photovoltaic power to push forward the deployment of renewable energy. Different tariffs are applied for different types of renewable energy to support various kinds of technologies (Table 3.2). In the two years after FIT started in July 2012, 11.8 GW of renewable energy capacity was installed and connected to the grid.

Korea

Korea is highly dependent on imported fossil fuels for energy. In 2013, 71.7 percent of electricity supply originated from fossil fuel combustion (IEA, 2014a), and 99.0 percent of the fossil fuels consumed in the country were imported (IEA, 2014b). Nuclear power has a relatively large share, 25.7 percent, compared to other East Asian regions. Though renewable energy has been supported by policies such as the FIT and RPS, its share in the overall fuel mix is still low, around 1% (excluding conventional hydro energy) in total.

Renewable energy technologies were supported by a FIT until 2011, which was replaced by the RPS in 2012. This was mainly because tariff spending on the FIT in Korea was not shared by the consumers but supported by a special government budget that ran into financing issues.

Korea adopted its latest National Energy Plan for 2030 in January 2014. Nuclear power remains important to the electricity supply, but its originally

Table 3.2 FIT tariff and installed capacity of renewable energy in Japan

Technology	Tariff (JPY/kWh)			Installed capacity (July 2012 – July 2014) (MW)
	2012	2013	2014	
PV (smaller than 10 kW)	42	38	37	2482.5
PV (larger than 10 kW)	40	36	32	9145.1
Wind (smaller than 20 kW)	55	55	55	0.003
Wind (larger than 20 kW)	22	22	22	111.7
Small hydro (smaller than 200 kW)	34	34	34	2.9
Small hydro (200–1,000 kW)	29	29	29	4.2
Geothermal (smaller than 1,5000 kW)	40	40	40	0.2
Biogas	39	39	39	6.3
Solid biomass (unutilized wood)	32	32	32	13.7
Solid biomass (wood and processed residue from agriculture)	24	24	24	15.1
Waste	17	17	17	53.7

Source: Agency for Natural Resources and Energy, Japan (2014).

planned share that had been outlined before the Fukushima accident will be reduced because concerns over the safety issues of nuclear power are now widespread. In the National Energy Plan 2014, the share of nuclear is set to be 29 percent of total electricity generation in 2035. The capacity of nuclear power is planned to increase to 32.9 GW by 2022 and be maintained at that level until 2035 (World Nuclear Association, 2014). Renewable energy is assumed to provide 10 percent of total electricity in 2022 and 11 percent of primary energy consumption in 2035.

Taiwan

Similar to Japan and Korea, Taiwan is highly dependent on imported fossil fuels. The high share of fossil fuels contributes to both Taiwan's carbon emissions and its security of energy supply. Nuclear power has been regarded as an important energy source to deal with these problems, but since the Fukushima accident faces public opposition. Renewable energy is also an important energy source in this context and has been supported by a FIT since 2009.

In 2011, 78.6 percent of electricity was generated from fossil fuel combustion (Bureau of Energy, Taiwan, 2014), and 98.7 percent of fossil fuels consumed in Taiwan were imported (IEA, 2014b). Nuclear power accounted for 16.7 percent and renewable energy, including conventional hydroelectric power, accounted for 3.6 percent of the electricity supply.

The Taiwanese government published a New Energy Policy of Taiwan in June 2014 (Bureau of Energy, Taiwan, 2014). In the plan, a steady reduction of nuclear energy and full-scale promotion of renewable energy are anticipated. There would be no extension to the life span of existing nuclear plants, and no more new nuclear plants would be built. The capacity of renewable energy, which was 3,615 MW in 2012, is planned to reach 9,952 MW by 2025 and 12,502 MW by 2030.

3.3   Modeling method

In this chapter we model the choice and diffusion of power technology in East Asia using the E3ME-Asia model (see Chapter 2, or Cambridge Econometrics, 2014), complemented by a simulation model of power technology diffusion, FTT:Power (Mercure, 2012). E3ME-Asia provides the demand for electricity, given industrial activity, household income, and electricity prices in 53 regions, including China, Japan, Korea and Taiwan. FTT:Power takes this demand as an input and, with given electricity sector policies such as carbon taxes or technology support mechanisms, determines the technology mix and calculates GHG emissions. The combined model has recently been used for studying the impacts of climate policy instruments for emission reductions worldwide by using the E3MG-FTT:Power framework (an old version of E3ME) that operates under 21 regions (Mercure et al., 2014). However, is now integrated to the current version of E3ME-Asia with 53 regions.

The dynamical equation

FTT:Power is composed of two parts; the choice of investors and the diffusion of technology. The choice of investors is represented by using a method related to discrete choice theory, a binary logit (see the appendix in Mercure et al., 2014), involving sets of distributed diverse agents making cost comparisons between available options. These choices are used to drive the diffusion of technology options according to the rate of replacement (using life expectancies) and the rate of construction. Technical constraints, such as those related to the predictability and/or flexibility of power sources, may not allow particular compositions to arise, due to grid stability problems (e.g., 100 percent wind power); it is assumed that investors, seeking to avoid stranded assets, have the foresight to avoid making such investment errors. Representing technology choice and using a matrix of preferences between every possible pair of options F_{ij}, a matrix of timescales of technological change A_{ij} and technical constraints G_{ij}, the central equation driving FTT:Power is a set of non-linear finite differences equations:

$$\Delta S_i = \sum_j S_i S_j \left(A_{ij}F_{ij}G_{ij} - A_{ji}F_{ji}G_{ji} \right)\frac{1}{\tau}\Delta t. \tag{3.1}$$

This equation generates, for two competing technologies, slow diffusion at low penetration, and then fast diffusion at intermediate stages before saturating at high penetration. It represents, however, the competition between 24 possible technology options (see Mercure (2012) for a full list of technology options) that can produce more complex patterns – including, for instance, the technology ladder where series of intermediate technologies may diffuse in and out of the system.

Timescales of diffusion

The diffusion of technologies in FTT:Power, expressed by Eq. 3.1, follows simple population dynamics. Eq. 3.1 can either be called a 'replicator dynamics' (as in evolutionary theory) or 'Lotka-Volterra' (as in population biology) equation. As is commonly done in survival analysis (and demography), one may define survival functions for technologies, corresponding to the probability of survival over years. By also determining a differential rate of upscaling for these technologies, one may derive dynamics of technological change that respect (1) the statistical lifetime of technologies and (2) the rate at which they can be replaced, beyond what is related to investor choices. This theory is explained in detail elsewhere (Mercure, 2013), and leads to Eq. 3.1.

Natural resource use

The diffusion of renewable power technologies in FTT:Power is limited by the availability of natural resources using cost-supply curves. In this framework, costs increasing with increasing levels of development are fed into costs that influence investor choices, limiting adoption when costs become prohibitive. For this purpose an extensive assessment of renewable energy resources was carried out on the basis of both literature – with some of the results taken from land-use models – and calculations by the authors (Mercure and Salas, 2012). This is included in the terms for investor choices F_{ij}.

In the case of non-renewable resources (fossil and nuclear fuels), a more complex depletion algorithm is used that generates path-dependent scenarios of depletion when given the price history (Mercure and Salas, 2013). In this calculation, the cost distribution of non-renewable resources consumed, and the cost distribution left for future consumption, depends on the price history of the commodity; thus, the price is determined as that generating the required supply. This methodology can reproduce depletion dynamics that are consistent with classic peak oil theory depletion profiles, however, including both conventional and unconventional resources as well as some of the dynamics of the global market. Fuel costs are included in the calculation of levelized costs carried out by investors.

Peak demand, energy storage and grid stability

Grid flexibility issues, peak demand, and energy storage are understood in FTT as simple limits to the shares of every technology beyond which the system becomes unstable. Broadly speaking, three types of electricity generation exist: (1) *baseload* systems, which we define as having an output that cannot be changed rapidly (in several hours or days, e.g., nuclear and coal), (2) *flexible* systems, which can change their output rapidly enough to compensate for rapid changes in demand or variable supply (in minutes, e.g., gas turbines, oil generators, or hydro), and (3) *variable* systems, renewables systems that have an uncontrollable variable output (e.g., wind, solar, and wave). To maintain stability and supply demand, a grid cannot be uniquely composed of variable or baseload systems; the difference between the supply of baseload together with variable systems and the demand must be buffered by flexible systems, which can switch on and off at the right times. An additional constraint arises related to the profile of the daily demand, which requires further flexibility. However, flexibility can also be provided by storage of electricity, which can displace the time profile of the (demand–variable supply) profile and loosens the constraint.

These limits are compactly expressed as inequalities for different types of share, also shown schematically in Figure 3.1:

$$S_{flex}CF_{flex} + S_{var}CF_{var} + S_{base}CF_{base} = \overline{CF} \le \overline{CF}_{rated}, \tag{3.2}$$

$$S_{flex}CF_{flex} + S_{var}CF_{var} \ge \overline{CF}\left(\frac{\Delta D}{D} + \frac{U_{var}T_D}{D} + \frac{E_s}{D}\right), \tag{3.3}$$

$$S_{flex} - S_{var} \ge \left(\frac{\Delta U_D}{U_{tot}} - \frac{U_s}{U_{tot}}\right), \tag{3.4}$$

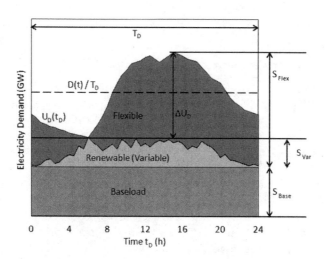

Figure 3.1 Simple representation of the share limits for grid stability, associated with equations (3.2–3.5).

$$S_{base} + S_{var} \leq \left(\overline{CF} - \frac{1}{2} \frac{\Delta U_D}{U_{tot}} + \frac{U_s}{U_{tot}} \right) \tag{3.5}$$

where S_{flex}, S_{base}, and S_{var} stand for the total shares of flexible, baseload, and variable systems, respectively. $\frac{\Delta U_D}{U_{tot}}$ stands for the peak load to total capacity ratio, and $\frac{U_s}{U_{tot}}$ stands for the ratio of electricity storage production capacity to total capacity. $\overline{CF}$ is the weighted average capacity factor and $\frac{\Delta D}{D}$ is the peak to average electricity demand ratio. $\frac{U_{var} T_D}{D}$ is the total generation that would be produced by variables were they to have 100 percent capacity factors, and $\frac{E_s}{D}$ is the total energy storage to total demand ratio. $\overline{CF}_{rated}$ is the weighted average factory-rated capacity factors.

Because operating flexible generators in order to backup variable renewables leads to lower capacity factors – as they run only a fraction of the time every day – these inequalities also determine the maximum capacity factors that can be used for flexible technologies.

Thus, because of the share limits, as long as flexibility exists in ample supply no restrictions constrain the development of any technologies. However, when a system ventures near one or more of its share limits, some types of share exchanges become prohibited in Eq. 3.1.

This can lead to several possibilities. For instance, the variable renewables market may separate from the baseload market, where variable technologies compete for the amount of shares allowed by the amount of flexibility available; this can take place at a different price level compared to baseload technologies. Similarly, the market for flexible generation can also form a sub-market at a different price level in order to accommodate the amount of renewables or peak demand. It is often the case that increases in renewable energy are limited by the degree of flexibility and storage. A focus on renewable energy needs to be combined with increases in its storage capacity and demand management to enable further growth.[1]

Linkage between FTT: Power and E3ME-Asia

The two models, FTT:Power and E3ME-Asia, are fully integrated within a single framework. While E3ME-Asia iterates within a year, it estimates the electricity demand for each region, and FTT:Power estimates how the demand will be met. Prices of different fuels are also passed from E3ME-Asia to FTT:Power to calculate the cost of electricity generated through technologies that use fuels. Given this information, FTT:Power determines how the electricity demands can be met by 24 technology options. The price of electricity, investment cost for new plants, and fuel use are then passed from FTT:Power to E3ME-Asia. The price of electricity affects the demand, and the demand is fed back into the iteration process. Investment costs outline the intermediate demand from the power sector to other industries through an input–output (I–O) relationship. Owing to data limitations, investment in the power sector is treated the same for all types of energy-generating technology. Fuel use is used to calculate emission levels.

3.4 The scenarios

Baseline assumptions

The decision about whether or not to build nuclear power plants in the four East Asian countries was assumed to be political rather than market-driven. Therefore, the electricity supply from nuclear power plants is set exogenously and is not solved endogenously by FTT:Power. The forecast period considered is 2015 to 2030.

In Japan, electricity supply through nuclear power until 2013 follows the historical data from IEA (2014a) and IAEA (2014). Supply in 2014 is set to zero, because no nuclear power station was online at the time of the analysis. There are 48 operational – but offline – nuclear reactors in Japan, of which 18 are currently undergoing safety evaluations. The two reactors at the Sendai Nuclear Power Plant, Sendai No. 1 and No. 2, have gone through all the safety evaluation processes and are assumed to restart from 2015. The other 16 reactors that have already applied for the safety check are assumed to restart from 2016 in our baseline. The other 30 are assumed to restart from 2017, excluding those that are suspected not to be able to withstand seismic activity. All the reactors will stop operating when, after 40 years, they reach the end of their lifetimes.

China, Korea, and Taiwan follow the historical data until 2013, and are then assumed to pursue their national plans as described in Section 3.2., that is, China increasing the capacity of nuclear power to 40 GW by 2015, 58 GW by 2020, and 200 GW by 2030; Korea increasing the capacity of nuclear power to 32.9 GW by 2022 and maintaining that level until 2035; and Taiwan shutting down existing plants at the end of their 40-year life span.

Being members of the International Energy Agency, Japan and Korea are not expected to increase the capacity of their oil-fired power plants. Taiwan is also following this guideline by not having increased the capacity of oil-fired power plants since 2000 (Bureau of Energy, Taiwan, 2013). Therefore, in this analysis, these three countries keep the current capacity of their oil-fired power plants exogenous from 2014 onwards. According to each country's national plan, large-scale hydropower plants are also set to exogenous capacity, because the construction of new dams is not only subject to available natural resources but also to the social context.

Policies that support renewable energy production are also considered in the baseline. According to the IEA (2014c), Japan, China, and Taiwan have FIT schemes, whereas Korea has an RPS scheme, which forces its power companies to purchase a certain proportion of electricity generated from renewable energy. Electricity from renewable energy would be bought from the cheapest provider until the amount meets the obligation and the purchase price would be the minimum to meet the target. In our modeling, the price achieved through RPS is set exogenously at a level that meets the target and is treated the same as that achieved through FIT. The schemes differ in terms of technologies covered as well as tariff rates or targets, and these factors are taken into account in the baseline.

Other inputs, including historical economic statistics, follow the general assumptions for E3ME-Asia.[2]

Scenario 1: limiting the share of nuclear power (S1)

In this scenario, the share of electricity supply from nuclear power plants is solved endogenously from 2015 onward by FTT:Power, with the restriction of not increasing the share of nuclear power in the electricity supply for China and Korea. Because Japan has a zero share of nuclear power in 2014, the share remains zero in the whole period afterwards. Taiwan is planning to stop further increases in nuclear power in the baseline and so this scenario is the same as the baseline. The scenario is analyzed for each country and then the policies are integrated to see if there are any spill-over effects between the countries.

Scenario 2: limiting the share of coal-fired power (S2)

In this scenario, the share of electricity supply from conventional coal-fired power plants is restricted to not increase above current levels, and plants are left to operate until the end of their lifetime. Other assumptions, including the capacity of nuclear and oil-fired power plants and support for renewable energy, are held as in the baseline.

Scenario 3: limiting both nuclear and coal-fired power (S3)

In this scenario, keeping all other baseline assumptions, S1 and S2 are combined; that is, both nuclear power and coal-fired power are restricted not to increase their share in electricity supply. The scenarios above are summarized in Table 3.3.

Table 3.3 Names of scenarios

Scenario						Description
	Jp	*Cn*	*Kr*	*Tw*	*Ea**	
Baseline	Base					Reference case with current policies
S1	S1Jp	S1Cn	S1Kr	(Same as base)	S1Ea	Limiting the share of nuclear power
S2	S2Jp	S2Cn	S2Kr	S2Tw	S2Ea	Limiting the share of coal-fired power
S3	S3Jp	S3Cn	S3Kr	(Same as S2Tw)	S3Ea	Limiting the share of nuclear and coal-fired power

Note: *Ea corresponds to setting the same restrictions simultaneously in each country.

In this chapter, we are not showing the results for 'Ea' scenario groups because the results for the power sector do not differ from those scenarios that put constraints on individual countries; there are no cross-border interactions, such as the trade of electricity. Economic impacts differ and will be analyzed in Chapter 4.

3.5   Modeling results

China

Electricity supplied by each technology in each scenario for China is shown in Figure 3.2. Although the baseline for China includes a support scheme for renewables, the share of renewable energy does not increase significantly. The reason behind this is that, although renewable energy grows in absolute terms, coal – which is the baseload technology dominating China's power sector – grows even faster to supply the rapidly increasing electricity demand. This condition makes further diffusion of renewable energy comparatively difficult. In S1, this situation does not change significantly because nuclear energy, which in China does not have a large share in the electricity supply, is substituted by coal – which is the least expensive energy source. Meanwhile, in S2, the share of coal-fired power stations decreases over time sufficiently to open room for the generation of renewable energy. However, owing to market-based decisions, nuclear power is not increased and can therefore not replenish the decrease in coal-fired power. Given the constraints to maintain grid stability, baseload technologies and variable renewable energy are competing against each other. The sum of the capacity of both technologies cannot exceed the minimum demand in a day. When both coal-fired and nuclear power are restricted, which is the case in S3, renewable energy gets a higher share than in S2 as the baseload technologies decrease further. However, the entire decrease in baseload technologies is not covered by renewable energy and some part is substituted by gas power plants, a flexible power system.

The dominating technology in renewable energies (excluding hydro energy) is solid biomass, given the support from the government and huge resource availability. The second is onshore wind and the third is solar PV.

Japan

Electricity supplied by each technology in each scenario for Japan is shown in Figure 3.3. As in described above for China, the largest increase in the share of renewables in Japan is in S3. In this scenario, the share of energy depending on coal and nuclear power, both baseload technologies, decreases. When electricity supply is dominated by baseload technologies, there is restricted market space for (variable) renewable energy sources that depends on the available flexibility; and these can now compete in a sub-market determined by grid stability. Nuclear power is also a baseload technology, but in S1 the share increase of renewables

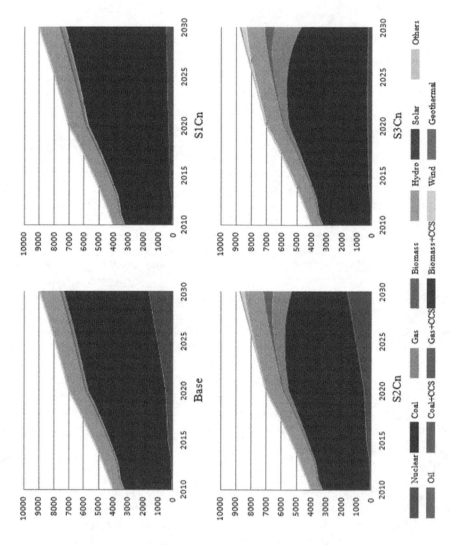

Figure 3.2 Electricity supply by technology (TWh) in China.

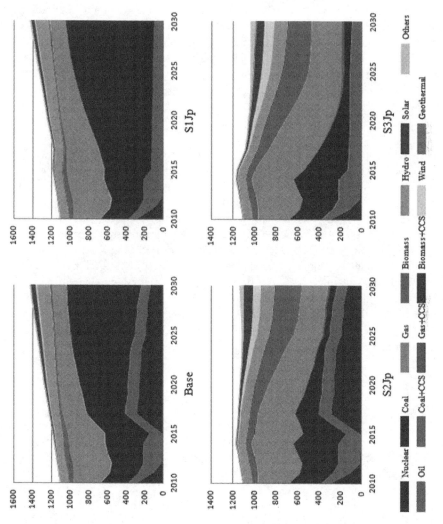

Figure 3.3 Electricity supply by technology (TWh) in Japan.

remains comparatively small, not able to reach the 22 to 24 percent share that was the referred target of renewable energies' (including conventional hydro energy) share in Japan's most recent national plan (Agency for Natural Resources and Energy, Japan, 2014). This is due to coal power not being restricted in S1. In addition, because coal is the cheapest technology, coal-fired power substitutes the share of nuclear energy, thereby resulting in a total share of baseload technologies that is higher than in S2. Meanwhile, in S2, the capacity of nuclear power is held exogenously and coal is predominantly replaced by flexible gas power, resulting in a considerable decrease of the total baseload share. The total share of renewable energy, including conventional hydro energy, is above the referred target in S2 and S3. The dominating technology is solid biomass. Japan has large biomass resources that are currently not used, which could be used for generating electricity as the electricity price rises and biomass becomes profitable.

Korea

Electricity supplied by each technology in each scenario for Korea is shown in Figure 3.4. The trend in Korea is similar to that of Japan, with S3 having the largest increase in share of renewables. Korea has a share of nuclear energy that is larger than Japan's, but the total share of baseload technologies is similar to that of Japan and the basic structure of the power mix is essentially the same. The share of renewables, however, becomes significantly higher than in the other three countries in all the scenarios. This is due to biogas being included with renewables – mainly using methane gas from landfills – and becoming competitive, increasing its share. The other reason for the high share of renewable energy in S2 and S3 is gas-fired power, a flexible technology that can deal with the variability of renewable energy that is starting to dominate the power sector. The national target for renewable energy, 10 percent of total electricity generation in 2022, is met only in S3.

Taiwan

Electricity supplied by each technology in each scenario for Taiwan is shown in Figure 3.5. Following a path similar to Japan and Korea, the share of renewables in Taiwan becomes the largest in S2. Because Taiwan has decided not to increase nuclear capacity, other than two plants that are under construction, reduction in coal-fired power is substituted by gas and renewables. Regarding the national targets, in 2025 the capacity of renewable energy is 7,239 MW in total, not meeting the target of 9,952 MW. However, in 2030 it increases to 23,678 MW, that is, twice the target 12,502 MW for that year. This is because, after going through the slow diffusion at low penetrations, fast diffusion at intermediate stages is realized. In S2, this intermediate stage starts even earlier and the total capacity of renewable energies reaches 35,977 MW in 2025, high above the national target. The high share of renewable energy is supported by the diffusion of flexible gas-fired power, substituting coal-fired power as well.

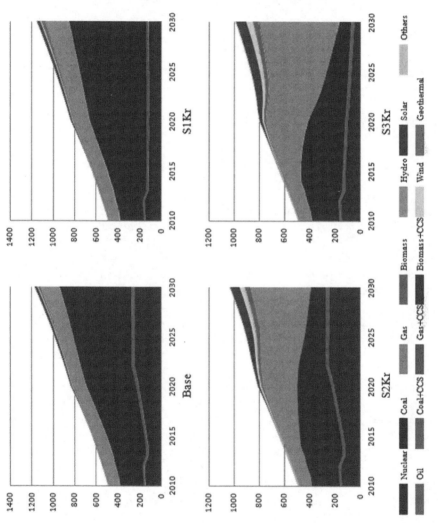

Figure 3.4 Electricity supply by technology (TWh) in Korea.

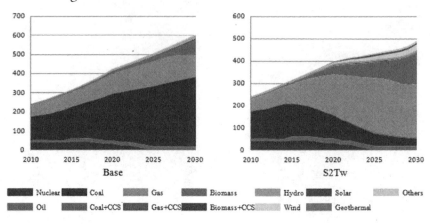

Figure 3.5 Electricity supply by technology (TWh) in Taiwan.

3.6   Conclusions

The model analysis using FTT:Power and E3ME indicates that, in the power sector, a phasing out of nuclear power is likely to result in increases in conventional energy sources and, on its own, does not contribute much to the diffusion of renewable energy. In contrast, phasing out coal-fired power plants results in substantial increases in renewable energy. This is because coal-fired power is a very low-cost baseload technology that dominates the power sector in each country, leaving little market space for renewable energy technologies. It may, thus, be important to regulate the share of coal-fired power generation in the power sector to enable a significant increase in renewable energy sources.

Without stronger support for renewable energy or the regulation of coal-fired power, decreasing nuclear power does not contribute to an increase in renewable energy; this is because most nuclear power would be replaced by coal-fired power generation, also a baseload technology.

In this study, the level of flexibility of technologies other than those related to electricity generation in the power system – such as transmission and distribution grids, and storage – are assumed to maintain the level of 2012. Support for further diffusion of flexible low-carbon technologies (e.g., gas turbines or biomass gasification), electricity storage, and demand-side management may be necessary to enable the further diffusion of renewable energy systems while maintaining grid stability (including by regulating traditional coal-fired power generation).

In the next chapter, we discuss the economic implications of these scenarios.

Notes

1 Note that the parameters for storage also implicitly represent the flexibility that is obtained through international trade of flexible generation capacity (e.g., importing Scandinavian hydro in Germany). In this assumption, the amount of electricity

traded sums to zero through the day. Since international trade of electricity is not covered in this version of the model, it is taken as an exogenous assumption.

2 See Cambridge Econometrics (2014) for more detail.

References

Agency for Natural Resources and Energy, Japan (2014). 'Feed-in tariff scheme.' http://www.enecho.meti.go.jp/category/saving_and_new/saiene/kaitori/index.html (accessed June 15, 2014; in Japanese).

Bureau of Energy, Taipei (2013). *Energy Statistics Handbook 2012* (second edition). Taipei: Bureau of Energy, Ministry of Economic Affairs,

Bureau of Energy, Taiwan (2014). 'New energy policy of Taiwan.' http://web3.moeaboe.gov.tw/ecw/english/content/Content.aspx?menu_id=969 (accessed June 14, 2014).

Cambridge Econometrics (2014). *E3ME Manual.* http://www.camecon.com/Libraries/Downloadable_Files/E3ME_Manual.sflb.ashx (accessed June 14, 2014).

International Atomic Energy Agency (IAEA) (2014). PRIS country statistics. http://www.iaea.org/PRIS/CountryStatistics/CountryStatisticsLandingPage.aspx (accessed June 28, 2014).

International Energy Agency (IEA) (2014a). *Electricity Information* (2014 Edition). Paris: International Energy Agency.

International Energy Agency (IEA) (2014b). *Energy Balances of OECD/Non-OECD countries.* Paris: International Energy Agency.

International Energy Agency (IEA) (2014c). *IEA/IRENA Joint Policies and Measures Database.* http://www.iea.org/policiesandmeasures/renewableenergy/ (accessed June 15, 2014).

International Energy Agency (IEA) (2014d). *World Energy Outlook 2014.* Paris: International Energy Agency.

Japan Nuclear Technology Institute (2014). 'Operation of nuclear power plant.' http://www.gengikyo.jp/facility/powerplant.html (accessed June 12, 2014; in Japanese).

Japan Renewable Energy Foundation (2014). 'Evaluation of estimate "Nuclear power plant stop caused capital outflow of 3600 billion yen." ' http://jref.or.jp/images/pdf/20140313/JREF_Proposal_fuelcost_2014MAR13.pdf (accessed June 15, 2014; in Japanese).

Mercure, J.-F. (2013). 'An age structured demographic theory of technological change.' *4th International Conference on Sustainability Transitions, Zurich, Switzerland, 2013.* http://arxiv.org/abs/1304.3602 (accessed June 15, 2014).

Mercure, J.-F. (2012). 'FTT:Power: A global model of the power sector with induced technological change and natural resource depletion.' *Energy Policy*, 48, 799–811. http://www.scopus.com/inward/record.url?eid=2-s2.0–84865029965&partnerID=40&md5=726905af5d2ba28060a3fea9488daec7 (accessed June 15, 2014).

Mercure, J.-F., and Salas, P. (2012). 'An assessment of global energy resource economic potentials.' *Energy*, 46(1), 322–336. http://dx.doi.org/10.1016/j.energy.2012.08.018 (accessed June 15, 2014).

Mercure, J.-F., and Salas, P. (2013). 'On the global economic potentials and marginal costs of non-renewable resources and the price of energy commodities.' *Energy Policy*, 63, 469–483. http://dx.doi.org/10.1016/j.enpol.2013.08.040 (accessed June 15, 2014).

Mercure, J.-F., Salas, P., Foley, A., Chewpreecha, U., Pollitt, H., Holden, P.B., and Edwards, N.R. (2014). 'The dynamics of technology diffusion and the impacts of climate policy instruments in the decarbonisation of the global electricity sector.' *Energy Policy*, http://dx.doi.org/10.1016/j.enpol.2014.06.029 (accessed June 15, 2014).

Renewable Energy Policy Network for the 21st Century (REN21) (2013). *Renewables 2013 Global Status Report*. http://www.ren21.net/portals/0/documents/resources/gsr/2013/gsr2013_lowres.pdf (accessed June 15, 2014).

World Nuclear Association (2014). 'Country profiles.' http://www.world-nuclear.org/info/Country-Profiles/ (accessed June 28, 2014).

4 Modeling the power sector in East Asia

Economic and environmental impacts of the choices of power sources

Yuki Ogawa, Jean-François Mercure,
Soocheol Lee, Hector Pollitt, Ken'ichi Matsumoto
and Akihiro Chiashi

4.1 Introduction

In Chapter 3, we analyzed three scenarios for the future of energy in East Asian countries, specifically: limiting the share of nuclear power, limiting the share of coal-fired power, and limiting the share of both nuclear and coal-fired power. The economic impacts of these scenarios in East Asia are not immediately or intuitively obvious to predict. This is due to many interacting factors: phasing out inexpensive energy systems, such as nuclear and coal-fired plants, drives up the total costs of supplying electricity in the power sector and, thus, is most likely to lead to higher prices of electricity. This, in turn, may decrease the welfare of consumers and may also reduce international trade competitiveness through higher export prices. Meanwhile, investment in low-carbon technology often has beneficial impacts on employment (see, for instance, Wei et al., 2010 and Cambridge Econometrics et al., 2013), since new technologies often involve higher levels of technological complexity and sophistication, research and development activities, and increased demand in interrelated sectors across the economy. Furthermore, most East Asian countries rely heavily on expensive energy imports, and a low-carbon energy transition could contribute significantly in reducing these costs. These two positive contributions may counterbalance the welfare loss that arises from higher electricity prices through the transition.

Before our work here, Pollitt et al. (2014) assessed three scenarios for the share of nuclear power in Japan by using the global macro-econometric model E3MG (the energy-environment-economy (E3) model at the global level, a predecessor to E3ME). Their analysis, which is discussed in depth in Chapter 5, revealed that the cost of denuclearization to the Japanese GDP is close to zero, and the impact on employment is slightly positive, driven by the effect of alternative investment in renwables. Here, we analyze the economic impacts that arise from the energy scenarios studied in Chapter 3 in China, Japan, Korea and Taiwan by using E3ME-Asia and show the net impacts that result from both increased energy prices and investment and decreased fuel imports.

In Section 4.2, we give an overview of the economic linkages that exist between the FTT:Power sector model and the macroeconomy in the E3ME-Asia model.

Section 4.3 provides the economic impacts from E3ME-Asia for each electricity policy and technology scenario as defined in the previous chapter. Section 4.4 discusses the findings.

4.2   Linkage between the electricity sector described by the FTT:Power model and the macroeconomy shown by the E3ME model: an overview

The price-demand interaction

The demand for electricity is calculated in E3ME-Asia by using a set of econo-metric equations that takes into account macro-econometric indicators and reads as follows:[1]

$$\Delta \log D_{ij} = \beta_{ij}^0 + \beta_{ij}^1 \Delta \log \Upsilon_{ij} + \beta_{ij}^2 \Delta \log P_{ij} + \beta_{ij}^3 \Delta \log TPI_{ij} + \varepsilon_{ij}.$$

Demand for electricity is represented as D_{ij} in industrial sector i and region j. Υ_{ij} is economic output, P_{ij} is the price of electricity, and TPI_{ij} is a measure of technological progress. β_{ij}^k are the parameters estimated from historical data. In general, electricity demand increases for higher economic output and/or lower electricity prices. However, technological progress can – unlike GDP – only increase and, when it does, energy demand is decreased. The factor TPI_{ij} cumulates increases in technology investments that, in part, involve systems with ever-improving energy efficiency spilling over into the energy sector in the form of reduced demand. It is thus assumed that the world does not readopt previously abandoned models of technology; hence the equation is asymmetric and, therefore, path-dependent.

The price of electricity involves the cost of operating the electricity sector. When demand changes, as noted in Chapter 3, the power sector model FTT:Power determines the technology mix (or energy mix) that supplies the demand, thereby generating the total cost of supplying electricity. This cost itself influences the price of electricity, which – again – changes demand. The convergence between the two models on supply and price constitutes the price–demand interaction. A policy that influences the technology mix thus also influences electricity prices and demand. In particular, in cases where renewables that cost more are introduced into the grid, electricity consumption will be reduced, providing a double contribution to reducing emissions. Furthermore, increases in electricity demand may also generate higher operating costs due to depletion of renewable and non-renewable resources, which therefore also influence the price. These interactions are complicated but crucial in order to correctly simulate the behavior of the system.

The investment feedback

Investing new capital into the electricity sector has a spillover effect across other sectors of the economy. It employs additional labor in various sectors, such as construction, engineering, cement, mining, and so forth, of which the output also stimulates further tertiary sectors and so on. New technologies tend to be more capital-intensive than old technologies, and may also involve higher levels of investment in research and development. All of these can contribute to short-term aggregate demand in the economy, leading to higher levels of employment and income.

In the longer term, there is also a technology feedback through the learning curves that are embodied in the FTT:Power model. As the technologies become established, their capital costs are gradually reduced over time; this can lead to lower electricity prices in the future and higher real incomes. Thus, a policy that supports an energy transition in FTT:Power has the potential to promote investment in new technologies, which can contribute positively to both employment and long-term economic growth.

The fuel-use feedback

East Asian countries, in particular Japan, Korea, and Taiwan, which are situated on islands and peninsulas, have modest amounts of fossil fuel reserves. Therefore, electricity sectors that predominantly depend of fossil fuels need to import them. This is particularly the case for Japan, Taiwan, and Korea. Meanwhile, in the case of China, domestic extraction of fossil fuels does not match its consumption and, thus, fossil fuel imports are also required. These imports are costly and result in high operation costs. Reductions in fossil fuel imports not only reduce operation costs but also contribute to restoring the trade balance and international competitiveness. This is further discussed in Section 4.3.

In the FTT:Power of E3ME-Asia model, fuel demand is estimated on the basis of the power mix used and the thermal efficiencies of each technology. In most cases, it is assumed that any marginal changes in fuel consumption are met by changes in import volumes. This treatment means that domestic supply of fossil fuels is effectively fixed and does not change between scenarios.

4.3   Modeling results

In this section, we look into the economic and environmental impacts that result from the scenarios analyzed in Chapter 3, that is, the impacts of limiting the share of nuclear power (S1), of limiting the share of coal-fired power (S2), and of limiting the share of both nuclear and coal-fired power (S3).

China

The results for each scenario for China are shown in Figure 4.1. In S1, China experiences a slight drop in GDP. This is due to the reduced investment in the electricity sector because coal-fired power plants, which are replacing nuclear power plants, are less capital-intensive. This loss of investment reduces current economic activity in the E3ME-Asia model, as we discuss in Chapter 5.

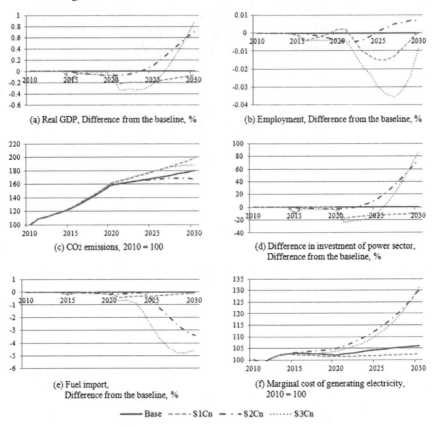

Figure 4.1 Economic and environmental indicators for China.

In S2, although the marginal cost of generating electricity is increased by almost 30 percent from baseline, GDP and other economic indicators increase. This is because investment in the electricity sector increases, substituting coal-fired power plants for other more capital-intensive technologies. In S3, China gets even higher GDP than in S2. This is because not only the coal-fired power but also the nuclear power is substituted by other expensive technologies which have more spillover effect than the former two technologies.

Japan

The results for each scenario for Japan are shown in Figure 4.2. S1 has a moderate negative effect on the economy during the simulated 15-year period due

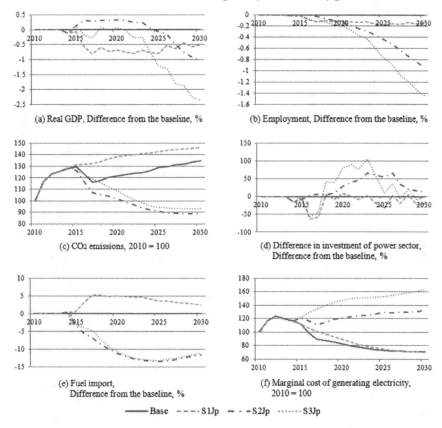

Figure 4.2 Economic and environmental indicators for Japan.

to increases in electricity prices and imports of fossil fuels. CO_2 emissions increase over this period because generation of nuclear power is mainly replaced by that from fossil fuels. Restrictions on coal-fired power significantly reduce imports of fossil fuels, impacting positively on GDP, while also increasing the price of electricity, impacting negatively impact on GDP. In S2, CO_2 emissions fall dramatically by more than 25 percent from the baseline level by 2030 – a substantial reduction for a single regulating factor.

Although phasing out coal power has a slight overall negative impact on GDP, it should be noted that this negative effect will be lessened if other East Asian countries adopt a similar policy at the same time.

Korea

The results for each scenario for Korea are shown in Figure 4.3. Unlike Japan, GDP in Korea, by 2030, gains in S1. Reducing the share of nuclear or coal

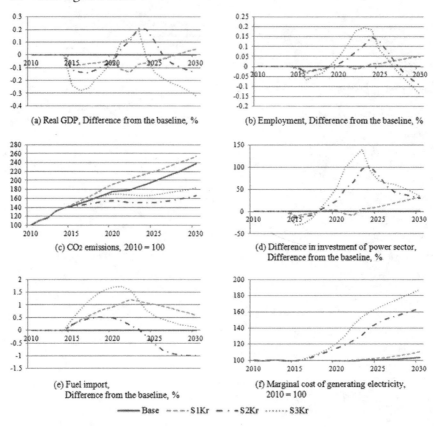

(a) Real GDP, Difference from the baseline, %

(b) Employment, Difference from the baseline, %

(c) CO2 emissions, 2010 = 100

(d) Difference in investment of power sector,
Difference from the baseline, %

(e) Fuel import,
Difference from the baseline, %

(f) Marginal cost of generating electricity,
2010 = 100

——— Base ― ― ― S1Kr ― · ― S2Kr ········ S3Kr

Figure 4.3 Economic and environmental indicators for Korea.

power leads to switching towards other technologies in the power sector. Switching requires investment in new power plants, which has a spillover effect to the national economy. In S2, the decrease in coal imports has a positive effect on the economy as well. These positive impacts compensate for the negative impacts that an increase in electricity prices have.

Taiwan

The results for each scenario for Taiwan are shown in Figure 4.4. For Taiwan, only the S2 scenario is analyzed, since the S1 scenario is the same as the baseline, and the S3 scenario is the same as the S2 scenario (see Chapter 3 for details). A reduction of coal-fired power generation turns out to benefit the economy through reduced coal imports and increased investment. With a reduction of more than 40 percent compared to the baseline level in 2030, Taiwan is predicted to accomplish the largest relative reduction in the emissions of CO_2 among the four countries analyzed.

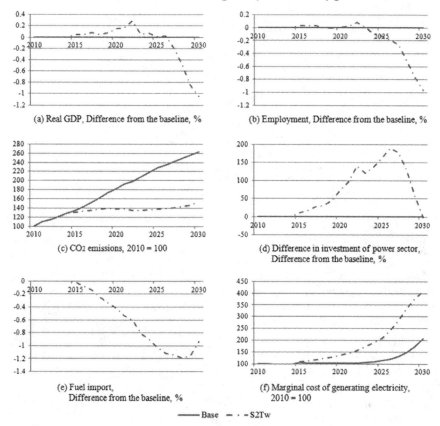

(a) Real GDP, Difference from the baseline, %

(b) Employment, Difference from the baseline, %

(c) CO2 emissions, 2010 = 100

(d) Difference in investment of power sector, Difference from the baseline, %

(e) Fuel import, Difference from the baseline, %

(f) Marginal cost of generating electricity, 2010 = 100

———— Base — · —S2Tw

Figure 4.4 Economic and environmental indicators for Taiwan.

Simultaneous restriction in the four countries

There are three different kinds of spillover effect when the restrictions are implemented simultaneously in all four countries. The first is the spillover effect from China and Japan to Korea and Taiwan. China and Japan have considerably larger economies than Korea and Taiwan. If the GDP of China or Japan decreases, both countries would import less from Korea and Taiwan, thereby triggering a decrease in the GDP of the latter two countries. In S2 and S3, there is a big investment stimulus in China to replace coal-fired power, leading to two potential outcomes. On the one hand, the GDPs of the three other countries – not that of China – increase because China's imports from those countries increase. On the other hand, the other three countries could show a GDP decrease and reduced imports from China, resulting in a slight decrease in China's GDP.

Table 4.1 Real GDP in 2030 by scenario in each country from the baseline level (%)

	S1, individual*	S1, Ea§	S2, individual	S2, Ea	S3, individual	S3, Ea
Cn	−0.06	−0.06	0.71	0.66	0.89	0.83
Jp	−0.51	−0.52	−1.04	−1.05	−2.36	−2.22
Kr	0.05	0.03	−0.14	−0.11	−0.32	−0.33
Tw	–	−0.03	−1.05	−0.95	–	−0.99

* individual means that each policy is implemented only in the subject country.
§ Ea means that each policy is implemented simultaneously in all four countries.

The second effect results from the electricity price. When only one region implements one scenario, only that country has to face an increase in the price of electricity. Higher electricity prices would make this country's products less competitive. However, if one restriction is applied to all four countries at the same time, all four countries would face price increases at the same time; thus, the competitiveness between them would not deteriorate.

The last effect is from technology learning. The cost of each technology is assumed to decrease as its cumulative installed capacity grows worldwide in FTT:Power. When one scenario is implemented at the same time in four countries, restricted technology will have less cumulative capacity, leading to higher cost. Technologies other than the restricted one will get more cumulative capacity, resulting in lower cost. However, the total cost of producing electricity becomes higher than the scenario implemented in a single country. This is because cost reduction of technologies other than the restricted one is not enough to compensate for the cost increase of restricted technology. Cost increases in the power sector would have a negative effect on the economy through higher electricity prices. Having these two effects in all countries and all cases, except in Japan in S1 and China in S3, simultaneous restrictions yields a better effect on GDP compared with individual restriction (as seen in Table 4.1). This result implies that, if the four countries cooperate with each other, they can reduce both the dependence on nuclear power and the dependence on coal-fired power while suffering smaller economic losses or even seeing economic benefits.

4.4   Conclusions

Our model analysis suggests that the elimination of nuclear-derived energy production in East Asia does not have a large impact on East Asian economy, with changes in GDP ranging between 0.6 percent and 0.3 percent compared to the baseline level. Regarding the environmental aspect, effects on CO_2

emission rates would be negative compared to the baseline. The Fukushima accident revealed the risks of using nuclear power, but our analysis suggests this risk can be mitigated, as the number of nuclear power plants is reduced, with modest economic loss.

The regulation of coal-fired power can be an effective measure to reduce CO_2 emissions from the power sector, but it can result in a burden to the economy through increased operation costs and prices of electricity, coal being the least cost energy source. Reducing imports of coal can have a positive effect on countries who are fuel importers. If the restriction on coal-fired power plants is implemented in all four countries simultaneously, the negative effect on GDP becomes lower in Japan, Korea and Taiwan, which face severe international trade competition with the price of electricity becoming a determinant of comparative competitiveness. The economic impact of restriction on both nuclear and coal-fired power can be positive, or, even if it comes to be negative, it would be small.

In the power sector, reducing coal-fired power as a baseload technology creates market space for the diffusion of renewables while maintaining grid stability. Power generation from renewable energy requires substantially more investment and is labor-intensive compared to coal-fired power generation. Investments and up-scaling costs of renewable energy can spill over across sectors, which can significantly benefit the economy, unlike fossil fuel costs. It should be noted that the high investment, which positively benefits the economy, when the renewables are first built to diffuse is considered in the period analyzed here, while negative effects of the higher electricity price would remain after 2030.

Overall model results indicate that these positive effects from reducing nuclear power, coal-fired power, or both, could compensate for all the negative impacts on economy due to increased prices of electricity when their mitigation impacts make this option more affordable.

Note

1 Δlog indicates differences of the logarithms of the quantities.

References

Cambridge Econometrics, Ernst & Young, Exergia, COWI, and Institute for Employment Research at Warwick University. (2013). *Employment Effects of Selected Scenarios of the Energy Roadmap 2050.* http://ec.europa.eu/energy/observatory/studies/doc/2013_report_employment_effects_roadmap_2050.pdf (accessed June 15, 2014).

International Energy Agency (IEA) (2014). *IEA/IRENA Joint Policies and Measures Database.* http://www.iea.org/policiesandmeasures/renewableenergy/ (accessed June 15, 2014).

Pollitt, H., Park, S-J., Lee, S., and Ueta, K. (2014). 'An economic and environmental assessment of future electricity generation mixes in Japan – an assessment using the E3MG macro-econometric model.' *Energy Policy*, 67, pp. 243–254. http://www.sciencedirect.com/science/article/pii/S0301421513012627 (accessed June 15, 2014).

Wei, M., Patadia S., and Kammen, M. (2010). 'Putting renewables and energy efficiency to work: How many jobs can the clean energy industry generate in the US?' *Energy Policy*, 38, pp. 919–931.

5 The environmental and macroeconomic implications of phasing out nuclear power in Japan

E3MG vs CGE modeling results

Soocheol Lee, Hector Pollitt, Park Seung-Joon, and Kazuhiro Ueta

5.1 Introduction

In this chapter we focus solely on the energy sector in Japan. The reason for this lies in the distinctive circumstances in Japan that have resulted from the Fukushima Daiichi Nuclear Power Accident in 2011. In contrast to some East Asian countries that may consider increasing the share of nuclear energy in their national energy mix, the focus in Japan is primarily on reducing the proportion of nuclear power. This remains the case even after the change of government from the Democratic Party of Japan (DPJ) to the Liberal Democratic Party (LDP) in late 2012.

We explore possible future scenarios in which the share of nuclear power in Japan is reduced and assess the macroeconomic implications of these scenarios. We also discuss how policy relating to nuclear energy interacts with the carbon targets that have been set in Japan. The analysis builds on two sets of model results: the first, which was published in the former administration's official government report, used a set of CGE models (Energy and Environment Council, 2012a), whereas the second, which was first published in the academic journal *Energy Policy* (Pollitt et al, 2014), used the E3MG model – an older version of the E3ME-Asia model that is used throughout this book. Both modeling exercises assess the three scenarios that were defined by the former Japanese government under Prime Minister Yoshihiko Noda in 2012 for an open, public discussion about future energy policy.

The following section, Section 5.2, discusses the policy context and the recent debates about nuclear power in Japan (and elsewhere). This discussion builds upon the more general policy introduction provided in the first section of this book. The 'levelized cost' method of comparing the costs of electricity generation is described in Section 5.3, the different types of modeling are discussed in Section 5.4, the scenarios are described in Section 5.5, and the results are presented in Section 5.6. In Section 5.7, we discuss the conclusions that can be drawn from the exercise and ways in which the results could be applied to other East Asian countries.

5.2   Policy background

Nuclear policy in Japan

In 2010, nuclear power provided 26 percent of Japan's electricity. This very high share – one of the highest in the world at the time (besides that of France) – can be explained by some of the key economic and political features of Japan, in particular the lack of domestic fossil fuel reserves and an established technological advantage in the generation of nuclear power. The June 2010 *Basic Energy Plan* assumed that nuclear power would continue to play a central role in Japan's energy mix, and that its share would rise to 53 percent by 2030.

However, the Fukushima accident in March 2011 changed the political context fundamentally because the public became immediately aware of the risks associated with nuclear power plants (NPP). The government (the centrist DPJ was in power at the time) responded to public concerns by reviewing the *Basic Energy Plan*.

In summer 2011, the government passed the Act on Special Measures Concerning Procurement of Electricity from Renewable Energy Sources (the Feed-in Tariff or FIT law) and, shortly afterwards, set up the Energy and Environment Council under the National Policy Unit chaired by the prime minister. The Energy and Environment Council published the so-called *Options* report in June 2012 (Energy and Environment Council, 2012a), which proposed three possible future scenarios for the share of nuclear power in electricity generation:

- No nuclear power
- A 15 percent share of nuclear power
- A 20–25 percent share of nuclear power

The report included some estimates of potential costs on the basis of a modeling exercise that was carried out in Japan; these are discussed later in this chapter. The public consultation portion of the report found very strong support for phasing out nuclear power altogether, despite the slightly higher costs associated with this option.

The findings of this consultation led to the *Innovative Strategy for the Energy and Environment* (Energy and Environment Council, 2012c, p. 2). The stated goal of this strategy was to 'implement all conceivable policy resources to enable zero nuclear power in the 2030s.' There were three principles for achieving this goal:

- The 40 year maximum lifetime of nuclear plants rule will be stringently applied
- Only those nuclear power plants whose safety has been verified by the Nuclear Regulation Authority will be permitted to operate
- No construction of new nuclear power plants will be permitted

Nevertheless, nuclear power generation was not seen as a key issue in the national elections at the end of 2012 (lower house) and July 2013 (upper house). In the elections, the conservative LDP defeated the DPJ government and returned to power. Previously, the LDP had been a strong supporter of nuclear power.

Policy impacts on the rest of East Asia and the rest of the world

The effects of the Fukushima accident were also felt in other East Asian countries. In Taiwan, opposition to nuclear power has been increasing since 2011, especially with regards to the newest Lungmen Nuclear Power Plant. The Korean government revised downwards its nuclear target in late 2013 (29 percent in 2035 compared to the previous plan of 59 percent in 2030; in 2013 the share was 27.6 percent). Although the impact of the Fukushima accident in Japan had no major impact on China's nuclear energy policy, some slowing down of construction projects has been observed.

The Fukushima accident also led to policy changes outside the East Asian region. Most notably, in Germany the current policy is now to phase out nuclear power completely. Reducing the generation of nuclear power in some countries has changed their power mix and affected global energy markets. Increased demand for natural gas in Japan and Germany has led to higher gas prices for the rest of the world (outside the US). Countries have also been affected by changes in the price of coal as a result of increased environmental regulation and exports of coal from the US (where shale gas has displaced local coal consumption). These examples highlight the importance of considering impacts in the rest of the world as well. However, this chapter only deals with the special case of Japan.

Interaction with climate policy

In many countries, such as China, nuclear power forms a key component of climate change policy. In Europe, the *Energy Roadmap 2050* (European Commission, 2011) suggests that nuclear plants will still generate 16 percent of electricity in 2050 (diversified supply scenario), despite current political uncertainty and the expected development of renewable technologies. In the discussion of the scenarios, the *Energy Roadmap 2050* notes that the share of nuclear power could be greater than 16 percent if key technologies, such as carbon capture and storage, were delayed.

In Japan, the increased use of nuclear power generation was also a key element in meeting climate change targets, in particular the previous administration's Copenhagen pledge that emissions in 2020 would be 25 percent lower than the 1990 level. Given the concerns about the economic effects of increases in electricity prices, it is reasonable to ask how phasing out nuclear power might affect the cost of meeting climate change targets.

Unfortunately, there could be particularly steep rises in the costs of electricity generation in Japan (excluding external costs), because an increase of the generation of nuclear power – with low fuel costs – was to play a key role in the power mix (see e.g. Duscha et al., 2013; and the discussion of levelized costs in

Section 5.3 following). At present, the share of renewable energy within Japan's electricity generation is quite low (10.7 percent in 2013, including conventional hydropower) and, under the current policy, nuclear power plants are to be replaced mainly by gas-fired stations.

Consequently, a shift away from nuclear power would lead to higher emissions from the power generation sector. This in turn means that other economic sectors would have to reduce their emissions to a much greater extent in order to meet the Copenhagen target. The September 2012 *Innovative Strategy* itself recognized this dilemma and estimated that phasing out the generation of nuclear power could lead to an increase in emissions of 16–20 percent, making the Copenhagen target much more difficult to achieve. Just before the 2013 UN Conference of the Parties in Warsaw, the present government eased Japan's greenhouse gas (GHG) reduction target (i.e., to reduce emissions by 3.8 percent by 2020 below the levels of 2005, meaning a 3.1 percent *increase* from the levels of 1990), assuming that no nuclear power plants are operating by 2020. However, in 2015 the Japanese government did announce a more stringent CO_2 target for 2030.

5.3   The 'levelized' cost of nuclear energy

The levelized (unit) cost is a common way of comparing the costs of different ways of generating electricity. Total levelized costs include the costs of building a plant and operating it over its lifetime, including (assumed) fuel costs. In the absence of regulation, one would expect to see a direct relationship between the average levelized cost of the power sector and the long-run price of electricity.[1] The levelized costs are, therefore, a very important factor in the investment decisions made by the power-generating companies.

For nuclear power, most of the levelized cost consists of the initial capital outlay; the marginal cost of generation is very low due to low unit fuel costs. There is, therefore, quite a big difference between the levelized cost of new plants and the cost of existing plants, regardless of the age of the plant. However, there is also a potential additional cost of nuclear power that is not usually taken into account when calculating levelized costs: namely the large human and physical damages that are incurred in the event of an accident (whether compensated in monetary terms or not). After the Fukushima accident, there were demands for these costs also to be taken into account.

In December 2011 the governmental Cost Estimation and Review Committee published a report that showed the levelized generation cost of nuclear power to be at least 8.9 yen/kWh (taking into account the assumed costs of damage caused by a nuclear accident. They changed this cost to 9.0 yen/kWh afterwards.). This compared to 9.5 yen/kWh for coal or 10.7 yen/kWh for gas (Cost Estimation and Review Committee 2011; Matsuo 2012).

Table 5.1 shows the current and projected levelized costs for different methods of electricity generation in Japan based on the information in this report. The E3MG modeling described below used the same information. The table distinguishes between the levelized costs for existing plants (i.e. excluding capital costs)

Table 5.1 Levelized costs for selected types of power generation in Japan, yen/kWh

	Existing plants in 2010*	*Future plants (2010)*	*Future plants (2020)*	*Future plants (2030)*
Nuclear	6.4	9.0	9.0	9.0
Coal	8.1	9.5	10.2	10.3
Gas (LNG)	10.0	10.7	10.4	10.9
Solar (plants)	10.5	38.0	19.1	16.0
Solar (residential)	7.4	35.9	15.4	12.0
Onshore wind	3.6	13.6	13.3	13.1
Offshore wind	–	–	16.2	15.9

Note:* The cost of existing plants is the levelized costs net of the capital costs.

Sources: Adapted from Cost Estimation and Review Committee (2011) and the Energy and Environment Council (2012b)

and future plants. Clearly, there is a substantial difference between these two measures for capital-intensive technologies, including the generation of nuclear and renewable energy. Because of the difference, high costs might be incurred if existing capacity were replaced before the end of its expected lifetime. The levelized cost of renewables (notably solar) is expected to decrease over time as new production methods are found and factories are able to benefit from economies of scale. The report by the Energy and Environment Council (2012b, p. 14) provides further details of how the values were estimated.

5.4 The modeling approaches

Previous analysis in the Options report

Upon publication, the *Options* report (Energy and Environment Council, 2012a) included model simulation results of the scenarios provided by the:

- National Institute for Environmental Studies (NIES)
- Osaka University (Prof. Ban Kanemi)
- Keio University (Prof. Nomura Koji)
- Research Institute of Innovative Technology for the Earth (RITE, see Homma and Akimoto, 2013).

Each modeling group was asked to use identical modeling assumptions so that results between the models could be compared. These are the same scenarios as those described later in this chapter. The details of the scenarios were discussed in Ban (2013). Further information about each of the CGE models used may be found on the respective websites of the institutions involved.

The E3MG model

The E3MG model used in Pollitt et al. (2014) is, essentially, an earlier version of the E3ME model described in Chapter 2; it was developed jointly by the University of Cambridge and Cambridge Econometrics. E3MG had a more limited geographical disaggregation than E3ME, but this made no difference to an analysis restricted to Japan. Another difference between the two models is that E3MG did not include the FTT:Power model of the power sector. However, this difference had no effect on the modeling of the scenarios described in this chapter because in order to match the scenario assumptions the power sector was treated as being exogenous.

E3MG has itself been used extensively for policy analysis and research purposes. Among other uses, it has provided inputs to the United Nations Framework Convention on Climate Change (UNFCCC) negotiations. The model has been used repeatedly for assessing the economic and labor market effects of international scenarios of decarbonization (Barker et al., 2005, 2006; Barker, Foxon, and Scrieciu, 2008; Barker and Scrieciu, 2009). E3MG was applied in Barker et al. (2012) to provide an economic assessment of the IEA's 450 ppm scenario, which is one of the standard global scenarios for meeting the two degrees climate target (see IEA, 2010).

Comparison of approaches

A basic feature of this book is the combination and comparison of different modeling approaches. For example, in Chapters 3 and 4, we first applied a simulation model (using E3ME-Asia linked to FTT:Power). We proceed in the present chapter by presenting and comparing the results from two different types of model.

The comparison between E3MG and CGE models is relevant to the interpretation of the results presented in this chapter. In particular, as noted in Chapter 2, the optimization approach of the CGE models typically means that model results are determined by supply-side factors that are largely fixed. By contrast, E3MG allows unused resources to be utilized (for example through an investment program) to boost economic activity and employment. This feature of E3MG does not always guarantee a positive outcome in the scenarios with higher investment, but it does admit the possibility of such an outcome.

The condition of the Japanese economy, which has been below its potential for more than two decades (though it may now be recovering), provides a very good reason for applying a non-equilibrium approach, such as that offered by the E3MG model. However, it is the comparison of results between the different modeling approaches that is of particular interest.

5.5   Scenarios

The analysis carried out by the CGE models was based on a 'business-as-usual' (BAU) case and three scenarios with varying shares of nuclear power in 2030 (0 percent, 15 percent, and 20–25 percent). CO_2 emissions in these scenarios are

Table 5.2 Assumptions for tuning the economic models (in 2030)

	2010	2030 (Scenarios for nuclear share)				
		BAU (24%)	0%	15%	20%	25%
Electricity generated (trillion kWh)	1.100	1.124	1.101	1.132	1.133	1.135
Fuel mix for electricity generation						
Nuclear share	26%	24%	0%	15%	20%	25%
Share of combustion power	63%	65%	62%	54%	48%	48%
Coal	24%	26%	20%	20%	17%	17%
LNG	29%	32%	37%	29%	26%	26%
Oil	10%	7%	6%	5%	5%	5%
Renewable energy share	10%	10%	38%	31%	31%	26%
Solar	–	0%	8%	7%	7%	6%
Wind	–	0%	10%	7%	7%	4%
Hydropower and geothermal	–	9%	16%	14%	14%	14%
Biomass	–	1%	4%	3%	3%	3%
CO_2 emissions ($MtCO_2$)	–	999	836	825	795	789

Sources: Ban (2013, p. 38), Energy and Environment Council (2012a), as interpreted in Pollitt et al. (2014).

restricted, so that there are larger shares of renewable energy when nuclear energy is reduced (see Table 5.2 and the appendix to this chapter). In each case, any change in generation cost is reflected fully in the price that is charged to electricity consumers, with the result that the scenarios are expected to lead to higher electricity prices and lower levels of GDP. For the modeling exercise, it was also assumed (implicitly) that a 'carbon tax' is raised in order to represent the burden of energy conservation.[2] In the scenario featuring 0 percent nuclear energy, there is also additional investment in energy efficiency and grid infrastructure to support the higher share of renewables.

The same scenarios were assessed with E3MG, except that a 25 percent share of nuclear energy was used instead of a range of 20–25 percent. The appendix in Pollitt et al. (2014) contains a very detailed set of calculations showing how the different power mixes affect levelized costs of electricity generation in each scenario and the amount of investment required in each case. The levelized costs are then translated into higher electricity prices that are set as an input to the model while the investment is also added in. The power sector is treated as exogenous and set to match the scenario assumptions. Imports of fossil fuels are automatically set to match the change in demand from power generation.

The analysis using E3MG was extended to include a range of carbon-reduction targets (no target, –10 percent, –15 percent, and –25 percent, all compared to 1990 levels) for the Japanese economy. The E3MG modeling thus considered whether the carbon targets would be economically compatible with a reduced share of nuclear power in electricity generation. To meet the targets for a given power sector fuel mix, a basic carbon tax was applied to all other sectors of the economy. The revenues from the tax were used to reduce income tax rates, so that the scenarios were revenue neutral. This is one example of environmental tax reform, a concept that is discussed extensively in the second part of this book (see Chapter 8).

The nuclear energy scenarios were originally designed by the Japanese government, and we view them as plausible policy scenarios, but it is important to note that they were somewhat controversial. Some of the modeling groups have argued that the scenarios are inherently inconsistent and, therefore, unrealistic, showing instead their own alternative scenarios.[3]

5.6 Results

Results from the CGE analysis

The *Options* report (Energy and Environment Council, 2012a) provided estimates of impacts on electricity prices and GDP. These are shown in Table 5.3 as the annual growth rates recorded in each scenario by each of the four CGE models used in the analysis. In all cases, electricity prices increase as the share of nuclear energy falls, which in turn leads to reductions in GDP due to a combination of weaker domestic demand (lower real incomes leading to lower rates of expenditure) and reduced competitiveness with impacts on international trade.

Table 5.3 Changes to annual growth rates of electricity prices and GDP from the models

	Increase in electricity prices (% per year)			Annual GDP growth rate (% per year)		
Nuclear share	0%	15%	25%	0%	15%	25%
NIES	1.7%	1.7%	1.7%	1.04%	1.08%	1.08%
Osaka University	2.0%	1.7%	0.9%	0.87%	0.90%	0.92%
Keio University	3.8%	3.0%	3.0%	0.88%	0.94%	0.95%
RITE	3.5%	3.0%	3.0%	0.49%	0.63%	0.64%
E3MG (see next section)	2.9%	2.5%	2.5%	1.07%	1.07%	1.07%

Source: Adapted from the Energy and Environment Council (2012a). E3MG results from Pollitt et al. (2014).

It is important to note that electricity prices are expected to increase in all scenarios, including the baseline case over the period up to 2030. The differences in electricity price between the scenarios turn out to be much smaller than the large changes that had been predicted by some industry and media groups. The impacts on GDP are also quite small overall, with the exception of the results from RITE. The overall conclusion was that the aggregate GDP impacts would not be major (Ban, 2013). The CGE models used do not show employment effects.

Results from the E3MG model

Pollitt et al. (2014) gives a detailed report of the E3MG results and first discusses the impact of a reduction in the share of nuclear energy on CO_2 emissions in 2020, showing that the impact is substantial (see Table 5.4). The paper also points out that the impact of CO_2 is expected to grow over time if no further policies are implemented.

Table 5.4 also shows the carbon taxes that would need to be levied on all sectors other than electricity to meet the various carbon-reduction targets, together with impact on GDP (see below). It should be noted that, even without a carbon tax, the current suggested GHG reduction target for Japan (+3.8 percent compared to 1990 levels) would be met. There is a clear pattern that, as the carbon target becomes

Table 5.4 CO_2 emissions in 2020 in each E3MG scenario

Carbon target	Nuclear share in 2020 (%)	Nuclear share in 2030 (%)	Energy CO_2 emissions in 2020 compared to 1990 (%)	Carbon tax rate (yen/ tC) in 2020 (2010 prices)	Carbon tax rate (yen/ tCO_2) in 2020 (2010 prices)	GDP in 2030 compared to baseline (%)
None	25.7	25	−3.8	0	0	0.00
None	20.7	15	−2.7	0	0	0.00
None	14.5	0	−1.1	0	0	−0.04
−10%	25.7	25	−10.0	5,582	1,522	+0.24
−10%	20.7	15	−10.0	7,462	2,035	+0.29
−10%	14.5	0	−10.0	9,285	2,532	+0.34
−15%	25.7	25	−15.0	14,773	4,029	+0.45
−15%	20.7	15	−15.0	17,292	4,716	+0.50
−15%	14.5	0	−15.0	20,262	5,526	+0.55
−25%	25.7	25	−25.0	45,034	12,282	+0.79
−25%	20.7	15	−25.0	49,801	13,582	+0.82
−25%	14.5	0	−25.0	56,838	15,501	+0.86

Sources: Reproduced from Pollitt et al. (2014); outcomes are based on E3MG model results.

Notes: tC refers to tons of carbon.

more stringent and the share of nuclear power generation falls, the carbon price increases, although a more stringent carbon target has a larger effect than a reduction in the share of nuclear energy. In the extreme case the carbon tax rate rises to 56,838 yen/tC, which at the time was around 435 euro/tC. In comparison, the current carbon tax rate in Japan is 289 yen/tCO$_2$.[4]

The paper provides five factors that may affect the GDP in the scenarios:

- Changes in the level of consumption and imports of fossil fuels
- Changes in electricity prices
- Investment in new power plants (plus energy efficiency and grid improvements)
- The carbon tax rate on non-power sectors required to meet the emissions targets
- The use of revenues from the carbon tax

As the share of nuclear power falls (without any restriction on GHG reduction), there is a combination of positive and negative effects. Higher imports of fuels and higher electricity prices will lead to a worse outcome for GDP, whereas higher investment levels could provide an economic stimulus. In a similar manner, levying a carbon tax would be expected to reduce GDP, whereas using the revenues to reduce other taxes would have a beneficial effect (see Chapter 8).

The results for GDP and employment from E3MG are shown in Table 5.5 as the percentage change from the case with a 25 percent nuclear power generation share in 2030. The model suggests that a reduction in the share of nuclear energy in the power mix leads to a just slightly lower GDP but also to an increase in employment and a corresponding reduction in unemployment. In both cases, however, the scale of the impacts is very small, particularly when spread over the period to 2030.

When the carbon targets (and a carbon tax) are added in the scenarios, E3MG shows that there is a possible strong double-dividend effect, with GDP increasing

Table 5.5 Macroeconomic impacts of reducing the share of nuclear power without GHG reduction target (2030, percentage change from 25% share)

	15% nuclear share	0% nuclear share
GDP	0.00	−0.04
Employment	0.01	0.07
Consumption	0.00	−0.38
Investment	0.10	1.47
Exports	0.00	−0.01
Imports	0.08	0.43
Price level	0.00	0.33

Sources: Reproduced from Pollitt et al. (2014).

as the level of emissions in 2020 falls. This is primarily due to a reduction in fossil fuel imports. The negative competitiveness effects that are associated with carbon pricing are also apparent in Japan, but not so strong due to Japan's low trade ratios.

The sectoral results from E3MG follow similar patterns compared with those described in other chapters (see, e.g., Chapters 4 and 8). The sectors that benefit most from a reduced share of nuclear energy are those that produce the investment equipment required to construct renewable energy plants and to replace existing power plants (see Pollitt et al., 2014 for estimates of the quantitative effects of investment in renewable energy). Their supply chains also benefit. Sectors that lose out are those that supply consumption goods because, although GDP and investment increase, consumption falls. However, when the carbon tax is introduced with revenue recycling through reduced income tax rates, many of the consumption goods sectors benefit again, albeit at the expense of the fossil fuel sectors (both inside and outside Japan).

5.7 Conclusions

Comparison of model results

E3MG and the CGE models were used to assess the same scenarios of a reduced share of nuclear power in electricity generation and, so, it is possible to compare the results from both modeling approaches. In the case described here, they are not very different. E3MG predicts no loss of GDP, whereas the CGE approach shows a small loss of GDP if the share of nuclear power generation falls to 15 percent (see Table 5.6). Moreover, both modeling approaches predict a small loss of GDP if the share of nuclear power generation is reduced to zero, although in the case of E3MG it is so small it is effectively zero. Furthermore, E3MG predicts a small increase in employment, whereas the CGE models do not report impact on employment.

Table 5.6 Percentage difference in GDP in 2030, compared to BAU[5] (25% case for E3MG)

	15% nuclear share	*0% nuclear share*
Macro-econometric model		
E3MG	0.00	−0.04
CGE models		
NIES	−0.31	−1.26
Osaka University	−2.08	−2.56
Keio University	−1.44	−2.56
RITE	−4.93	−7.39

Sources: Energy and Environment Council (2012a), Pollitt et al. (2014).

Overall, four out of the five modeling exercises show that, despite higher electricity prices, reducing the share of nuclear power in the energy mix to 15 percent by 2030 would have only a modest impact on GDP. The loss of GDP would be somewhat greater if nuclear energy was completely phased out by 2030, but the loss is only just over 2.5 percent in four of the five exercises.

The interaction with climate policy

An important message from the E3MG modeling is the strong interaction between the power mix and climate policy. This is also an important message from this book. The fact that we discuss the power sector and environmental tax reform in separate parts of the book does not mean that they should be considered in isolation from each other.

It is of course be possible to reduce emissions in other ways than through a carbon tax, for example through increased energy efficiency (see Chapter 6), although improved efficiency is already assumed in the 0 percent nuclear energy case.[6] It is certainly recognized in general (e.g., Grubb, 2014) that a combination of policies is required to meet more ambitious carbon targets, with carbon pricing being a necessary component but not sufficient on its own. The need for a combination of policies and policy cooperation with related countries or regions is also consistent with other findings in this book.

The E3MG results suggest that a carbon tax with revenue recycling will not do harm to the Japanese economy, with possible double dividends and an increase in GDP of up to 0.8 percent compared to baseline. However, the carbon prices required to meet the targets are both very high from a political perspective and could have severe competitiveness impacts on certain industries (see Chapter 13), so there may still be strong arguments against introducing the taxes. Therefore, some instruments to curb the negative competitiveness impact, such as a policy mix with low-carbon subsidies and border tax adjustment, probably need to be considered (see Chapter 14) in order to ease political resistance to carbon taxation.

Appendix

Table 5.A1 Summary of scenario results (from the *Options* report)

		2010	2030			
			0% NPP		15% NPP	20–25% NPP
			Before additional measures	After additional measures		
Composition of electricity generation	NPP share	26%	0% (−25%)	0% (−25%)	15% (−10%)	20–25% (−5%– 1%)
	Renewables	10%	30% (+20%)	35% (+25%)	30% (+20%)	30–25% (+20 –+15%)
	Combustion	63%	70% (+5%)	65% (+0%)	55% (−10%)	50% (−15%)
	Coal	24%	28% (+4%)	21% (−3%)	20% (−4%)	18% (−6%)
	LNG	29%	36% (+7%)	38% (+9%)	29% (+0%)	27% (−2%)
	Oil	10%	6% (−4%)	6% (−4%)	5% (−5%)	5% (−5%)
Energy conservation	Electricity generation	1.1 trn kWh	1.0 trn kWh	1.0 trn kWh	1.0 trn kWh	1.0 trn kWh
	End energy consumption	0.39 bn kL	0.31 bn kL	0.30 bn kL	0.31 bn kL	0.31 bn kL
NPP	Dependence on NPP	26%	0% (−25%)	0% (−25%)	15% (−10%)	20–25% (−5%–1%)
Energy security	Dependence on fossil fuels	63%	70% (+5%)	65% (+0%)	55% (−10%)	50% (−15%)
	Imported fuel values (total primary energy supply)	17 trn yen	17 trn yen	16 trn Yen	16 trn yen	15 trn yen
			Promoting stronger shift to gas			
Climate policy	Renewable energy share	10%	30% (+20%)	35% (+25%)	30% (+20%)	30–25% (+20 –+15%)
	Non-fossil energy share	37%	30% (−5%)	35% (+0%)	45% (+10%)	50% (+15%)
	Coal to gas in combustion power plants including CHP	1:1.2	1:1.3	1:1.8	1:1.5	1:1.5

(*Continued*)

Table 5.A1 (Continued)

		2010	2030			
			0% NPP		15% NPP	20–25% NPP
			Before additional measures	After additional measures		
GHG emission	2030	–	-16%	-23%	-23%	-25%
	2020	–	+0% (0% NPP), -5% (14% NPP)	-0% (0% NPP), -7% (14% NPP)	-9% (21% NPP)	-10–11% (23–26% NPP)
Generation costs (yen/kWh)		8.6	–	15.1 (+6.5)	14.1 (+5.5)	14.1 (+5.5)
Transmission investment (trn yen, accumulated to 2030)			3.4	5.2	3.4	3.4–2.7
Energy saving investment (trn yen, accumulated to 2030)			80 (saving 60)	100 (saving 70)	80 (saving 60)	80 (saving 60)
Household electricity price in 2030 (10 thousand yen/month)						
NIES		1.0	–	1.4	1.4	1.4
Osaka Univ.			–	1.5	1.4	1.2
Keio Univ.			–	2.1	1.8	1.8
RITE			–	2.0	1.8	1.8
Real GDP in 2030 (trn yen)						
NIES		511	636 (2030 BAU)	628	634	634
Osaka Univ.			624 (2030 BAU)	608	611	614
Keio Univ.			625 (2030 BAU)	609	616	617
RITE			609 (2030 BAU)	564	579	581

Source: Energy and Environment Council (2012a), edited by authors.

Note 1: The exchange rate was 90.90 JPY/USD and 122.33 JPY/EUR on January 27, 2013.

Note 2: Numbers in parenthesis indicate difference from reference case.

Notes

1 In a liberalized energy market, short-run electricity prices will mainly be determined by marginal costs, which exclude capital costs. In Europe, this has caused problems for power companies who have become unable to recoup their investment costs. However, we assume that this situation will not continue indefinitely.
2 In the Energy and Environment Council (2012a), footnote 4 of table 2 (p. 14) states, 'In the economic modeling analysis, the economic burden resulting from energy conservation efforts was represented as a carbon tax, and the energy prices include this carbon tax. Note that the electricity prices in this table also include the carbon tax.'
3 For further information, see the summary in Pollitt et al. (2014), which references Homma and Akimoto (2013), McLellan et al. (2013) and Zhang et al. (2012).
4 Note that the carbon tax shown in this paragraph is not comparable with results in Chapter 8 due to different sectoral coverage.
5 The BAU used by the CGE models had a 24 percent nuclear share in 2030, so is very similar to the 25 percent case for E3MG.
6 A carbon tax, as modelled here and in the CGE scenarios, could boost energy efficiency, but other policies such as public investment programs could also lead to greater efficiency (see Chapter 8).

References

Ban, K. (2013). 'The relationship between energy policy and economic growth.' Keizai Seminar No. 669, pp. 35–41 (in Japanese).

Barker, T., Anger, A., Chewpreecha, U., and Pollitt, H. (2012). 'A new economics approach to modelling policies to achieve global 2020 targets for climate stabilisation.' In 'Economic policies of the new thinking in economics.' Special issue, *International Review of Applied Economics, 26*(2), pp. 205–211.

Barker, T., Foxon, T., and Scrieciu, S. S. (2008). 'Achieving the G8 50% target: Modelling induced and accelerated technological change using the macro-econometric model E3MG.' In Strachan, N., Foxon, T. and Fujino J. (Eds.), 'Modelling long-term scenarios for low-carbon societies.' Special issue, *Climate Policy, 8* (Supplementary Issue 1), pp. S30–S45.

Barker, T., Pan, H., Köhler, J., Warren, R., and Winne, S. (2005). 'Avoiding dangerous climate change by inducing technological progress: scenarios using a large-scale econometric model.' In Schellnhuber, H. J., Cramer, W., Nakicenovic, N., Wigley, T., and Yohe, G. (Eds.), *Avoiding Dangerous Climate Change.* Cambridge: Cambridge University Press, Chapter 38.

Barker, T., Pan, H., Köhler, J., Warren, R., and Winne, S. (2006). 'Decarbonizing the global economy with induced technological change: Scenarios to 2100 using E3MG.' In Edenhofer, O., Lessmann, K., Kemfert, K., Grubb, M., and Köhler, J. (Eds.), 'Induced technological change: Exploring its implications for the economics of atmospheric stabilization.' Special issue, *Energy Journal, 27*(special issue 2006), pp. 241–258.

Barker, T., and Scrieciu, S. S. (2009). 'Unilateral climate change mitigation, carbon leakage and competitiveness: an application to the European Union.' *International Journal of Global Warming, 1*(4), pp. 405–417.

Cost Estimation and Review Committee (2011, December 19). 'The report of the cost estimation and review committee.' The Energy and Environment Council,

Cost Estimation and Review Committee. http://www.cas.go.jp/jp/seisaku/npu/policy09/archive02_hokoku.html (in Japanese).

Duscha, V., Schumacher, K., Schleich, J., and Buisson, P. (2013). 'Costs of meeting international climate targets without nuclear power.' *Climate Policy, 14*(3), pp. 327–352. http://dx.doi.org/10.1080/14693062.2014.852018.

Energy and Environment Council (2012a, July 29). 'Options for energy and the environment.' http://www.cas.go.jp/jp/seisaku/npu/policy09/archive01.html (in Japanese).

Energy and Environment Council (2012b). 'Options for energy and the environment, the Energy and Environment Council Decision on June 29, 2012.' National Policy Unit (outline of 2012a in English).

Energy and Environment Council (2012c). 'Innovative strategy for energy and the environment.' http://www.cas.go.jp/jp/seisaku/npu/policy09/archive01.html (in Japanese).

European Commission (2011). Energy Roadmap 2050, COM (2011) 885 final. Brussels. http://ec.europa.eu/clima/policies/roadmap/index_en.htm (accessed May 17, 2015).

Grubb, M. (2014). *Planetary Economics.* Abingdon, UK; New York: Routledge.

Homma, T., and Akimoto, K. (2013). 'Analysis of Japan's energy and environment strategy after the Fukushima nuclear plant accident.' *Energy Policy, 62*, pp. 1216–1225.

International Energy Agency (IEA) (2010). *World Energy Outlook.* Paris: IEA.

Matsuo, Y. (2012). 'Summary and evaluation of cost calculation for nuclear power generation by the cost estimation and review committee.' Institute for Energy Economics Japan (IEEJ). http://eneken.ieej.or.jp/data/4337.pdf (accessed May 17, 2015).

McLellan, B., Zhang, Q., Utama, N. A., Farzaneh, H., and Ishihara, K. N. (2013). 'Analysis of Japan's post-Fukushima energy strategy.' *Energy Strategy Reviews, 2*(2), pp. 190–198.

Pollitt, H., Lee, S., Park, S.-J., and Ueta, K. (2014). 'An economic and environmental assessment of future electricity generation mixes in Japan: An assessment using the E3MG macro-econometric model.' *Energy Policy, 67*, pp. 243–254.

Zhang, Q., Ishihara, K. N., Mclellan, B. C., and Tezuka, T. (2012). 'Scenario analysis on future electricity supply and demand in Japan.' *Energy, 38*(1), pp. 376–385.

6 Energy efficiency policies in East Asia

Macroeconomic implications and interactions with existing climate policies

Unnada Chewpreecha, Seonghee Kim, Lisa Ryan, and Sunhee Suk

6.1 Introduction

The previous chapters have considered ways in which East Asia's future energy requirements might be met through different mixes of technology. However, apart from responses to changes in price, the amount of energy required in the scenarios that were modelled is taken as given. In this chapter, we assess how East Asia's total energy requirements might be reduced through energy efficiency measures.

Grubb, Neuhoff, and Hourcade (2014) introduced the three pillars of policy to reduce greenhouse gas (GHG) emissions: standards and engagement, markets and pricing, and strategic investment for technological progress. We have already considered the policies designed to encourage progress in renewable energy technologies in Chapters 3 and 4, and the second part of this book focuses exclusively on the second pillar (price mechanisms). Implementing policies across all three pillars to improve energy efficiency and make the best use of existing technologies is widely accepted as one of the most cost-effective means to reduce CO_2 emissions. This chapter uses the E3ME-Asia macroeconomic model to examine the macroeconomic and CO_2-emission impacts of introducing additional energy efficiency targets and policies in East Asia.

There are considerable benefits from improving energy efficiency. It is estimated that energy efficiency improvements can avoid 22–24 Gt CO_2-equivalent between 2015 and 2030 relative to a baseline scenario and assuming a carbon price of US$ 70 per ton. This is equivalent to about one-fifth of all cost-effective emission reduction measures over that period (UNEP, 2014).

However, the benefits are not limited to energy and GHG emission savings. There are significant economic and social effects known as the 'multiple benefits of energy efficiency' (IEA, 2014a) that should result from improved energy efficiency. The increased disposable income from reduced energy bills can lead to increased consumption across all sectors, leading to a rise in economic activity and employment. For businesses, less money spent on energy means a better cash flow and more funds available for reinvestment or profits and increasing productivity. Increased investment in energy efficiency equipment and services by consumers and businesses

---

Box 6.1   Definitions

Energy efficiency improvements involve technical or behavioral changes that result in less energy consumption while delivering the same or better energy services. Energy efficiency measures can take place on the supply side of the energy system, in the generation, transmission, and distribution of energy, and on the demand side, where the main energy-using sectors are buildings (residential commercial), transport, industry, and appliances and lighting. The energy saved or *the energy-demand reduction from energy efficiency* improvements can be quantified as the difference between the energy used to deliver a service with and without the energy efficiency improvement. The *cost-effective supply of energy efficiency* can be defined as the investment opportunities for which the sum of the benefits, stemming from avoided energy consumption, outweighs the investment costs over a specified period of time (IEA, 2013a).

---

results in a rise in economic activity in these sectors, leading to potential competitive advantages and increased exports. The public budget can also benefit, either directly through energy bill reductions in the public sector, or from increased tax and other revenues through the rise in economic activity. On the social side, energy efficiency improvements in previously cold homes can lead to health benefits for the residents. And, in countries with pressure on energy supply, energy efficiency improvements on generation, transmission, and distribution of energy can provide access to energy for a greater number of consumers (IEA, 2014a). Moreover, the multiple benefits of energy efficiency can lead to rebound effects (see Box 6.1).

An empirical study identifies the expected payback time for energy saving investment among companies in China, Japan, and Korea (Liu, Suk, and Yamamoto, 2014). The results indicate that companies in the three countries expect investment in energy savings to become profitable in a short period. Payback times of less than three years were expected by the companies that were surveyed in China and Korea, while Japanese companies expected slightly longer payback times, averaging three to five years (Liu, Suk, and Yamamoto, 2014).

The significant benefits of energy efficiency, that is, of the uptake of energy efficiency measures, are generally less than the estimated potential for cost-effective measures. This is due to a number of well-documented barriers to investment in energy efficiency, which include several market failures, such as split incentives, imperfect information, and externalities where the price of energy is low, as well as other barriers, such as human inertia, access to finance, and the small size of projects for investors (Ryan et al., 2011).

Policies are needed to address these barriers, and many governments have implemented a range of energy-efficiency policy measures in energy-using sectors. A combination of regulatory, informational, and financial measures is needed to fully overcome the market failures in the current system. The main drivers of energy efficiency are energy prices, policy, consumer preferences, and multiple

Box 6.2   Rebound effects

Rebound effects occur when, after the implementation of an energy efficiency measure, more energy is consumed than the technical potential of
the energy efficiency measure would indicate. For example, if insulation is
installed in a home, the energy saving attributed to the measures is usually calculated as the energy consumption of the home with and without
insulation. However, if the home was cold before it was insulated because
of heating losses, it might be that the residents prefer to keep the heat level
in the home higher after the home is insulated, because they find it more
comfortable and they know the home will retain more heat with the added
insulation. In this case, the energy savings would be less than expected
prior to the insulation; this would be counted as a rebound effect. In the
past, rebound effects were considered in a negative light. However, there is
increasing recognition that the increased welfare associated with the multiple benefits may more than offset the 'lost' energy savings, and therefore
rebound effects can, in fact, be positive in economic terms.

benefits (IEA, 2013a). Policy packages that target these drivers are likely to have
most success in exploiting the potential of energy efficiency in order to reduce
energy consumption.

This chapter estimates the effects of energy efficiency policies in East Asian
economies. Section 6.2 describes the policies that are currently in place in each
country. Sections 6.3 and 6.4 describe the modeling approach that was applied
and the scenarios that were assessed. Results are presented in Section 6.5, with
Sections 6.6 and 6.7 providing further discussion.

6.2   Current energy efficiency policies in East Asia

This section outlines current energy efficiency policies in China, Japan, and Korea.
These three East Asian countries rank in the top ten countries globally in terms of
total energy consumption and GHG emissions and accounted for around 30 percent of the world's energy-related CO_2 emissions in 2010. Energy efficiency is a
key pillar of energy and climate-change strategies in each country, and we can see
a diverse range of policies in place.

China

In 2010, the National People's Congress approved the Outline of the 12th Five-Year
Plan for National Economic and Social Development (State Council of the People's
Republic of China, 2010; see Figure 6.1). This outline includes binding targets on
energy savings and GHG emission reductions from 2011 to 2015: a reduction of
energy consumption per unit of GDP by 16 percent and a reduction of CO_2 emission
intensity (per unit of GDP) by 17 percent. Energy consumption per unit of GDP

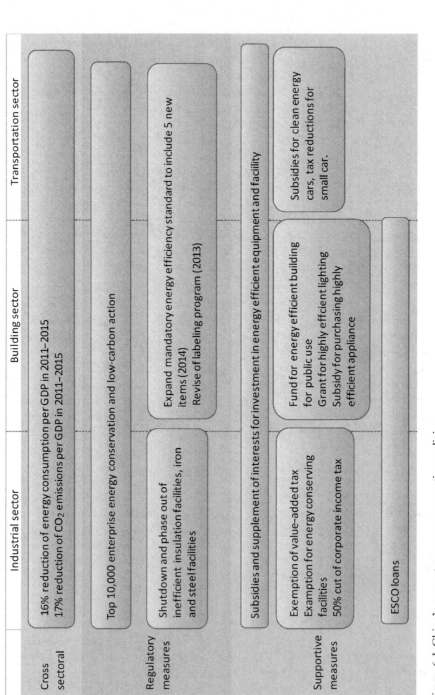

Figure 6.1 China's current energy conservation policies.

improved from 56.7 toe per million RMB in 2010 to 51.7 toe per million RMB in 2013 (reaching 55 percent of the national target). In 2014, China set a 3.9 percent annual reduction target for 2014 and 2015, in order to meet the national energy saving target and reduce emissions of particulates (PM2.5).

Strong governmental leadership is an important feature of Chinese energy conservation policy. For example, accountability and assessment mechanisms of energy conservation targets are a key component of the energy management system. The Top 1,000 Enterprises Energy Conservation Project launched in 2006 has expanded into the Top 10,000 Enterprises Energy Conservation Project and now covers 17,000 enterprises. This scheme reinforces energy conservation targets, and the government assesses the performance of each company in meeting their energy conservation targets and implementing the energy-saving measures. The results of the assessments are published.

Public benefit projects for energy-saving products were implemented in 2009 and are subsidy programs to promote energy-efficient home appliances, automobiles, electric motors, and lighting products. In 2013, the focus of the programs was shifted from home electric appliances to industrial equipment, such as transformers, compressors and pumps, and so on.

Japan

Figure 6.2 shows current energy conservation policies in Japan, a country that pioneered the establishment of a national energy conservation law in 1979. This law was triggered by the two oil crises in the 1970s. The Act on the Rational Use of Energy requires industrial and transport companies to report their energy efficiency measures and improvements in their overall energy efficiency to the government every year. Also, companies must set targets to reduce their energy consumption by around 1 percent each year. In 2013, the energy conservation law was amended. The two main changes were to: (1) help smooth electricity demand over the day to deal with peak demand electricity, and (2) expand the scope of the Top Runner Program. Since 2014, companies have been required to report electricity consumption at different times of day. Companies that implement measures to reduce electricity consumption from the grid are considered to be in compliance with the energy conservation law.

The Top Runner Program was amended to add products that contribute to improving the energy efficiency of houses, buildings, and other equipment. Construction materials were added, and insulation standards for insulation materials were specified. Commercial electric refrigerators and freezers, and multifunction devices, such as printers, electric water heaters (heat pump water heaters), and light-emitting diode (LED) lamps were also added to the program.

Korea

Figure 6.3 shows current energy conservation policies in Korea; the country has strengthened its sectoral demand management measures. The 5th Energy

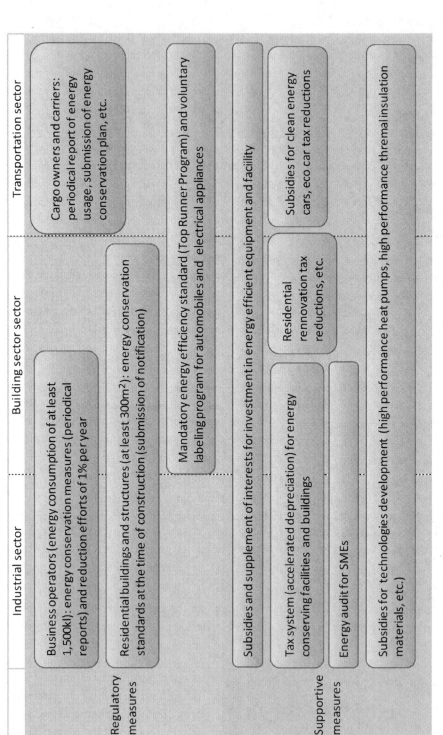

Figure 6.2 Current energy conservation policies in Japan.

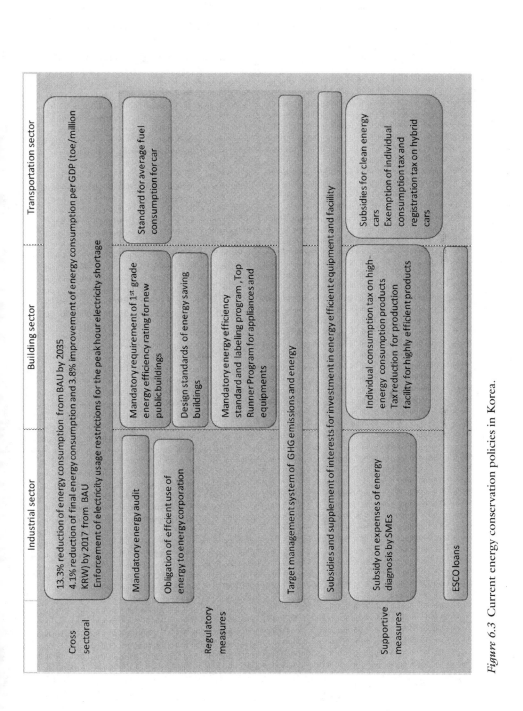

Figure 6.3 Current energy conservation policies in Korea.

Efficiency Basic Strategy was adopted in December 2014 to achieve the national energy efficiency targets of a 13.3 percent reduction in final energy consumption and a 15 percent reduction in electricity consumption by 2035, compared to a baseline scenario. This target was set in the second National Energy Master Plan, which was adopted in January 2014. The 2014 strategy set intermediate targets of a 4.1 percent reduction in final energy consumption, and a 3.8 percent improvement in energy consumption per unit of GDP (toe/million KRW) by 2017 compared to baseline.

Korea has suffered electricity shortages caused by problems at nuclear power plants and delays in the construction of a new coal power plant due to resistance from local residents. After blackouts in 2011, the focus of energy demand management shifted to electricity savings. A GHG and energy target management system was introduced in 2010.

In January, 2015 the Korean emission trading scheme (ETS) was implemented. Companies and facilities, which were previously covered by the GHG and energy target management system, moved to ETS. According to the 2014 strategy, the Korean government will introduce agreements to promote non-utility generation in electricity-intensive industries. Fuel efficiency standards will also be strengthened to reach the levels of developed countries, including Japan and the EU, by 2020. In addition, the scope of a fuel-efficiency labeling scheme will be expanded to include heavy-duty vehicles. For the buildings sector, building codes for energy efficiency will be strengthened to mandate zero-energy buildings for construction by 2025.

6.3   Assessment of the macroeconomic impacts of energy efficiency policies by using the E3ME-Asia modeling approach

In this chapter, the E3ME-Asia model is applied to provide estimates of the macroeconomic impacts of energy efficiency measures in East Asia. The model has previously been applied extensively to energy efficiency to estimate both the economic and employment implications of energy efficiency programs, including the EU's 2020 and 2030 targets. E3ME-Asia has the following key distinctions that make it appropriate for investigating energy efficiency:

- Its non-equilibrium and non-optimization properties allow for the possibility that zero-cost or negative-cost efficiency options can exist and can draw upon unproductive capital and labor resources in both short and long terms.
- The full integration of the economic national accounts, energy system, and emissions in E3ME-Asia allows for analysis of energy and climate policies in parallel, as well as taking into account the rebound effects of energy efficiency.
- The E3 modular approach allows for incorporation of detailed input from external sources.
- The annual time profile of the model allows for an evaluation of the impacts in the short and long runs, rather than the net benefits over a time period.

The model is described more generally in Chapter 2.

Energy savings are entered into E3ME-Asia exogenously, alongside the investment costs for each policy. These policies are assumed to be additional to the model baseline, which already includes policies that were announced up to 2012 (the International Energy Agency's *World Energy Outlook 2013* current policy scenario; see IEA 2013b for more information). The next section describes how we form the energy efficiency scenario.

Figures 6.4 and 6.5 provide conceptual frameworks for interpreting the main macroeconomic impacts of energy efficiency in E3ME-Asia. The impacts are derived from two sets of effects – those from energy savings (Figure 6.4) and those from investment in energy efficiency (Figure 6.5). Energy savings create reduced demand for energy, which can be met either by reductions in energy imports or reductions in the domestic supply of energy. These savings translate to cost savings to industries and households. Industry can improve its price competitiveness if it chooses to pass on these savings through to the final product prices. Alternatively, companies can choose to retain cost savings and increase their profitability. For households, savings on energy bills mean that they have more disposable income to spend on other goods and services.

The rebound effects in energy demand come from increased economic activities as a result of the initial energy savings.

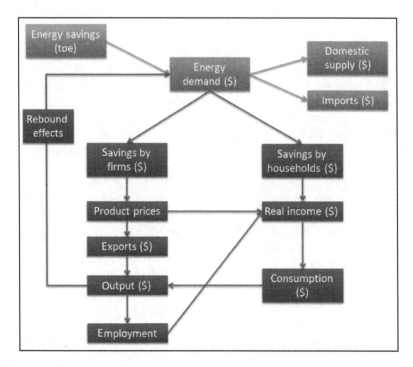

Figure 6.4 Main macroeconomic impacts of energy savings.

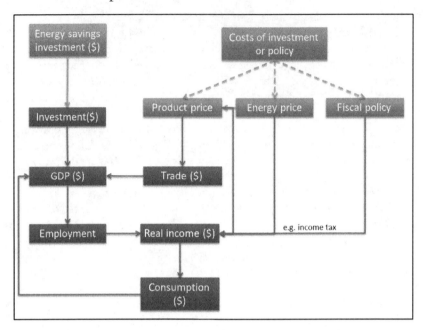

Figure 6.5 Main macroeconomic impacts of energy efficiency investment and policies.

The bottom left part of Figure 6.5 shows the loop by which investments in energy efficiency may lead to multiplier effects in the model (i.e., it includes direct, indirect, and induced effects). On their own, these investments lead to an increase in GDP and rate of employment. However, when the costs of implementing the energy efficiency programs are taken into account, the net impact on GDP will become smaller, possibly negative.

Depending on the policy assumptions, the cost of the program can be paid through higher product prices, higher energy prices, or fiscal adjustment if the government is funding the investment directly. Higher product prices lead to negative real impacts through reductions in consumer spending and worsening in the competitiveness of industries. Higher energy prices would have a similar effect, while the impacts of government backing would depend on how the energy-efficient products are financed (e.g., which tax increases to pay for them, or how spending is reduced).

6.4   Energy efficiency scenarios

In this chapter we take a top-down approach to defining energy efficiency scenarios in East Asia, based on information gathered from the two OECD/IEA publications: 'Energy Efficiency Outlook' (IEA, 2014c, Chapter 8) and 'Investment in Energy Efficiency' (IEA, 2014b, Chapter 4). In contrast to a bottom-up approach, where energy savings from individual measures are used as modeling inputs, our top-down approach looks at the differences in total final energy consumption between the IEA's 'New Policies Scenario' and 'Current Policies Scenario' (IEA, 2014c) and, on the basis of information gathered from the publication,[1] attributes around 62 percent of the savings in energy consumption to end-use efficiency. Owing to the IEA's country-level coverage, it is only possible in this chapter to model energy efficiency scenarios for China and Japan. However, many of the conclusions could also be applied to Korea.

The IEA's New Policies Scenario takes into account both policies and measures that have been already adopted (i.e., that are already in the E3ME-Asia baseline) as well as measures that have been proposed in 2013 and 2014 but have yet to be put into effect (see Table 6.1).

Table 6.2 provides a summary of the energy savings, that is, differences between the IEA's (2014c) Current Policies Scenario and New Policies Scenario that can be attributed to energy efficiency in 2020. The shares are estimated at global level from the information provided in the Energy Efficiency Outlook (IEA, 2014c).

Using these global share assumptions and the energy balances in the WEO's two scenarios, we estimate total energy efficiency savings to be 39.1 mtoe[2] and 1.6 mtoe in China and Japan respectively by 2020 (see Table 6.3).

Table 6.1 Selected energy efficiency policies in China and Japan announced or introduced in 2013 and 2014 in the New Policies Scenario (IEA, 2014c)

Country	Sector	Selected energy efficiency measures in East Asia
China	General	Acceleration of the efficient use of coal by supporting the aim to reduce coal use in several provinces, e.g. by phasing out small, inefficient coal-fired boilers.
	Industry	Phase out outdated production capacity in the steel, cement, and glass industries, including the closure or upgrade of coal-fired boilers.
	Buildings	More than 50% of new buildings to comply with 'green' building standards from 2015, with 400 million m^2 of buildings in northern China to be retrofitted.
	Transportation	Phase out (from 2015) less efficient 'yellow label' vehicles produced before 2005.
Japan	Building and industries	Extension of, among others, the Top Runner Program to, e.g., commercial electric refrigerators and freezers, heat pump water heaters, self-ballasted (LED) lamps, and three-phase induction motors; announced targets for newly constructed buildings to be net-zero energy on average by 2030.

Sources: IEA (2014c, Chapter 8).

Table 6.2 Global energy savings in 2020 from energy efficiency (% of total energy savings between IEA's (2014c) Current Policies Scenario and New Policies Scenario)

	Buildings	*Transport*	*Industry + others*
Coal	40%	–	39%
Oil	27%	53%	57%
Gas	38%	–	64%
Electricity	58%	–	70%
Heat	25%	–	100%
Other renewables	0%	–	100%
Other fuels	40%	–	–

Sources: IEA (2014c, Chapter 8).

Note: Figures show share of energy savings that are attributable to explicit energy efficiency measures. A share of 100% implies that no savings are achieved through other measures.

Table 6.3 Estimates for energy-efficiency savings in 2020, China and Japan (mtoe differences between Current Policies Scenario and New Policies Scenario)

	China	*Japan*
Industry	**−16.0**	**−0.5**
Coal	−5.9	−0.1
Oil	−1.3	−0.1
Gas	−0.5	−0.1
Electricity	−6.8	−0.1
Heat	−1.4	0.0
Bioenergy	−0.1	−0.1
Transportation	**−10.0**	**−0.3**
Oil	−10.0	−0.3
Buildings	**−11.2**	**−0.8**
Coal	−1.2	0.0
Oil	−0.5	−0.1
Gas	−0.7	−0.1
Electricity	−8.7	−0.6
Other	**−1.9**	**0.0**
Total	**−39.1**	**−1.6**

Sources: IEA (2014c) and own calculations.

Table 6.4 Average additional annual energy efficiency investment in China and Japan in the New Policies Scenario, 2014–2020 (2012 billion US$)

2012 billion US$	China	Japan
Industry	**3.2**	**0**
Energy intensive	1.6	0
Non-energy intensive	1.6	0
Transportation	**8.4**	**3.2**
Road	8.4	3.2
Others	0	0
Buildings	**2**	**2.4**
Total	**13.6**	**5.6**

Sources: IEA (2014b, 2014c) and own calculations.

In terms of energy efficiency investment, the IEA (2014b) publication provides detailed annual average energy efficiency investments for China and Japan in the New Policies Scenario. The investment numbers have been adjusted to take into account energy efficiency investment in the Current Policies Scenario, which could be due to existing energy efficiency policies (adopted in 2013) or techno-economically driven (i.e., it would happen without a policy). Based on this adjustment, around 40 percent of global total energy efficiency investments reported in the New Policies Scenarios is considered to be additional to the Current Policies Scenarios that is used to form the E3ME-Asia baseline. The share of energy efficiency investment in the baseline is assumed to be the same in all countries. Table 6.4 provides annual estimates of investment in energy efficiency in China and Japan over the period 2014 to 2020.

It is important to stress that our energy efficiency scenario reflects only additional policies that were announced after 2013 and are yet to be implemented (IEA, 2014c, New Policies Scenario). Energy efficiency measures adopted in 2013 are already included in our E3ME-Asia baseline (IEA, 2014c, Current Policies Scenario). This explains why the energy savings and required investments in our energy efficiency scenario are relatively small. The result should not be interpreted as suggesting there are not much larger potential gains in efficiency.

Both energy savings and investments in the New Policies Scenario form modeling inputs for the energy efficiency scenario modelled in this chapter. As in other chapters, the E3ME-Asia baseline was made consistent with the IEA's Current Policies Scenario from *World Energy Outlook* (2014c). This baseline case was used as a benchmark for the comparison of results.

It is necessary to make further assumptions on how these energy efficiency investments are paid for; we assume:

- Businesses pay for all industry as well as half of transportation and buildings investment by passing on the resulting costs through higher product prices.

- Households pay for the other half of transportation and buildings investment, meaning that they have less income to spend on other goods and services.

As mentioned earlier in the chapter, if these energy efficiency measures were to be introduced together with carbon taxation, governments could use the carbon tax revenues to fund the investments and, therefore, to reduce the cost burden on industry and households. However, to keep the scenario simple, we assume no carbon pricing in either the baseline or the scenario, and that all the energy efficiency measures are introduced due to regulation.

In addition, we assume that there is no change to global energy prices or to policies outside China and Japan, compared to the baseline.

6.5   Modeling outcomes

Table 6.5 summarizes the results from the modeling exercise for China and Japan in 2020. The table shows the impacts on GDP and employment for the additional energy efficiency policies in the IEA (2014c) New Policies Scenario. The E3ME-Asia results show that both countries benefit from the energy efficiency measures, even in the short time scale of the policies (2014–2020) and relatively limited scale of investment.

The more detailed results for China and Japan in Table 6.6 suggest that the increases in GDP in both countries are driven by the additional investment that is

Table 6.5 Impacts on GDP and employment in 2020 of energy efficiency policies in the IEA (2014c) New Policies Scenario, % difference from baseline

	China	*Japan*
GDP	0.11	0.13
Employment	0.02	0.04

Sources: Authors' estimates using the E3ME-Asia model.

Table 6.6 Detailed macroeconomic impacts in 2020, % difference from baseline

	China	*Japan*
GDP	0.11	0.13
Consumption	−0.04	0.03
Investment	0.45	0.47
Exports	0.12	0.03
Imports	0.23	0.04
Consumer price	0.04	−0.07

Sources: Authors' estimates using the E3ME-Asia model.

required. These additional investments stimulate domestic demand and employment opportunities in both countries.

The contrast in the consumer spending results for China (negative) and Japan
(positive) reflects the nature of energy efficiency investment and our assumptions
about how these investments are paid for. In China, consumer prices rise because
the cost of investment in industrial energy efficiency is assumed to be passed on to
final product prices; in Japan, the IEA figures suggest no additional energy efficiency
investment by industry during the period 2014–2020 compared to what is already
included in the baseline (inclusive of energy saving measures implemented by 2013).

In both countries, we assume that half of the costs of investment in transportation
and buildings are paid for by households. It should be noted that we have treated
household investment as an increase in gross fixed capital formation (i.e., investment) rather than as a boost in consumption of durable goods. The results in 2020
show that, despite this assumption, the negative impacts on household consumption are limited because energy efficiency measures create jobs and boost average
incomes. Beyond 2020, benefits from the energy savings are expected to continue.

Total imports increase for both China and Japan in the energy efficiency scenario. The increases are mostly due to the advanced manufacturing sectors that
supply investment goods related to energy efficiency. Imports of fossil fuels are
reduced in both countries by a small amount; this is more important for Japan,
which is more reliant on energy imports (see Chapter 7). However, in both countries there is an apparent reduction in energy import dependency, which could
improve domestic energy security (see Chapter 7).

The net reductions in total energy demand (Table 6.7) include both the initial
reductions from the energy efficiency measures estimated by the IEA (2014c; see
Table 6.3) and the rebound in demand from economic activities generated by higher
investment and savings in energy bills. Although the reductions in emissions are
quite small, because of the limited number of additional policies announced during
2013–2014 and the short time scale of the scenario (period 2014–2020), the results
clearly show the potential of energy savings caused by these measures and their contribution to meeting the CO_2 reduction/intensity targets for both countries.

6.6   Limitations of our approach

Our approach of modeling energy efficiency in this chapter has two main
limitations.

Table 6.7 The energy and CO_2 impacts in 2020 of energy
efficiency policies, % difference from baseline

	Japan	China
Total final energy consumption	–0.55	–1.73
CO_2	–0.58	–1.95

Sources: Authors' estimates using the E3ME-Asia model.

First, due to the lack of detailed information on specific energy efficiency measures in East Asia, it was not possible to model the economic impacts of energy efficiency at the individual policy level. Instead, we relied on top-down information from the IEA, together with some basic assumptions, to estimate the amount of total energy savings and associated investment in China and Japan. A more comprehensive approach would require estimates of energy savings, which could be derived either from using an energy system model or another bottom-up analysis. It would also need information on the associated costs and investment of each measure to form inputs to the E3ME-Asia model.

The second limitation relates to the labor market. As a non-optimization model, E3ME-Asia is well-suited for modeling energy efficiency. The model allows for the possibility of spare economic capacity that can be used in each country, but it is unable to take into account putative effects of bottlenecks in specific industries. For example, the baseline labor market projections include unemployed workers who, under the right economic conditions, could be moved into employment. However, the model assumes that, as long as there are people available to work, then they can take on new jobs, regardless of the skills required. A further micro-based supplementary analysis would be required to further investigate the skills mismatch issue.

6.7 Overall conclusions

This chapter examines the economic impacts following the introduction of some additional energy efficiency targets and policies (the IEA New Policies Scenario) in East Asia compared with a baseline scenario (the IEA Current Policies Scenario). We use the E3ME-Asia model to carry out this analysis. One of the key features of E3ME-Asia, unlike the more common CGE modeling approach, is that it does not rely on theoretical economic assumptions about optimizing behavior. This makes E3ME-Asia a particularly suitable tool for assessing low-cost and negative-cost (i.e., net benefit) energy efficiency measures.

Although the input assumptions in our energy efficiency scenario are quite stylized, we demonstrate that the limited additional energy efficiency measures that were modelled give the Chinese and Japanese economies a small boost through investments that stimulate demand and create jobs. The energy efficiency measures can also help to reduce the countries' reliance on fossil fuel imports and their exposure to international movements in energy prices (see Chapter 7). Even when the rebound effects are taken in account, the energy efficiency programs reduce energy demand and CO_2 emissions.

Grubb et al. (2014) described the three pillars of policy reform that are required to meet ambitious emission reduction targets. Chapters 3 and 4 focused on policies promoting development of new technologies – and in the second part of this book we shift attention to market-based instruments, the second pillar. However, the high carbon prices that are discussed in Chapter 8 also emphasize the important role of first pillar regulatory measures in promoting energy efficiency that we assess in this chapter. The implementation of energy efficiency programs would lead to lower carbon prices for the East Asian economies while also boosting GDP and employment.

Notes

1 Energy efficiency in energy supply (power generation and refineries) is more limited as less new infrastructure (which is generally more efficient than the existing stock) is built in the New Policies Scenarios than in the Current Policies Scenarios. Other energy savings from non-efficiency include fuel and technology switching and reduced energy service demand.
2 Mtoe stands for million tons of oil equivalent. For example, the difference between total final consumption of coal by industry in China in 2020 in the Current Policies Scenario and New Policies Scenario (IEA, 2014c) is 15 mtoe, of which we assumed 39 percent to be attributed to energy efficiency, i.e. 5.9 mtoe.

References

Grubb, M., Neuhoff, K., and Hourcade, J. C. (2014). *Planetary Economics*. New York: Routledge.

International Energy Association (IEA) (2013a). *Energy Efficiency Market Report 2013*. Paris: OECD/IEA.

International Energy Association (IEA) (2013b). *World Energy Outlook 2013*. Paris: OECD/IEA.

International Energy Association (IEA) (2014a). *The Multiple Benefits of Energy Efficiency*. Paris: OECD/IEA.

International Energy Association (IEA) (2014b). *World Energy Investment Outlook*. Paris: OECD/IEA.

International Energy Association (IEA) (2014c). *World Energy Outlook 2014*. Paris: OECD/IEA.

Liu, X. B., Suk, S. H., and Yamamoto, R. (2014). 'The feasibility of pricing of carbon emissions in three Northeast Asian countries: Japan, China and the Republic of Korea.' Policy Brief, No. 29, Institute for Global Environmental Strategies. http://pub.iges.or.jp/modules/envirolib/upload/5260/attach/PB_29_E_0403.pdf (accessed May 17, 2015)

Ryan, L., Moarif, S., Levina, E., and Baron, R. (2011). *Energy Efficiency Policy and Carbon Pricing*. IEA Information Paper, Energy Efficiency Series. Paris: OECD/IEA. http://www.iea.org/publications/freepublications/publication/EE_Carbon_Pricing.pdf (accessed May 17, 2015).

State Council of the People's Republic of China (2010). People's Republic of Economic and Social Development Twelfth Five-Year Plan. Beijing: Chinese Central Government.

United Nations Environment Programme (UNEP) (2014). *The Emissions Gap Report 2014: A UNEP Synthesis Report*. Nairobi: UNEP.

7 Energy structure and energy security under climate mitigation scenarios in East Asia

Ken'ichi Matsumoto

7.1 Introduction

Climate change is currently one of the most significant global environmental issues in society, and policy discussions from mid- to long-term perspectives are continuing in the international arena, including the United Nations Framework Convention on Climate Change. Energy has also been a significant global issue; for example, due to fluctuations in price and limited supply. In recent years, energy demand has increased dramatically in large emerging countries accompanying the growth in economy and population, and demand is expected to increase further (BP, 2013; IEA, 2013). As a result, there are growing concerns about tight energy supplies in the future. In addition, since production and reserves of fossil fuels, such as crude oil and natural gas, are located in a small number of countries (BP, 2013), countries poor in energy resources and dependent on fuel imports, like East Asian countries, will face substantial price fluctuation and geopolitical risks.

Climate change measures[1] aim to reduce greenhouse gas (GHG) emissions, often with a focus on CO_2 reduction. Energy savings and shifts to low-carbon energy – namely, shifts from coal to natural gas, and from fossil fuels to renewables – have been implemented to reduce emissions. Further promoting energy savings and the use of renewables is required to realize larger reductions in GHG emissions. If the saving of energy and use of renewables, which are basically domestic energy, are enhanced as climate change measures, the volume and dependence of energy imports will decrease. Climate change policy can, therefore, also improve energy security.

Energy security is an important issue in its own right. When considering the energy security of a country, especially one that relies on foreign sources of energy, risk diversification is necessary to reduce the country's risk of not being able to obtain enough energy resources for its economic activity. The ways of diversifying the risks are, for example, diversification of supply and fuel types, and industrial globalization (Neff, 1997).

In this chapter, we analyze the energy structure and energy security in three East Asian countries (China, Japan, and Korea) by introducing climate change measures using a computable general equilibrium (CGE) model. The CGE model ensures that the analysis covers the whole economy in a consistent manner. The

Herfindahl index is applied to compare the diversity of energy types in each scenario (see Section 7.3 for details). This chapter focuses on the narrowly defined 'energy security' (see the following). Similar analysis on a global scale has been carried out by Matsumoto (2013).

Comprehensive research on energy security has been performed targeting Asian (mainly Northeast Asian) countries as a part of the Asian Energy Security project (see the 'Special Section: Asian Energy Security' in *Energy Policy*, *39*(11) – the overview is in von Hippel et al., 2011b). The authors analyze the issue for some Asian countries, such as Japan, Korea (North and South), and China, and the region as a whole from either the narrowly defined (i.e., energy security from energy supply)[2] or broadly defined energy security (i.e., energy security not only from energy supply, but also from economy, technology, environment, society and culture, and military) using the LEAP (Long-range Energy Alternatives Planning) software system (von Hippel, Savage, and Hayes, 2011a; von Hippel et al., 2011c). The results from multiple energy pathways within a country or a region are compared in order to indicate which pathway is preferable, depending on different measures of energy security, such as cost, energy output, fuels imports/exports, technological development, and GHG emissions. In addition, other external methods, such as diversification indices and qualitative analysis, can be applied using the results from LEAP to further analyze energy security (von Hippel et al., 2011a).

Section 7.2 describes the model and scenarios. In Section 7.3, we show the results of the analysis, particularly on energy demand. Finally, in Section 7.4, we draw conclusions.

7.2 Methods

Model

The model used in this study is a recursive dynamic CGE model on a global scale, incorporating energy and environmental components, that is based on the work of, for example Masui et al. (2011), Matsumoto (2013), and Matsumoto and Masui (2011). Here, an overview of the model is described; for more details of the model, see Matsumoto, Tachiiri, and Kawamiya (2015).

The model is disaggregated into 24 geographical regions and 21 types of economic goods/services (Tables 7.1 and 7.2). Basically, one sector produces one type of good/service. However, the electric power sector (the ELY sector in Table 7.2) is divided into detailed technologies, including thermal (coal-, oil-, and gas-fired), hydro, nuclear, solar, wind, geothermal, biomass, waste, and other renewable power generation methods. In addition, carbon capture and storage (CCS) can be selected by thermal and biomass power generation as an advanced technology. Each industrial sector in the economy is represented by a nested constant elasticity of substitution (CES) production function.

Each industrial sector produces goods/services that are delivered for the international market and/or the domestic market, by taking inputs of production

Table 7.1 Region definitions

Code	Region
AUS	Australia
NZL	New Zealand
JPN	Japan
CAN	Canada
USA	United States of America
E15	15 Western EU countries
RUS	Russia
E10	10 Eastern EU countries
XRE	Other Europe
KOR	Korea
CHN	China and Hong Kong
XRA	Other Asia-Pacific
IDN	Indonesia
THA	Thailand
XSE	Other Southeast Asia
IND	India
XSA	Other South Asia
MEX	Mexico
ARG	Argentina
BRA	Brazil
XLM	Other Latin America
XME	The Middle East
ZAF	South Africa
XAF	Other Africa

Note: In this chapter, we focus on China, Japan, and Korea for the analysis.

factors and intermediate inputs. The Armington assumption (Armington, 1969) is applied for international trade.

In each domestic market, the supplied goods/services are consumed as final consumption, investment, and/or intermediate input for industrial sectors. The total investment demand in each period is set exogenously to meet a prescribed future economic growth rate (see the 'Reference Scenario' section, following). The model uses a putty–clay approach for forming capital.

Each region has a final demand sector that is assumed to own all production factors, and supplies them to the industrial sectors through the economy's factor markets to receive its income. The final demand sector distributes income

Table 7.2 Commodity/sector definitions

Code	Commodities/sectors
Energy commodities/sectors	
COA	Coal
OIL	Crude oil
GAS	Natural gas
P_C	Petroleum products
GDT	Gas manufacture and distribution
ELY	Electric power*
Non-energy commodities/sectors	
AGR	Agriculture
LVK	Livestock
FRS	Forestry
FSH	Fishery
EIS	Energy-intensive industries
OMN	Other mineral mining
M_M	Metals and manufacturing
FOD	Food processing
OMF	Other manufacturing
CNS	Construction
TRT	Transportation
CMN	Communication
WTR	Water
OSG	Governmental services
SER	Other services

Note: The electric power sector consists of thermal power (i.e., coal-, oil-, and gas-fired), hydropower, nuclear power, solar power, wind power, geothermal power, biomass power, waste power, and other renewables. In addition, thermal power and biomass power with CCS technology are available.

between final consumption and savings. The final consumption for each good/service is determined to maximize the utility represented by a CES function.

The model is calibrated to reproduce economic activity and energy levels in the base year (2001) using the following data sources: the Global Trade Analysis Project (GTAP) 6 (Dimaranan, 2006) for economic activity levels, the Emission Database for Global Atmospheric Research v4.0 (European Commission Joint Research Centre, 2010) for GHG emissions, and the International Energy Agency energy balances (IEA, 2009a,b) for energy.

Several assumptions are included to expand the model to a dynamic structure. Demographic assumptions are based on the medium variant of the United Nations' *World Population Prospects* (UN, 2011). Future economic growth assumptions to determine the amount of investment are based on the Sustainability First scenario of the *Global Environment Outlook 4* (UNEP, 2007). And technological improvement is based on the *Special Report on Emission Scenarios* (SRES) B2 scenario (Nakicenovic and Swart, 2000). These assumptions are applied to both the reference scenario and policy scenarios. The simulation periods of this study are those between the base year (2001) and 2050.

In the emission reduction cases (i.e., the policy scenarios explained in the 'Policy Scenarios' section), global GHG emissions are assigned to regions in proportion to their population in 2050. Between the base year and 2050, regional GHG emission limits are set by linear interpolation of the emissions in the base year and the limits in 2050. Global emissions trading is also applied in the model.

Scenarios

Reference Scenario

As a first step in the process of developing policy scenarios (see the 'Policy Scenarios' section), we develop a 'no climate policy' reference scenario. In this reference scenario, GHG emissions and concentrations and radiative forcing exceed those of the policy scenarios. The reference scenario assumes that no policies and measures solely aimed at controlling GHG emissions are introduced beyond those that are in place already and that the existing policies are not renewed when they expire. The reference scenario is based upon the assumptions explained in the 'Model' section.

The following details summarize the reference scenario. The global population grows from 6.1 billion to 9.2 billion between 2001 and 2050. Global GDP grows from $30 trillion to $102 trillion in the same period. In 2050, primary energy demand in the world reaches 849 EJ/year, and China becomes the largest economy both in terms of GDP and energy demand, followed by the US. Globally, fossil fuel demand – particularly that of coal – increases continuously because of its relatively low cost. Consequently, annual CO_2 emissions become 17.5 GtC in 2050.

Policy scenarios

In this chapter, the Representative Concentration Pathways (RCPs) are used for the climate change policy scenarios[3]. RCPs are the first step toward the Fifth Assessment Report of the Intergovernmental Panel on Climate Change, and one of the latest families of climate policy scenario. RCPs are defined by radiative forcing levels in 2100 and consist of four scenarios, namely the lowest (2.6 W/m²; van Vuuren et al., 2011a), the highest (8.5 W/m²; Riahi et al., 2011), and the two middle scenarios of 4.5 W/m² (Thomson et al., 2011) and 6 W/m² (Masui et al., 2011). In this study, these policy scenarios (Figure 7.1) are analyzed using the CGE model.[4]

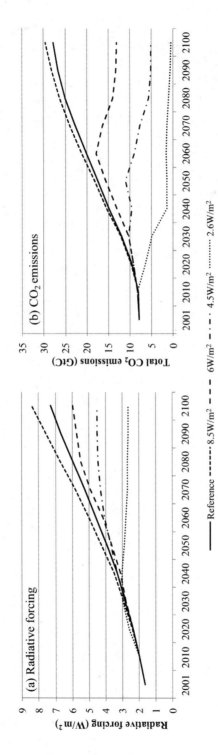

Figure 7.1 (a) Radiative forcing levels and (b) corresponding total CO_2 emissions.

Source: Figures 2 and 3 in Matsumoto (2013).

Note: Since these radiative forcing and emission pathways are our calculation, they are different from the original RCPs.

Legend: Reference ——— 8.5W/m² - - - - - 6W/m² - - - 4.5W/m² ········ 2.6W/m²

It should be noted that energy structure is not exogenously controlled or fixed as shares[5] when running both the reference and policy scenarios. It is, instead, allowed to change endogenously in response to the scenario inputs based on the costs and elasticity parameters in the model.

7.3   Results and discussion

Carbon prices are used in the model to reduce emissions. The carbon prices in the policy scenarios in 2050 are $0.78/tCO_2$, $39.50/tCO_2$, and $209/tCO_2$, respectively in the 6 W/m² , 4.5 W/m² , and 2.6 W/m² scenarios. The carbon price in the 6 W/m² scenario is very low because of the low reduction in emissions compared to the reference scenario in 2050, whereas the carbon price in the 2.6 W/m² scenario is high because of the high emission reduction compared to reference scenario.

Regarding primary energy in Asian countries, demand increases in China and Korea in all scenarios (including the reference scenario) until 2050, whereas it decreases in Japan (Table 7.3). The decrease in Japan is due to its falling population and because it is already a developed country. Comparing the scenarios, primary energy demand is lower in the more ambitious scenarios. In addition, the energy structure in each country changes drastically between scenarios, especially in the 2.6 W/m² scenario (Figure 7.2). In the reference scenario, fossil fuels occupy more than 90 percent of the primary energy demand in China and Korea, and 76 percent of that in Japan in 2050. This is because of the dependence on coal, the price of which is relatively low in the no-GHG-constraint situation. In the policy scenarios, however, the share of fossil fuels – especially that of coal – decreases, and instead, the share of renewables increases. The share of renewables is remarkably high in the 2.6 W/m² scenario.

As a metric for energy security implications of different patterns of energy demand, we use the Herfindahl index (Eq. 7.1), which is based on diversity indices in economic and financial analysis (Neff, 1997; von Hippel et al, 2011a). The index has a maximum value of one when there is only one energy type and goes down with increasing diversity of energy types. This means that a lower value of the index indicates dependence on more-diverse energy sources.

$$H = \Sigma_i x_i^2 \qquad (7.1)$$

Table 7.3 Total primary energy demand (EJ)

	2001	2050			
		Reference	6 W/m²	4.5 W/m²	2.6 W/m²
China	53.5	275.6	261.0	149.8	73.5
Japan	19.9	12.1	11.7	11.6	9.3
Korea	9.1	13.3	12.1	11.5	7.2

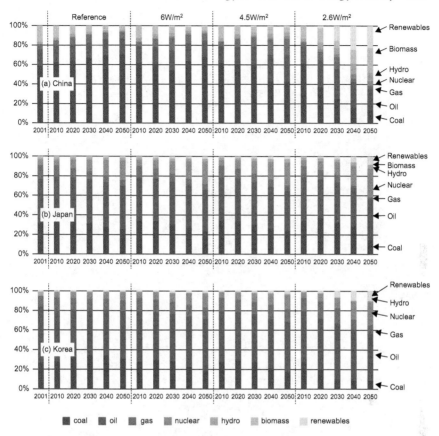

Figure 7.2 Structure of primary energy in East Asian countries.

Note: 'Renewables' in the figure include all renewables except hydropower and biomass.

H: Herfindahl index; x_i: the fraction of primary energy demand by energy type i.

Applying the index to the scenarios, the values change from 2001 to 2050 as shown in Figure 7.3. In the reference scenario, diversity worsens in China, whereas it improves in Japan and Korea. The resulting pattern is due to China using more coal in the future, whereas Japan and Korea use other energy sources. The level of diversity improves in all the policy scenarios in all countries compared to the reference scenario. Among the policy scenarios, values for the index are lower in the lower emissions cases. Japan is an exception as the index value in the 2.6 W/m² scenario is slightly larger than in the other policy scenarios, but this is due to Japan's high renewable share in the strictest scenario, so it does not really represent a worsening of energy security.

Finally, observing net imports of fossil fuel in the three countries, we see increases in China and Korea in 2050 compared to the 2001 level in the reference scenario, whereas there are decreases in Japan. Although China was a net exporter

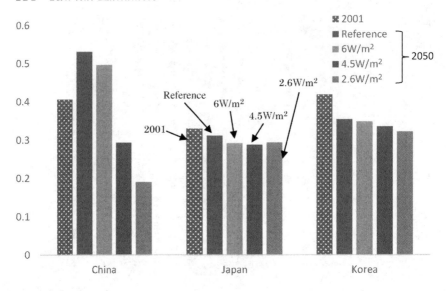

Figure 7.3 Herfindahl index in East Asian countries.

of coal in the base year, it soon becomes a net importer because of increasing domestic consumption. Trade patterns are quite similar between the scenarios, but the amount traded falls in each case (compared to the reference scenario in 2050) by, respectively, for China, Japan, and Korea:

- 4.6 percent, 9.4 percent, and 8.9 percent in the 6 W/m² scenario
- 24.4 percent, 11.5 percent, and 14.2 percent in the 4.5 W/m² scenario
- 74.9 percent, 37.1 percent, and 53.9 percent in the 2.6 W/m² scenario

Trade in coal and oil falls most in the low-emission scenarios. In contrast, for natural gas, the highest net imports are observed in the 4.5 W/m² scenario and the lowest import volumes in the 2.6 W/m² scenario. This is due to the relative carbon intensity of each fuel. Natural gas has the lowest carbon intensity, so use of gas is promoted to reduce GHG emissions. However, in order to reduce GHG emissions enough to achieve the lowest 2.6 W/m² scenario, the transition to low-carbon-intensive fossil fuels is not enough, and a reduction of the total amount of fossil fuels is also required.

From the above analysis, we can see that it is necessary to decrease the dependence on fossil fuels, and increase the share of renewable and nuclear energies[6] (compared to the reference scenario) to reduce GHG emissions. It is clear that this outcome is also linked to a reduction in the volume of trade in fossil fuels. That is, the self-sufficiency of energy supply will increase by promoting climate change measures. The three East Asian countries are all net importers of fossil fuels. Thus, such a situation can improve their energy security.

7.4   Concluding remarks

In this study, we have analyzed the change in energy structure and the impacts on energy security when introducing climate change policies by using a CGE model. In the analysis, we used the RCP-based scenarios for the policy scenarios and compared them with a reference scenario.

Overall, to reduce GHG emissions, East Asian countries need to shift their energy structures from those based on fossil fuels to those that use more renewables. The stricter the emission reduction, the larger the required shifts. The analysis shows that these shifts will also improve self-sufficiency in the energy supply and, consequently, that they are effective from the point of energy security.

Between the three countries, some differences can be seen. Since Japan is already one of the most-developed countries in the world, and its population is declining, the shares of fossil fuel use and imports (as well as total primary energy demand) decrease over time, and energy security improves even in the reference scenario. However, the effect of reducing GHG emissions further to enhance renewables and to improve energy security is still clear in the results.

China is a net exporter of coal in the base year, but soon becomes a net importer. Unlike Japan, the Herfindahl index for China increases in the reference scenario because of large increases in the use of fossil fuels, particularly coal. By introducing the carbon reduction measures, the index significantly improves because China's share in renewables increases and that of coal decreases.

Korea is in between the two situations. Total primary energy demand increases in Korea over time in the reference scenario, and the share of nuclear energy increases simultaneously. Consequently, Korea's energy security improves. However, as the use of renewables and nuclear energy are enhanced in the policy scenarios, further improvements to Korea's energy security can be realized.

In this study, future energy sources under different climate mitigation scenarios are selected by the price mechanism, in order to understand endogenously changing energy structure and energy security by scenario. However, as indicated in the scenarios described in Chapters 3 and 4 of this book (see also Chapter 1), the introduction of some energy sources, such as nuclear power and renewables, depends greatly on political and social conditions. Particularly, nuclear power is recently a very controversial energy source considering its sustainability and risks, although it is a low-carbon energy source. In such cases, the future energy structure will change and, thus, the degree of energy security will also be affected.

Notes

1   In this study, only mitigation measures are considered as climate change measures (policies), while adaptation measures are not considered.
2   It can be referred to as energy dependency.
3   See Moss et al. (2010) and van Vuuren et al. (2011b) for the details of RCPs.
4   Since the model used in this study is different from those used in the original RCP analyses, the features used differ. The radiative forcing of the 8.5 W/m² scenario is higher than that of the reference scenario of this study, meaning that it is required

to increase GHG emissions from it. Therefore, we do not show the result of the 8.5 W/m² scenario below.

5   E.g. p percent or e GWh of nuclear power generation in country A in year Υ.
6   Although nuclear power is a low-carbon energy source like renewables, it is not currently fully sustainable, as existing nuclear power generation uses uranium, which is an exhaustible resource. In addition, nuclear power generation carries environmental risks through accident and nuclear waste.

References

Armington, P.S. (1969). 'A theory of demand for products distinguished by place of production.' *International Monetary Fund Staff Papers*, 16, pp. 159–178.

BP (2013). *Statistical Review of World Energy June 2013*. http://www.bp.com/statisticalreview (accessed March 3, 2014).

Dimaranan, B. V. (Ed.) (2006). *Global Trade, Assistance, and Production: The GTAP 6 Data Base*. West Lafayette, IN: Center for Global Trade Analysis, Purdue University.

European Commission Joint Research Centre (2010). *Emission Database for Global Atmospheric Research (EDGAR) Release Version 4.0*. http://edgar.jrc.ec.europa.eu/index.php (accessed November 11, 2012).

International Energy Agency (IEA) (2009a). *Energy Balances of Non-OECD Countries: 2009 Edition*. Paris: IEA Publications.

International Energy Agency (IEA) (2009b). *Energy Balances of OECD Countries: 2009 Edition*. Paris: IEA Publications.

International Energy Agency (IEA) (2013). *World Energy Outlook 2013*. Paris: IEA Publications.

Masui, T., Matsumoto, K., Hijioka, Y., Kinoshita, T., Nozawa, T., Ishiwatari, S., Kato, E., Shukla, P. R., Yamagata, Y., and Kainuma, M. (2011). 'An emission pathway for stabilization at 6 Wm⁻² radiative forcing.' *Climatic Change*, *109*(1–2), pp. 59–76.

Matsumoto, K. (2013). 'Change in energy structure and energy security under climate mitigation scenarios.' In Leal, W., and Voudouris, V. (Eds.) *Global Energy Policy and Security*. London: Springer, pp. 45–57.

Matsumoto, K., and Masui T. (2011). 'Analyzing long-term impacts of carbon tax based on the imputed price applying the AIM/CGE model.' *Management of Environmental Quality*, *22*(1), pp. 33–47.

Matsumoto, K., Tachiiri, K., and Kawamiya, M. (2015). 'Impact of climate model uncertainties on socioeconomics: A case study with a medium mitigation scenario.' *Computers & Operations Research*, http://dx.doi.org/10.1016/j.cor.2015.01.011.

Moss, R. H., Edmonds, J. A., Hibbard, K. A., Manning, M. R., Rose, S. K., van Vuuren, D. P., Carter, T. R., Emori, S., Kainuma, M., Kram, T., Meehl, G. A., Mitchell, J. F., Nakicenovic, N., Riahi, K., Smith, S. J., Stouffer, R. J., Thomson, A. M., Weyant, J. P., and Wilbanks, T. J. (2010). 'The next generation of scenarios for climate change research and assessment.' *Nature*, 463, pp. 747–756.

Nakicenovic, N., and Swart, R. (Eds.) (2000). *Special Report on Emissions Scenarios*. Cambridge, UK: Cambridge University Press.

Neff, T. L. (1997). *Improving Energy Security in Pacific Asia: Diversification and Risk Reduction for Fossil and Nuclear Fuels*. Commissioned by the Pacific Asia Regional Energy Security (PARES) Project. http://oldsite.nautilus.org/archives/papers/energy/NeffPARES.pdf (accessed March 5, 2011).

Riahi, K., Rao, S., Krey, V., Cho, C., Chirkov, V., Fischer, G., Kindermann, G., Nakicenovic, N., and Rafai, P. (2011). 'RCP8.5: A scenario of comparatively high greenhouse gas emissions.' *Climatic Change*, *109*(1–2), pp. 33–57.

Thomson, A. M., Calvin, K. V., Smith, S. J., Kyle, G. P., Volke, A., Patel, P., Delgado-Arias, S., Bond-Lamberty, B., Wise, M. A., Clarke, L. E., and Edmonds, J. A. (2011). 'RCP4.5: A pathway for stabilization of radiative forcing by 2100.' *Climatic Change*, *109*(1–2), pp. 77–94.

United Nations (UN) (2011). *World Population Prospects: The 2010 Revision*. New York: United Nations Publication.

United Nations Environment Programme (UNEP) (2007). *Global Environment Outlook 4*. Valletta, Malta: Progress Press.

Van Vuuren, D. P., Edmonds, J., Kainuma, M., Riahi, K., Thomson, A., Hibbard, K., Hurtt, G. C., Kram, T., Krey, V., Lamarque, J.-F., Masui, T., Meinshausen, M., Nakicenovic, N., Smith, J. S., and Rose, S. K. (2011a). 'Representative Concentration Pathways: An overview.' *Climatic Change*, *109*(1–2), pp. 5–31.

Van Vuuren, D. P., Stehfest, E., den Elzen, M.G.J., Kram, T., van Vilet, J., Deetman, S., Isaac, M., Goldewijk, K. K., Hof, A., Beltran, A.M., Oostenrijk, R., and van Ruijven, B. (2011b). 'RCP2.6: Exploring the possibility to keep global mean temperature change below 2°C.' *Climatic Change*, *109*(1–2), pp. 95–116.

Von Hippel, D., Savage, T., and Hayes, P. (2011a). 'Introduction to the Asian Energy Security project: Project organization and methodologies.' *Energy Policy*, *39*(11), pp. 6712–6718.

Von Hippel, D., Savage, T., and Hayes, P. (2011b). 'Overview of the Northeast Asia energy situation.' *Energy Policy*, *39*(11), pp. 6703–6711.

Von Hippel, D., Suzuki, T., Williams, J. H., Savage, T., and Hayes, P. (2011c). 'Energy security and sustainability in Northeast Asia.' *Energy Policy*, *39*(11), pp. 6719–6730.

Introduction to Part 2

Environmental taxation in East Asia

Two economic methods of environmental policy reform are typically recommended by environmental economists as effective and desirable from economic, environmental, and energy viewpoints: emissions trading schemes (ETS) and environmental tax reform (ETR). A representative example of ETS is the large-scale European Union cap-and-trade system (EU ETS), which was implemented in 2005 and from which various effects have been reported. ETR entails increased taxation of energy and those goods that increase environmental load, thereby allowing decreased tax burdens in other areas such as labor taxes. Such policies have been implemented in Germany and several Northern European countries, and there are indications that they may materialize 'double dividends' of improved environmental and economic outcomes (through increases in GDP and employment, etc.). Movement toward introducing such measures in advanced industrial countries of East Asia, such as Japan and Korea, has begun in recent years.

In 2012, Japan became the first Asian country to introduce a carbon tax in the form of an additional tax on oil, coal, and natural gas. The tax is quite low, however, at only 289 yen (about 3 US$) per ton of emitted carbon dioxide and, because revenue from this tax is not explicitly slated for application to lowering other taxes, this cannot be regarded as environmental tax reform and has no prospect for a double dividend.

Korea is implementing an ETS in 2015. Due to industry opposition, however, this will be implemented in a weakened form. Taiwan, too, has continued efforts at implementing policies to effectively combat climate change despite strong political opposition. In China as well, there has been at least some progress toward implementing international climate change policies. For several years now, the government has been considering implementation of a carbon tax. A CO_2 emissions-trading market has already been established in Shenzhen, and occasional pilot markets can be seen in other cities. There are plans in place for nationwide emissions trading to begin around 2020.

In this section we consider many different types of ETR. We first investigate in Chapter 8 whether a double dividend might be possible from ETR in East Asia. The results from our modelling are compared to the wider literature in Chapter 9. Chapter 10 assesses how carbon taxes might be used as revenue-raising instruments, either in a world of fiscal constraints or to allow the development of national social security systems.

The next two chapters in this part of the book address social considerations. Chapter 11 examines the effects of ETR on income distributions, which are often cited as a barrier to reform. The analysis suggests some alternative ways of using carbon tax revenues that could offset negative distributional effects. Chapter 12 introduces an innovative new modelling approach that links the proceeds of carbon taxes to investment in human capital, which could provide educational services and equip national workforces for the transition to a low-carbon economy.

Finally we turn attention to the tricky issue of industrial competitiveness. Chapter 13 goes beyond the analysis that can be offered by the modelling to consider industry sectors at a much higher level of detail. The last chapter in this section (Chapter 14) considers whether Border Tax Adjustments could provide a solution to issues of competitiveness and carbon leakage.

8 The double dividend of an environmental tax reform in East Asian economies

Park Seung-Joon, Yuki Ogawa, Takeshi Kawakatsu, and Hector Pollitt

8.1 Introduction and policy background

In this chapter we analyze quantitatively the environmental and economic effects of environmental tax reform (ETR) in four East Asian economies: China, Japan, Korea, and Taiwan. We use a model-based approach to assess a set of scenarios in which carbon taxes are raised and various existing taxes are reduced to compensate.

The E3ME-Asia model that we apply is global in nature, but our analysis is carried out at the national level. This reflects the policy situation; although an international emissions trading scheme based on global cooperation for climate protection has been pursued, attempts to expand and develop the Kyoto Protocol have ended in stalemate due to conflicting national interests. Therefore, in our scenarios, each country introduces domestic policy instruments so as to achieve its own GHG reduction target, which was pledged after the Copenhagen Accord. Among those domestic policy instruments, we choose the domestic carbon tax, possibly harmonized with other countries, as a very important instrument to achieve the GHG reduction target.

In this exercise, we focus on carbon taxes within the four East Asian countries. Carbon taxes are increasingly gaining attention in East Asia because they are relatively easy to introduce due to their low administrative costs, even in developing countries. Developing countries are seeking ways to increase tax revenues so as to be able to provide better public services as their development progresses.

Higher taxes on consumption, income, corporate profits, or higher social security contributions from labor would distort the allocation of resources and bring about economic loss. A carbon tax on energy products, however, would internalize the externality (of environmental cost) caused by the burning of fossil fuels, raising environmental and economic efficiency and contributing to government budgets with revenues.

In this chapter we consider how the revenues from carbon taxes could be used. If the revenues are used to reduce other existing distortional taxes, economic efficiency, as shown by indicators such as GDP or employment, may be improved further. This is called the 'double dividend of an environmental tax reform,' meaning that there are positive effects on both the environment and the economy. And, if the carbon tax is introduced together with other countries, possibly with the same tax rate as in other countries, the effectiveness and efficiency of this policy may be enhanced.

The remainder of this chapter is structured as follows. In Section 8.2, we introduce the economic literature and explain the issues concerning the double dividend. In Section 8.3, we explain the key features of E3ME-Asia that are related to ETR analysis. The policy scenarios for the analysis are introduced in Section 8.4, and the results are shown in Section 8.5. Section 8.6 discusses the results in further depth and Section 8.7 concludes.

8.2   Existing discussion and literature

There has been broad discussion about the possibility of double dividends from ETR, supported by many theoretical and quantitative model analyses, but most of this analysis has been carried out either in Europe or North America.

Much of the focus of this work has been on whether a 'strong' double dividend (in which there are improvements to both environment and economy) exists. Opponents have argued, while supporting the possibility of 'weak' double dividend,[1] that there will be no strong double dividend, supporting their discussion by mathematical equilibrium models showing the so-called 'tax interaction effects.' According to this argument, higher environmental taxes will lead to increased general prices and reduced real wage rates, resulting in lower labor supply.[2] Though many quantitative results from empirical[3] analyses, such as computable general equilibrium models (CGE) or macro-econometric models, confirmed the argument of opponents, there are also many simulation results showing that a strong double dividend is possible (see, e.g., Bosquet, 2000; Andersen and Ekins, 2009).

Despite there being a wide range of published papers on the topic in Europe or North America, we find in East Asia very few papers, and those mostly use CGE models (see, e.g., Park, Yamazaki, and Takeda, 2012 for the Asia-Pacific region; Zhang and Zhang, 2013 for China; Takeda, 2007 for Japan; Kim and Kim, 2010 for Korea; and Bor, 2010 for Taiwan). CGE models tend to have pessimistic results for any environmental policy due to their supply-oriented nature and the assumption of equilibrium in all markets, including the labor market (if not explicitly designed otherwise). Macro-econometric models, meanwhile, based on Keynesian theory, stressing market non-equilibrium and the importance of demand-side factors, can produce different results. These models can find that environmental investment caused by environmental regulation (including environmental taxes) and tax reductions via revenue recycling may boost aggregate demand, thereby triggering multiplier effects.

The meaning of an internationally harmonized carbon tax is discussed by Nordhaus (2005). It means that countries will together introduce domestic carbon taxes, possibly with the same tax rate as in other countries. This approach is regarded as the most efficient way of reducing the externality of carbon emissions, because the marginal abatement cost of CO_2 will be the same across all countries and industries. Furthermore, in the context of climate negotiation stalemate, the unified carbon tax rate is worth seeking because it can avoid the difficult problems of carbon leakage and industrial competitiveness.

In this chapter, we analyze the economic and environmental effects of environmental tax reforms in the four East Asian economies, focusing on the double dividend, using the E3ME-Asia model described in Chapter 2 and in the next section.

8.3 The E3ME-Asia model

As the main structure of E3ME-Asia was explained in Chapter 2, the focus in this section is how E3ME-Asia can be used to assess ETR. Further information about the E3ME-Asia model, including the full technical manual (Cambridge Econometrics, 2014) can be found at the model website, http://www.e3me.com.

The original E3ME model was designed to assess energy and climate policy in Europe and was later merged with the global E3MG model, which had data for major economies outside Europe. It has now been developed further into the E3ME-Asia model, employing detailed data from East Asian economies. E3ME-Asia is a macro-econometric simulation model based on post-Keynesian economic theory, which allows for imperfect price adjustment, market disequilibrium, and limited rationality of economic actors. Owing to the detailed database about taxes on income, labor, energy, and so on, E3ME-Asia is very suitable for analyses of ETR, which consist of newer or higher taxes on energy products and recycling of the revenues via reduction of other taxes. The carbon tax will reduce fossil fuel consumption and CO_2 emissions due to price effects and (in many cases) due to reduced economic activity levels (such as GDP or employment).

Revenue recycling through the reduction of the rate of social security contributions on wages (also referred to as labor tax rates) may lead to increased labor demand. Wage rates depend on wage-bargaining functions, which are affected by overall labor market conditions and inflation, and will also affect employment decisions. These wage-rate functions are empirically estimated for each sector and each country. Reduced income tax rates and reduced consumption tax rates (VAT rates) will directly lead to increased consumption expenditure through the estimated consumption functions.

One of the most notable applications of the E3ME model (a predecessor to E3ME-Asia) was the COMETR research project (Andersen and Ekins, 2009), in which E3ME was used for ex-post assessment of economic and competitiveness effects of some of the first examples of ETR in Europe. The modeling results are described in Barker et al. (2007) and Barker et al. (2009), and elaborated further in the context of households in Ekins et al. (2011). They suggest that a small but strong double dividend effect is possible in Europe.

More recently, E3ME-Asia (and its global predecessor, E3MG) has been widely used to analyze environmental policy around the world. The model has also been used repeatedly to assess decarbonization pathways at different international levels (Barker et al., 2005, 2006; Barker, Foxon, and Scrieciu, 2008; Barker and Scrieciu, 2009) and in the UK (Dagoumas and Barker, 2010). Most recently, E3MG has been applied as described by Barker et al. (2012) to provide an economic assessment of the International Energy Association's (IEA) 450 ppm scenario (IEA, 2010). In all of these studies, taxation has been a key policy input, with assumptions about revenue neutrality included in the scenarios.

In Japan, E3MG has been applied for an assessment of the economic costs of meeting Japan's Copenhagen pledge of reducing GHG emissions by 25 percent below 1990 level by 2020 (see Lee, Pollitt, and Ueta, 2012). The model results showed this to incur a modest economic cost that could be turned into a modest benefit if efficient revenue recycling methods were used. In the most recent publication using E3MG, the interaction between the share of nuclear power in Japan's energy mix and its carbon targets was discussed (Pollitt et al, 2014).

8.4   Scenarios

We analyze the effects of introducing carbon taxes in four East Asian economies. Two sets of scenarios are assessed: one set in which each country acts independently, and one set in which there is coordination across the four countries. In today's context, where global harmonization seems difficult, the results of this model analysis seeking the East Asian harmonization could have substantial implication in the discussion of climate policy.

The carbon tax rates are set to meet the official voluntary targets for each country. The taxes are applied to all fossil energy products used in all economic sectors. The tax revenue accrues to the domestic government that introduced the carbon tax, without any international fiscal flows.

The official GHG reduction targets for the four countries are as follows:[4]

- China: to reduce GHG intensity (i.e., CO_2 emissions per unit of real GDP) by 40 percent in 2020
- Japan: to reduce GHG emissions in 2020 by 3.8 percent from the 2005 level
- Korea: to reduce GHG emissions in 2020 by 30 percent from the baseline level
- Taiwan: to reduce GHG emissions in 2020 to the 2005 level.

As E3ME-Asia does not cover the non-CO_2 GHG emissions in detail, we apply the target values shown above to CO_2 emissions only. As increases in GDP and CO_2 emissions are anticipated in our baseline scenario (based on the IEA's *World Energy Outlook 2013*), the reduction of CO_2 emissions in 2020 on the basis of national targets is substantial for Japan, Korea, and Taiwan (11 percent for Japan, 30 percent for Korea, and 42 percent for Taiwan), whereas it is only 5 percent for China, owing to the efficiency improvements predicted in the baseline scenario.

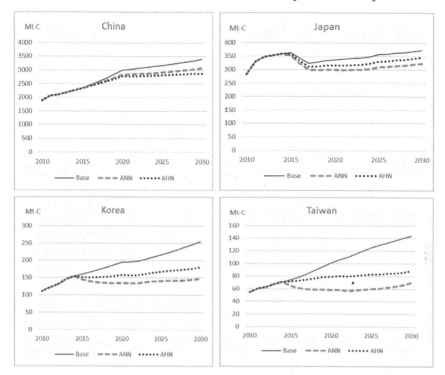

Figure 8.1 CO$_2$ emissions in China, Japan, Korea, and Taiwan.

Source: Authors' own calculations using E3ME-Asia.

ANN: Four countries introduce carbon tax to achieve the national target without revenue recycling.

AHN: Four countries introduce harmonized carbon tax without revenue recycling.

There are three levels of carbon tax: zero (baseline), endogenously set carbon tax rate to achieve the national reduction target in 2020 (-N- scenarios), and harmonized carbon tax rates (-H- scenarios). The carbon taxes are introduced gradually. For the -N- scenarios, reduction targets for each year from 2015 to 2020 are set (typically on a 'linear stepping-up' basis), and the necessary carbon tax rate for each year is endogenously calculated. For the -H- scenarios, we calculate the harmonized carbon tax rate with which the four countries' total emissions reductions will be the same as the sum of each country's reduction quantity in the ANN scenario (explained in the following; 8.2 percent from total baseline CO$_2$ emissions).[5] The tax rate amounts to 82.09 US$/tCO$_2$ (nominal value in 2020). After 2020, the carbon tax rate is set to increase annually by +1.7 percent in all the scenarios, reflecting the baseline inflation rates from 2020 to 2030[6] in E3ME-Asia.

Each government recycles the revenues from the carbon tax by reducing (a) consumption tax (or value added tax; -C scenario), (b) income tax (-I scenario), (c) employers' social security contributions (-L scenario, i.e., reduction in labor

Table 8.1 Scenarios

Country of C-tax

A-: four countries

J-: only Japan

K-: only Korea

C-: only China

T-: only Taiwan

Carbon tax rate

B: baseline (no carbon tax)

N-: rates to achieve national emission reduction targets

-H-: harmonized rate

Revenue recycling, other tax to be reduced

-N: no recycling

-C: consumption tax

-I: income tax

-L: employer's social security contribution (SSC)

Country	All	A-	A-	C-	C-	J-	J-	K-	K-	T-	T-
Tax Rate	B	-N-	-H-	-N-	-H-	-N-	-H-	-N-	-H-	-N-	-H-
Recycling: -N	B	ANN	AHN	CNN	CHN	JNN	JHN	KNN	KHN	TNN	THN
-C	B			CNC	CHC	JNC	JHC	KNC	KHC	TNC	THC
-I	B			CNI	CHI	JNI	JHI	KNI	KHI	TNI	THI
-L	B			CNL	CHL	JNL	JHL	KNL	KHL	TNL	THL

costs), or (d) does not recycle the revenue at all, thereby improving the balance of its budget (-N scenario, as in 'no recycling').[7] The recycling will be done on the basis of 'revenue neutrality' as long as the revenue of the tax to be reduced is positive. However, especially in transition countries such as China or Taiwan, there may be neither comparable income tax nor social security contributions, so the potential of revenue recycling by reducing them is limited. When these tax rates reach zero, the remaining carbon tax revenue will not be recycled in the model.

In this chapter, we do not apply 'lump-sum recycling,' which is usually assumed in existing CGE model analyses, as it is not easy to distribute money to all citizens with conventional instruments for taxation policy. Lump-sum recycling will, however, be analyzed in Chapter 11. We also do not apply the revenue recycling through capital taxes, which, again, is often applied in CGE analysis, because in the E3ME-Asia model there is no explicit production function including capital, and there is no variable explicitly defined as sectoral capital.

The scenarios are named as a combination of the letters described previously and in Table 8.1. For example, the scenario 'KHC' refers to a carbon tax introduced only in Korea, at the harmonized rate and with the revenues recycled through reductions in the consumption tax (VAT).

The baseline is essentially based on the IEA's *World Energy Outlook 2013*, but reflecting the current and future situations about nuclear power plants capacity[8] and renewable energy promotion.[9] We analyze the effect of ETR in comparison to the baseline (difference in percentage).

8.5 Results

Four countries

When all of the four countries achieve their national CO_2 reduction targets the carbon tax rate in 2020 for China, Japan, Korea, and Taiwan is 52.44, 153.70, 213.37, and 495.44 (US\$/tCO_2), respectively. These tax rates are endogenously calculated for the ANN scenario, and we apply the same rates for all other single-country -N- scenarios. It should be noted that, with different revenue-recycling methods, the reductions in CO_2 emissions may differ slightly between the scenarios due to economic effects.[10] After 2020, these carbon tax rates are simply inflated by 1.7 percent annually and, although they are quite high, it is assumed that no other relevant policy (e.g., for energy efficiency, see Chapter 6) is introduced. In reality, however, a portfolio of policies would be implemented.

According to the model results (Table 8.2), the economic effects of the carbon tax are modestly negative in 2020 and 2030 in all four economies. The rates of employment also fall slightly in all cases, with the exception of China in 2030, where the demands for investment in renewables create enough jobs to offset the negative economic effects.

The harmonized carbon tax rate of 82.09 US\$/tCO_2 was calculated so that the sum of CO_2 reductions in the four countries is the same as the sum in the ANN scenario. This rate is used in the AHN scenario and, in this scenario, the

Table 8.2 The ANN scenario

ANN	2020				2030			
from baseline (%)	China	Japan	Korea	Taiwan	China	Japan	Korea	Taiwan
Real GDP	−0.90	−1.23	−0.94	−2.13	−0.44	−1.11	−0.41	−2.41
CO_2	−5.35	−11.20	−30.21	−42.34	−9.70	−13.28	−42.44	−51.83
Employment	−0.14	−0.49	−0.39	−2.81	0.01	−0.89	−0.33	−1.61
Consumption	−1.35	−2.46	−3.30	−7.04	−0.79	−2.61	−2.03	−5.25
Investment	−0.95	−0.80	−1.30	−2.08	−0.17	−0.31	−0.66	−3.99
Export	−0.17	0.01	−0.11	0.74	−0.40	−0.40	−0.64	−0.17
Import	0.12	−2.14	−1.93	−2.74	−0.29	−2.49	−2.21	−2.19
Import: oil, gas, etc.	0.04	0.00	0.00	−4.54	0.04	−0.17	0.00	−3.38
Consumption price	2.86	3.69	3.91	9.26	1.26	2.41	2.16	5.50
Nominal wage and salaries	1.78	1.45	1.03	2.13	0.76	0.50	0.44	3.52
Carbon tax rate ($US\$/tCO_2$)	52.44	153.70	213.37	495.44	62.07	181.92	252.54	586.41

Source: Authors' own calculations using E3ME-Asia.

Table 8.3 The AHN scenario

AHN	2020				2030			
from baseline (%)	China	Japan	Korea	Taiwan	China	Japan	Korea	Taiwan
Real GDP	−1.29	−0.59	−0.35	0.13	−0.16	−0.62	−0.12	−0.49
CO_2	−7.29	−6.44	−18.70	−21.07	−15.62	−7.24	−29.41	−38.91
Employment	−0.23	−0.25	−0.15	−0.31	0.06	−0.48	−0.19	−0.48
Consumption	−2.13	−1.29	−1.58	−1.28	−0.96	−1.36	−1.00	−1.55
Investment	−1.25	−0.42	−0.85	0.08	0.91	−0.24	−0.08	1.04
Export	−0.04	0.19	0.21	1.28	−0.24	−0.22	−0.43	−0.05
Import	0.28	−1.17	−1.00	−0.11	−0.29	−1.22	−1.24	−0.62
Import: oil, gas, etc.	0.02	−0.01	0.00	−1.78	0.03	−0.13	0.00	−0.87
Consumption price	4.52	1.94	1.83	1.57	1.65	1.17	1.04	1.83
Nominal wage and salaries	2.77	0.74	0.50	0.44	1.13	0.25	0.17	0.76
Carbon tax rate ($US\$/tCO_2$)	82.09	82.09	82.09	82.09	97.16	97.16	97.16	97.16

Source: Authors' own calculations using E3ME-Asia.

reduction requirements and economic burdens are substantially eased for Japan, Korea, and Taiwan because of China's intensified effort to reduce CO_2 emissions.

Although China's reduction of CO_2 emissions only increased by 1.94 percent (from 5.35 percent to 7.29 percent), in absolute terms this change is large. For China, the direct economic cost of the carbon tax in 2020 is slightly higher in the AHN scenario than in the ANN scenario. In 2030, however, China's economy shows better performance in AHN than in ANN, mainly because of increased investment and technological improvements due to the energy shift.

China

The model results for China are summarized in Tables 8.4 and 8.5. In the scenario where only China introduces a carbon tax – at the rate of 52.44 US$/tCO$_2$ to achieve the national CO_2 target (CNN) – the negative impact on the main real economic indicators is quite small (e.g. for China's GDP it is –0.86 percent in 2020). With the higher carbon tax rate of 82.09 US$/tCO$_2$, the negative economic impacts in 2020 increase and, especially, the drop in consumption is remarkable. We observe no significant difference in China's economic values regarding CNN or CHN compared with ANN or AHN, respectively.

Table 8.4 China: scenarios with a carbon tax rate to achieve the national target

China	2020				2030			
from baseline (%)	CNN	CNC	CNI	CNL	CNN	CNC	CNI	CNL
Real GDP	–0.86	1.55	–0.68	–0.86	–0.30	2.17	–0.14	–0.30
CO_2	–5.34	–4.93	–5.32	–5.34	–9.69	–9.72	–9.65	–9.69
Employment	–0.16	0.89	–0.15	–0.16	0.04	0.20	0.05	0.04
Consumption	–1.43	6.43	–0.96	–1.43	–0.63	4.75	–0.27	–0.63
Investment	–0.86	–1.50	–0.78	–0.86	–0.22	0.57	–0.15	–0.22
Export	0.03	–0.42	0.04	0.03	–0.10	0.24	–0.08	–0.10
Import	0.17	0.60	0.27	0.17	–0.29	0.80	–0.19	–0.29
Import: oil, gas, etc.	0.00	0.01	0.00	0.00	0.01	0.00	0.01	0.01
Consumption price	2.96	–8.99	2.94	2.96	1.07	–6.49	1.04	1.07
Nominal wage and salaries	1.81	–3.79	1.84	1.81	0.72	–3.42	0.78	0.72
Carbon tax rate (US$/tCO$_2$)	52.44	52.44	52.44	52.44	62.07	62.07	62.07	62.07

Source: Authors' own calculations using E3ME-Asia.

Table 8.5 China: scenarios with a harmonized carbon tax rate

China	2020				2030			
from baseline (%)	*CHN*	*CHC*	*CHI*	*CHL*	*CHN*	*CHC*	*CHI*	*CHL*
Real GDP	–1.27	2.73	–1.10	–1.27	–0.09	3.75	0.07	–0.09
CO_2	–7.29	–6.81	–7.27	–7.29	–15.62	–15.80	–15.59	–15.62
Employment	–0.23	1.42	–0.22	–0.23	0.08	0.30	0.08	0.08
Consumption	–2.17	10.80	–1.71	–2.17	–0.88	7.33	–0.52	–0.88
Investment	–1.21	–2.19	–1.13	–1.21	0.91	2.40	0.98	0.91
Export	0.06	–0.62	0.07	0.06	–0.11	0.47	–0.10	–0.11
Import	0.30	1.05	0.40	0.30	–0.28	1.46	–0.18	–0.28
Import: oil, gas, etc.	0.00	0.01	0.00	0.00	0.01	–0.01	0.01	0.01
Consumption price	4.57	–14.05	4.53	4.57	1.55	–9.61	1.53	1.55
Nominal wage and salaries	2.78	–5.75	2.81	2.78	1.10	–4.98	1.16	1.10
Carbon tax rate ($US\$/tCO_2$)	82.09	82.09	82.09	82.09	97.16	97.16	97.16	97.16

Source: Authors' own calculations using E3ME-Asia.

Considering the -H- scenarios, if the government recycles the revenues by reducing VAT (CHC), the main economic indicators, including GDP, employment, and consumption, show improved results and there is a strong double dividend.

As there are no significant social security contributions in China, the recycling choice CNL is not an option. Direct income tax revenue is also low, meaning that CNI is close to CNN (and there can be no strong double dividend).

The final point to note is that, when the revenues can all be recycled, economic performance is better in the scenario with the higher carbon tax rate and, thus, a higher potential of revenue recycling (compare CNC with CHC).

In 2030, the performance in all scenarios improves compared to 2020, as companies and individuals have more time to adapt to the high carbon prices.

Japan

The model results for Japan are summarized in Tables 8.6 and 8.7.

In the scenario in which only Japan introduces a carbon tax so as to achieve the national CO_2 target (JNN), the negative impact on the main real economic indicators is substantial (e.g., in 2020, –1.25 percent for real GDP, –2.48 percent in consumption) because of the fairly high carbon tax rate (153.70 $US\$/tCO_2$).

Table 8.6 Japan: scenarios with a carbon tax rate to achieve the national target

Japan	2020				2030			
from baseline (%)	JNN	JNC	JNI	JNL	JNN	JNC	JNI	JNL
Real GDP	−1.25	1.45	1.17	−0.70	−0.99	2.80	1.83	−0.19
CO_2	−11.22	−8.42	−9.03	−10.72	−13.20	−9.26	−10.40	−12.36
Employment	−0.50	0.53	0.47	0.09	−0.87	1.23	0.72	−0.19
Consumption	−2.48	2.32	1.46	−1.23	−2.53	3.89	1.92	−0.80
Investment	−0.81	−0.55	0.38	−1.57	−0.28	0.31	1.07	−1.21
Export	0.00	0.01	0.22	−0.08	−0.19	0.23	0.24	−0.25
Import	−2.16	−0.38	−0.38	−1.92	−2.46	−0.32	−0.71	−2.21
Import: oil, gas, etc.	−0.01	−0.04	−0.04	−0.02	−0.07	−0.05	−0.05	−0.07
Consumption price	3.72	−3.19	2.39	2.33	2.31	−3.72	2.00	0.70
Nominal wage and salaries	1.47	−0.91	2.58	2.10	0.42	−1.17	2.92	0.61
Carbon tax rate (US\$/tCO_2)	153.70	153.70	153.70	153.70	181.92	181.92	181.92	181.92

Source: Authors' own calculations using E3ME-Asia.

Table 8.7 Japan: scenarios with a harmonized carbon tax rate

Japan	2020				2030			
from baseline (%)	JHN	JHC	JHI	JHL	JHN	JHC	JHI	JHL
Real GDP	−0.64	0.79	0.68	−0.34	−0.52	1.55	1.06	−0.08
CO_2	−6.50	−4.92	−5.27	−6.21	−7.15	−4.65	−5.49	−6.63
Employment	−0.27	0.27	0.25	0.05	−0.46	0.68	0.42	−0.08
Consumption	−1.32	1.23	0.83	−0.63	−1.28	2.26	1.21	−0.31
Investment	−0.45	−0.33	0.20	−0.86	−0.19	0.09	0.56	−0.72
Export	0.00	−0.01	0.12	−0.04	−0.11	0.11	0.13	−0.14
Import	−1.25	−0.31	−0.28	−1.11	−1.24	−0.03	−0.24	−1.08
Import: oil, gas, etc.	−0.01	−0.02	−0.02	−0.01	−0.04	−0.03	−0.03	−0.04
Consumption price	1.97	−1.76	1.25	1.22	1.10	−2.27	0.96	0.21
Nominal wage and salaries	0.74	−0.49	1.34	1.11	0.16	−0.77	1.55	0.28
Carbon tax rate (US\$/tCO_2)	82.09	82.09	82.09	82.09	97.16	97.16	97.16	97.16

Source: Authors' own calculations using E3ME-Asia.

With the lower rate of 82.09 US$/tCO$_2$, the negative economic impacts in 2020 become far smaller. We observe no significant difference in economic values of Japan in JNN or JHN, compared to ANN or AHN, respectively.

Japan has enough existing tax revenue from VAT, income tax, and social security contributions to neutralize the carbon tax revenue. If the government recycles the revenue through a reduction of VAT or income tax (JNC, JNI; JHC, JHI), the main economic indicators, such as real GDP, employment, or consumption, show a strong double dividend (compared to the JNN or JHN scenarios without revenue recycling). When social security contributions (JNL, JHL) are reduced, however, we observe just a weak double dividend. In cases with positive double dividends, economic performance is better in the scenario with a higher carbon tax rate and, thus, higher potential of revenue recycling.

Korea

The calculation results for Korea are summarized in Tables 8.8 and 8.9. In the scenario in which only Korea introduces the carbon tax so as to achieve the national CO$_2$ target (KNN), the impact on main real economic indicators is substantial (e.g., –1.00 percent for real GDP, –3.28 percent in consumption in 2020), because of the high carbon tax rate (213.37 US$/tCO$_2$). With a lower

Table 8.8 Korea: scenarios with a carbon tax rate to achieve the national target

Korea	2020				2030			
from baseline (%)	KNN	KNC	KNI	KNL	KNN	KNC	KNI	KNL
Real GDP	–1.00	2.88	0.76	–0.83	–0.26	1.41	1.04	–0.13
CO$_2$	–30.14	–27.11	–29.10	–30.08	–42.29	–40.02	–41.03	–42.14
Employment	–0.45	2.58	0.56	0.28	–0.22	1.13	–0.04	0.53
Consumption	–3.28	6.06	0.83	–2.80	–2.04	2.11	0.93	–1.67
Investment	–1.42	0.04	–0.47	–1.47	–0.48	2.34	0.68	–0.49
Export	–0.19	–0.08	–0.13	–0.19	–0.16	0.06	–0.06	–0.16
Import	–1.94	–0.26	–1.12	–1.86	–2.02	0.45	–0.87	–1.89
Import: oil, gas, etc.	0.00	0.00	0.00	0.00	0.00	0.00	0.00	0.00
Consumption price	3.87	–5.73	4.25	3.76	2.14	–1.39	2.91	2.15
Nominal wage and salaries	0.94	0.72	2.00	2.21	0.39	1.92	1.39	1.69
Carbon tax rate (US$/tCO$_2$)	213.37	213.37	213.37	213.37	252.54	252.54	252.54	252.54

Source: Authors' own calculations using E3ME-Asia.

Table 8.9 Korea: scenarios with a harmonized carbon tax rate

Korea	2020				2030			
from baseline (%)	*KHN*	*KHC*	*KHI*	*KHL*	*KHN*	*KHC*	*KHI*	*KHL*
Real GDP	−0.50	1.11	0.29	−0.33	0.01	0.76	0.61	0.14
CO_2	−18.61	−17.12	−18.12	−18.53	−29.52	−28.37	−28.72	−29.33
Employment	−0.28	0.98	0.17	0.45	−0.06	0.45	0.02	0.70
Consumption	−1.58	2.29	0.29	−1.09	−1.00	0.85	0.38	−0.63
Investment	−1.05	−0.42	−0.63	−1.09	0.17	1.37	0.71	0.17
Export	−0.11	−0.06	−0.08	−0.10	−0.08	0.00	−0.04	−0.09
Import	−1.10	−0.39	−0.73	−1.01	−1.10	−0.04	−0.56	−0.97
Import: oil, gas, etc.	0.00	0.00	0.00	0.00	0.00	0.00	0.00	0.00
Consumption price	1.79	−2.25	1.96	1.68	1.06	−0.55	1.41	1.06
Nominal wage and salaries	0.33	0.22	0.80	1.60	0.24	0.81	0.69	1.54
Carbon tax rate ($US\$/tCO_2$)	82.09	82.09	82.09	82.09	97.16	97.16	97.16	97.16

Source: Authors' own calculations using E3ME-Asia.

carbon tax rate of 82.09 US$/tCO$_2$, the negative economic impacts in 2020 become far smaller. We observe no significant difference in Korea's economic values in KNN or KHN, compared to ANN or AHN, respectively.

If the government recycles revenue by reducing VAT or income tax (KNC, KNI; KHC, KHI), the main economic indicators, such as real GDP, employment, or consumption, show strong double dividends compared to the baseline. When social security contributions are reduced, we observe just weak double dividends, mainly because social security contributions in Korea are still very low, limiting the capacity of revenue recycling (the SSC rate will reach zero in KNL and KHL). In cases of positive double dividends, economic performance is better in a scenario with a higher carbon tax rate and thus a higher potential of revenue recycling (compare, e.g., KNI and KHI).

Taiwan

The calculation results for Taiwan are summarized in Tables 8.10 and 8.11. In the scenario in which only Taiwan introduces carbon tax so as to achieve the national CO$_2$ target (TNN), the economic impacts are significant (e.g., −2.49 percent for real GDP) due to the high carbon tax rate (495.44 US$/tCO$_2$). With the lower carbon tax rate of 82.09 US$/tCO$_2$, the negative economic impacts in

Table 8.10 Taiwan: scenarios with a carbon tax rate to achieve the national target

Taiwan	2020				2030			
from baseline (%)	TNN	TNC	TNI	TNL	TNN	TNC	TNI	TNL
Real GDP	−2.49	1.10	5.32	−0.78	−2.53	2.67	6.92	0.14
CO_2	−43.71	−2.39	−41.10	−43.20	−52.18	−50.72	−49.81	−51.51
Employment	−3.17	0.10	2.11	1.26	−1.74	2.51	4.92	3.03
Consumption	−7.61	−0.24	8.49	−4.16	−5.83	4.18	12.63	−0.82
Investment	−2.35	−0.91	1.25	−1.93	−3.66	−1.71	−0.07	−3.10
Export	0.03	0.06	0.29	−0.07	0.06	0.11	0.33	−0.02
Import	−3.43	−2.08	−0.17	−3.00	−2.27	−0.35	1.68	−1.59
Import: oil, gas, etc.	−0.26	−0.19	−0.11	−0.23	−0.30	−0.18	−0.08	−0.24
Consumption price	10.01	0.38	2.97	6.54	6.29	−5.07	−2.61	0.98
Nominal wage and salaries	2.33	0.75	3.91	6.45	4.10	−0.55	1.75	4.81
Carbon tax rate ($US\$/tCO_2$)	495.44	495.44	495.44	495.44	586.41	586.41	586.41	586.41

Source: Authors' own calculations using E3ME-Asia.

Table 8.11 Taiwan: scenarios a with harmonized carbon tax rate

Taiwan	2020				2030			
from baseline (%)	THN	THC	THI	THL	THN	THC	THI	THL
Real GDP	−0.18	2.74	1.57	0.73	−0.47	2.94	1.60	0.92
CO_2	−22.41	−20.89	−21.60	−22.06	−38.88	−37.91	−38.29	−38.54
Employment	−0.62	2.23	0.59	2.18	−0.50	2.15	0.96	1.99
Consumption	−1.43	4.67	2.21	0.45	−1.70	4.94	2.33	0.91
Investment	−0.17	1.04	0.63	0.01	0.95	1.72	1.63	1.12
Export	−0.01	0.01	0.05	−0.08	0.08	0.10	0.14	0.03
Import	−1.04	0.14	−0.29	−0.80	−0.68	0.55	0.17	−0.35
Import: oil, gas, etc.	−0.09	−0.04	−0.05	−0.07	−0.08	−0.01	−0.04	−0.06
Consumption price	1.74	−5.50	0.28	0.19	2.03	−5.07	−0.07	−0.58
Nominal wage and salaries	0.34	−0.42	0.75	3.20	1.02	−2.17	0.43	1.51
Carbon tax rate ($US\$/tCO_2$)	82.09	82.09	82.09	82.09	97.16	97.16	97.16	97.16

Source: Authors' own calculations using E3ME-Asia.

2020 become far smaller. We observe no significant difference in Taiwan's economic values in TNN or THN compared to ANN or AHN, respectively.

If the government recycles the revenue through a reduction of income taxes (TNI, THI), the main economic indicators, such as real GDP, employment, or consumption, show remarkable improvements, with strong double dividends of real GDP. In scenarios with higher carbon tax rates, the carbon tax revenue is higher than VAT or social security contribution revenue, so the possibility of revenue recycling is limited (TNC, TNL). However, with lower tax rates, existing VAT or social security contribution revenues are larger than the carbon tax revenue, enabling full revenue recycling (THC, THL).

In cases with positive double dividends, economic performance is better in a scenario with a higher carbon tax rate and, thus, a higher potential of revenue recycling (compare, e.g., TNI and THI).

8.6 Discussion

As analyzed using E3ME-Asia, with results shown in the previous sections, we summarize our findings as follows:

1   To achieve the national targets for Japan, Korea, and Taiwan, high carbon tax rates are required. This means that the national targets are fairly ambitious to be achieved through a carbon tax only.
2   The economic burden of reducing CO_2 emissions is by no means intolerable (around 0–2 percent), even if the required carbon tax rate is high and the revenue is not recycled.
3   If China contributes to the higher share of CO_2 reductions with the same tax rates as the other three countries (harmonized carbon tax), the economic burden for the other countries will be substantially eased, even if the reduced CO_2 emissions of all four countries together is the same.
4   The results of a single-country carbon tax and four-country carbon tax are not much different for the country that introduces it.
5   A positive double dividend is most likely if revenue is recycled through a reduction in VAT. Whether we obtain a positive double dividend by using other options for revenue recycling is country-specific, especially when it comes to the revenue from existing taxes and SSC.
6   Reduced CO_2 emissions and a higher carbon tax rate do not necessarily translate into a higher economic burden, especially when a strong double dividend is observed.

For points (1) and (2), the required carbon tax rates are 153.70 US$/tCO$_2$ for Japan, 213.37 US$/tCO$_2$ for Korea, and 495.44 US$/tCO$_2$ for Taiwan in 2020. This means that the pledged national CO_2 reduction targets are severe compared to baseline emission levels – especially for Korea and Taiwan, for which high growth in production and emissions is anticipated – and it is not easy to reduce CO_2 emissions over only six years through the stepwise introduction of carbon tax only. However, despite the high carbon tax rates, the drop in real GDP is rather limited (–0.86 percent in China, –1.25 percent in Japan, –1.00 percent in Korea, and –2.86 percent in Taiwan in 2020). The reason for this is that the carbon tax – when introduced as an indirect tax – does not prohibit core industrial activities, and even when the carbon tax increases the price of energy-intensive goods, consumers can choose goods that are less energy intensive.

As for point (3), the national target for 2020 is much easier to achieve for China than for the other three countries. The reduction of CO_2 emissions by 40 percent is mostly achieved with a lower carbon tax rate (52.44 US$/$tCO_2$). However, if all four countries apply the same carbon tax rate (82.09 US$/$tCO_2$), China's carbon tax rate and amount of CO_2 reduction are significantly higher and, therefore, it would be possible for the other three countries to have lower carbon tax rates that would contain the negative impact on GDP or employment (see Tables 8.2 and 8.3).

Regarding point (4), if we compare the main macro-economic indicators (such as real GDP or employment) in four-country carbon tax (AHN) and single-country carbon tax (-HN) scenarios, the results are not significantly different; that is, the variation is less than 0.4 percent. The impact on some industrial sectors may differ strongly, but this is not the scope of this chapter (see Chapters 13 and 17).

For point (5), we believe the differences regarding positive double dividends are remarkable compared to other publications, especially when considering studies that have used CGE models. With CGE models, the revenue recycling through a reduction of labor tax (employers' social security contributions) often shows better results than through a reduction of income tax or VAT. This is usually explained in a neoclassical context in that a tax on a narrower tax base with a higher tax rate (in this case, carbon tax) will cause heavier deadweight loss than a tax on a wider tax base with a lower tax rate (in this case, VAT or income tax). Therefore, a switch of taxation from income or general consumption to energy will not have a positive economic impact, whereas – especially when assuming disequilibrium in the labor market – reduced labor costs through reduced SSC will raise labor demand, resulting in favorable economic results.

Our results from using the E3ME-Asia model can be explained as follows. The reduction of SSC does not necessarily lead to a significantly lower wage rate to induce more employment, and does not lead to higher income or consumption either. In our macro-econometric model where no 'optimal equilibrium' is assumed, the existing VAT (and, similarly, income tax) has a worse impact on the economy than a carbon tax with the same revenue. This is because the latter can be avoided by consumers by buying relatively cheaper goods, whereas the former cannot be avoided, and so expenditures will drop directly (see Chapter 10).

As for point (6), if we can have a strong double dividend, even in scenarios with a high carbon tax rate, we can say that more ambitious CO_2 reduction targets – which require higher carbon taxes – will not necessarily be harmful for the economy.

However, these results are observed within the scope of our scenario assumptions. We cannot say that these observations always hold with far higher carbon tax rates.

8.7 Conclusion

We have analyzed the economic impact of CO_2-reduction policies, specifically the introduction of a carbon tax for four East Asian economies, by using the E3ME-Asia macro-econometric model. The economic burden of introducing a carbon tax in order to reduce CO_2 emissions is not a serious one, even if the necessary reduction effort is significant and there are increases in energy prices. The GHG reduction pledges of Korea or Taiwan are fairly ambitious, resulting in rather high carbon tax rates. If China contributes to a higher share of CO_2 reductions by applying the same tax rates as the other three countries, the reduction burden for the other countries are eased significantly.

The possibility of a positive double dividend is created by revenue recycling, especially through a VAT reduction in these four East Asian countries. A positive double dividend due to other recycling options is country-specific. Moreover, an ambitious reduction effort does not necessarily translate into a higher economic burden (in the range of our scenario calculations), especially in the case of a strong double dividend.

These results are remarkably contrasted to those of other studies, especially those that are based on supply-side-oriented CGE models with a neoclassical foundation. However, according to our analyses, the significant reduction of CO_2 emissions in the medium-term is possible – including positive economic effects.

Notes

1 A 'weak' double dividend means that the negative economic effect from an environmental tax will be eased when the revenue of it is used to reduce another existing distorting tax, but the total economic effect of ETR is still negative.
2 The argument of opponents such as Bovenberg, Parry, or Goulder is summarized and criticized in Goodstein (2003).
3 Though simulation analyses using computer models such as CGEs are often referred to as 'empirical,' many of them lack empirical basis.
4 Based on national reduction targets reported to UNFCCC (UNFCCC homepage; http://unfccc.int/meetings/copenhagen_dec_2009/items/5264.php; http://unfccc.int/meetings/cop_15/copenhagen_accord/items/5265.php). The reduction target of Taiwan for 2020 is based on Taiwan's official document written in Chinese (http://estc10.estc.tw/ghgrule/organization/division_2.asp), which is slightly different from the homepage of Taiwan's government in English (http://unfccc.epa.gov.tw/unfccc/eglish/05_faq/p1_faq.html).
5 Because the carbon tax rate used is rounded off to the second decimal point, the combined reduction of all four countries may not be exactly the same in ANN and AHN. The annual carbon tax rates from 2015 to 2020 are 37.25, 53.16, 60.39, 67.63, 74.86, and 82.09 \$/tCO_2.

6 The baseline inflation rates of the GDP deflator are 1.78 percent for China, 0.99 percent for Japan, 1.59 percent for Korea, and 0.85 percent for Taiwan. We apply the same increase of carbon tax rate (1.7 percent) for all four countries.

7 In this case, the revenue will not vanish in the model. As IS balance identity holds, $(S - I) + (T - G) = (X - M)$, the improvement in budget balance (tax minus government spending) will lead to a reduction in net savings and/or to an increase of net exports. The 'no recycling' scenario is not easy to introduce in a CGE model.

8 We assume that in Japan the lifetime of a nuclear power plant is limited to 40 years. Nuclear power plants in Japan, all of which are offline in 2014, will gradually restart after investigation by the Nuclear Regulation Committee by 2017, except for eight reactors whose safety status is highly questionable.

9 The effect of existing promotion schemes for renewables, such as feed-in tariffs (FIT) in China, Japan, or Taiwan and renewable portfolio standards (RPS) in Korea, are input into the FTT:Power model (Mercure, 2012) to calculate the baseline composition of electricity generation (see Chapter 3).

10 In other analyses (especially CGE), carbon prices will be endogenously adjusted in different scenarios with different economic performances to keep the emission rate constant. However, for two reasons we apply a different calculation. First, we think our method is more realistic regarding carbon tax, and second, the 'target run' calculation used in our E3ME-Asia analysis is very time-consuming to apply for each individual scenario.

References

Andersen, M. S., and Ekins P. (2009). *Carbon-Energy Taxation: Lessons from Europe.* Oxford: IEA.

Barker, T., Anger, A., Chewpreecha, U., and Pollitt, H. (2012). 'A new economics approach to modelling policies to achieve global 2020 targets for climate stabilisation.' In 'Economic policies of the new thinking in economics.' Special issue, *International Review of Applied Economics*, 26(2), pp. 205–211.

Barker, T., Ekins, P., Junankar, S., Pollitt, H., and Summerton, P. (2009). 'The competitiveness effects of European environmental tax reforms.' *European Review of Energy Markets*, 3(1), pp. 1–33.

Barker, T., Foxon, T., and Scrieciu, S. S. (2008). 'Achieving the G8 50% target: Modelling induced and accelerated technological change using the macroeconometric model E3MG.' In 'Modelling long-term scenarios for low-carbon societies.' Special issue, *Climate Policy*, 8(Supplementary Issue 1), pp. S30–S45.

Barker, T., Junankar, S., Pollitt, H., and Summerton, P. (2007). 'Carbon leakage from unilateral environmental tax reforms in Europe, 1995–2005.' *Energy Policy*, 35, pp. 6281–6292.

Barker, T., Pan, H., Köhler, J., Warren R., and Winne, S. (2005). 'Avoiding dangerous climate change by inducing technological progress: Scenarios using a large-scale econometric model.' In Schellnhuber, H. J., Cramer, W., Nakicenovic, N., Wigley, T., and Yohe, G. (Eds.), *Avoiding Dangerous Climate Change*. Cambridge: Cambridge University Press.

Barker, T., Pan, H., Köhler, J., Warren, R., and Winne, S. (2006). 'Decarbonizing the global economy with induced technological change: Scenarios to 2100 using E3MG.' In Edenhofer, O., Lessmann, K., Kemfert, K., Grubb, M., and Köhler, J. (Eds.), 'Induced technological change: Exploring its implications for the economics of atmospheric stabilization.' Special issue, *Energy Journal*, *27*(special issue 2006), pp. 241–258.

Barker, T., and Scrieciu, SS. (2009). 'Unilateral climate change mitigation, carbon leakage and competitiveness: An application to the European Union.' *International Journal of Global Warming*, *1*(4), pp. 405–417.

Bor, Y. J. (2010). 'Energy taxation and the double dividend effect in Taiwan's energy conservation policy: An empirical study using a computable general equilibrium model.' *Energy Policy*, *38*(5), pp. 2086–2100.

Bosquet, B. (2000). 'Environmental tax reform: Does it work? A survey of the empirical evidence.' *Ecological Economics*, *1*(34), pp. 19–32.

Cambridge Econometrics (2014). *E3ME Manual, Version 6.0*. http://www.e3me. com. (accessed on May 17, 2015)

Dagoumas, A., and Barker, T. (2010). 'Pathways to a low-carbon economy for the UK with the macro-econometric E3MG model.' *Energy Policy*, *38*(6), pp. 3067–3077.

Ekins, P., Pollitt, H., Barton, J., and Blobel, D. (2011). 'The implications for households of environmental tax reform (ETR) in Europe.' *Ecological Economics*, *70*(12), pp. 2472–2485.

Goodstein, E. (2003). 'The death of the Pigouvian tax? Policy implications from the double-dividend debate.' *Land Economics*, *79*(3), pp. 402–414.

International Energy Agency (IEA) (2010). *World Energy Outlook 2010*. Paris: IEA.

International Energy Agency (IEA) (2013). *World Energy Outlook 2013*. Paris: IEA.

Kim, S.-R., and Kim, J.-Y. (2010). *The Design and Economic Effects of Green Fiscal Reform in Korea*. Seoul: Korea Institute of Public Finance. (In Korean).

Lee, S., Pollitt, H., and Ueta, K. (2012). 'A model-based econometric assessment of Japanese environmental tax reform.' *Scientific World Journal*, *2012*(2012), article ID 835917.

Mercure, J.-F. (2012). 'FTT:Power: A global model of the power sector with induced technological change and natural resource depletion.' *Energy Policy*, 48, 799–811.

Nordhaus, W. (2005). 'Life after Kyoto: Alternative approaches to global warming policies.' Yale University working paper, http://www.econ.yale.edu/~nordhaus/kyoto_long_2005.pdf (accessed on November 7, 2007).

Park, S.-J., Yamazaki, M., and Takeda, S. (2012). 'Environmental tax reform: Major findings and policy implications from a multi-regional economic simulation analysis.' Background Policy Paper for *Low Carbon Green Growth Roadmap for Asia and the Pacific*, Bangkok: United Nations.

Pollitt, H., Lee, S., Park, S.-J., and Ueta, K. (2014). 'An economic and environmental assessment of future electricity generation mixes in Japan: An assessment using the E3MG macro-econometric model.' *Energy Policy*, 67, pp. 243–254.

Takeda, S. (2007). 'The double dividend from carbon regulations in Japan.' *Journal of the Japanese and International Economies*, *21*(3), pp. 336–364.

Zhang, J.-H., and Zhang, W.-Z. (2013). 'Will carbon tax yield employment double dividend for China?' *International Journal of Business and Social Research*, *3*(4), pp. 124–131.

9 The macroeconomic impacts of environmental tax reform

A comparison of model results

Hector Pollitt, Soocheol Lee, Park Seung-Joon, Yongsung Cho, and Emiko Inoue

9.1 Introduction

In Chapter 8, we presented results from the E3ME-Asia model. We showed that there can be a strong double dividend if the revenues from carbon taxes are used to reduce other taxes. In this chapter, we compare our findings with those described in the wider economic literature about environmental tax reform (ETR).

Most current analysis in East Asia has been carried out by using computable general equilibrium (CGE) models. In this chapter we attempt to explain how E3ME-Asia differs in its approach to CGE models, and how the differences in approach could lead the models to reach different (and sometimes opposite) conclusions about the economic impacts of ETR. The discussion is quite technical in nature and more policy-focused readers may be tempted to skip parts of this chapter. However, for users of modeling results, including policy makers, this chapter plays a key role in helping to interpret the results from the models and to understand the underlying assumptions that can drive these results. Therefore, this chapter is, in our view, one of the most important ones in this book.

In addition to the short description provided in Chapter 8, the E3ME-Asia model has been introduced in Chapter 2, which is why we do not provide a further general description here. Instead, we focus our discussion on how the key features of the different modeling approaches affect their results.

Although our comparison in this chapter inevitably focuses on the differences in approach, it is important to emphasize that there are also many similarities between the models. In particular, the accounting balances and the national accounting structure form the framework for all the models. This ensures that accounting identities (e.g., the calculation of GDP) are consistent in all cases and that supply and demand balance within all the modeling frameworks. There are also similarities between the data used in the models and the types of indicator that the models report in their outputs. As we shall discuss in the following sections, the main difference between models lies in how they accommodate human behavior.

In the following, we compare the results from the E3ME-Asia model (Cambridge Econometrics, 2014) with a selection of results from studies in which

CGE models have been used (Section 9.2). These comparisons are further discussed in Section 9.3, whereas Section 9.4 provides concluding remarks.

9.2 Comparing the results from E3ME-Asia with CGE analyses

We divided our comparison of the impacts of ETR into four parts. First of all, we consider the carbon prices that are required to meet the national targets. Second, we compare the effects of the carbon taxes on East Asia's economies. Third, we consider how the different revenue recycling methods affect the results. And, last, we compare the sectoral results from the two modeling approaches.

Comparison of carbon prices

Various model comparison studies have been carried out to assess how emission levels respond to carbon pricing (see, e.g., outputs from the Energy Modeling Forum and IPCC meta-analysis). However, these studies are often quite descriptive and can only go so far in explaining why differences occur between different modeling approaches; they do not often discuss in depth the technical reasons for obtaining the differences in results. The study by Barker, Qureshi, and Köhler (2006) is an exception, as it investigates in some detail the impacts of induced technological change (i.e., new technologies being developed in response to policy measures) on model outcomes.

In this book, it is impossible to fully scientifically compare the different modeling approaches, as we did not run the same ETR scenarios used in the E3ME-Asia model in a CGE model. Instead, we look at some of the wider literature,[1] which means that we combine results for different countries, time periods, and revenue recycling methods.

In general, we can see a wide variation in the results from the models, which is not surprising, given the wide range of different contexts covered. It is also apparent that the carbon prices that are required for a given reduction in emissions in the E3ME-Asia model are generally near the top end of the range of model outcomes.

There are several possible explanations for the differences, and it is difficult to rule any of them out when comparing such a broad range of studies. For example, baseline energy prices are important, as a higher baseline energy price means that the proportional cost increase from a specific carbon tax rate (per ton of CO_2) is less and, therefore, the response to the increase in costs is less. As these studies were carried out at different times, and energy prices vary a lot over time, this possibility cannot be ignored. However, we have not found a systematic difference in assumptions regarding the energy price between the inputs of the E3ME-Asia and the CGE models.

This leaves four main possible reasons for differences in the carbon prices, which relate to the parameters of the models and their underlying structures.

The first is the value of the fuel price elasticities used in the models. These elasticities determine how much (in percentage terms) fuel consumption changes in response to a percentage change in fuel prices (e.g., from a carbon tax). A higher price elasticity means that consumption is more responsive to changes in price and a lower carbon price is needed to reach the emission reduction targets. For most sectors in the E3ME-Asia model, the long-run fuel price elasticities are close to –0.3 (see Table 9.1), meaning that a 1 percent price increase leads to an eventual 0.3 percent fall in consumption. The long-run elasticity is larger in magnitude for the road transport sector (–0.7), as past data have shown that vehicle efficiency can be improved in response to higher fuel prices. The substitution elasticities that are used in CGE models can vary between models but are often based on the same data sets and econometric estimates. So this factor could explain differences between individual sets of model results but is unlikely to be a general cause of differences.

The second possible factor relates to the degree of switching between energy inputs that is allowed in the models. Here, the greatest opportunities lie in the power sector, where, for example, coal could be replaced with gas, or gas with renewables. We know that the FTT:Power model that is incorporated to E3ME-Asia is relatively unresponsive to changes in prices (especially in the short run) when no other policies are implemented (see Chapter 3). However, many CGE models, especially those without a 'bottom-up' (technological) power sector sub-model, allow flexible price responsiveness in the power mix. The treatment of fuel switching in the models could therefore explain at least part of the difference in results. Fuel switching is likely to be particularly important for China, where a large share of total emissions relates to the use of coal in the power sector.

Related to this point is the third reason, which is how the models treat technology. Many CGE models are static and treat technology as fixed, or at least do not treat it explicitly. As shown in Barker et al. (2006), allowing for the possibility of induced technological change can have a major impact on the carbon prices that are required to achieve a given reduction in emissions. In E3ME-Asia, the FTT:Power component includes learning curves that make switching to low-carbon power sources cheaper (especially in the long run) under scenarios with high emission reductions (unless resource constraints are breached); the model's equations for fuel consumption by other sectors also incorporate endogenous technological progress. It is important to note, however, that these features imply lower carbon prices for E3ME-Asia than in other models, so if the carbon prices in E3ME-Asia are higher than those in other models, it means that the impacts of technological change are outweighed by those of other factors.

The last possibility relates to how the models deal with transition effects. This point is related to the price elasticities described previously. In most CGE models, equilibrium is assumed in each calculation period (e.g., every year), and therefore, it is assumed that companies and individuals are able to adjust their behavior to any price change within each period. In summary, in the CGE modeling framework, 2020 may be considered 'long-term.' In contrast, E3ME-Asia, which allows non-equilibrium outcomes, has at first a short-term effect, which then develops into a longer-term outcome over time.[2] For example, if gasoline prices increase, drivers have only limited scope to immediately reduce fuel consumption; but, if the time horizon is extended, they will at some point be able to purchase a more fuel-efficient vehicle. In this way, the results for E3ME-Asia include a mixture of the short-term and long-term elasticities that we see in Table 9.1. On its own, this difference in treatment suggests that E3ME-Asia requires higher carbon prices to get the same reduction in emissions, especially in the short run.

The impacts of the carbon taxes as part of ETR

Figure 9.1 shows how reductions in emissions link to changes in GDP in the different modeling approaches. The E3ME-Asia results are from Chapter 8 and the

Table 9.1 Approximate price elasticities in the E3ME-Asia model

	E3ME-Asia (short run)	E3ME-Asia (long run)
Power generation	–	–
Industry	–0.15	–0.30
Road transportation	–0.01	–0.70
Households	–0.10	–0.20

Notes: The power sector in E3ME-Asia is modeled using the FTT:Power model (see Chapter 3).

Source: E3ME-Asia model.

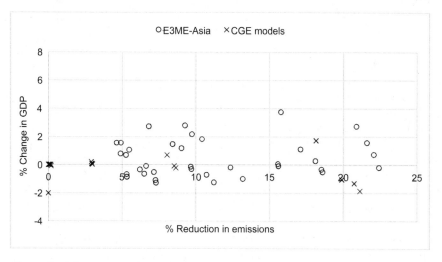

Figure 9.1 The impact of changes in emissions on GDP.

CGE results have been pulled from the literature. Again, we must emphasize that the figure includes results for different East Asian countries across different time periods and with different revenue recycling measures, so the figure should not be used to draw quantitative conclusions.

However, we again see a general trend in differences. The macro-level outputs are perhaps where the differences between the two sets of model results are most stark. In most cases the CGE model predicts either a small reduction in GDP (i.e., no double dividend) or a small increase in exceptional circumstances.[3] Other macroeconomic indicators – including trade volumes, household consumption, and welfare – follow a similar pattern. E3ME-Asia suggests that, in many of the revenue-recycling scenarios, there will be a double dividend of higher GDP combined with less CO_2 emissions.

To understand the differences between the results, we must look into the different mechanisms that are involved in each modeling approach. Some other modeling results discussed in Chapter 8 and other studies published so far can also help with this comparison. For example, we can see from the results of the harmonized carbon tax rate scenarios with no revenue recycling (-HN) discussed in Chapter 8 that the carbon tax on its own (i.e., with no revenue recycling) causes GDP to fall in the E3ME-Asia model, but we can also see that the fall is compensated by the positive impact of the reduction of other tax rates. The question is, how does all this happen and why is it not consistent between the different models?

Let's start by considering how human behavior is represented in the two modeling frameworks. In the CGE model, it is assumed that all 'agents' (individuals or companies) behave in an optimal manner. For example, households are assumed to maximize their 'utility,'[4] and firms are assumed to maximize their profits. All agents are assumed to have all necessary information available to make their decisions. Aggregating from the micro to the macro, these features lead to several key properties of the model. Prices will always adjust fully so that demand is equal to supply and that both are equal to potential supply, meaning that the economy is effectively running at full capacity. As the constraint on output is the level of potential supply (e.g., limited by the amounts of labor or capital) in the system, the models are often described as supply-oriented.

In contrast, within the E3ME-Asia framework there is no assumption about human behavior being optimized. Instead, using the model's econometric equations, it is assumed that behavioral patterns in the past are an accurate representation of the future. So, instead of assuming that prices adjust to the levels necessary to obtain supply–demand equilibrium, prices are determined by the outcomes of the econometric equations. In the domestic price equations in E3ME-Asia, prices are influenced by unit costs and technology, as well as how close the sector is to capacity (e.g., wages may rise when unemployment rates are low). Unless a specific capacity constraint is breached, it is assumed that the level of supply in the economy will adjust to meet the level of demand. This is why the model is sometimes described as demand-oriented. Within the

E3ME-Asia framework, supply is always equal to demand, but it may be less than potential supply, and the starting point is one where production levels are below their potential.

Understanding this distinction is key for understanding the differences in the model results. In the case of the CGE model, the starting position (initial equilibrium) is very often deemed optimal. Once a constraint is added (e.g., a binding carbon reduction target), it is not usually possible to improve upon the starting point, and the impacts must be either neutral or negative. The exception to this rule is when the baseline includes distortions from existing taxes, in which case it is possible to achieve a better reallocation of resources if this distortion is reduced (see the discussion in Section 9.3 of Teng and Jotzo, 2014). However, the model is always assessing a reallocation of resources rather than the effects of bringing resources in and out of the economic system. In contrast, in the E3ME-Asia model, there are almost always spare resources in the economy that could be drawn upon under the right conditions and, if these conditions are met, an increase in GDP is possible.

The ETR scenario provides a clear illustration of this mechanism. As the countries in East Asia are net importers of fuel, a carbon tax (with revenue recycling) effectively provides the opportunity to shift spending from imported fuels to goods that are produced domestically. In the CGE model, this substitution effect cannot take place without displacing or 'crowding out' other activity, because the economy is already operating at full capacity.[5] In E3ME-Asia, however, the capacity is available if required.

This pattern is exactly what we see in the results, with the CGE model showing quite large changes in both exports and imports but, overall, a small reduction in GDP due to the new, suboptimal allocation of resources. In the E3ME-Asia results, however, reallocation of resources takes place, but the number of resources used is also increased, leading to higher overall GDP. The outcome is illustrated most clearly in the ETR scenario results for the labor market; increases in employment rates, decreases in unemployment rates, and increases in labor market participation rates (as described in Chapter 8).

For policy makers, the discussion above gives some indication of when it might be appropriate to apply one of the two different modeling approaches. The CGE analysis is usually carried out to obtain long-term estimates of the impacts of a policy, and it is carried out over a period of time in which it is possible for the economy to return to a long-run equilibrium state. It may also be reasonable to use the CGE analysis for periods of economic boom when the economy is operating at full capacity. Alternatively, the analysis offered by the macro-econometric E3ME-Asia model provides both short-run outcomes and also an estimate of long-term impacts, assuming that full economic capacity will not be reached, even in the long run. Therefore, the macro-econometric approach would be much more suitable for analysis of an economy in recession. Thus, there remains a subjective element in deciding which model to use, and there are some merits in using the two approaches in tandem.

The impacts of the different revenue recycling methods

In Chapter 8, we saw that the choice of revenue recycling method can have a very important impact on the outcomes from the analysis. For example, a strong double dividend was found under some methods of revenue recycling but not others.

There are relatively few studies in which CGE models have been used that compare different revenue recycling methods in East Asia (Park, Yamazaki, and Takeda, 2012 provides a good example), but we can draw the tentative conclusion that the spread of results is much greater when using the E3ME-Asia model than when using a CGE model.

This difference would reflect the underlying assumptions of the two models. As the CGE modeling framework assumes that all resources are being used, the impacts we see from substitution effects are quite small. In contrast, in the E3ME-Asia modeling we see resources being brought in and out of productive use, so it is not surprising that the potential range of impacts is larger.

One particularly illustrative area is the treatment of labor markets in the two modeling approaches.[6] A standard CGE model assumes that wages adjust to ensure market clearing in all countries; that is, there is no involuntary unemployment. This means that reducing labor taxes (employers' social security contributions) does not lead to higher levels of employment; instead, wages adjust upwards and the effect is similar to that of reducing income tax rates.[7]

In contrast, the response of wage rates in the E3ME-Asia model is determined by a set of econometric equations. It is possible in these equations that the model parameters produce results similar to those seen in the CGE model (e.g., in cases of full employment), but typically, this is not the case. Instead, the adjustment in wages is partial and takes time to come into effect. Higher levels of employment and lower levels of unemployment are, to some extent, consequences of the slow upward adjustment in wages. Similarly, the responses in wage rates to changes in inflation and direct tax rates are important in determining the effects of reducing consumption, labor, and income taxes. That is, while most CGE models show very similar results for scenarios with reductions in consumption or labor taxes, in E3ME-Asia those results may differ.

In summary, the mechanisms that determine the spread of results in the two models are the same ones that lead to the differences in results described in the previous section. Ultimately, this again comes down to assumptions about optimization and behavioral patterns. For example, in the CGE model all workers accept a certain wage rate, which ensures that they are employed; whereas in the E3ME-Asia model wage rates are set on the basis of historical patterns – and there are some workers who may be unemployed.

Sectoral impacts

It is always difficult to directly compare the sectoral results from macroeconomic models, as all models use slightly different classifications; but some consistency in data is enforced by the adoption of standardized international classifications.

Our review of model results shows a degree of consistency between the different approaches, at least when considering them in a qualitative manner. For both models, the sectors whose outputs fall are usually those whose products have become more expensive – that is, those that supply energy and those that are intensive users of energy and pass these costs on to customers. The sectors in which output increases are those of agriculture, food, transportation, and services, which benefit from the effects of a shift in household spending away from energy-intensive goods. The impact on construction is typically broadly neutral.

One area of disagreement between the models is the scale of the impact on the energy-intensive industries, where impacts can have positive or negative effects. On the positive side, many energy-intensive products are used to build the investment goods (e.g., energy-efficient homes or renewable-energy-related equipment) that are required to reduce emissions. On the negative side, these sectors may be very open to competitiveness effects and carbon leakage (see Chapter 13). Typically, CGE models show much larger negative effects. These impacts are largely the result of changes in trade patterns, and differences between the model results reflect model parameters for import substitution rates rather than differences in model structure. This is a topic we pick up in much more detail in Chapters 18 and 19.

9.3   Discussion

There has been an almost endless discussion about the failure of economists to agree with each other on key economic issues. At times it has been seen as a source of embarrassment for the profession and an obstruction to academic progress (Blinder, 1989); this chapter explores the reasons for some of the disagreement. We have compared the results from two modeling approaches that embody different schools of macroeconomic theory. On the one hand, we have the CGE models, which are neoclassical in approach. They represent the long-term part of what has been called 'the new neoclassical synthesis' (Goodfriend and King, 1997) that shapes current mainstream macroeconomics, and they share features with many other macroeconomic models commonly in use. On the other hand, we have the E3ME-Asia model, derived from a post-Keynesian background, which is quite different in its general approach. Notable differences between the models include the treatment of price formation and the interaction of supply and demand. These factors drive the differences in results and conclusions that are obtained by using the two modeling approaches.

However, these differences are, in fact, themselves the result of a more fundamental difference in modeling assumptions. In the CGE model, it is assumed that individuals and firms behave so as to optimize their own welfare, whereas the E3ME-Asia model assumes that future human behavior can best be approximated by projecting forward historical patterns, which are based on econometric estimates.

The aim of this chapter is not to determine which approach is the better one as, clearly, each has certain advantages and disadvantages. For example, it is difficult to justify assumptions about perfect information of current and future events in CGE models; but operators of macro-econometric models have never been able to dismiss the 'Lucas critique' (Lucas, 1976), which states that behavior responds to changes in policy, and extrapolations of past behavior may, therefore, be invalid. These debates have been going for almost as long as those disciplines of macroeconomics have existed.

Our intentions in this chapter are more practical in nature: to provide the reader with a basic understanding of how the different types of model work, how to interpret the results of future modeling exercises, and what questions to ask when making these interpretations. One point that should now be clear to the reader is that the descriptions of the models used in assessments, often provided only in technical annexes or external references, are an important part of the overall story.

The final point to raise is that carrying out these model comparison exercises can be highly valuable (see also Chapter 5). By combining models from different schools of thought, it is possible to obtain a range of putative outcomes in response to policy impacts. For example, from this chapter we can see that, regardless of approach, the macroeconomic impacts of ETR are likely to be small, even if we do not know whether they will be positive or negative. If we then take into account that the primary reason for introducing ETR is environmental rather than economic, a broadly neutral macroeconomic outcome can be seen as supportive of the policy.

9.4   Conclusions

In this chapter we have compared the results from Chapter 8 with some of those based on CGE analyses in the wider economic literature. We have explained the most important reasons for the differences between the results from the two different types of macroeconomic model. It is clear that the underlying assumptions of the models can be very important in determining the quantitative outcomes and even the direction of the results. Educating policy makers about this fact is one of the main aims of this book.

We can, however, still draw some firm conclusions from the analysis that has been carried out, despite the overall differences in results. In most cases, we see only relatively minor impacts on GDP (which may be positive or negative), but large reductions in CO_2 emissions. The pattern of impacts across sectors is also mostly consistent between the two modeling approaches, with energy suppliers and energy-intensive users losing out, and the service sectors gaining.

To conclude, we have not been able to find a definitive answer to the question of whether ETR in the East Asian countries being considered will result in strong double dividends or not, but our findings are generally supportive of the policy. In the following chapters, we turn attention to some other potential costs and benefits of ETR and, more generally, carbon taxation, starting with how carbon taxes could be used to reduce government deficits.

Notes

1 Sources reviewed include Park, Yamazaki, and Takeda (2012), Cao (2007), and Li et al. (2013).
2 Typically, this time period is 3–4 years; it is estimated as part of the econometric equations.
3 The increases are when revenues are used to reduce capital taxes (see Park et al., 2012).
4 Broadly speaking, economic welfare.
5 Furthermore, in most CGE models trade balances are fixed due to closure rule problems.
6 See Barker, De-Ramon, and Pollitt (2009) for a discussion of the role of labor markets in a similar modeling exercise.
7 In a CGE model that allows disequilibrium in the labor market through exogenous wage rates, a strong double dividend in employment can be observed. Cambridge Econometrics et al (2013) includes an example with the GEM-E3 model, which is compared to E3ME.

References

Barker, T. S., De-Ramon, S., and Pollitt, H. (2009). 'Revenue recycling and labour markets: effects on costs of policies for sustainability.' In Bosetti, V., Gerlagh, R., and Schleicher, S. (Eds.), *Modelling Transitions to Sustainable Development.* Cheltenham, UK: Edward Elgar. Pp. 104–126.

Barker, T. S., Qureshi, M. S., and Köhler, J. (2006). 'The costs of greenhouse gas mitigation with induced technological change: A meta-analysis of estimates in the literature.'

4CMR Working Paper, Cambridge Centre for Climate Change Mitigation Research, Cambridge: University of Cambridge.

Blinder, A. S. (1989). *Macroeconomics under Debate.* New York: Harvester Wheatsheaf.

Cambridge Econometrics (2014). *E3ME Manual, Version 6.* http://www.e3me.com.

Cambridge Econometrics, Ernst & Young, E3MLab, Exergia, Warwick Institute for Employment Research, and COWI (2013). *Employment Effects of Selected Scenarios of the Energy Roadmap 2050.* Report submitted to the European Commission (DG ENER), https://ec.europa.eu/energy/sites/ener/files/documents/2013_report_employment_effects_roadmap_2050_2.pdf (accessed May 17, 2015).

Cao, J. (2007). 'Essays on environmental tax policy analysis: Dynamic computable general equilibrium approaches applied to China.' PhD dissertation, Committee on Higher Degrees in Public Policy, Harvard University.

Goodfriend, M., and King, R. J. (1997). 'The new neoclassical synthesis and the role of monetary policy.' *NBER Macroeconomics Annual*, 12, pp. 231–283. http://www.nber.org/chapters/c11040.pdf (accessed May 17, 2015).

Li, A. J., Zhang, A., Li, X., unknown author, and Peng, S. (2013). 'How large are the impacts of carbon motivated border tax adjustments on China and how to mitigate?' Beijing Normal University School of Economics and Business Administration, Working Paper No. 53.

Lucas, R. (1976). 'Econometric policy evaluation: A critique.' In Brunner, K., and Meltzer, A. (Eds.), *The Phillips Curve and Labor Markets*. Amsterdam: North-Holland. Pp. 19–46.

Park, S. J., Yamazaki, M., and Takeda, S. (2012). 'Low carbon green growth roadmap for Asia and the Pacific – environmental tax reform: Major findings and policy implications from a multi-regional economic simulation analysis.' Bangkok: United Nations. http://www.unescap.org/sites/default/files/2.%20Environmental-Tax-Reform.pdf (accessed May 17, 2015).

Teng, F., and Jotzo, F. (2014). 'Reaping the Economic Benefits of Decarbonization for China.' CCEP Working Paper No. 1413, Crawford School of Public Policy, Australian National University.

10 Environmental taxes and fiscal deficits

Hector Pollitt, Park Seung-Joon,
Takeshi Kawakatsu, and Jiro Sakurai

10.1 Introduction

Environmental tax reform (ETR) involves the substitution of one tax with another that specifically taxes environmentally damaging activities, without any net impact on the government budget balance. In Chapter 8 we assessed the potential of ETR in four East Asian countries (China, Japan, Korea, and Taiwan) and showed that the macroeconomic impacts of ETR are quite small and could, in some circumstances, be positive.

After initially being applied in countries of northern Europe in the early 1990s (see Andersen and Ekins, 2009), the popularity of ETR as a policy grew throughout Europe (and globally over the past 10–15 years) as economists convinced policy makers that market-based mechanisms are an efficient way to reduce pollution. However, according to experiences in Europe, ETR has never been without controversy, as targeted industries have cited competitiveness effects (see Chapter 13) and lobbied for special protection from the taxes. In many cases, specific exemptions to ETR have reduced both their effectiveness and revenue-raising powers.

But one of the most pervasive arguments against ETR raised in Europe is that individuals and companies simply do not trust policy makers to enforce revenue neutrality. Rather than ETR being presented as a tax reform, it is perceived as a tax increase, a view that is pushed by groups lobbying on behalf of the affected industries. In some cases, this has been a legitimate argument; for example the reduction in labor taxes that was associated with the UK's Climate Change Levy was reversed a year later.

After escalating energy prices and the economic and financial crisis, ETR became politically infeasible in many European countries. The subsequent focus on government deficits and the shift to austerity has also made ETR difficult in practice for three reasons:

- Policy makers have other economic priorities.
- It is difficult to introduce new taxes in times of slow growth and high unemployment.
- Reducing existing taxes is difficult when faced with a large fiscal deficit.

However, even if introducing ETR is not possible, there may still be a role for environmental taxation. Many countries (e.g., the US, certain European countries) remain under pressure, either politically or from creditors or international agencies, to improve their fiscal position. In East Asia, Japan stands out for its high debt levels (see the next section). Usually, fiscal balances are improved through a combination of spending cuts and tax increases. Regarding tax increases, the question may change from:

'Is it better to increase one tax and reduce another?'
to
'Which tax is it better to increase?'

In this chapter, we explore whether the current economic and fiscal positions in the four East Asian countries under consideration provide the grounds for introducing (or increasing) taxes on carbon emissions without including an offset reduction in other taxes. As current growth rates, fiscal deficits, and public debt levels vary considerably between countries, the analysis is carried out at a national level.

In the next section, we summarize the economic and fiscal conditions in each country. We then present three options to raise tax revenues in each country in Sections 10.3 and 10.4, expanding on the modeling that was presented in Chapter 8 and following an approach used previously in Europe (Pollitt et al., 2012) and the US (RFF, 2013). The final two sections in the chapter draw the results together and provide recommendations on future taxation in each country.

10.2   The economic and fiscal position in East Asia

China

With rapid economic growth, China's general government expenditure (Figure 10.1) has expanded since 1995, and the absolute scale of government expenditure in 2011 was 15 times larger than in 1995. In addition to the increase in social security expenses since the late 1990s, this pattern reflects an increase of defense expenditures. The share of government expenditure in nominal GDP was 12.7 percent in 1995, but it increased to 24 percent in 2011 – almost the same level as that of Korea. However, the share is clearly lower than that of major advanced economies.

China's budget balance improved in the period after 2000, and in 2007, it became positive (Figure 10.2). However, in 2008 it became negative again due to the financial crisis and the subsequent government stimulus package. In 2009, China recorded a budget deficit equal to 3 percent of GDP but, after that, it improved to 1.3 percent in 2011.

The general gross government debt in China has increased since 1995 (Figure 10.3). Although it can be difficult to determine from the official statistics, the debt to GDP ratio has been between 15 percent and 20 percent since 2000, but increased to 33.5 percent in 2010. It was 28.7 percent in 2011, which is a little higher than equivalent measures in Korea and Taiwan, but less than that of most major advanced economies.

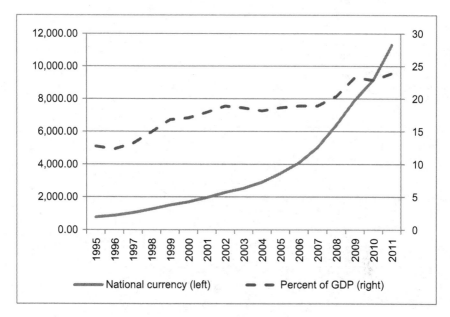

Figure 10.1 China: general government expenditure (bn).
Source: Made from *IMF World Economic Outlook Database*, April 2014.

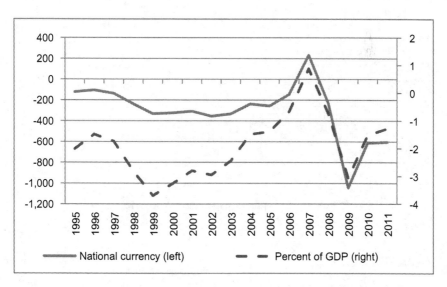

Figure 10.2 China: general government net lending (bn).
Source: Made from *IMF World Economic Outlook Database*, April 2014.

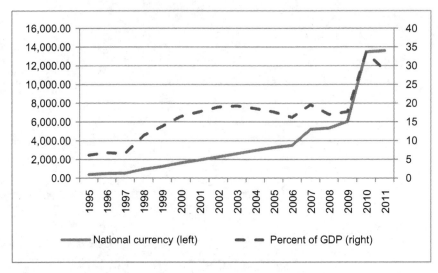

Figure 10.3 China: general government gross debt (bn).

Source: Made from *IMF World Economic Outlook Database*, April 2014.

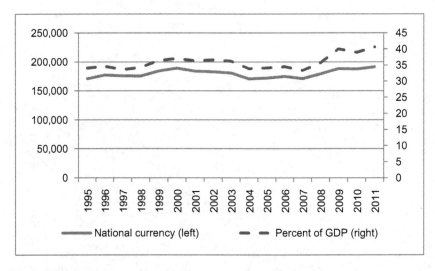

Figure 10.4 Japan: general government expenditure (bn).

Source: Made from *IMF World Economic Outlook Database*, April 2014.

Japan

General government[1] expenditure in Japan decreased after 2001 but started to increase again from 2009 (Figure 10.4). In addition to the increase in social security expenditures, the pattern reflects fiscal measures of unprecedented scale due to the global financial crisis. The share of government expenditure in

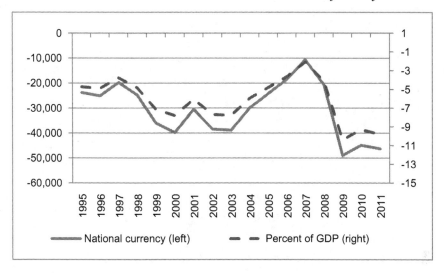

Figure 10.5 Japan: general government net lending (bn).
Source: Made from *IMF World Economic Outlook Database*, April 2014.

nominal GDP remained at around 30 percent in the period 1995–2008, but it has increased to around 40 percent since 2009. Nevertheless, this share is still lower than that of many other major developed economies (and roughly comparable to that of the US).

Japan recorded a budget deficit equal to 9.8 percent of GDP in 2011 (Figure 10.5). The government balance has always been negative in Japan, and the public deficit averaged 6.2 percent of GDP between 1995 and 2011. The deficit improved over the period 2004–2007, but it increased again to 10.4 percent in 2009.

Reflecting the constant trend in deficits, the debt-to-GDP ratio increased from 95.1 percent in 1995 to 229.8 percent in 2011 (Figure 10.6). As a result, Japan has had the highest debt-to-GDP ratio among major advanced economies since 1999. Fortunately for Japan, the vast majority of this debt is held domestically (e.g., in pension funds), and so the country does not face external pressures to reduce its public debt. However, it is possible that the picture will change in the future, when pensioners start using their savings and if Japanese import volumes (including of fossil fuels) increase.

Korea

Korea's general government expenditure has been increasing since 1995, but its share in nominal GDP has remained almost constant (in the range of 15 percent to 23 percent; see Figure 10.7). That share is clearly lower than for other major

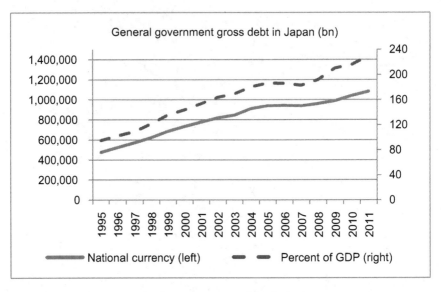

Figure 10.6 Japan: general government gross debt (bn).

Source: Made from *IMF World Economic Outlook Database*, April 2014.

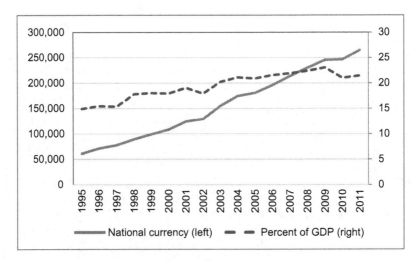

Figure 10.7 Korea: general government expenditure (bn).

Source: Made from *IMF World Economic Outlook Database*, April 2014.

developed economies, which means that the general tax burden is also lower. However, as its social security system is still less developed than other advanced economies, higher public revenue may become necessary in the future.

In recent history, Korea's budget balance (general government net lending; see Figure 10.8) has always been positive, in the range of about 0 percent to 4 percent. This is due to a combination of factors, including accruals of pension

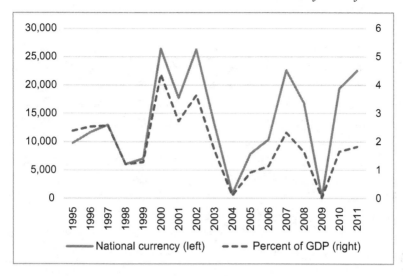

Figure 10.8 Korea: general government net lending (bn).
Source: Made from *IMF World Economic Outlook Database*, April 2014.

contributions when the country's social security system was developed. External factors have also been responsible. The Asian Currency Crisis in 1997 had a devastating impact on the Korean economy, resulting in a large drop in GDP (–5.7 percent in 1998). During the crisis, Korea had to manage its public budget in line with the conditions specified to receive IMF support, such as a positive budget balance, even in the severe economic downturn. Quick recovery led to a fiscal surplus in the period 2000–2002 (of about 3 percent to 4 percent of GDP), followed by a drop in surplus in 2003 and 2004. From 2005, the government's net lending increased again towards the peak of 2007, followed by a decline in 2008 reflecting the economic shock from the global financial crisis. Still, even in the middle of the downturn, Korea maintained a positive fiscal balance.

Korea's government debt (general government gross debt; see Figure 10.9) includes the accrued liabilities from public pensions as well as the received annual contributions, so its debt level has gradually increased despite the positive budget balance. Nevertheless, Korea's gross debt was only 34.2 percent of GDP in 2011, which is relatively low compared with other major industrialized countries.

Taiwan

Taiwan's absolute level of government expenditure has expanded since 1995 (Figure 10.10). The share of government expenditure in GDP has also gradually increased over this period, from around 15 percent to 20 percent. Even so, Taiwan's government is remarkably smaller than those of other major developed countries, meaning that there is a lower tax burden for its citizens and businesses. Still, similar to other emerging economies, Taiwan's social security system is still under construction and, therefore, the country may require higher spending and revenue in the future.

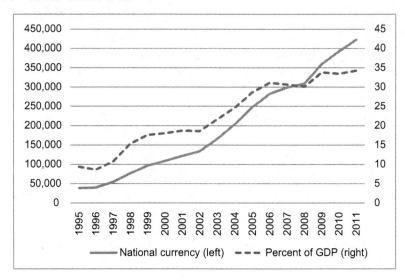

Figure 10.9 Korea: general government gross debt (bn).

Source: Made from *IMF World Economic Outlook Database*, April 2014.

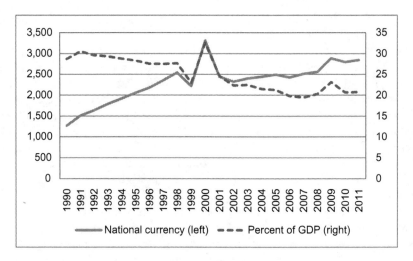

Figure 10.10 Taiwan: general government expenditure (bn).

Source: Made from *IMF World Economic Outlook Database*, April 2014.

Taiwan's budget balance (general government net lending; see Figure 10.11) has always been negative, in the range of about –2 percent to –9 percent, but Taiwan does not rely heavily on foreign debt. Therefore, during both the Asian Currency Crisis (1997) and the global financial crisis (2008), Taiwan was affected less than other Asian countries such as Korea. Still, soon after hitting the historical peak of the government's net borrowing in 1997, the government

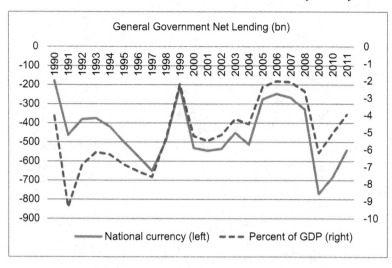

Figure 10.11 Taiwan: general government net lending (bn).
Source: Made from *IMF World Economic Outlook Database*, April 2014.

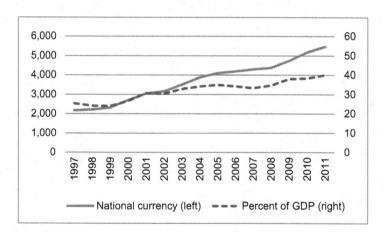

Figure 10.12 Taiwan: general government gross debt (bn).
Source: Made from *IMF World Economic Outlook Database*, April 2014.

promptly (and temporarily) consolidated its fiscal position in 1998 and 1999. The deficit steeply increased again in 2000. From 2005, a positive economic trend enabled Taiwan to reduce its annual deficit, but the economic shock following the collapse of Lehman Brothers and the global economic downturn resulted in a spike of net borrowing in 2009. Continuous net borrowing has led to a continuous accumulation of government debt (general government gross debt; see Figure 10.12). Gross debt was about 40 percent of GDP in

2011, close to Taiwan's legal debt limit. However, Taiwan's public finances are generally considered to be sound because the country became free of foreign debt in 2011 (Liu, 2011).

10.3   The scenarios

In this chapter, we apply the E3ME-Asia model to assess the macroeconomic effects following the increase of different taxes. The starting point for the analysis is the same reference case and the same set of scenarios that were adopted in Chapter 8. In each country, the same carbon tax is applied as in Chapter 8 (to meet national emissions targets), the difference here being that we focus on the '-NN' scenarios in which no revenues are recycled and they are all instead used to reduce the public deficit. As shown in Chapter 8, these scenarios have negative results on GDP and employment in all four countries.

The results from these scenarios are then compared to three sets of similar scenarios in which the standard rates of income tax, VAT (or sales tax), and labor taxes are increased *so as to produce the same amount of revenue* in each year of the projection period. The comparison of results thus shows the relative costs and benefits over time of reducing public deficits in different ways. The ultimate question addressed is whether a carbon tax represents an efficient way of reducing public deficits.

The VAT rate in E3ME-Asia is also defined as a single rate in each country, although variations of this rate are allowed for different product groups. In the scenario, an increase in VAT is applied equally across all consumer products so that they see the same proportionate increase in price.

The income tax rate in E3ME-Asia is defined as a single rate in each country that is levied on all earned wage income, regardless of the individual's total income. When this rate is adjusted, it effectively assumes a similar proportional increase in tax payments across all income tax bands. The impact of an increase in the tax rate is to reduce household disposable income. There may also be a small reduction in labor supply as the tax acts as a disincentive to work.

The labor tax, also referred to in some countries as 'employers' social security contributions,' is a tax on wages that is paid by the employer and, therefore, increases the cost of labor. A single rate (as a proportion of wages) is applied for each country.

Table 10.1 summarizes the scenarios. A separate set of scenarios was run for each country so that all impacts are the result of domestic policy.

10.4   Modeling results

China

In China, the revenues from each of the tax increases account for around 4 percent of GDP in 2020 (see Table 10.1). The expected scale of the impacts, therefore, also is around 4 percent, depending on factors such as import shares, multiplier effects, and changes to savings ratios.

Table 10.1 Summary of scenarios

Scenario	Revenues raised (% GDP, 2020)				Description
	China	Japan	Korea	Taiwan	
Reference case	0.0	0.0	0.0	0.0	Baseline in Chapter 8
S1	4.0	2.8	3.8	13.6	Carbon tax (-NN scenarios in Chapter 8)
S2	4.0	2.8	3.8	13.6	Increase in VAT rate
S3	4.0	2.8	3.8	13.6	Increase in income tax rate
S4	4.0	2.8	3.8	13.6	Increase in labor tax rate

Note: Revenues are presented as a share of nominal GDP in 2020.

Source: Authors' own calculations.

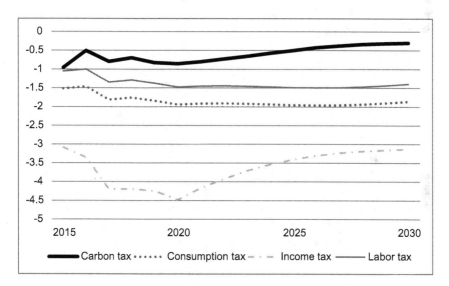

Figure 10.13 China: impact on GDP (% from base).

Note: The line for the consumption tax was smoothed to strip out short-term volatility, but the 2030 figure was not changed.

Source: Authors' own calculations.

Under the carbon tax, the reduction in GDP is initially around 1 percent, although this moves close to zero by 2030 (Figure 10.13). There are two important factors here: the large share of imports in energy products to China and the induced investment in the electricity sector (particularly in renewables). These two factors mean that the carbon tax results are less negative than those for increases in other taxes; the loss of GDP for consumption and labor taxes is around 2 percent, whereas for income taxes the loss is around 3–4 percent.

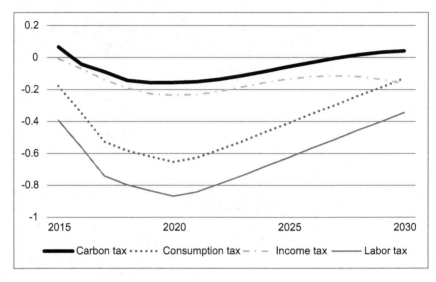

Figure 10.14 China: impact on employment (% from base).

Source: Authors' own calculations.

Note: The line for the consumption tax was smoothed to strip out short-term volatility, but the 2030 figure was not changed.

The projected changes in employment for China range from just above zero to a 1 percent reduction by 2030 (Figure 10.14). The carbon tax could lead to a very small increase in the overall rate of employment by 2030 due to the large number of jobs created in constructing and installing renewable energy equipment. However, increases in income taxes and VAT rates have a negative impact of around –0.2 percent on employment by the end of the projection period. Least favorable of all for employment is the labor tax, which directly increases the cost of labor and leads to reductions in employment. In 2020, employment is more than 0.8 percent lower than in the reference case in this scenario.

Japan

In Japan, each tax increase generates revenues equal to 2.8 percent of GDP in 2020 (Table 10.1). Although the carbon tax rate used for Japan is higher than that for China, Japan's lower carbon intensity means that the potential macro-economic effects are smaller overall.

The smallest impacts on GDP come from the labor tax increase and the introduction of the carbon tax (around a 1 percent decrease in GDP by 2030), of which the labor tax increase produces the most favorable results (especially around 2020) (Figure 10.15). If VAT or income tax rates were increased, the

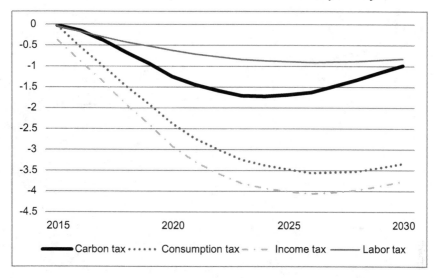

Figure 10.15 Japan: impact on GDP (% from base).
Source: Authors' own calculations.

negative impact on GDP could be around 4 percent, which is more than the original tax increase due to multiplier effects. The main reason for the multiplier effects is that the Japanese economy has quite low trade ratios, so unless particular products (e.g., fuels) are targeted, it is domestic activity – rather than imports – that is most affected by a loss of real household income.

The negative impact on employment is less pronounced – up to 1 percent in the labor tax and carbon tax scenarios, and up to 2 percent if income taxes or consumption taxes are increased (Figure 10.16). It is perhaps surprising (and counterintuitive) that a tax on labor leads to the lowest reduction in labor demand, but the E3ME-Asia parameters suggest that labor costs play only a small role in determining employment levels (and changes in output are much more important). However, as discussed in other chapters, it is important to note that E3ME-Asia's historical database is dominated by a period of low or no price/wage growth in Japan, and relationships can be expected to change if prices started to increase on a 'normal' trajectory. Therefore, the employment reductions in the labor tax scenario could be an underestimate and we suggest that further analysis is carried out in this area.

Korea

The tax increases in Korea amount to 3.8 percent of GDP in 2020, similar to China and higher than in Japan (Table 10.1). However, in most cases, the GDP impacts are smaller than for Japan, although the patterns between the tax scenarios

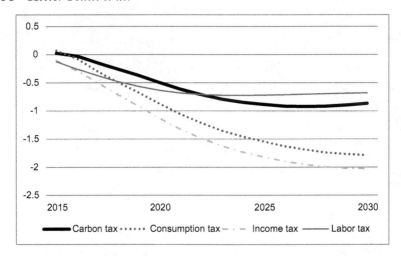

Figure 10.16 Japan: impact on employment (% from base).
Source: Authors' own calculations.

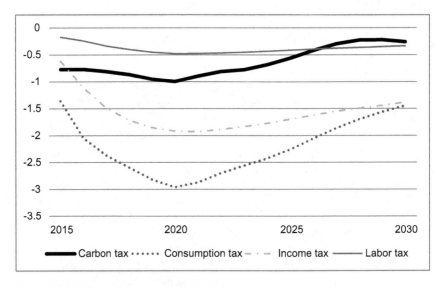

Figure 10.17 Korea: impact on GDP (% from base).
Source: Authors' own calculations.

are similar. The reason for this is that Korea has much higher trade ratios; therefore, a larger share of the loss of demand is met by imports rather than reductions
in domestic production. Overall, the cost to GDP of implementing the taxes is
around 0.5 percent in 2030 for the carbon tax and labor tax scenarios, and
1.5 percent for the income tax and consumption tax scenarios (Figure 10.17).

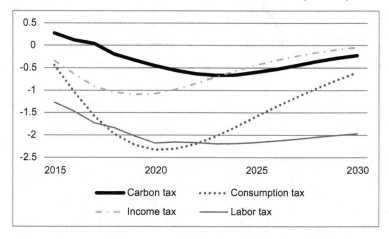

Figure 10.18 Korea: impact on employment (% from base).
Source: Authors' own calculations.

The employment effects for Korea show a pattern that differs substantially from those for Japan. During the forecast period, the loss of employment from carbon tax accounts for at most 0.5 percent, whereas by 2030 impacts on employment from consumption and income taxes are also getting quite small (although there may be large short-term adjustment effects; see Figure 10.18). In contrast to the results for Japan, the largest loss of employment occurs in the labor tax scenario, where there is a reduction in employment of 2 percent that persists until 2030. The results suggest that raising labor costs could have large and permanent effects on employment in Korea. Again, Korea's high trade ratios are likely to make the country more exposed to this type of competitiveness effect.

Taiwan

Like Korea, Taiwan is a country that is highly exposed to international trade. The scale of the tax increases in Taiwan is also much bigger than in the other countries, accounting for 13.6 percent of GDP in 2020 (Table 10.1).

The range of impacts on GDP for Taiwan is large, and the modeling results should be viewed as indicative only for this scale of change (Figure 10.19). However, the results quite clearly show that the carbon tax, followed by labor taxes, have the smallest impacts on GDP, and that consumption and income taxes have a substantial negative impact, all increasing – albeit at different rates – in the period 2015–2030. In the case of Taiwan, the high trade ratios do not translate to a reduction in domestic demand being offset by imports; instead, multiplier effects dominate and lead to further losses of GDP.

Turning to the employment results, there is a similarly clear message. The carbon tax could lead to loss of employment of about 2 percent, but for all other tax increases the reduction is about 10 percent by 2030 (Figure 10.20).

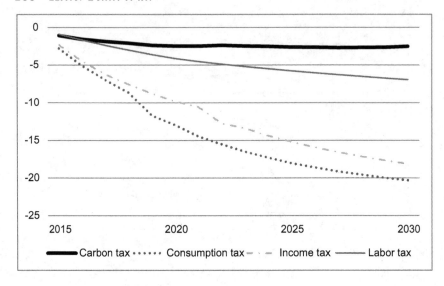

Figure 10.19 Taiwan: impact on GDP (% from base).

Source: Authors' own calculations.

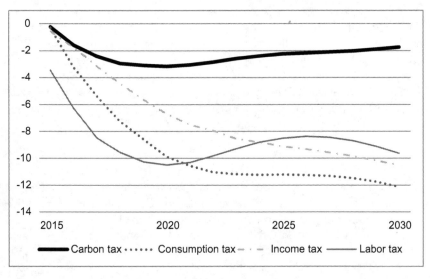

Figure 10.20 Taiwan: impact on employment (% from base).

Source: Authors' own calculations.

10.5   Discussion

In this analysis, we have considered four ways of increasing tax revenues. It was assumed that the revenues raised from these tax increases are used to reduce government debt levels.

In all four countries being discussed, the choice of how to raise the revenues can have a substantial effect on the economy in terms of GDP loss and reduction in employment. Some of the key issues are discussed below, followed by how negative employment effects could be limited.

Loss of domestic production versus loss of imports

One important way to reduce the loss of output is by targeting consumption of imports rather than that of products which are produced domestically. For the East Asian countries, the carbon taxes do this in a reasonably effective manner, as most fossil fuels are imported (coal in China is an important exception). However, in countries with high trade ratios (e.g., Korea), it is less important to target particular products because a large share of domestic demand is met by imports anyway.

National import ratios are very important for determining the impact of any tax increases that affect aggregate demand. In the case of income tax increases (see Table 10.2), the negative relationship between import ratios and the impact on GDP is quite clear, with a simple correlation of −0.656 between the import ratio and the relative GDP impact (with China being the outlier). For carbon taxes, the relationship is less clear cut, as the primary impact on demand focuses on products that are imported anyway, but import ratios still have an important effect on determining the size of the indirect impacts.

The importance of import penetration rates was also one of the key findings in the previous analyses that were carried out in Europe and the US (Pollitt et al., 2012; RFF, 2013). It should be noted that, in an equilibrium-based world, exchange rates would adjust in response to different rates of international trade, cancelling out import effects. However, this assumption is not adopted in E3ME-Asia, and exchange rates are held as exogenous. International financial flows typically account for a much larger volume of currency exchange than export/import volumes, and so, in our view, this assumption is not unreasonable.

Table 10.2 How import ratios affect the GDP impacts

Country	Income tax (% GDP)	GDP impact (% GDP)	Relative GDP impact GDP impact/ income tax	Import ratio (imports/GDP)
China	4.0	−0.9	−0.2	0.26
Japan	2.8	−1.2	−0.4	0.24
Korea	3.8	−1.0	−0.3	0.49
Taiwan	13.6	−2.5	−0.2	0.64

Source: Authors' own calculations.

Taxing profits

In a standard multiplier analysis, taxes and imports are two important system leakages that lead to lower multiplier values. Another important leakage is company profits. In a CGE model, profit margins are typically maintained because increases in costs are fully realized as an increase in the final product price. However, in E3ME-Asia, international competition can mean that not all cost increases are passed on, even in the long run.

It is of course recognized that, in reality, increased profits can lead to higher real economic activity, for example, through additional investment (an important driver of long-term growth). Future versions of the E3ME-Asia model are aiming to better acknowledge this linkage, but even so, it is expected that only a small share of profits contributes to current activity. The reason for this is the high rate of savings associated with profits. Aside from companies retaining profits themselves (as has been witnessed in recent years with the accumulation of large sums of cash in large firms), profits that are paid out through dividends are subject to high savings rates, often in pension funds.

The implication is that, in the modeling, a tax that reduces profit levels has less impact on GDP than one that targets household incomes. The carbon tax (when applied to business) and labor tax both meet this criterion.

Employment effects

Employment levels are generally determined by two things: the level of economic output and the relative labor costs (wage rates plus labor taxes). Both of these can be affected by the taxes modeled in this chapter, and the interaction between wages and prices in the wider economy is important.

The first point to note is that the relative importance of the two factors can vary quite considerably between countries. For example, in Japan the results suggest that labor costs are not an important determinant of employment levels, whereas in the other three countries they clearly are. The policy message is quite clear: national circumstances must be taken into account in policy design.

Table 10.3 demonstrates the differences between the four East Asian countries by showing average long-run elasticities in the E3ME employment

Table 10.3 Output and labor cost elasticities in E3ME

	Output	*Labor costs*
China	0.17	–0.08
Japan	0.68	–0.20
Korea	0.52	–0.59
Taiwan	0.64	–0.30

Source: Authors' own calculations.

equations. Higher numbers indicate a larger response in employment to changes in economic output and labor costs. The table shows that employment is quite unresponsive in China (possibly due to the large share of agricultural employment and rapid growth led by high productivity increases), whereas in Japan, employment responds well to output, rather than labor costs. Within these national averages, there are further differences between economic sectors.

The situation becomes more complex when indirect effects are taken into account. Each of the taxes modeled affects the economy in a different way. An increase in the VAT rate leads directly to higher rates of inflation. Whether this feeds into a higher nominal wage rate (and possible further inflationary impacts) could depend on labor market characteristics, notably the strength of the workforce's bargaining position (e.g., degree of unionization). If wages do not respond, however, real wage rates will fall and employment could increase (albeit in worse-paid jobs). Upon an increase of the income tax rate, one important question is whether employees will demand higher wages to compensate for their loss of take-home income. Again, this could have an important bearing on the net impact on employment.

10.6 Conclusions

There are obvious parallels between the analysis that was carried out in this chapter and the scenarios that were assessed in Chapter 8. Leaving aside some non-linearities and absolute limits,[2] the results are consistent in that the worst taxes to increase in the modeling discussed in this chapter are usually the best ones to decrease in the modeling discussed in Chapter 8. The double dividend results seen in Chapter 8 are represented here by showing that increasing other taxes has a worse economic effect than increasing carbon taxes.

The fiscal situations in China, Japan, Korea, and Taiwan vary considerably. Japan, on the one hand, has a very high level of public debt and no clear plan on how to repay it. China, on the other hand, has only a modest public debt that is likely to be eroded (in relative terms) by high rates of future economic growth. These country-specific differences mean that the requirements to reduce public deficits will be quite different in the four countries assessed, as will the ways in which each country can do so. At present, only Japan has a pressing need to address levels of public debt, although other countries in East Asia are expected to face higher social costs in future.

A key conclusion from this analysis is that the expected impacts of tax increases also vary substantially between countries. In this chapter, our model results identified the most important factors, but there are, of course, a variety of other possible factors, both within and outside the modeling framework.

The evidence from this chapter shows that the carbon tax as a means to reduce fiscal deficit should be considered, because much of the economic pain will be borne by a loss of import demand rather than domestic economic activity. The modeling results show that the impact a carbon tax has on GDP is less than that of raised income or consumption taxes (VAT), and its impact on employment is often better than that of raised labor taxes.

The possible exception here is Japan, the country with the largest public debt, and, in order to cover it, the one that is most likely to need to raise taxes. The model results for Japan show that raising a labor tax could yield better GDP and, possibly, better employment results than raising a carbon tax; although it seems that further analysis of the nature of the Japanese labor market is required. Without this analysis, we recommend careful consideration concerning the use of carbon tax revenues in Japan (as carried out in Chapter 8) in order to find a way that stimulates GDP and employment without worsening the government balance.

Overall, however, the economic case in favor of a carbon tax is quite strong in this chapter, even in the absence of the revenue recycling measures that are discussed in Chapters 8 and 9. If the potential environmental benefits are also factored in, the case becomes stronger still. The next chapters consider ways to further improve implementation and political acceptance of carbon taxes in East Asia by considering some of the social implications.

Notes

1 General government expenditure consists of central and subnational governments, and the social security funds controlled by these units.
2 In particular, in Chapter 8 it was impossible to reduce tax rates to below zero, whereas in this chapter all taxes may be increased.

References

Andersen, M. S., and Ekins, P. (2009). *Carbon Energy Taxation: Lessons from Europe.* Oxford; New York: Oxford University Press.

IMF World Economic Outlook Database (2014 April) http://www.imf.org/external/pubs/ft/weo/2014/01/weodata/index.aspx (accessed June 13, 2015).

Liu, Philip (2011, September 16). 'Taiwan becomes a foreign-debt free nation.' China Economic News Service. http://cens.com/cens/html/en/news/news_inner_37777.html (accessed June 1, 2015).

Pollitt, H., Zhao, Y., Ward, J., Smale, R., Krahe, M., and Jacobs, M. (2012). 'The potential role for carbon pricing in reducing European deficits.' *Global Policy,* 3(3), pp. 1–22. http://www.globalpolicyjournal.com/sites/default/files/pdf/Pollit%20et%20al%20-%20The%20Potential%20Role%20for%20Carbon%20Pricing%20in%20Reducing%20European%20Deficits%2009.12_0.pdf (accessed May 17, 2015).

Resources for the Future (RFF) (2013). *Deficit Reduction and Carbon Taxes: Budgetary, Economic, and Distributional Impacts.* RFF seminar report. http://www.rff.org/Events/Pages/The-Role-of-a-Carbon-Tax-in-Tax-Reform-and-Deficit-Reduction.aspx (accessed May 17, 2015).

11 The distributional effects of low carbon policies in Japan and South Korea

Unnada Chewpreecha and Tae-Yeoun Lee

11.1 Introduction

Discussions on pollution control policies and environmental taxation have traditionally focused on efficiency effects, such as social optimality or cost effectiveness. Recently, however, the distribution of policy costs across socio-economic groups has received increased attention. The fairness of the policy itself is an important issue, and a very unfair or uneven policy burden on a particular group in society may render the policy politically infeasible. In this chapter, we consider the impacts of environmental tax reform (ETR) on different household groups. The impacts on industry, which are closely linked to trade effects, are discussed in Chapter 13.

It is important to note that ETR can affect both household incomes and the purchasing power of those incomes. Most early studies of distributional effects focused on the cost burdens (e.g., through higher fuel costs) to different socio-economic groups, based on their expenditure patterns and the relative weighting of energy-intensive products in those patterns. More recent works, however, have put more emphasis on how household incomes could change as a result of ETR, for example through different methods of revenue recycling. The impacts of environmental regulation on returns to capital and labor have also been investigated.

Our focus in this chapter is the social distributional impact of the ETR that we introduced in Chapter 8. We use the results from the E3ME-Asia model for Japan and Korea; data limitations make the analysis problematic for China and Taiwan.

Recently, income inequality has widened in both Japan and Korea, and economic disparity has become a social problem (see Section 11.2). Furthermore, according to previous studies that assessed the impact of environmental measures, energy taxes can have a significant impact on the incomes of low-income households, meaning that the taxes are regressive overall. We therefore consider the impacts of the ETR in Chapter 8 on income distribution in both countries and also assess how the revenues could be used to reduce the potential burden for low-income households.

The remainder of this chapter is organized as follows. In Section 11.2, we describe income inequality and features of households' consumption expenditure by five income classes in East Asia, with a focus on Japan and Korea. Section 11.3 analyzes the distributional effects of ETR in Japan and Korea using the E3ME-Asia model. Section 11.4 summarizes the scenarios we investigated and Section 11.5 presents the impacts on income distribution. We discuss how ETR could be used to improve income distribution in Section 11.6 and consider the political implications of our findings in Section 11.7.

11.2   Distributional effects of low carbon policies in East Asia

The Gini coefficient is often used to analyze the degree of economic inequality in a country. It has a possible range of values from zero to one, with zero indicating that all individuals have the same income, and one indicating that one individual receives all the income. Silber (1989) constructs a method for analyzing the main factors that determine changes in the Gini coefficient.

Figure 11.1 shows that in 2007 the country with the lowest GINI coefficient was Slovenia, while the country with the highest GINI coefficient was Chile (coefficient levels in 2007 are represented by the bars in the chart). Disposable income inequality rose in 15 of the 32 OECD countries (Israel and Switzerland

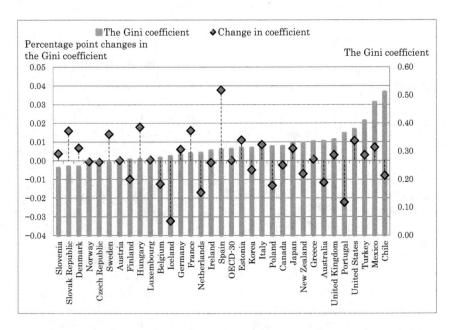

Figure 11.1 The Gini coefficient of household disposable incomes in 2007 and percentage point changes in the Gini coefficient of household disposable incomes between 2007 and 2011.

Source: OECD, 2014.

are missing due to data limitations) between 2007 and 2011. The Gini coefficients of Korea and Japan in 2007, which were 0.312 and 0.329 respectively, were higher than the average of OECD 30 countries. Disposable income inequality fell very slightly in Korea but rose considerably in Japan between 2007 and 2011.

Moreover, the OECD's[1] estimates of annual percentage changes in household disposable income in this period give us an indication of changes in income in different income groups. The figures show that (nominal) incomes in poorer households fell by more than the average in Japan and increased by less than the average in Korea. In other words, at the bottom end of the income scale, both countries became more unequal.

Next, we look closely at the current situation of income and expenditure in Japanese and Korean households. Figure 11.2 shows current patterns of monthly income and expenditure by quintile income groups in Korea. Both income and expenditure are increasing in nominal terms in all income groups over the period 2003–2013, but we can see very low saving rates (and often negative saving rates) in the lowest income group (unit-of-1). We also see that the higher-income groups and worker households have tended to gain more over time, both in relative and – especially – absolute terms.

The share of utility costs[2] in income ranges from less than 4 percent to more than 22 percent in Korea (see Figure 11.3), and there is a clear pattern that the share of utility costs in lower-income groups is higher than that for upper groups. The share of costs is also higher for low-income households and in non-working households, including retired workers and people who are economically inactive. This finding is consistent with analysis carried out for other countries (see below). It means that the economic burden of the carbon tax is likely to fall more on the poorer households and it will, overall, be regressive.

Next, we turn to the situation in Japan. Figure 11.4 shows the current patterns of monthly income and expenditure in workers' households by quintile income groups in Japan.[3] Both income and expenditure decrease slightly over time in all income groups because of deflation, but the lower-income groups tend to show smaller changes, at least in absolute terms. The largest relative drops in income were in the second and third quintiles, and the largest drop in expenditure was in the middle quintile.

The share of utility costs in income is in the range of 5 percent to 9 percent in Japan (see Figure 11.5). The share of utility costs in lower-income groups is higher than the share for upper groups. Moreover, the share of utility costs in income has tended to increase in all income groups over time, with a larger increase in the lower-income groups.

Moreover, when comparing the two countries, we can see that the share of utility costs in Korean households is higher than the share in Japanese households. This means that the impacts of a carbon tax could be stronger for Korean households. In both cases, the impacts seem likely to be felt more strongly in the lower-income groups. Therefore, according to the current situation in both countries, we can assume that new carbon or energy taxes are regressive overall.

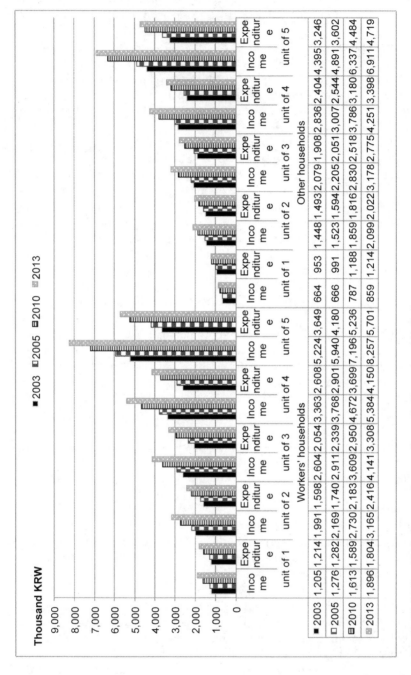

Figure 11.2 Monthly income and expenditures in Korea by quintile income group.

Source: KOSIS, 2014.

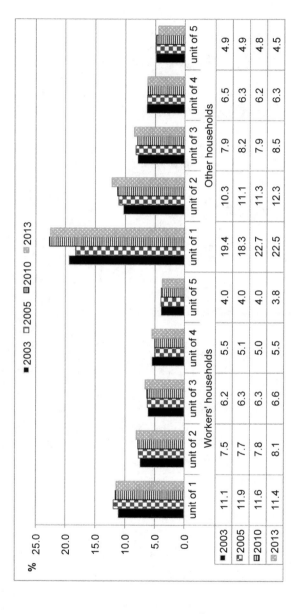

	Workers' households						Other households				
	unit of 1	unit of 2	unit of 3	unit of 4	unit of 5		unit of 1	unit of 2	unit of 3	unit of 4	unit of 5
2003	11.1	7.5	6.2	5.5	4.0		19.4	10.3	7.9	6.5	4.9
2005	11.9	7.7	6.3	5.1	4.0		18.3	11.1	8.2	6.3	4.9
2010	11.6	7.8	6.3	5.0	4.0		22.7	11.3	7.9	6.2	4.8
2013	11.4	8.1	6.6	5.5	3.8		22.5	12.3	8.5	6.3	4.5

Figure 11.3 The share of utility costs in consumption expenditures in Korea by income group.

Source: KOSIS, 2014.

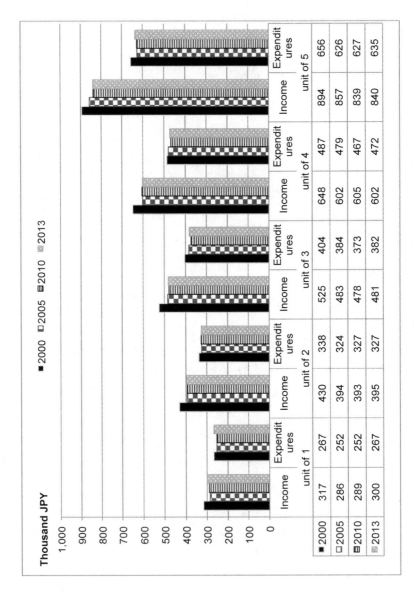

Figure 11.4 Monthly income and expenditures of workers' households in Japan by quintile income group.

Source: e-STAT, 2014.

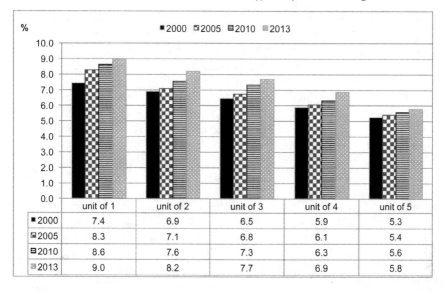

%	unit of 1	unit of 2	unit of 3	unit of 4	unit of 5
■ 2000	7.4	6.9	6.5	5.9	5.3
▨ 2005	8.3	7.1	6.8	6.1	5.4
▤ 2010	8.6	7.6	7.3	6.3	5.6
▨ 2013	9.0	8.2	7.7	6.9	5.8

Figure 11.5 The share of utility costs in consumption expenditures in Japan by income group.

Source: e-STAT, 2014.

Previous research about the distributional impacts of carbon taxes

The distributional implications of ETR depend on several different factors, such as the types of fuel being taxed and, in particular, how the revenues from the taxes are recycled back to the economy. There is quite a wide range of studies that have considered the effects of different types of ETR. Most of these studies show that carbon or energy taxes are regressive overall, but it is also important to note that the findings depend on the country that has been assessed and whether the taxes are applied to motor fuels or to residential heating.[4]

For instance, Speck (1999) showed that carbon or energy taxes are, in general, mildly regressive and that impacts on low-income households are less than expected. The paper also notes that the effects depend on which fuel is taxed and on revenue recycling methods. Ekins et al. (2011) used a previous version of the E3ME-Asia model to produce similar results, although the analysis in this study was only carried out for countries of the European Union.

Fujikawa and Watanabe (2004) analyzed the impacts on regional and household income distribution of a carbon tax in Japan. The authors show that the carbon tax can increase households' expenses and that it is overall regressive, as the price elasticity of utility costs is relatively small. Shimoda and Watanabe (2006) also analyzed the impacts of a carbon tax in Japan on low-income households and obtained the result that the carbon tax is regressive.

Tiezzi (2005) calculated the welfare effects and the distributive impact of a carbon tax on Italian households. She found that a carbon tax results in welfare loss and that the impact on households is not small. However, the distribution of welfare loss across different levels of total monthly expenditure groups did not suggest that the tax is regressive.

Callan et al. (2009) and Bureau (2011) analyzed the effects of carbon taxes and revenue recycling across household income groups in Ireland. They found that the carbon tax is regressive, but if the tax revenue is used to increase social benefits, households in lower-income groups could end up better off.

Heerden et al. (2006) analyzed the impacts of a carbon tax in South Africa using a CGE model. They found the potential for double or triple dividend[5] if the revenues raised from an energy-related environmental tax are recycled back to households and industries by lowering existing taxes. For instance, they found a triple dividend of decreasing emissions, increasing GDP, and decreasing poverty when the revenue of the environmental taxes is recycled through a reduction in food prices.

To summarize, in many previous studies the introduction of a carbon tax was found to be (usually mildly) regressive. However, if the revenues from the carbon tax are recycled so that existing distortions in the conventional tax system are removed (see also Chapter 8), it is possible to increase all incomes. If the revenue recycling focuses on low-income groups, it is possible to make ETR neutral or progressive overall.

11.3   Assessment of distributional effects using the E3ME-Asia model

E3ME-Asia's model of distributional income is relatively basic, including income quintiles and some specific socio-economic groups. The analytical framework was originally developed for European countries and has since been extended to cover non-European regions where data permit. The analysis of distributional income sits outside the main modeling framework because the time-series data required to estimate econometric parameters are not available. This means, for example, that there is no feedback from the distributional analysis to aggregate household expenditure and the different savings rates of each income group. The framework is linked in only one direction to the results of the main model.

The approach is based on two components. The first of these is the income component. For each socio-economic group, the shares of income from wages, benefit payments (pensions and non-pension benefits),[6] and other income (minus tax deductions) are scaled in line with the aggregate model results for wages, benefits, and so on. For example, a scenario that includes increases in benefit rates would show positive results for low-income groups who rely more on benefits. Formally, the income part of the modeling is given as:

$$SERI_{ij} = SRWC_{ij} \times RWS_j + SRBC_{ij} \times \left(0.3 \times RBEN_j\right) + SRPC_{ij}$$
$$\times \left(0.7 \times RBEN_j\right) + SRRC_{ij} \times RRI_j - SRTC_{ij} \times RDTX_j$$
$$- SRTC_{ij} \times REES_j$$

where
$SERI_{ij}$ average disposable income per year in current prices for socio-economic group i in region j
$SRWC_{ij}$ share of income from wages for socio-economic group i in region j
RWS_j E3ME-Asia result for total wages and salaries in region j
$SRBC_{ij}$ share of income from benefit payments for socio-economic group i in region j
$RBEN_j$ E3ME-Asia result for total benefit payments in region j (assuming a 70 percent share of total payments to go towards pensions and a 30 percent share to go towards non-pension-related benefit payments)[7]
$SRPC_{ij}$ share of income from pension payments for socio-economic group i in region j
$SRRC_{ij}$ share of income from 'other sources' for socio-economic group i in region j
RRI_j E3ME-Asia model result for 'other' incomes in region j
$SRTC_{ij}$ share of tax payments from income for socio-economic group i in region j
$RDTX_j$ E3ME-Asia result for total direct tax revenues in region j
$REES_j$ E3ME-Asia result for total employees' social security contribution revenues in region j

The second part of the distributional analysis in E3ME-Asia links household expenditure survey data to the model results for consumer prices by product group. This feature is mainly used to assess the effects of higher energy prices on different socio-economic groups as, in many countries, low-income households use a larger share of their incomes for space heating (see previous section). A rise in energy costs would therefore reduce their real incomes disproportionately, through the equation below.

$$PSE_{ij} = \frac{\sum(BSEC_{ijk} \times VCR_{kj})}{\sum(BSEC_{ijk} \times CR_{kj})}$$

where
PSE_{ij} average price deflator for socio-economic group i in region j
$BSEC_{ijk}$ share of product k in total consumption for socio-economic group i in region j
VCR_{kj} E3ME-Asia result for spending on product k in region j (current prices)
CR_{kj} E3ME-Asia result for spending on product k in region j (constant prices)

The distributional effects in E3ME-Asia are derived from real income effects that are calculated from current price income and the price deflator for each socio-economic group.

$$SRRI_{ij} = \frac{SERI_{ij}}{PSE_{ij}}$$

where

$SRRI_{ij}$ average real disposable income per year for socioeconomic group i in region j

The Gini coefficient is also calculated in E3ME-Asia for each country. The calculation is based on real incomes, because the usual method of calculating coefficients by using nominal incomes would not be suitable in scenarios where prices change. The results from the model scenarios should instead be interpreted as changes in price that are equivalent to changes in real income and, thus, lead to new Gini coefficients. It should be noted that, unlike micro-simulation models, E3ME-Asia does not contain micro-data on individual income distribution, and therefore, the calculation of Gini coefficients is based on quintiles. For the sake of consistency, the results for Gini coefficients in the E3ME-Asia baseline are calibrated to the Gini coefficients published by the World Bank (2014) and Eurostat (2014) for Europe.

To illustrate the distributional impacts from climate policy in E3ME-Asia, we first consider a scenario with a high carbon price and no revenue recycling. The carbon price results in higher energy prices for consumers (e.g., heating fuels and gasoline for cars) and also for products that use energy as an input. According to the household budget survey data that are used in the model, lower-income groups usually spend higher shares of their income on energy for heating than higher-income groups. Therefore, average price inflation (PSE) becomes relatively higher for low-income groups. As a result, real disposable income ($SRRI$) for the lower-income groups decreases by more than for groups with higher incomes.

If the revenues from the carbon taxes are recycled back into the economy, income distribution will also be affected depending on the chosen revenue recycling method. For example, revenue recycling through income tax reductions would benefit higher-income groups more because they have a higher share of their income from employment or earned income ($SRWC$) and, subsequently, pay a higher amount of income tax. So, despite overall net-positive impacts on GDP (see Chapter 8), this method of revenue recycling can produce a worse outcome in terms of income distribution.

Data on income distribution

The structure and format of data on household incomes and expenditure vary between countries. In most countries, data come from surveys such as the figures published in household budget surveys. Owing to the non-uniform nature of data sources, the raw data must be processed to convert them into the E3ME-Asia classifications for socio-economic groups and the model's categories of consumer spending.

In Japan and Korea, for example, due to data limitations, the analysis can only cover six (average, and five quintiles) out of E3ME-Asia's 14 socio-economic groups. In this analysis, we obtained Japanese distributional data from the Family Income and Expenditure Survey (e-Stat, 2014)[8] and Korean distributional data from the Household Income and Expenditure Survey (KOSIS, 2014).[9]

Limitations of the E3ME-Asia approach

The E3ME-Asia calculation of distributional effects is derived from macro-level indicators. This approach allows for consistency with other macroeconomic variables within the model, but it means that the analysis in E3ME-Asia cannot provide the same level of detail compared with results from a micro-level simulation model,[10] which is a modeling tool that is designed specifically for this type of analysis.

It should be made clear that there are many limitations to the E3ME-Asia approach, reflecting the available data, the macro nature of the approach, and the lack of feedback from distributional analysis to the rest of E3ME-Asia model. These include:

- It is not possible to estimate different responses to higher energy costs among the groups. For example, it is often suggested that high-income households have access to finances in order to pay for energy-efficient equipment, which could be reflected by a higher price elasticity. In E3ME-Asia, all income groups implicitly have the same elasticity.
- It is not possible to consider how changes in wage rates affect particular social groups. For example, there is no linkage between sectoral employment and socio-economic groups (as the distributional data do not link to sector of employment), and it is not possible to address differences in wages within sectors.
- The approach cannot address heterogeneity in the groups. For example, model results suggest that higher costs for motor fuels often affect low-income households less, as they are less likely to own a car. But low-income households that do own cars will still be affected.

In summary, the results should be considered carefully in the context of the scenarios modeled and, at times, perhaps viewed with caution. Nevertheless, the approach is able to give at least an indication of the types of distributional effect expected, possibly suggesting grounds for further analysis with a more specialized tool. An example of this type of distributional analysis is provided in Ekins et al. (2011).

11.4 Scenarios

We start with some of the scenarios from Chapter 8 (see Table 11.1) for which the results are presented in Section 11.5. We then develop some new scenarios, which are presented in Section 11.6.

Table 11.1 ETR scenario summary (Chapter 8)

Country	Carbon tax rate	No revenue recycling (N)	Consumption tax reductions (C)	Income tax reductions (I)	Labor tax reductions (L)
Japan (J)	National target (N)	JNN	JNC	JNI	JNL
Japan (J)	Harmonized carbon tax rate (H)	JHN	JHC	JHI	JHL
Korea (K)	National target (N)	KNN	KNC	KNI	KNL
Korea (K)	Harmonized carbon tax rate (H)	KHN	KHC	KHI	KHL

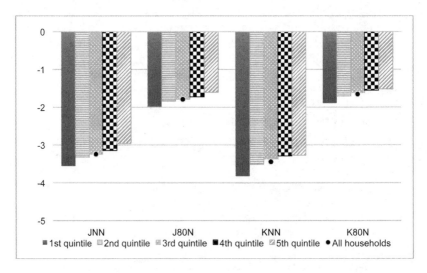

Figure 11.6 Carbon tax impact on real disposable income, 2020 (% differences from baseline).

Source: E3ME-Asia, Cambridge Econometrics (2014).

11.5   Distributional effects in the scenarios described in Chapter 8

As expected, a carbon tax without revenue recycling has a regressive impact on income distribution (see Figure 11.6), because lower-income households spend a larger share of income on energy. The distributional impacts are more obvious in the national target cases, where the carbon tax rates are higher ($154/tCO$_2$ in Japan and $213/tCO$_2$ in Korea; see Chapter 8). Although the introduction of the carbon taxes reduces real income in all groups, it is the lower-income groups that experience larger reductions in their real disposable incomes because of higher energy prices. However, the pattern is not completely negative, as household spending patterns in Korea and Japan reveal that higher-income groups spend a bigger share of their budget on private transport, including motor fuels.

Next we turn our attention to the impact of ETR (i.e., carbon tax with revenue recycling) on the distribution of household income (see Figure 11.7); again, as

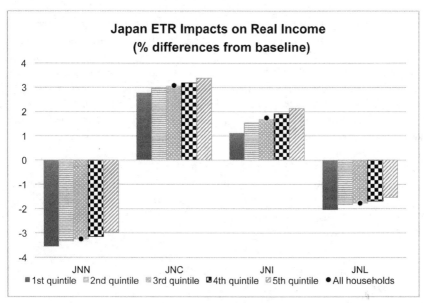

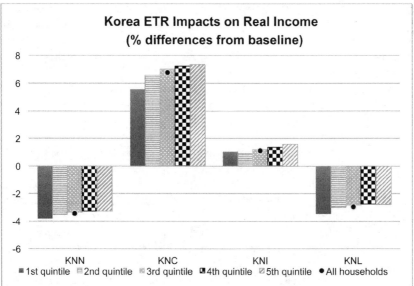

Figure 11.7 Japan and Korea ETR impacts on real income, 2020 (% differences from baseline with no carbon tax).

Source: E3ME-Asia, Cambridge Econometrics (2014).

modelled in Chapter 8. The E3ME-Asia results show that all methods of revenue recycling improve real household income compared to the case without revenue recycling.

For Korea, the labor tax scenario does not have much of a positive impact because the tax rate is already close to zero, meaning that only a small share of the revenues is recycled. We see a similar result for Japan, in which household incomes are still lower than in the baseline; this is because much of the benefit in this scenario accrues to industry rather than to households. A discussion on the Japanese labor market and how it impacts on these scenarios is provided in Chapter 10.

In all ETR cases, the relative impacts on income distribution in Japan and Korea do not change much compared with the no-revenue-recycling case. The higher-income groups benefit more from ETR in all the Chapter 8 scenarios. These groups earn more and consume more; their benefits may be only slightly higher in relative terms, but they are much higher in absolute terms.

The additional demand for employment can also favor higher-income groups. New opportunities could either be for higher skill and higher-paid jobs or for lower skill and lower-paid jobs. Lower-income households also include those comprising retired, disabled or handicapped, or inactive workers and, therefore, would not benefit from additional employment demand brought about by the reduction in taxes.

11.6   Alternative ETRs to address the income distribution issue

In this section, we investigate two additional possibilities for revenue recycling that are designed to directly address the distributional impacts of carbon taxes. First, we investigate the use of a basic income payment as a method of revenue recycling. Second, we look at using carbon revenues to increase benefit payments to all households.

Basic income payment means that revenues from the carbon tax are given back to each household equally, regardless of their socio-economic status – that is, at a fixed amount of payment (e.g., $100 per household). It is not means tested, so both high-income and low-income households receive the same amount, but for the lower-income groups, these payments form a larger share of their income. In modeling circles, this is sometimes referred to as 'lump-sum' payments. It is important to note that in the model, the basic income payment has been added to income rather than wealth (meaning that most of it is spent rather than saved and therefore adds to consumption). As introduced in Chapter 2 and described further in Chapter 9 the modelling approach differs from the standard CGE model, which has strong supply constraints, and this type of boost is met with a higher price response.

Benefit payments in E3ME-Asia are defined as regional social security benefits, other than in kind, paid by the general government. They comprise: social security benefits in cash, privately funded social benefits (e.g., retirement pensions paid

Table 11.2 Alternative ETR scenarios

Country	Carbon tax	Basic income payment (P)	Benefit payment (B)
Japan (J)	National target (N)	JNP	JNB
Korea (K)	National target (N)	KNP	KNB

by an autonomous pension fund), unfunded employee social benefits, and social assistance benefits in cash (e.g., child allowance, welfare affairs, and services).

We have chosen these two examples because they are expected to benefit lower-income households disproportionately. Table 11.2 summarizes the two additional ETR scenarios.

In the short run, both these alternative scenarios produce good results for average household incomes (see Figure 11.8), but they would not be expected to perform so well in the long run. The reason is the timing of labor market responses, particularly on the supply side. Whereas lower income tax rates provide an incentive to work, the basic payment does not, and higher benefits provide a disincentive. In addition, higher benefit rates can boost wages in the short run but, again, this is unlikely to last in the long term. So although we see positive short-term demand stimulus in these scenarios, long-term growth rates are likely be lower.

However, our focus here is on the distribution of incomes. The two alternative ETR methods both produce more equal outcomes regarding income distribution for Japan, although they are unable to entirely reverse all the distributional impacts. For Korea, the basic tax payment reverses the negative distributional effects of the carbon tax, but the higher benefit rate does not have much positive impact. This last result, showing that inequality increases further when benefits are increased, is surprising. Closer examination of the model results suggests that higher benefit rates push up wages in low-paid sectors – including food production – which are passed on as higher costs to goods and services that also constitute a larger share of expenditure for low-income households. Although this result is unlikely to persist in the long term, it does highlight the fact that increases in benefits need to be targeted well.

Table 11.3 summaries the impacts on GDP, the Gini coefficient, and CO_2 emissions for each scenario in Japan. With the exception of reductions in labor taxes, GDP improves in all ETR scenarios compared to the case without revenue recycling (see Chapter 8). Benefits and basic payments produce short-term results that are comparable to the other revenue recycling methods because they directly boost income and the spending power of households. The Gini coefficients indicate that these two alternative ETR scenarios could produce better outcomes in terms of income distribution (apart from non-targeted benefit rates in Korea).

Revenue recycling results in higher levels of economic activity, leading to higher levels of CO_2 emissions compared to the cases without revenue recycling. However, the results do not suggest that the basic payments or the benefit rates produce results that are much different to the other revenue recycling methods.

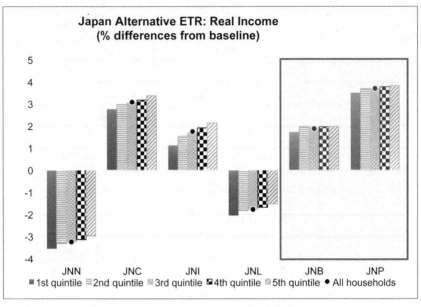

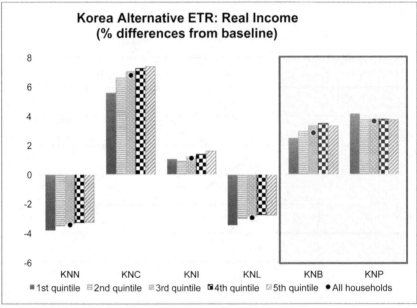

Figure 11.8 Alternative ETR for Japan and Korea: impacts on real income, 2020 (% differences from baseline).

Source: E3ME-Asia, Cambridge Econometrics (2014).

Table 11.3 ETR impacts on GDP, Gini coefficient, and CO_2; summary (2020)

	Japan			Korea			
	GDP	Gini	CO_2	GDP	Gini	CO_2	
	% difference from baseline	percentage point difference	% difference from baseline	% difference from baseline	percentage point difference	% difference from baseline	
JNN	−1.2	0.09	−11.2	−1.0	0.08	−30.1	KNN
JNC	1.5	0.09	−8.4	2.9	0.24	−27.1	KNC
JNI	1.2	0.15	−9.0	0.8	0.09	−29.1	KNI
JNL	−0.7	0.08	−10.7	−0.8	0.10	−30.1	KNL
JNB	1.3	0.04	−8.9	2.7	0.14	−28.5	KNB
JNP	1.2	0.09	−9.0	0.8	−0.09	−29.1	KNP

11.7   Conclusion

The E3ME-Asia results confirm that introducing a carbon tax without revenue recycling is likely to widen the distribution of income in Korea and Japan. The ETR scenarios in Chapter 8 include revenue recycling measures and produce better macroeconomic outcomes for all income groups in Japan and Korea, but the measures are still regressive in all cases. A reduction in the standard rate of income tax provides little benefit to those who do not earn labor income, whereas a reduction in VAT benefits all households proportionately, making no real difference overall. In the case of labor taxes, a reduction in the rate paid can lead to a higher demand for jobs, benefitting those who move into employment, but there is less benefit to other groups.

In this chapter, two alternative methods of revenue recycling were introduced. First, using carbon tax revenues to increase benefit payments, and second, using the revenues to make a basic income (lump-sum) payment to all households. Both of these methods show that it is possible to address distributional impacts while retaining positive GDP impacts. However, the results for Korea indicate that changes to benefits must be targeted in order to avoid unintended knock-on effects.

Although the two alternative methods presented here provide examples of ETR that can address income distribution, policy makers should also consider a longer-term approach to address income imbalances that exist in an economy. One example we have already considered is the possible role for energy efficiency (see Chapter 6). In the next chapter, we investigate another option and explore how revenues from carbon taxes can be used to invest in human capital. This could lead to a more balanced society in the long run.

In conclusion, we have shown in this chapter that the careful use of the revenues from ETR could lead to an improvement in income distribution in the short run. We now turn our attention to how these revenues could be used to address any longer-term imbalances in East Asia's economies.

Notes

1 See the OECD's income distribution database (OECD, 2014).
2 This includes electricity and gas bills, water bills, and related expenditure.
3 In Japan, we can only use workers' household data.
4 The energy expenditure share is defined as either energy/income or energy/expenditure. This is an important distinction. If we use the latter definition, energy taxes tend to be almost proportional. This measure corresponds to the 'lifecycle consumption hypothesis,' and takes into account the fact that richer households save a larger part of their income. Applying the two measures to VAT, we see that it is regressive when using the income definition, but proportional when using the expenditure measure, for the same reason.
5 In general, the term 'triple dividends' is used when revenue-neutral green tax reforms (Pigovian tax) can produce three types of benefit simultaneously.
6 This is any benefits that can be counted as non-wage income; mostly this is pensions, but it also includes other benefits (e.g., child benefits, unemployment benefits).
7 This is roughly estimated from income (by source) data for Japan and Korea.
8 Also you can find the dataset at the following site: Statistics Bureau, Family Income and Expenditure Survey. http://www.stat.go.jp/english/data/kakei/index.htm (August 9, 2014).
9 KOSIS: Average monthly income & expenditure by age of household head. http://kosis.kr/statHtml/statHtml.do?orgId=101&tblId=DT_1L9H020&language=en&conn_path=I3 (August 5, 2014).
10 Microsimulation is a general term for modelling the behaviour and interactions of micro units (persons, households, firms, etc.). Microsimulation models are considered to be more suitable at providing the distributional impacts of tax or benefit policies because the analysis is carried out at micro level (e.g., households). The EUROMOD model (Sutherland, 1997; Navicke, Rastrgina, and Sutherland, 2013) is an example of a microsimulation model. There are ongoing efforts to link it to E3ME, in order to provide a comprehensive modelling framework that covers both the macro and micro aspects of the analysis.

References

Bureau. B. (2011). 'Distributional effects of a carbon tax on car fuels in France.' *Energy Economics*, 33(1), pp. 121–130.
Callan, T., Lyons, S., Scott, S., Tol, R. and Verde, S. (2009). 'The distributional implications of a carbon tax in Ireland.' *Energy Policy*, 37(2), pp. 407–412.
Cambridge Econometrics (2014). *E3ME Technical Manual, Version 6.0*. http://www.camecon.com/Libraries/Downloadable_Files/E3ME_Manual.sflb.ashx (accessed August 20, 2014).
Ekins, P., Pollitt, H., Barton, J., and Blobel, D. (2011). 'The implications for households of environmental tax reform (ETR) in Europe.' *Ecological Economics*, 70(12), pp. 2472–2485.
e-Stat (2014). 'Family income and expenditure survey.' *Portal site of Official Statistics of Japan*. http://www.e-stat.go.jp/ (accessed August 9, 2014; in Japanese).

Eurostat (2014). 'Your key to European statistics.' European Commission. http://ec.europa.eu/eurostat (accessed August 20, 2014).

Fujikawa, K., and Watanabe, T. (2004). 'The burden of carbon tax by income group and region.' In Society of Environmental Economics and Policy Studies (Ed.), *Environmental Tax* (pp. 93–106). Tokyo, Toyo Keizai (in Japanese).

Heerden, J., Gerlagh, R., Blignaut, J., Horridge, M., Mabugu, S.H., and Mabugu, M. (2006). 'Searching for triple dividends in South Africa: Fighting CO_2 pollution and poverty while promoting growth.' *Energy Journal*, *27*(2), pp. 113–141.

Korean Statistical Information Service (KOSIS) (2014). 'Monthly income and expenditures in Korea by quintile income group'. Korean Statistical Information Service. http://kosis.kr/statHtml/statHtml.do?orgId=101&tblId=DT_1L9H006&conn_path=I3 (accessed August 8, 2014; in Korean).

Navicke, N., Rastrgina, O., and Sutherland, H. (2013). 'Using EUROMOD to nowcast poverty risk in the European Union.' Eurostat, European Commission. http://bookshop.europa.eu/en/using-euromod-to-nowcast-poverty-risk-in-the-european-union-pbKSRA13010/ (accessed August 20, 2014).

Organization for Economic Co-operation and Development (OECD). (2014). Income distribution database. http://www.oecd.org/social/income-distribution-database.htm (accessed August 9, 2014).

Shimoda, M., and Watanabe, T. (2006). 'Re-examination of the scheduled carbon tax on the basis of IO analysis: A quantitative analysis on household burden by income class and by region.' *Shogaku Kenkyu, the Business Review of Aichi Gakuin University*, *46*(3), pp. 151–166 (in Japanese).

Silber, J. (1989). 'Factor components, population subgroups and the computation of the Gini index of inequality.' *Review of Economics and Statistics*, *71*(1), pp. 107–115.

Speck, S. (1999). 'Energy and carbon taxes and their distributional implications.' *Energy Policy*, *27*(11), pp. 659–667.

Sutherland, H. (1997). 'Policy simulation at the European level: A guide to EUROMOD.' ISER Microsimulation Unit Research Notes, MU/RN/24.

Tiezzi, S. (2005). 'The welfare effects and the distributive impact of carbon taxation on Italian households.' *Energy Policy*, *33*(12), pp. 1597–1612.

World Bank (2014). 'World development indicators.' World Data Bank. http://data.worldbank.org/data-catalog/world-development-indicators (accessed August 9, 2014).

12 Human capital and environmental taxation in Japan and Korea

Tae-Yeoun Lee, Hector Pollitt, Sung-in Na, and Unnada Chewpreecha

12.1 Introduction

In Chapter 8, we considered the possible economic implications of environmental tax reform (ETR) in the four East Asian economies. The scenarios that were assessed in that chapter looked at the impacts of increasing environmental taxes and of using the revenues to reduce other tax rates.

Many studies have shown that the ways in which the revenues from environmental taxes are used are very important in determining the overall macroeconomic outcomes of fiscal reform. The 'recycling' of revenues back into the economy can take many different forms, for example, by offsetting other taxes (as in Chapter 8) or through higher rates of government expenditure. Several modeling studies have considered uses of revenues to boost rates of physical investment (Goulder, 1995; De Mooij, 2000; Bosque, 2000 and etc.; see Section 12.2 for more details); however, very few studies have assessed the possibility of increased spending on education in order to boost human capital.

Revenue recycling is used to reduce the economic short-term shocks from carbon or energy taxes. In East Asian countries, it is expected that the population will decrease in the future. Thus, in order to achieve both environmental protection and economic growth, it is necessary to increase productivity per capita, energy efficiency, and so forth, by increasing spending on education.

In this chapter, we consider the long-term effects of revenue recycling through education investment to boost human capital. To our knowledge, this policy has not been assessed previously for any country in the world. The methodological approach that we apply using the E3ME-Asia model is also new.

The remainder of this chapter is organized as follows. In Section 12.2, we describe private and public spending on education, and the returns of education (wages, productivity, etc.) in East Asian countries, with a focus on Japan and Korea. Sections 12.3 and 12.4 analyze the effects of human capital investment in East Asia using the E3ME-Asia model. Section 12.5 presents results of the long-term effects of revenue recycling on human capital investment. We discuss how ETR can be used to improve labor productivity in future by boosting human capital in Section 12.6, and the political implications of our conclusions in Section 12.7.

12.2   Background and previous research

The current status of education and training to boost human capital in Japan and Korea

First, we review the population prospects and trends in East Asian countries. According to United Nations (2014), total population in Japan peaked in 2010 and is now decreasing. Moreover, the share of population aged 0–64 was 80 percent in 2010, but will be reduced to about 60 percent in 2050. Although the total populations of China, Korea, and Taiwan may increase in the coming decades, these countries' populations will grow older, as in Japan. This means that a shortage of labor is expected in the future. To overcome labor shortages without excessive immigration, an improvement in labor productivity is necessary.

We therefore discuss how East Asian countries can enhance the quality and quantity of available labor. In order to develop skilled workforces, well-designed education and job training systems, and policies that encourage and enable individuals to participate in learning are required.

In most labor market analysis, educational attainment is used as a proxy measure of human capital and the level of an individual's skill. Education investment to boost human capital can be divided into three stages according to age:

* preschool (preschool program)[1]
* school (schooling)
* post-school (job training)

The returns of human capital investment are different at each stage (see Heckman, 2000). In this chapter, we use 'education' when referring to that part of the population still in school and 'job training' to part of the population who work, that is, those who have left school.

In the following paragraphs, we review education and job training by focusing mainly on Japan and Korea.[2] As education through to junior high school is compulsory in Japan and Korea, the net school enrolment ratios of primary education (elementary school) and secondary education (junior high school, high school, college, etc.)[3] were 90–100 percent in 2012 (World Bank, 2014). Since 2000, tertiary education (university) attainment rates have increased and were higher than the average for OECD countries in 2013 (OECD, 2013). As shown in Figure 12.1, tertiary education attainment rates of adults (defined as 25–64 year-olds)[4] in Japan and Korea are 46 percent and 40 percent respectively. Especially in Korea, tertiary education attainment rates of younger adults increased to about 64 percent in 2011. However, the gap in attainment between younger and older adults in Japan and Korea is 28 and 51 percentage points[5] respectively, which is considerably higher than the OECD average (Figure 12.1).

Next, we review whether educational attainment affects unemployment (Table 12.1). According to the OECD data for 2013 upon which the table is based on, employment rates (unemployment rates) are highest (lowest) among

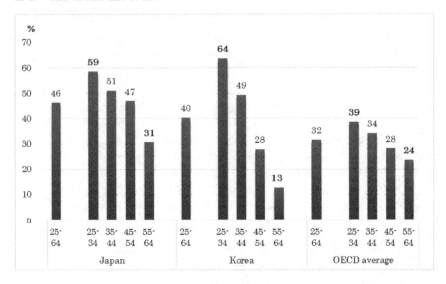

Figure 12.1 Percentage of the population that has attained tertiary education by age group, 2011.

Source: OECD (2013), Table A1.3a. See Annex 3 for notes (http://www.oecd.org/edu/eag.htm).

people with tertiary education across OECD countries. In 2011, the average unemployment rate of adults with upper secondary or post-secondary non-tertiary education in OECD countries was 7.3 percent. The unemployment rates of individuals with upper secondary or post-secondary non-tertiary education in Korea and Japan are lower than the OECD average, at 3.4 and 5.3 percent, respectively. As shown in Table 12.1, unemployment rates among younger adults are higher than among middle-aged adults at all levels of education. The gap between the two age groups is the smallest among tertiary educated individuals: 6.9 percent of younger adults are unemployed compared to 3.9 percent of middle-aged adults across OECD countries. Unemployment rates by age and educational attainment in Japan and Korea are lower than the OECD average, but the pattern between age and educational groups is the same as for other OECD countries.

The data also show that spending more time in education affects earnings. The OECD data for 2013 summarized the relative earnings of adults with income from employment by educational attainment; earnings of younger adults with tertiary education were 22 percent (Japan) and 23 percent (Korea) higher than those of younger adults with post-secondary non-tertiary education. However, earnings of younger adults with lower upper secondary education were 9 percent (Japan) and 15 percent (Korea) less than those of individuals with post-secondary non-tertiary education.

In this chapter, we also consider training schemes in the two countries. There are two types of job training: on-the-job training (On-JT) and off-the-job training (Off-JT). These are defined on the website BusinessDictionary.com

Table 12.1 Status of the labor market sorted by age and educational attainment of the worker, 2011

| | Adults (25- to 64-year-olds) | | | | Younger adults (25- to 34-year-olds) | | | | Middle-aged adults (35- to 44-year-olds) | | | |
| | Upper secondary or post-secondary non-tertiary education | | Tertiary education | | Upper secondary or post-secondary non-tertiary education | | Tertiary education | | Upper secondary or post-secondary non-tertiary education | | Tertiary education | |
	Employ-ment rate	Unemploy-ment rate	Employ-ment rate	Unemploy-ment rate	Employ-ment rate	Unemploy-ment rate	Employ-ment rate	Unemploy-ment rate	Employ-ment rate	Unemploy-ment rate	Employ-ment rate	Unemploy-ment rate
Japan	73	5.3	79	3.5	75	7.5	80	4.6	79	5.2	80	3.1
Korea	71	3.4	77	2.9	63	6.2	75	4.6	74	3.1	78	1.9
OECD average	74	7.3	83	4.8	76	9.5	82	6.9	81	6.8	88	3.9

Note: Employment and unemployment rates are given in %.

Source: OECD (2013), Table A5.5a and A5.5c. See Annex 3 for notes (http://www.oecd.org/edu/eag.htm).

Table 12.2 Off-JT

		Implementation rate of Off-JT	Participation rate of employees	Average learning time in Off-JT	Annual cost per worker
		2013	2013	Hours (Japan: 2007, Korea: 2013)	2013
Japan	Regular worker	69.9%	44.9%	34.6	13,000 JPY
	Non-regular worker	34.1%	18.9%	16.5	
Korea	Regular worker	62.0%	51.5%	36	27,700 KRW
	Non-regular worker		37.3%	28	

Source: e-Stat, 2014a; KOSIS, 2014a.

as 'employee receives training at the place of work, while doing the job' and 'employee receives training at a location different from their normal work environment' respectively.[6] In 2013, implementation[7] of Off-JT for office-based employment was 69.9 percent and 62 percent for regular workers in Japan and Korea respectively (Table 12.2), whereas it was only available for 34 percent of non-regular workers in Japan (but also 62 percent in Korea)[8]. In the places where Off-JT is implemented, the figures suggest that 44.9 percent of regular workers in Japan and 51.5 percent in Korea participate, but only 18.9 percent of non-regular workers in Japan and 37.3 percent in Korea participate.

Finally, we look at trends in productivity in Japan and Korea. As in most other countries, GDP per hour worked (a proxy for labor productivity, in US$) has been increasing over time in Japan and Korea. However, labor productivity per working hour was lower than the OECD average in 2013 in both countries (Figure 12.2). Korean productivity remains substantially less than the OECD average and about half that of the United States, although the average Korean employee works around 2,092 hours per year, or 420 hours more than the OECD average (1,765 hours for Japanese workers).[9] This leads to work–life balance issues in the labor market, in which overwork may cause a decrease in working efficiency and concentration owing to a lack of rest and leisure time.

To summarize, rates of participation in the labor market and rates of employment among tertiary-educated adults are higher than equivalent rates for less-educated adults. Although labor productivity, partly as a result of education and job training, is increasing in Japan and Korea – other factors (such as overwork) are reducing productivity. The figures suggest that there is the potential for education and training to raise productivity further.

Educational inequality recently became a social issue in Japan and Korea because it has become clear that parents' incomes and educational achievements

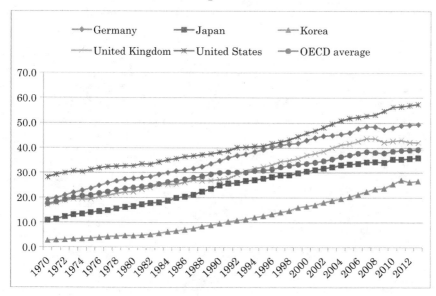

Figure 12.2 Productivity: GDP per hour worked (USD, constant prices, 2005 PPPs).
Source: OECD (2014)

affect the educational opportunities of their children. Using similar data to that in Chapter 11, we can see that the share of education spending in total consumption of low-income households is less than half that of high-income households (Table 12.3). A vicious cycle of poverty and social disparity due to a lower level of income can be found in Japan and Korea, where less education spending in lower-income households may enhance disparities in the next generation (Cingano, 2014).

It should be noted that there is an argument by Becker (1962), Becker and Becker (1998), and Sweetman (2002) that higher education can increase labor productivity, but that sometimes, it may enhance social disparities. However, we think that investment in education in order to support socially disadvantaged groups not only increases productivity but also diminishes these disparities.

Previous research about the double dividend and investment in human capital

We summarized the discussion about 'double dividends' in Chapter 8. The term was first used by Pearce (1991); further research related to double dividends has been conducted by Goulder (1995), De Mooij (2000), Bosque (2000), Bento and Jacobsen (2007) and others. For Japan, the effect of double dividend was analyzed by Park (2002), Kawase et al. (2003), and Takeda (2007) using a computable general equilibrium (CGE) model; however, they obtained different results, in that some studies show that labor income tax

Table 12.3 Monthly real income, expenditure and education spending in Japan and Korea (workers' household of two-or-more-persons, 2013)

Japan (10,000 JPY)	1st income quintile	2nd income quintile	3rd income quintile	4th income quintile	5th income quintile
Income	30.00	39.50	48.11	60.21	83.97
Expenditure	26.66	32.66	38.24	47.21	63.55
Consumption exp.	22.49	26.34	29.85	35.76	45.14
Education	0.80	1.26	1.56	2.37	3.53
Ed./con. exp (%)	**3.6**	**4.8**	**5.2**	**6.6**	**7.8**

Korea (10,000 KRW)	1st income quintile		2nd income quintile		3rd income quintile		4th income quintile		5th income quintile	
	worker	others	worker	others	worker	others	worker	others	worker	others
Income	189.6	85.9	316.5	209.9	414.1	317.8	538.4	425.1	825.7	691.1
Expenditure	180.4	121.4	260.7	202.2	330.8	277.5	415.0	339.8	570.1	471.9
Consumption exp.	148.9	103.0	210.1	165.3	256.7	219.7	310.0	267.4	389.4	355.9
Education	11.8	4.9	19.7	13.0	31.1	24.6	41.0	32.5	51.4	43.8
Ed./Con. exp (%)	**7.9**	**4.8**	**9.4**	**7.9**	**12.1**	**11.2**	**13.2**	**12.2**	**13.2**	**12.3**

Notes: Ed/Con. exp is the share of educational expenditure in consumption.

Source: e-Stat (2014b); KOSIS (2014b).

reduction has the effect of strong double dividend, whereas others attribute this effect to capital tax reduction.

In this chapter, we move beyond the basic definition of double dividend to consider the additional benefits of investment in human capital. Oueslati (2014) and Abdullah and Morley (2014) analyzed the 'triple dividend' effects of carbon taxes. They found that a carbon tax, under the certain conditions, would cut CO_2 emissions, increase economic growth, and reduce economic poverty.

There is also a quite substantial literature about the benefits of training and education. Again we must distinguish three levels of education: preschool, school, and post-school. Mincer (1958) and Becker (1962) estimated the relation between the level of education, income, and productivity. Heckman (2000) and Heckman et al. (2006) analyzed the effect of education by the length of time in education. Also, Higuchi et al. (2005) and Higuchi (2013) analyzed the effects of education and training within a company in Japan. In addition, Higuchi et al. (2005) found job training to increase the wage rates of workers who attend Off-JT to have a positive effect by improving productivity. In Korea, Hwang (2012) analyzed the relationship between the performance of a company and its investment in education and training. According to those studies, investment in education and job training yield a positive return.

Many studies analyze and demonstrate the positive effect that governmental support has on education and training within a company, such as Holzer et al. (1993), Gorg and Strobl (2006), and Lee and Yoo (2011). However, Leuven and Oosterbeek (2000), Abramovsky et al. (2011) and Kim (2009) find empirically that the impact of governmental support in education and job training within a company is negative or, at least, uncertain.

In summary, a number of studies have come to the conclusion that investing in education and job training yields positive returns; however, some studies obtained different results in their analysis on the impact that governmental support has in education and job training within a company. In the next section, we try to account for the effect that investment in school education and post-school education, such as job training, has on productivity. We note that there are many assumptions, only some of which are laid out clearly in the reviewed literature. For example, while personal productivity and ability can be enhanced by investing in education, productivity also depends on other factors, such as individual ability. It is clear that this is an area with the potential for further research.

12.3 Modeling human capital investment effects using E3ME-Asia

Methods

This section assesses the possibility of modeling human capital investment by combining the economic framework provided by the E3ME-Asia macro-econometric model with recent advances in measuring the returns to education. Our starting point is the scenarios that were assessed in Chapter 8, which we then modify to use some of the revenues from the environmental taxes to increase funding for various types of education. The results are compared to both the reference case and the more traditional forms of ETR that are considered in Chapter 8. We then assess the possibility of creating a triple dividend[10] of better environmental outcomes, higher economic production, and a more educated workforce (with social benefits),[11] and assess whether education-led green growth is a sensible strategy in Japan and Korea.

Recent work on estimating the economic returns to education (Gambin et al., 2014) has highlighted several difficulties in estimating the returns at the macro level, such as those noted previously; the return on education depends on personal ability. It should be made clear that we do not try to address all of these issues in this exercise, but further refinements to the methodology could be made in future.

Figure 12.3 outlines the basic approach to the modeling, showing how the revenue recycling can affect both aggregate demand and potential supply. We then apply two additional scenarios each for Japan and Korea, in which some of the revenues from carbon taxation are used to increase (a) spending on school education, or (b) spending on job training. In this chapter, 'education' is rather concerned with school students, whereas 'training' is used when referring to working people. A share of the tax revenues is diverted to the education sector and is represented as an increase in public expenditure in the model (but still maintaining overall revenue neutrality). A corresponding increase in labor productivity is entered exogenously.

In the analysis below we model two labor-market scenarios. In scenario (a), with higher spending on education, we also reduce labor market participation rates to reflect the additional time students spend in full-time studies. However, in scenario (b), with additional work-place training, we assume that the people who receive the training are still able to work.

At this point in the discussion we must return to the differences between E3ME-Asia and the more common CGE modeling approach (see Chapter 2). In a CGE model, where output is determined by supply-side constraints, an increase in labor productivity is guaranteed to lead to an increase in levels of economic production. However, in E3ME-Asia, there will only be an increase in output if there is the demand for the additional products.

The labor market in E3ME-Asia is constrained by the available working-age population and, as the economy approaches full employment, wages increase resulting in cost-push inflation. Despite being usually regarded as largely demand driven, E3ME-Asia does include a measure of expected capacity in other markets through its 'normal' output equations. Normal output represents firms' expectations of future output levels based on developments in the rest of the economy and technology. In the model, it affects price-setting behavior, investment, and import shares; if the expected capacity of future supply increases, then prices are reduced and investment may be delayed, whereas imports may also be reduced if more goods can be sourced domestically.

We follow a Cobb-Douglas style assumption that a 1 percent increase in labor productivity leads to a 1 percent increase in potential output. Whether actual

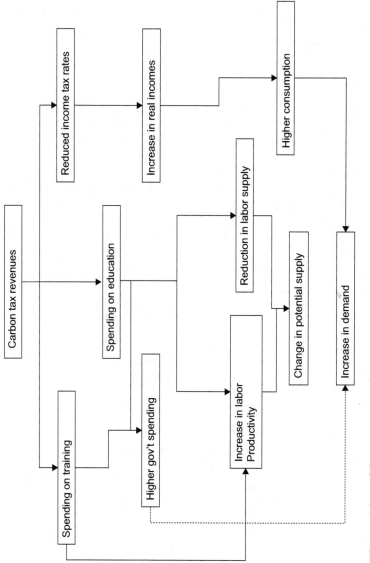

Figure 12.3 Modeling returns to education and training.

output increases by 1 percent depends on the price-setting behavior of the firms involved and whether this creates an increase in aggregate demand.

In this exercise, we have assumed that labor productivity increases across the economy, but it would be possible to restrict the gains to selected economic sectors, for example, to reflect particular training schemes. A formal definition of the relevant equation sets can be found in the model manual (Cambridge Econometrics, 2014). To our knowledge, this representation of labor productivity contributing to easing supply restrictions within a demand-driven framework has not been assessed previously.

Scenarios

The baseline case in this chapter is the same as the one used in Chapter 8. It is a business-as-usual case, in which we assume no additional policy, including in education. Our main 'standard' ETR scenario is also taken from Chapter 8; it is the case in which all East Asian countries meet their national emission reduction targets through ETR, using the revenues from carbon taxes to reduce income tax rates (Table 12.4). As in Chapter 8, the official GHG reduction targets in Japan and Korea are as follows:

- Japan: to reduce GHG emissions in 2020 by 3.8 percent from the 2005 level
- Korea: to reduce GHG emissions in 2020 by 30 percent from the baseline level

We then apply two additional scenarios each for Japan and Korea, in which some of the revenues are, instead, used to increase:

- spending on school education for school students
- spending on job training for working people

Table 12.4 Scenarios

Country of carbon tax	*CO_2-reduction targets*	*Revenue recycling*	*Name of scenario*
Baseline (no reduction)			
J: only Japan	N: national target	I: reduction in income tax	JNI
		E: spending on education	JNE
			JNT
K: only Korea		T: spending on job training	KNI
			KNE
			KNT

It should be noted that the share of revenues that is diverted to spending on education and training is, in fact, quite small (see Table 12.5), so all the tax-reform scenarios have a large reduction in income tax rates.

Data sources

The results from the scenarios depend on the data that are used. There are two critical inputs:

- the cost of the training/education
- the resulting increase in productivity

For the education inputs, we used data from the OECD (2013) report, whereas for information on training schemes, we used the Portal Site of Official Statistics of Japan (e-Stat, 2014a and 2014b) and the Korean Statistical Information Service (KOSIS, 2014a and 2014b) database.

In both cases it is necessary to make some supplementary calculations and assumptions to determine the model inputs. These are described in the following sections.

12.4 Estimating the costs of education/training and the potential efficiency gains

Estimating training costs

A key part of the scenarios is the formation of the estimates of the costs of providing the training and education and the expected gains in productivity. For both elements we must refer to micro-level analysis.

The sources of information for the training scenario are the Ministry of Health, Labor and Welfare data from the e-Stat database (see Table 12.2 in Section 12.2). We assume that 35 percent of Japanese workers are covered by the scheme, amounting to 21,189,700 people over the 17-year period from 2014 to 2030 (i.e., 1,246,450 people per year). At an average cost of 13,000 yen per person, this amounts to an annual cost of 16,203.89 million yen (kept constant in real terms over the period). It is assumed that the training is funded entirely by central government and that this figure is converted to US dollars for use within the model.

Higuchi et al. (2005) provides an estimate that there is a increase in productivity of 11 percent for each worker in the scheme. By multiplying the 11 percent productivity increase by the share of the workforce covered each year (35 percent divided by 17 years), we can estimate the boost to aggregate labor productivity. The estimated figure is 0.2265 percent, and it is assumed to be spread across all economic sectors.

The boosts to productivity are additional each year, so every year up to 2030 labor productivity in Japan increases by another 0.2265 percent compared to the baseline. To simplify the training scenario, we have assumed that the trained workers stay in the labor market (e.g., do not retire), although it is not difficult to modify this assumption.

For workplace training in Korea, the calculation is similar (for the dataset, see Table 12.2). We have assumed that, up to 2030, 32 percent of workers are covered by the training, meaning that 404,400 workers are trained each year. The cost to train each worker is 27,700 Won per annum and so the annual bill is 11.2bn Won, which is paid by the Korean government. The estimated increase in productivity for each worker enrolled in the scheme is around 12 percent, meaning that the resulting change to aggregate labor productivity is quite similar to that for Japan, 0.225 percent per annum (32 percent multiplied by 12 percent, divided by 17; Hwang, 2012). Again, the increases in productivity are allowed to accumulate over time so that, each year up to 2030, the Korean labor force becomes an additional 0.225 percent more productive, compared to the baseline.

Estimating education costs

The calculations for additional spending on education are slightly more complex. We assume that in both Japan and Korea there is a 20 percentage point increase in the number of students receiving tertiary education beyond the current level (60 percent and 64 percent in 2012, respectively and these levels are already quite high by international standards). This means an additional number of 222,612 and 98,372 students from each school year group in Japan and Korea, respectively. We have assumed that the courses last four years, meaning that by the time the measures are fully in place there will be almost 900,000 additional students in Japan and almost 400,000 additional students in Korea. We have assumed that students are not able both to work and start their courses at the age of 19, so labor market participation in the 15–19 and 20–24 age groups is reduced accordingly (assuming a 50 percent male/female split).

The cost of the education is estimated from the OECD figures for 2010 (OECD, 2013), using the average per year of tertiary education per pupil. The additional cost per annum is 16,015 US$ per student in Japan and 9,972 US$ per student in Korea (both 2010 prices). As the program starts in 2014, by 2017 it is in full operation. Costs also increase over this period, and after 2017 they are assumed to remain constant in real terms over the projection period (see 2020 values in Table 12.5). In our scenarios, this cost is entirely met by the national governments using a share of the carbon tax revenues. We note that, in reality, partial subsidies may be a more realistic policy. The remaining carbon tax revenues are used to reduce income tax rates, as in the JNI and KNI scenarios in Chapter 8.

The estimated increases in productivity also come from the OECD report (OECD, 2013). We assume a one-to-one relationship between changes in wages and changes in productivity, suggesting that graduates will be 22 percent (Japan) or 23 percent (Korea) more productive than they would have been without the additional education. Multiplying this figure by the share of the workforce that receives the education (once they have graduated after four years) gives the

Table 12.5 Use of carbon tax revenues in each scenario, 2020, current prices ($bn)

	Carbon tax rate (US$/ tCO₂)	Carbon tax revenues	Tertiary education costs	Training scheme costs	Revenues used for income tax reductions
Baseline	0.0	0.0	0.0	0.0	0.0
Japan: JNI	153.7	131.0	0.0	0.0	131.0
JNE	153.7	131.5	14.6	0.0	116.9
JNT	153.7	131.2	0.0	0.1	131.1
Korea: KNI	213.4	81.2	0.0	0.0	81.2
KNE	213.4	81.3	5.3	0.0	76.0
KNT	213.4	81.8	0.0	<0.1	81.8

Notes: Carbon tax revenues vary slightly between scenarios due to indirect impacts on GDP.

Sources: E3ME-Asia model, authors' calculations.

overall estimate of increase in labor market productivity. Again, this is applied evenly to all economic sectors.

Table 12.5 shows the revenues that are generated from the carbon taxes in 2020, the costs of providing the training and tertiary education (converted to current prices), and the remaining revenues used to reduce income tax rates. It is clear from the table that the costs of the training scheme are much lower than the costs of increasing rates of formal education.

12.5 E3ME-Asia results on human capital investment effects

Introduction to the carbon tax scenarios

The impacts of the carbon tax are discussed in Chapter 8. Here, we use the results for the scenarios in which the national emission reduction targets are met and the revenues from the carbon tax are used to reduce direct income tax rates. We compare the results of the other scenarios, in which a small share of the revenues is diverted to pay for the training or education, to the outcomes in this case. As a sensitivity test, we also evaluate the case where the carbon tax revenues are used to reduce income taxes. Further intuition about the results and the economic mechanisms involved are provided in the next section.

The carbon taxes are set to the same rates across all the scenarios for each country, matching the treatment in Chapter 8. This makes the results easier to interpret, but it should be noted that – in the scenarios with higher GDP – there could be a small increase in emissions, limiting slightly the reductions in emissions from the carbon taxes. This would mean that the carbon targets are narrowly missed and explains why the revenues from the carbon tax vary between scenarios in Table 12.5.

Table 12.6 Results for Japan

Japan	2020			2030		
from baseline (%)	JNI	JNE	JNT	JNI	JNE	JNT
RGDP Real GDP	1.17	1.73	1.47	1.83	3.15	3.64
RCO$_2$ CO$_2$ emission	−9.03	−8.72	−8.91	−10.40	−9.58	−9.00
REMP Employment	0.47	0.53	0.53	0.72	1.16	1.33
CR Consumption	1.54	1.88	2.38	1.92	3.15	4.61
RSK Investment	0.38	0.89	−0.02	1.07	2.26	0.39
RSX Export	0.22	0.36	0.13	0.24	0.47	0.14
RSM Import	−0.39	−0.16	−0.61	−0.71	−0.44	−1.49
RSG Government consumption	0.00	0.96	0.01	0.00	0.72	0.01
RRPD Real incomes	1.67	1.67	2.78	1.83	2.67	4.41
RTCA Carbon tax rate (USD/tCO$_2$)	**153.7**	**153.7**	**153.7**	**181.9**	**181.9**	**181.9**

Source: E3ME-Asia model.

Japan

The carbon tax plus revenue recycling (JNI) produces a double dividend for Japan, with an increase in GDP of around 1.8 percent compared to baseline by 2030. Employment increases by 0.7 percent (Table 12.6).

When some of the revenues are used to pay for education and training, the increases in GDP are larger, reaching more than 3 percent compared to baseline; employment also increases by up to 1.3 percent above baseline levels. Interestingly, the outcomes are quite similar for both the education and training cases, despite the increase in tertiary education being much more expensive; this largely reflects the fact that the productivity impacts are quite similar, while the training/ education costs are matched by additional spending in the education sector.

Emissions in all three cases are very similar, with the Japanese target (3.8 percent reduction in emissions below 2005 levels in 2020, or 9 percent below our baseline value) roughly met in all cases.

Korea

In Korea, the carbon tax plus revenue recycling leads to an increase in GDP of 0.8 percent in 2020 and 1.0 percent in 2030 (see Table 12.7). If some of the revenues are spent on tertiary education and training, the increases in GDP are small compared with those of Japan. The pattern for employment is fairly similar to that for GDP. Investing in education (rather than reducing income taxes) does not have much impact on employment levels because the two effects of higher

Table 12.7 Results for Korea

Korea		*2020*			*2030*		
	from baseline (%)	*KNI*	*KNE*	*KNT*	*KNI*	*KNE*	*KNT*
RGDP	Real GDP	0.76	0.89	0.77	1.04	1.14	1.15
RCO$_2$	CO$_2$ emission	−29.10	−29.09	−28.64	−41.03	−40.88	−40.36
REMP	Employment	0.56	0.48	0.50	−0.04	**−0.05**	0.29
CR	Consumption	0.83	0.48	1.19	0.93	0.99	2.27
RSK	Investment	−0.47	−0.53	−1.00	0.69	0.13	−1.35
RSX	Export	−0.13	−0.14	−0.15	−0.06	−0.09	−0.15
RSM	Import	−1.12	−1.15	−1.09	−0.87	−0.90	−0.57
RSG	Government consumption	0	2.70	0	0	2.01	0
RRPD	Real incomes	0.86	0.52	1.29	0.88	0.98	2.29
RTCA	Carbon tax rate (USD/tCO$_2$)	**213.4**	**213.4**	**213.4**	**252.5**	**252.5**	**252.5**

Source: E3ME-Asia model.

GDP and taking people out of the labor force roughly cancel each other; unemployment is lower, however, because a larger proportion of the people not in employment are, instead, in education. There is, in addition, a small benefit for employment in the training scenario. CO$_2$ emissions fall broadly in line with the Korean target in all scenarios.

In both countries, the results from the modeling show that the introduction of an environmental tax, the revenues of which are used to boost educational and training spending, could have long-term economic benefits in the form of a more productive workforce. However, there may be a significant time delay before the positive effects are realized due to the slow pace of change in the labor force. In this interim period, there may be an economic cost from higher energy prices that erodes domestic real incomes and harms economic competitiveness.

The analysis also suggests that it is important to carefully define the type of education that is boosted through the additional funding. This decision must be taken in the context of national education systems and potential future skills gaps in the domestic labor force.

12.6 How ETR can be used to improve human capital investment effects

One of the most interesting aspects of these scenarios is the interaction between the supply- and demand-side factors. The revenue recycling in the JNI and KNI scenarios that we have taken from Chapter 8 include mainly a boost to aggregate demand in the form of an increase in household incomes. In the education scenario, we divert some of that spending to government expenditure (in the form of spending on education) and, therefore, stimulate a different component of demand (i.e., government consumption rather than household consumption). In fact, this shift provides a small short-term stimulus because some of the money that households would have saved is used to pay for teachers' salaries and equipment in classrooms. In the training scenario, this effect also takes place, but the cost of the training is much less, and so the shift is much smaller.

The longer-term impacts on both the training and education scenarios result from the shifts on the supply side. Both the education and training scenarios provide a boost to potential economic output by improving the productivity of the labor force, although – in the case of the education scenario – there is a short-term cost from having fewer workers available. The increase in potential output affects firms' price-setting behavior, and they reduce prices to increase sales and use the excess capacity. It may also become possible to substitute imports with domestic production. Increased labor productivity on its own will not lead to higher employment levels, but if there is a boost to the wider economy then employment may increase.

As we saw when forming the scenario inputs, the potential increase in worker productivity is quite similar in both the education and training scenarios, but we saw in Table 12.5 that the training schemes are much cheaper. The training schemes may be more attractive to national governments, although it should be noted that the effects of increasing education spending and reducing income taxes roughly balance at macro level.

We should also note that in both the training and education scenarios, there may be non-economic benefits from having a better educated population; these factors are not taken into account in our analysis.

12.7   Conclusion

As carbon pricing gradually becomes established across the world, how to use the revenues is a very important question. Some previous model-based assessments have suggested the possibility of a 'double dividend' if the revenues are used to reduce existing taxes on labor or incomes, or to improve the physical capital stock.

The possibility of using the revenues to invest in human capital has not been explored extensively to date, in part because of difficulties in quantification. We have used a modified version of the E3ME-Asia macro-econometric model to assess the possibility for investment in human capital, drawing on micro-level analysis of education and training schemes. Although there are still many assumptions and possible refinements, we believe that the approach is in general robust and provides an accurate representation of investment in human capital.

Our analysis shows that this option could provide long-term economic, environmental, and social benefits (a 'triple dividend') if the revenues are used efficiently. Investing in human capital has the potential to boost long-term growth through increases in labor productivity, and the model results found GDP levels to be higher when some of the revenues are used this way rather than when all carbon tax revenues are used to reduce income tax rates. Also, in most cases, employment levels increase and unemployment levels decrease, the latter in part because more people are in education.

We tested two scenario variants. In the first case, formal tertiary education is expanded, and in the second, there is a focus on off-the-job training. The model results showed that the impacts on GDP are similar in each case, despite the cost to government of the tertiary education being much higher. This is because much of the education cost is in the form of salaries for teachers that are then spent in the domestic economy.

The conclusion from this chapter is, thus, that the carbon tax plus investment in human capital is a policy that merits serious consideration and further analysis.

Notes

1 Preschool is classified as pre-primary education (nursery and kindergarten) in the International Standard Classification of Education. School is defined as primary education up to tertiary education.
2 The reason for focusing on just these two countries is the availability of relevant data.
3 Secondary education includes lower secondary education (junior high school), upper secondary education (high school) and post-secondary non-tertiary education (college and vocational school). For more detail on the classification of the levels of education, see pages 22–23 of OECD (2013).
4 'Adults' refers to population at the age of 25–64; 'younger adults' refers to 25- to 34-year-olds; 'middle-aged adults' refers to 35- to 44-year-olds; 'upper age adults' refers to 45- to 54-year-olds; 'older adults' refers to 55- to 64-year-olds. The population at working age is the total population aged between 25 and 64, and middle-aged refers roughly to 45- to 64-year-olds, in general.
5 Percentage points is the absolute difference between two percentages.
6 Read more about the definitions of these terms on BusinessDictionary.com: http://www.businessdictionary.com/definition/on-the-job-training-OJT. html#ixzz3AX7MbOz0 and http://www.businessdictionary.com/definition/ off-the-job-training.html#ixzz3AX7hPXjG (accessed August 15, 2014).
7 Implementation means providing the opportunity for workers to participate in the training.
8 Asao (2011) defined regular worker 'as an employee who is hired directly by his/her employer without a predetermined period of employment, and works for scheduled hours', and non-regular workers 'as an employee who does not meet one of the conditions for regular employment. As the three conditions are open-ended, fulltime, and direct employment,' respectively.
9 See more at *Business Korea* (2014), 'Korean workers show lowest productivity in OECD, despite long overtime,' http://www.businesskorea.co.kr/article/3366/ work-life-balance-korean-workers-show-lowest-productivity-oecd-despite-long-overtime (accessed August 16, 2014).
10 In general, the term 'triple dividends' is used when revenue-neutral green tax reforms (Pigovian tax) can produce three types of benefits, simultaneously.
11 For more detail about impacts of investment in education, see Section 12.2.

References

Abramovsky, L., Battistin, E., Fitzsimons, E., Goodman, A., and Simpson H. (2011). 'Providing employers with incentives to train low-skilled workers: Evidence from the UK employer training pilots.' *Journal of Labor Economics*, 29(1), pp. 153–193.

Abdullah, S., and Morley, B. (2014). 'Environmental taxes and economic growth: Evidence from panel causality tests.' *Energy Economics*, *42*, pp. 27–33.

Asao, Yutaka (2011). 'Overview of non-regular employment in Japan.' JILPT (The Japan Institute for Labor Policy and Training) Report No. 10, pp. 1–42. http://www.jil. go.jp/english/reports/documents/jilpt-reports/no.10.pdf (accessed May 18, 2015).

Becker, Gary S. (1962). 'Investment in human capital: A theoretical analysis.' *Journal of Political Economy*, *70*(5), pp. 9–49.

Becker, G. S., and Becker, G. N. (1998). *The Economics of Life*. New York: McGraw-Hill.

Bento, A. M., and Jacobsen, M. (2007). 'Ricardian rents, environmental policy and the "double-dividend" hypothesis.' *Journal of Environmental Economics Management*, *53*(1), pp. 17–31.

Bosquet, B. (2000). 'Environmental tax reform: Does it work? A survey of the empirical evidence.' *Ecological Economics*, *34*(1), pp. 19–32.

Cambridge Econometrics (2014). *E3ME Technical Manual, Version 6.0*. http://www. camecon.com/Libraries/Downloadable_Files/E3ME_Manual.sflb.ashx (accessed August 20,2014).

Cingano, F. (2014). 'Trends in income inequality and its impact on economic growth.' OECD Social, Employment and Migration Working Papers. http:// dx.doi.org/10.1787/5jxrjncwxv6j-en (accessed December 23, 2014).

De Mooij, R. A. (2000). *Environmental Taxation and the Double Dividend*. Amsterdam: Elsevier Science and North Holland.

e-Stat (2014a). 'Basic survey of human resources development.' *Portal site of Official Statistics of Japan*. http://www.e-stat.go.jp/SG1/estat/GL08020101.do?_toGL0 8020101_&tstatCode=000001031190&requestSender=dsearch (accessed July 13, 2014; in Japanese).

e-Stat (2014b). 'Family income and expenditure survey.' *Portal site of Official Statistics of Japan*. http://www.e-stat.go.jp/ (accessed July 10, 2014; in Japanese).

Gambin, L., Beaven, R, Hogarth, T., May-Gillings, M., and Long, K. (2014). 'Methodological issues in estimating the value added of further education, higher education and skills: A review of relevant literature.' BIS Research Paper No. 166, Department for Business, Innovation and Skills, UK. https://www.gov.uk/government/organisations/department-for-business-innovation-skills (accessed June 29, 2014).

Goulder, L. H. (1995). 'Environmental taxation and the double dividend: A reader's guide.' *International Tax and Public Finance*, *2*(2), pp. 157–183.

Görg, H., and Strobl, E. (2006). 'Do government subsidies stimulate training expenditure? Microeconometric evidence from plant-level data.' *Southern Economic Journal*, *72*(4), pp. 860–876.

Heckman, J. (2000). 'Policies to foster human capital.' *Research in Economics*, *54*(1), pp. 3–56.

Heckman, J. J., Lochner, L. J., and Todd, P. E. (2006). 'Earnings functions, rates of return and treatment effects: The mincer equation and beyond.' NBER Working Paper No. 11544.

Higuchi, Y. (2013). 'The dynamics of poverty and the promotion of transition from non-regular to regular employment in Japan: Economic effects of minimum wage revision and job training support.' *Japanese Economic Review*, *64*(2), pp. 147–200.

Higuchi, Y., Kodama, T., and Abe, M. (2005). *Economic Analysis of Labor Market Design: Enhancing the Job-Matching Function*. Tokyo, Japan: Toyokeizai (in Japanese).

Holzer, Harry J., Block, Richard N., Cheatham, Marcus, and Knott, Jack H. (1993). 'Are training subsidies for firms effective? The Michigan experience.' *Industrial and Labor Relations Review*, *46*(4), pp. 625–636.

Human capital and environmental taxaction 209

Hwang, S.-R. (2012). 'Education and training investment and firm performance.' *HRD REVIEW*, 15(1), pp. 190–198 (in Korean).

Kawase, A., Kitaura, Y., and Hashimoto, K. (2003). 'Environmental taxes and double dividend: The simulation analysis by applied general equilibrium model.' *Public Choice Studies*, 41, pp. 5–23 (in Japanese).

Kim, A. (2009). 'The effect of government intervention on the market failure in firm training in Korea'. *Journal of Labour Economics*, 32(2), pp. 125–150 (in Korean).

Korean Statistical Information Service (KOSIS) (2014a). 'Experience of education or training & average hours educated or trained by employment type.' http://kosis.kr/statHtml/statHtml.do?orgId=101&tblId=DT_1DE7083&conn_path=I3 (accessed July 14, 2014; in Korean).

Korean Statistical Information Service (KOSIS) (2014b). 'Family Income and Expenditure Survey.' http://kosis.kr/statHtml/statHtml.do?orgId=101&tblId=DT_1L9H006&conn_path=I3 (accessed July 13, 2014; in Korean).

Lee, C. and Yoo, G. (2011). 'Training incentives in the Korean Levy-Grant System and the performance: Evidences from the KLIPS Data'. *KDI Journal of Economic Policy*, 33(3), pp. 87–120 (in Korean).

Leuven, E., and Oosterbeek, H. (2000). 'Evaluating the effect of tax deductions on training.' *Journal of Labor Economics*, 22(2), pp. 461–488.

Mincer, J. (1958). 'Investment in human capital and personal income distribution.' *Journal of Political Economy*, 66(4), pp. 281–302.

Organization for Economic Co-operation and Development (OECD) (2012). *Better Skills, Better Jobs, Better Lives: A Strategic Approach to Skills Policies*. OECD Publishing. http://dx.doi.org/10.1787/9789264177338-en (accessed July 24, 2014).

Organization for Economic Co-operation and Development (OECD) (2013). *Education at a Glance 2013: OECD Indicators*, OECD Publishing. http://dx.doi.org/10.1787/eag-2013-en (accessed January 25, 2014).

Organization for Economic Co-operation and Development (OECD) (2014). 'Level of GDP per capita and productivity'. OECD.StatsExtracts. stats.oecd.org/Index.aspx?DataSetCode=PDB_LV# (accessed August 18, 2014).

Oueslati, W. (2014). 'Environmental tax reform: Short-term versus long-term macroeconomic effects.' *Journal of Macroeconomics*, 40, pp. 190–201.

Park, S. J. (2002). 'A CGE analysis of environmental tax reform.' *Kokumin Keizai Zasshi (Journal of National Economics)*, Kobe University, Departmental Bulletin Paper, 186(2), pp. 1–16. (In Japanese).

Pearce, D. (1991). 'The role of carbon taxes in adjusting to global warming.' *Economic Journal*, 101(407), pp. 938–948.

Sweetman, Arthur (2002). 'Working smarter: Education and productivity.' *Review of Economic Performance and Social Progress*, 2, pp. 157–180. http://www.csls.ca/repsp/2/arthursweetman.pdf (accessed May 18, 2015).

Takeda, S. (2007). 'The double dividend from carbon regulations in Japan.' *Journal of the Japanese and International Economies*, 21(3), pp. 336–364.

United Nations (UN) (2014). World population prospects: The 2012 revision. http://esa.un.org/unpd/wpp/Excel-Data/population.htm (accessed August 18, 2014).

World Bank (2014). World development indicators: Education statistics. http://databank.worldbank.org/data/home.aspx (accessed August 23, 2014).

13 Competitiveness issues and carbon leakage

Hector Pollitt, Alicia Higson, Sung-in Na,
Seonghee Kim, Yuki Ogawa, and
Park Seung-Joon

13.1 Introduction

In Chapter 9, we concluded that the economic impacts of environmental tax reform (ETR) in East Asia would be limited in scope. In some cases they could even be positive, representing a double dividend from ETR. Furthermore, in Chapters 11 and 12, we showed the potential for social benefits. For the policy maker, this raises the question of why substantial ETR has not been implemented already in the East Asian countries.

This brings us to a crucial road block of who are the winners and losers from policy reform. The issue has already been discussed in the context of households in Chapter 11, when we considered the implications of reform from a social perspective. The concern in this chapter is industrial competitiveness. It is closely linked to international trade.

To a certain extent, the issue we address in this chapter is one of political economy. The modeling of ETR in Chapter 8 acknowledged only a limited role for institutional behavior[1] in determining policy success, and it was assumed that ETR is implemented successfully across all economic sectors. In reality, there will be interest groups lobbying both for and against the policies.

Given that it is inevitable that any policy reform will create winners and losers, the following typical features of the climate policy environment must be considered:

- Losers tend to oppose reform more strongly than winners provide support.
- There is an inherent bias to retain the status quo.
- Many potential losers from ETR have strong political ties.

These aspects should not be underestimated. First, there are two key features of human nature that exert a significant bias in the personal evaluation of policies: we tend to value losses more highly than gains, and we inherently prefer our current position as we aim to minimize regret and transaction cost (see e.g. Khaneman, 2012). These characteristics are compounded by the degree of resources that the potential losers from climate policy can draw on, from being established as existing organizations. While the winners of policy reform may be

(1) individual households, (2) firms that are unaware that they would benefit, or (3) new firms that do not yet exist, established organizations benefit from existing networks (e.g., industry bodies, trade unions) and are able to use these networks to gain political influence. The process of stakeholder engagement that is carried out in many countries has an inherent bias toward existing economic entities.

Arguments about a loss of competitiveness usually play a central role in this debate. The argument is quite simple and intuitively attractive. If there is a carbon or energy tax, then domestic firms will face higher input costs. If they operate in a competitive international market, an increase in costs will require domestic firms to charge higher prices, putting them at a disadvantage to producers in other countries with no ETR. The net result could be a substitution of domestic production with imports, leading to an economic loss (and loss of jobs) and limited or no environmental gain.[2] This series of events is termed 'carbon leakage';[3] it is a specific example of the 'pollution haven hypothesis' put forward by Copeland and Taylor (1994). In an extreme case, there could even be a net increase in carbon emissions if the country to which production shifts is more carbon intensive than the one that introduced the ETR.

The reality is more nuanced. The costs and time required to transport goods mean that it is not always possible or easy to substitute domestic production with imports. It is also rare that imports can provide a perfect substitute – and there are often reasons other than price for preferring a particular brand or home-grown product.

There has been an – often heated – ongoing debate about how one should define a sector that is at risk of carbon leakage. It seems obvious that it must be one that faces an increase in costs from environmental measures, but it must also be one where import substitution is a realistic threat (the sectors included are often referred to as 'energy-intensive trade-exposed,' or EITE sectors). Uncomfortably, these are rather fuzzy concepts that must be quantified in a fairly arbitrary manner. At times the issue has been highly controversial, as it is used to determine the list of sectors that should receive public support in the EU emission trading system (ETS). To these sectors, the decision of whether they are at risk of carbon leakage or not can be worth billions of euros.

At present, a sector in the EU is deemed at 'significant risk of carbon leakage' if:[4]

- Cost as a proportion of gross value added (GVA) increases by at least 5 percent and the sector has a trade intensity greater than 10 percent

Or has either:

- An increase in costs of more than 30 percent

or

- A trade ratio in excess of 30 percent

Although recognized as arbitrary in quantification, similar criteria could be applied to East Asian countries, for example based on the carbon prices that were estimated in Chapter 8.

The macroeconomic models that were used and discussed in Chapters 8 and 9 can also be used to address the question of carbon leakage and competitiveness. However, one must also recognize the limitations of the tools that are imposed by the available data (and, to a lesser extent, economic theory). The structure of this chapter is, therefore, as follows: first we analyze the results from the E3ME-Asia model to see if they show evidence of carbon leakage, then in Section 13.3 we outline the limitations of the modeling. We carry out a more detailed sector-specific assessment in Section 13.4. The final two sections of this chapter draw together the different strands of analysis to produce a broad set of overall policy conclusions.

13.2   Evidence from the modeling

If country A introduces a carbon tax, the formal definition of the rate of carbon leakage is:

(–1) × Increase in emissions in other countries
/ Decrease in emissions in country A

The rate of carbon leakage could be estimated for a single sector or for a whole country.

The true extent of carbon leakage is unknown, but one thing that is clear is that it varies by sector, country, and timeframe. Economists have, for the most part, relied on models to provide estimates of rates of carbon leakage, but the estimates that models produce can be highly dependent on assumptions relating to the mobility of capital and the degree of possible import substitution.

It is also possible to have negative rates of carbon leakage as a result of technology transfer. If environmental regulation stimulates the development of a new technology, this technology could be applied in other countries. A possible example of this phenomenon is the recent reduction in the cost of solar panels, which was a result of policy-induced demand from Europe but has made the technology more competitive globally. Further discussion of negative carbon leakage in the context of the E3ME-Asia model is provided in Barker et al. (2007), whereas Gerlagh and Kuik (2014) use a CGE model to show how carbon leakage and technology spillovers can offset each other. Overall, however, different studies have produced rates of carbon leakage ranging from less than 0 percent to more than 100 percent (i.e., just about anything).[5]

The assessment of the model results in this chapter builds on the modeling that was carried out in Chapter 8. We use the scenarios that considered the national emission reductions[6] in one country at a time and the variants that did not include revenue recycling in order to isolate as much as possible the potential

Table 13.1 Change in emissions, %, and estimated rate of carbon leakage, 2020

	CNN	JNN	KNN	TNN
China	−5.3	0.0	0.0	0.0
Japan	0.1	−11.2	0.0	0.0
Korea	−0.2	−0.1	−30.1	−0.1
Taiwan	0.9	0.0	0.0	−43.7
Rest of world	0.0	0.0	0.0	0.0
Estimated rate of carbon leakage (%)	0.7	−0.5	−0.8	−0.9

Note: See Chapter 8 for scenario definitions.

Sources: E3ME-Asia, Chapter 8 authors.

competitiveness effects of the carbon taxes. As a reminder about the scenario names in Chapter 8, CNN denotes a carbon tax introduced in China to meet the national target with no revenue recycling. JNN, KNN, and TNN denote the same scenarios for Japan, Korea, and Taiwan, respectively.

For each of the four East Asian countries under consideration, we examine the impact a carbon tax on one country has on emissions in each of the other three countries and the rest of the world in 2020. The outcomes for emissions from the E3ME-Asia scenarios described in Chapter 8 are provided in Table 13.1. Estimated rates of carbon leakage are provided in the bottom row.

The table shows that three of the four countries experience small *negative* rates of carbon leakage for their carbon taxes as a whole. This result will appear counter-intuitive to many economists but can be explained by the FTT model (see Chapter 3) and the crucial role of the power sector in decarbonizing the global economy. As one country invests in low-carbon equipment, learning and economies of scale reduce the costs for other countries to invest in the same equipment. This is an example of the potential positive effects of technology transfer. It offsets any carbon leakage effects at aggregate level.

At national level, we see only one example of carbon leakage – from the Chinese package. This is because China has a larger share of basic manufacturing that can be substituted more easily by production elsewhere (e.g., Taiwan). Even so, a carbon leakage rate of 0.7 percent is very small – although, again, it would be higher without technology transfer in the power sector.

In summary, we identify only low levels of carbon leakage from the modeling results. However, it would be somewhat misleading to conclude from the table that there is no carbon leakage. A more appropriate message would be that technology transfer in the power sector may be offsetting leakage effects within other sectors.

The sectoral output from E3ME-Asia provides an indication of some leakage effects. For example, when China introduces its carbon tax, emissions in the Japanese chemicals and non-metallic minerals sectors increase by around

0.5 percent. Emissions from chemicals in Korea increase by 2 percent, and Taiwan sees short-term impacts in the chemicals sector (2 percent) and in non-metallic mineral products (up to 15 percent). Other sectors see less impact, but it seems we cannot rule out carbon leakage altogether, although it is likely to occur only in specific sectors under specific circumstances.

13.3   Limitations of the modeling

The results from the macroeconomic modeling in Chapter 8 suggest that ETR will have only a very limited impact on GDP levels and the short analysis above suggests that carbon leakage will also only be modest at most. However, for two reasons, we believe this does not provide conclusive evidence that there will be no carbon leakage:

- As noted above, macroeconomic models have produced a wide range of possible rates of carbon leakage. A single set of results should not be viewed as definitive.
- It must be recognized that there are limitations to the level of detail that modeling can cover. It would be wrong to assume that there will not be larger localized impacts.

We focus now on the second of these issues. As discussed in the introduction to this chapter, researchers have put a lot of effort into determining ways to identify those economic sectors most at risk from carbon leakage. Typically, the analysis has been carried out at the '4-digit' level, which is much more detailed than the more aggregated '2-digit' level,[7] which is the maximum offered by most macroeconomic models. This is quite an important distinction, as the models make a simplifying assumption that sectoral production in any one country is 'homogenous.' This means that, for example, all production by the non-metallic mineral products sector is assumed to be identical in the modeling, when in reality, the sector comprises glass, cement, and other ceramics; all of which have different production processes. Whereas most people would accept that this assumption does not invalidate the modeling results (although aggregation bias should not be ignored altogether),[8] it must be recognized that there could be real-world impacts that the modeling in its limited resolution cannot identify.

The European Commission identifies nearly 150 sub-sectors in Europe as being at risk of leakage at the 4-digit level,[9] mainly because of their high trade ratios. Grubb, Neuhoff, and Hourcade (2014) notes that six sectors (dubbed the 'Big Six') account for a large share of industrial emissions in Europe; they also highlight the fact that the pattern is consistent across most other countries. The available statistics do not suggest that the case would be different for the East Asian economies, so we will also focus on these sectors as well:

- Iron and steel
- Aluminum

- Refining
- Cement and lime
- Basic inorganic chemicals
- Pulp and paper

In the E3ME-Asia model, these sectors fit mostly within broader sectors; for example iron and steel and aluminum form parts of the more aggregate basic metals sector, whereas cement and lime are part of non-metallic mineral products.

13.4   Detailed sectoral analysis

Whereas detailed econometric analysis of potential carbon leakage in these more precisely drawn sectors has been carried out in Europe, the data available for the East Asian countries are more likely to support a more qualitative assessment approach (which could supplement the more aggregated modelling carried out in Chapter 8). The first stage in our assessment is to estimate the share of energy costs in each sector's production costs; for this we use the most detailed input–output information that is available for each country. The input–output tables inform us of the value of the purchases for a single year of different fuels by each sector. As always when using national data, the sectors do not exactly match up, but we make use of the most detailed information available. One issue to note is that the input–output tables include all purchases, not just energy consumed. A correction must be made for the refineries sector, which purchases liquid oil to process rather than to consume.

The economic value of the fuels must be converted to energy content (by dividing by prices) and then carbon content – using standard Intergovernmental Panel on Climate Change (IPCC) coefficients. The carbon tax rate we use is, again, taken from Chapter 8, although this time we use the harmonized rate for all countries ($82.1/tCO_2$) to aid comparability between countries. Putting all these factors together gives us an estimate of the total direct increase in costs that result from the carbon tax. Our calculation brings us toward one of two metrics that are used by the EU ETS Directive to determine whether a 'sector or subsector shall be deemed to be exposed to a significant risk of carbon leakage.'[10]

Carbon costs / GVA = (direct + indirect costs) / GVA

However, the equation also notes that firms could also face indirect increases in costs. The clearest example is through higher prices charged for electricity. Again, we can combine the input–output information with the model results from Chapter 8 to provide an estimate of cost increase. This additional step is particularly important for the electricity-intensive aluminum sector. Owing to the level of complexity involved (partly in the calculation but, more specifically, in how such a wide range of cost increases could be measured in policy implementation), we do not take into account other indirect cost increases; the indications are that these would be quite small for these basic manufacturing sectors anyway.

Finally, we have also attempted to include CO_2 emissions from production processes (i.e., emissions not based on fuel consumption) using data from the E3ME-Asia model. As the data on process emissions is not highly disaggregated, there is a certain amount of guesswork involved in allocating emissions to sectors, but it is important for the cement and chemicals sectors that these are included.

Faced with an increase in costs, firms in the sector have the choice of raising prices or reducing profit margins. Which of these options they choose (or, more likely, how the options are combined) will depend on the sector's competitive position in international markets; for example, sectors that are highly exposed to trade may have less scope to raise prices. For this information we turn to international trade statistics and estimate trade shares based on the following ratio:

Trade intensity = (imports + exports) / (imports + turnover)

This is the second of the EU ETS Directive's criteria for determining whether a sector is vulnerable to carbon leakage. The numeric thresholds used to identify at-risk groups in the EU are summarized in Table 13.2.[11]

In our assessment, we estimate cost increases by dividing the increase in costs from the carbon tax by existing total costs (including taxes and labor) rather than by GVA. GVA includes labor costs, some taxes, and profits, but does not include material input costs. As, in our view, competitiveness is determined by all costs, using total costs provides a better indicator to use.

We do, however, maintain the 5 percent and 30 percent thresholds to distinguish small and large cost increases in our assessment, even though the cost calculation is different. These are fairly arbitrary boundaries that would need to be revised anyway for application in East Asia, as the European thresholds are unlikely to be suitable.

The estimated increase in electricity price is derived from the E3ME-Asia data on the assumption that all emissions costs are passed on; this tended to give

Table 13.2 Quantitative thresholds for being at risk of carbon leakage

		Trade intensity		
		<10%	*10–30%*	*>30%*
Carbon cost/ GVA	<5%	No	No	Yes
	5–30%	No	Yes	Yes
	>30%	Yes	Yes	Yes

more reliable results than the input–output information, which can include other purchases from companies in the electricity sector.

In order to investigate further the trade impact for the Big Six sectors, data on bilateral trade have been gathered from the UN's Commodity Trade Statistics Database.[12] The categories in this database do not perfectly map onto the input–output (IO) tables, and hence, the data calculated are only indicative of the direction and strength of trade between our chosen and partner countries for these sectors. The arising discussion is intended to supplement the trade ratio calculations and, together, provide an overview of the sector's vulnerability to carbon leakage.

It is worth noting at this stage that the trade patterns for refined petroleum are considerably different from those for the other five product categories. This is due to the nature of fuel refining that takes place in countries that are naturally endowed with a petroleum source. For example, whereas Saudi Arabia and Kuwait provide a large proportion of imports of refined fuel, very little other trade in petroleum takes place with the four East Asian countries.

The results of this exercise are described below.

China

The Chinese input–output table provides a detailed breakdown of eleven sectors that fit into the Big Six sectors we are assessing. Table 13.3 indicates that, in 2007, these sectors accounted for more than 12 percent of total production in China. Our analysis suggests that eight of these sectors see cost increases greater than 10 percent. In accordance with the threshold values presented in Table 13.2, one sector has a high increase in cost – paper and paper products (61 percent increase) – and would be deemed vulnerable solely on the basis of this increase. Refining, steel rolling, and colored metal rolling are all boundary cases. At the same time, only one sector – basic chemical materials – would be (due to a strong flow of imports) classified outright as vulnerable to carbon leakage on the basis of its trade intensity ratio. A further five sectors could also qualify based on the joint criteria, whereas colored metal compounds would be a boundary case.

In contrast, the cement sectors have a very low trade share as these goods are almost entirely produced domestically. This pattern is common across all the countries we analyzed and is due to the heavy nature of the final products.

Together, these indicators point to two sectors as obvious candidates for carbon leakage; basic chemical materials (which is also the largest sector by value-added), and paper and paper products. Both are discussed below in more detail.

China imports a large share of basic chemical products, and the modeling indicated that basic chemical products could be a sector vulnerable to carbon leakage. The top five importers represent 65 percent of the total import flow but no single country dominates. The countries are: Kazakhstan (20 percent),

Table 13.3 Competitive position in China of key sectors

Sector	Sub-sector	Share of total production (%)	Direct cost increase from carbon tax (%)	Direct plus indirect cost increase from carbon tax (%)[13]	Trade ratio (%)[14]
Pulp and paper	Paper and paper products	0.4	58.7	*61.0*	*10.4*
Refining	Processing of oil and nuclear	0.9	29.8	*33.0*	*10.2*
Basic inorganic chemical	Basic chemical materials	3.5	17.2	*19.6*	*38.6*
Cement and lime	Cement, lime, and gypsum	0.2	16.2	*23.2*	*1.4*
	Cement and lime products	1.3	8.2	*13.4*	*0.9*
Iron and steel	Iron	1.2	2.5	*5.7*	*2.1*
	Steel	2.2	2.7	*3.7*	*3.3*
	Steel rolling	0.7	23.0	*31.0*	*15.2*
	Ferrous alloy	0.4	9.7	*12.7*	*26.6*
Aluminum	Colored metal rolling	1.1	22.0	*32.1*	*19.2*
	Colored metals and compounds	1.0	2.8	*5.0*	*16.2*

Source: Calculations by authors from national input–output tables.

Australia (15 percent), the US (11 percent), Germany (10 percent), and Korea (9 percent). China's chemical exports are less concentrated, the most common destinations are the US, Japan, and Korea – and companies in these countries often compete. Overall, high trade levels and a high degree of competition suggest that the sector looks vulnerable to carbon leakage.

The paper and paper products sector has a low trade ratio; exports only account for 4 percent of domestic production and imports are less than 10 percent of total supply. China has a variety of trade partners but the transport costs for the sector's products suggest a lower exposure to carbon leakage.

Japan

Table 13.4 shows detailed input–output data for Japan, allowing us to assess the sectors at a high level of detail. For reasons of conciseness we do not show all sub-sectors that comprise the Big Six industries (these account for about 9 percent of total production in the Japanese economy) but have selected those that match closest our definitions. As Table 13.4 shows, these sub-sectors account for around 5.2 percent of total production.[15] Many of them see cost increases

Table 13.4 Competitive position in Japan of key sectors

Sector	Sub-sector	Share of total production (%)	Direct cost increase from carbon tax (%)	Direct plus indirect cost increase from carbon tax (%)[16]	Trade ratio (%)[17]
Pulp and paper	Pulp	0.1	7.4	8.7	27.6
	Paper	0.2	4.0	5.6	10.0
	Other paper items: paperboard, building paper, and paper products	0.5	0.7	1.0	6.0
Inorganic chemicals	Industrial soda chemicals	0.1	2.1	6.3	5.8
	Compressed gas and liquefied gas	0.0	0.5	5.3	2.3
	Salt	0.0	12.4	12.8	43.5
	Pigments and other industrial chemicals	0.1	2.4	3.0	33.5
Refining	Petroleum refinery products (incl. greases)	1.6	4.0	4.1	19.1
Cement and lime	Cement	0.0	28.6	31.1	6.6
	Other structural clay products	0.0	7.7	8.1	4.7
	Concrete, cement products, pottery, etc., and clay refractories	0.4	1.2	1.4	2.6
Iron and steel	Pig iron	0.2	36.7	37.4	1.9
	Ferrous alloys	0.0	15.3	16.7	60.2
	Crude steel and steel products	1.8	2.0	2.3	15.8
Aluminum	Aluminum (inc. regenerated aluminum)	0.1	1.8	2.0	54.6

Source: Calculations by authors from national input–output tables.

of less than 10 percent due to the relatively low carbon intensity of Japanese industry – including the electricity sector, which has a much smaller additional cost to pass on. The sectors that stand out as being conceivably at risk of carbon leakage (cement, pig iron, and, possibly, ferrous alloys) compose only a very small share of total production (around 0.3 percent) so any impact from the cost increases would have very limited wider impact.

Although not widely traded, the trade statistics show that Japan's main trading partners for the products at risk of carbon leakage are also in East and

Southeast Asia. In particular, China and Korea account for around half of trade in these products with Japan.

In summary we would expect Japan to have only very limited competitiveness and carbon leakage effects. Our analysis also suggests that a degree of cooperation and coordination would substantially reduce negative impacts further.

Korea

The Korean input–output table allows us to disaggregate twelve sub-sectors in our assessment sectors. These sectors account for 11 percent of total production in Korea. This is a relatively large share, but it reflects Korea's history of being competitive in energy-intensive sectors. However, our analysis suggests that only four of these sectors will see cost increases in excess of 5 percent in the carbon tax scenarios (see Table 13.5). The one that stands out is cement (at almost 60 percent). With regard to the trade ratio, the picture is much less positive, as most sectors surpass the 30 percent threshold by a large margin. Indeed, once

Table 13.5 Korea: competitive position of key sectors

Sector	Sub-sector	Share of total production (%)	Direct cost increase from carbon tax (%)	Direct plus indirect cost increase from carbon tax (%)[18]	Trade ratio (%)[19]
Pulp and paper	Pulp	0.0	0.5	7.5	92.7
	Paper	0.3	0.2	3.5	34.6
	Paper products	0.4	0.1	0.6	10.7
Refining	Petroleum products	3.9	6.6	7.0	57.0
Basic inorganic chemicals	Basic inorganic chemical products	0.3	2.4	4.7	62.7
Cement and lime	Cements	0.1	55.8	59.4	10.9
	Concrete products	0.3	0.6	1.4	0.6
Iron and steel	Primary iron, primary steel, and ferroalloys	1.8	21.9	23.1	81.3
	Hot-rolled steel plates and sheets	2.0	0.1	1.8	41.7
	Cold-rolled steel plates and sheets	0.5	0.2	1.1	50.8
Aluminum	Nonferrous metal ingots	0.5	0.6	3.1	68.4
	Primary nonferrous metal products	0.6	0.4	1.1	50.3

Source: Calculations by authors from national input–output tables.

the two metrics have been combined, only two sectors would not be at risk (i.e., paper products and concrete products).

As noted above, Japan and China are key trading partners for energy-intensive products in Korea. These two countries account for an especially large share of Korea's imports (87 percent of cement in 2013). Exports of these products are slightly more dispersed, with the US, Latin America, and the EU also being important trading partners in this respect. However, with high transport costs (especially for cement), it seems less likely that carbon pricing would have a large impact on trade on longer routes.

In summary, our analysis does not suggest that there will be strong competitiveness or carbon leakage effects in Korea. Only one product, primary iron, seems to be exposed. However, with high trade ratios across many products the issue needs to be considered carefully.

Taiwan

The input–output table from Taiwan allows us to identify nine separate sub-sectors that account for around 9 percent of total production. Cost increases for some of these sectors could be fairly large, with an increase of 10 percent or more in six of them. However, the largest increase is not much more than 20 percent (for cement), so one would not expect very large price increases. Indeed, none of the increases in cost surpass the 30 percent threshold.

However, the trade ratios reflect how actively Taiwan participates in international trade. Six of the trade ratios are considerably above the 30 percent threshold for a vulnerable sector, and of the remaining sectors, only one sector does not have a high trade ratio. This sector is cement products, which follows the same pattern as in other countries.

The combination of the two indicators leads us to the conclusion that only paper and cement products are not at risk from carbon leakage. All other sectors could face pressure.

Looking at Taiwan's trade data, we see that – for imports – its main trading partners for the products in Table 13.6 lie mainly within East Asia, as well as the US (e.g., those countries account for two-thirds of inorganic chemicals imports in 2013). Taiwan's export destinations are much more varied, with large shares of exports going to Southeast Asia and a few locations further afield as well. It is difficult to draw firm conclusions from these findings, but as Taiwan is a small country with large trade ratios, it seems that carbon leakage impacts could be important, even though the cost increases to energy-intensive sectors are not as high as in other countries.

Summary

The result of the analysis shown in the above tables is fairly crude and there are many subtleties we cannot capture. We should also bear in mind that data at this level of detail can be somewhat unreliable, and that we have combined

Table 13.6 Taiwan: competitive position of key sectors

Sector	Sub-sector	Share of total production (%)	Direct cost increase from carbon tax (%)	Direct plus indirect cost increase from carbon tax (%)[20]	Trade ratio (%)[21]
Pulp and paper	Pulp and paper	0.2	17.2	17.2	60.2
	Paper products	0.4	4.7	4.7	22.3
Refining	Petroleum refining products	3.6	19.8	19.8	47.3
Basic inorganic chemicals	Basic chemical materials	0.4	16.8	17.2	75.7
Cement and lime	Cement	0.1	23.4	23.4	25.3
	Cement products	0.3	13.1	13.1	0.4
Iron and steel	Pig iron and crude steel	0.7	4.9	15.6	45.9
	Primary iron and steel products	3.1	4.1	4.5	41.7
Aluminum	Aluminum	0.4	6.8	6.8	54.7

Source: Calculations by authors from national input–output tables.

data from several different sources. Nevertheless, our numbers provide a basic indication of what might happen to the most energy-intensive sectors if a carbon tax of $82.1/tCO_2$ was imposed upon them.

Table 13.7 picks out those sectors that appear to be most vulnerable in our analysis. We have defined them as sectors whose cost increases are 15 percent or more and current trade ratios bigger than 10 percent. It must be stressed that this does not exclude the possibility of leakage from other sectors; rather, it defines the scope of our searching.

We can see that the selected sectors account for a relatively small proportion of total production in each country, but this does not imply that they should be ignored in policy making. These sectors account for a much larger share of emissions in the region, and so carbon leakage could reduce significantly the effectiveness of the carbon taxes we have imposed.

It is clear that there are some consistent trends in outcomes. China features prominently because of its low existing fuel costs, meaning that the carbon tax has a larger relative effect. Taiwan also has five sectors in the list because of its high level of trade intensity. Also, the list of sectors is fairly short, although spread across the Big Six group; there are five steel-related sectors, and two each of paper and pulp, refining, chemicals, and cement. This immediately raises the question of whether these sectors should be treated specially and, more generally, how policy makers should respond.

Table 13.7 Summary: competitive position of the most vulnerable sectors

Country	Sector	Share of total production in home country (%)	Direct plus indirect cost increase from carbon tax (%)[22]	Trade ratio (%)[23]
China	Paper and paper products	0.4	*61.0*	*10.4*
China	Processing of oil and nuclear	0.9	*33.0*	*10.2*
China	Basic chemical materials	3.5	*19.6*	*38.6*
China	Steel rolling	0.7	*31.0*	*15.2*
China	Colored metal rolling	1.1	*32.1*	*19.2*
Japan	Ferrous alloys	0.0	*16.7*	*60.2*
Korea	Cements	0.1	*59.4*	*10.9*
Korea	Primary iron, primary steel, and ferroalloys	1.8	*23.1*	*81.3*
Taiwan	Pulp and paper	0.2	*17.2*	*60.2*
Taiwan	Petroleum-refining products	3.6	*19.8*	*47.3*
Taiwan	Basic chemical materials	0.4	*17.2*	*75.7*
Taiwan	Cement	0.1	*23.4*	*25.3*
Taiwan	Pig iron and crude steel	0.7	*15.6*	*45.9*

Source: Calculations by authors from national input–output table.

13.5 Possible policy responses

For sectors whose competitiveness effects appear to be limited, there is no requirement for remedial policy. The situation is much more difficult when competitiveness effects appear to be substantial. As described in Grubb, Neuhoff and Hourcade (2014), there are three ways in which prices could be adjusted to negate the competitiveness effect:

- Reduction of domestic costs
- Increase in import costs
- Adjustment of costs depending on origin/destination

In the past, the EU has opted for the first alternative by allocating ETS allowances to the sectors affected. However, this did not always have the desired effects and has had major unintended consequences within European industry (De Bruyn et al., 2010) while also substantially reducing the revenues available for recycling (which provided the positive economic results in Chapter 8). The second option would require the rest of the world to implement equal carbon pricing and so seems unlikely in reality.

This leaves us with the third alternative as a possible policy outcome in the form of border tax adjustments, which we assess in detail in the next chapter.

13.6 Conclusions

Climate change is a global phenomenon and, if dangerous levels of global warming are to be avoided, emissions must be reduced at global level. However, the prospects for a global carbon reduction policy still seem remote, so we must consider policies at national (or regional) level. National policies that substitute domestic production and levels of emissions with imports do not contribute to the overall effort to reduce global warming.

There is clearly the danger that unilateral carbon pricing and ETR potentially produces this type of result – one with a high cost to domestic industries and little or no global environmental benefit. Industrial firms are usually quick to point out that loss of international competitiveness and possible carbon leakage should be key concerns when implementing ETR. However, if East Asia is to decarbonize its economies, the industrial sector must contribute to reducing emissions.

In this chapter we have adopted a two-pronged approach to assess the potential competitiveness effects of ETR. First, we analyzed further the macro-level modeling results from Chapter 8. In general, the results showed that most reduction in carbon emissions is genuine and does not simply replace domestic emissions with those from other countries (i.e., there is zero or negative carbon leakage). This is an encouraging result for proponents of ETR.

However, we must recognize that the model results are based on assumptions, and there is widespread disagreement about the true extent of competitiveness effects and carbon leakage – including from economic models. Furthermore, the level of detail available in the models is limited by the data sets that they use, and previous analysis has suggested that, within a small number of very specific sectors, there may be much higher rates of carbon leakage. We, therefore, turned our attention to the situation for these sectors in East Asia.

Limitations in the available data mean that the analysis must be fairly qualitative in nature, but the results show that some specific sectors in East Asian countries could face a loss of competitiveness, particularly cement and basic iron production. Trade data suggest that these sectors can, in some cases, be vulnerable to carbon leakage, which raises the question of how policy should respond. Domestic subsidies may be attractive to industry but can create perverse incentive effects and eat into the revenues for recycling. So, in the absence of a global or even regional agreement on prices, we must turn our attention to border tax adjustments.

Notes

1 Broadly speaking, by 'institutional behavior,' we mean the role of interest groups, the media, and other political factors that feature in the policy process.
2 Remembering that, ultimately, it is global emissions levels that matter for global warming, not national totals.
3 This is carbon leakage in geographical terms, which is the most common meaning of the term. It is also possible to have carbon leakage between sectors if a good that is taxed is substituted by one that is not.
4 As the criteria are linked to the EU ETS, the carbon price may vary. In our analysis, we use the harmonized price from Chapter 8 as the basis for our analysis, which is higher than expected prices in Europe. For more information on the European perspective, see http://ec.europa.eu/clima/policies/ets/cap/leakage/index_en.htm.
5 There is now quite a wide range of literature on carbon leakage (see Quirion, 2010). As noted above, studies such as Barker et al. (2007) and Gerlagh and Kuik (2014) show how very low or negative rates of leakage are possible. At the other end of the scale, studies such as Babiker (2005) suggest that leakage rates above 100 percent are possible.
6 The choice of scenario is not important, as the pattern of results is consistent between scenarios.
7 A basic description of international data classifications is provided here: http://en.wikipedia.org/wiki/Industry_classification.
8 This is a tricky issue. In most cases, the weights for the relative sizes of the sectors mean that the price elasticities are accurate, but aggregation bias could occur if a sector combines commoditized products (which, in theory, should have an infinite elasticity) and differentiated products. McDaniel and Balistreri (2002) describe some of the uncertainties surrounding Armington trade elasticities.
9 See http://ec.europa.eu/clima/policies/ets/cap/leakage/docs/carbon_leakage_detailed_info_en.pdf.
10 Art. 10a (15–16) of the ETS Directive (European Parliament and of the Council, 2003).
11 In addition, if a product is close to meeting the criteria, then the qualitative context will also be taken into consideration.
12 Concerning Taiwanese data, a statement is available on the UN website, essentially stating that the 'other Asia nes' (not elsewhere specified) category can be used as a suitable proxy (http://comtrade.un.org/kb/article.aspx?id=10223).
13 Values in bold and italics are 30 percent or over; values in italics are between 5 and 29.9 percent.
14 Values in bold and italics are 30 percent or over; values in italics are between 10 and 29.9 percent.
15 The low value partly reflects the high level of detail of the Japanese IO table, which enabled us to focus our analysis on specific sub-sectors. In the case of other countries' IO tables our target activity may have been combined with ancillary sub-sectors, increasing the apparent importance of the sector.
16 Values in bold and italics are 30 percent or over; values in italics are between 5 and 29.9 percent.
17 Values in bold and italics are 30 percent or over; values in italics are between 10 and 29.9 percent.
18 Values in bold and italics are 30 percent or over; values in italics are between 5 and 29.9 percent.
19 Values in bold and italics are 30 percent or over; values in italics are between 10 and 29.9 percent.
20 Values in bold and italics are 30 percent or over; values in italics are between 5 and 29.9 percent.

21 Values in bold and italics are 30 percent or over; values in italics are between 10 and 29.9 percent.
22 Values in bold and italics are 30 percent or over; values in italics are between 5 and 29.9 percent.
23 Values in bold and italics are 30 percent or over; values in italics are between 10 and 29.9 percent.

References

Babiker, M. H. (2005). 'Climate change policy, market structure, and carbon leakage.' *Journal of International Economics*, *65*(2), pp. 421–445.

Barker, T. S., Junankar, S., Pollitt, H., and Summerton, P. (2007) 'Carbon leakage from unilateral environmental tax reforms in Europe, 1995–2005.' *Energy Policy*, 35, pp. 6281–6292.

Copeland, Brian R. and Taylor, M. Scott (1994). 'North–South trade and the environment.' *Quarterly Journal of Economics*, *109*(3), pp. 755–787.

De Bruyn, S., Markowska, A., de Jong, F., and Bles, M. (2010). 'Does the energy intensive industry obtain windfall profits through the EU ETS?' CE Delft, commissioned by the European Climate Foundation. http://www.ce.nl/publicatie/does_the_energy_intensive_industry_obtain_windfall_profits_through_the_eu_ets/1038 (accessed May 17, 2015).

European Parliament and of the Council. (2003). 'Establishing a scheme for greenhouse gas emission allowance trading within the community and amending council directive 96/61/EC.' Directive 2003/87/EC.

Gerlagh, R., and Kuik, O. (2014). 'Spill or leak? Carbon leakage with international technology spillovers: A CGE analysis.' *Energy Economics*, *45*, pp. 381–388.

Grubb, M., Neuhoff, K., and Hourcade, J. C. (2014). *Planetary Economics*. Abingdon, UK; New York: Routledge.

Kahneman, D. (2012). *Thinking, Fast and Slow*. London: Penguin.

McDaniel, C. A., and Balistreri, E. J. (2002). 'A discussion on Armington trade substitution elasticities.' USITC Office of Economics Working Paper No. 2002–01-A.

Quirion, P. (2010, July 2). 'Carbon leakage: Beyond competitiveness.' Paper presented at the Berlin seminar on energy and climate policy. http://climatepolicyinitiative.org/wp-content/uploads/2011/12/Quirion_Carbon-leakage.pdf (accessed May 17, 2015).

14 The role of border tax adjustments

Park Seung-Joon, Unnada Chewpreecha, and Hector Pollitt

14.1 Introduction

As we have seen in previous chapters, environmental tax reform (ETR) is an effective tool for curbing energy demand and the emissions of greenhouse gases (GHG) (see Chapter 8), and could play a key role in the phasing out of nuclear power (see Chapter 5) with negligible or slightly positive macroeconomic outcomes. However, the inevitable rise in energy prices may lead to serious concerns about industrial competitiveness (see Chapter 13).

If the carbon tax is not internationally harmonized, energy-intensive goods produced in a country with a significant carbon tax rate will become more expensive than those produced in other countries. Countries that do apply a carbon tax may struggle to compete with lower-cost imports and substitution of domestic production with imports might occur. Therefore, the concern is that the reduced competitiveness of domestic goods might lead to a worsening trade balance or the relocation of factories, ultimately impacting on employment levels. Although an IEA information paper suggested that 'changes in exchange rates, energy prices, labour and capital costs are, in many cases, far more significant in a company's decision about where to source supply or locate production than the existence of a carbon price' (Reinaud, 2008, p. 6), measures to reduce the differential in costs seem very important for the political acceptability of ETR.

In this chapter, we study the possibility of introducing a border tax adjustment (BTA) as a remedy to this problem.

14.2 Definition of BTA and its legal legitimacy

As discussed in Chapter 13, concerns regarding competitiveness have acted as a strong disincentive to introduce unilateral ETRs in the absence of sufficient international cooperation. Traditionally, early adopters of ETRs in Europe, such as the Scandinavian countries or Germany, have addressed the issue by introducing exemptions or reductions in carbon/energy tax rates, but this method significantly spoils the environmental effectiveness of these taxes. For this reason, some economists have proposed the introduction of other measures. For example, Stiglitz (2006) mentioned 'sanctions' and the 'energy tariff' (especially against the US) as incentives for cooperation and as instruments to level the playing field. As those concepts were discussed in a somewhat aggressive manner, opponents of the idea often claimed that the measures could be a trigger of trade war or are, indeed, disguised protectionism. When politicians, including former French President Nicolas Sarkozy, proposed the introduction of a carbon tax at Europe's borders during discussions about the EU's 2020 energy and climate package (at roughly the same time as France planned the introduction of a carbon tax), other political leaders in Europe criticized such a 'protective' measure (EurActiv, 2009).

In order to debate this issue more constructively, it is necessary to define what BTA is and to distinguish between non-discriminatory and discriminatory border measures. Namely, BTA is, as explained below, not a trade sanction measure against anti-environmental countries and it does not discriminate between trade partners. Other trade measures may be used as a sanction against any other country in a discriminatory manner (see Table 14.1).

Table 14.1 Border measures related to climate policies

	Concept	*Rules*	*Method*
Non-discriminatory	Border tax adjustment	GATT II: 2 (a) GATT IV:4 SCM agreement	Levy domestic indirect tax on imports and exempt it for exports.
Discriminatory	Anti-dumping duty Countervailing duty	GATT VI SCM agreement	Higher import duty on low-priced or subsidized imports.
	Import restrictions	GATT XX	To keep the effectiveness of domestic laws which are relevant to General Exception of GATT Art. XX ((b) to protect human, animal or plant life or health; (g) conservation of exhaustible natural resources).
	Border adjustments in relation to an emission trading scheme	GATT XX?	For example, importers need to submit emissions certificates for imports

Source: Park, 2014 (modified).

Border tax adjustment

BTA is not a special trade measure for protecting domestic industries but a practice concerning any indirect tax on any commodities that ensures a level playing field for domestic and foreign commodities according to the 'destination principle.' By imposing a domestic tax on imported goods and by refunding it on goods to be exported, BTA may appear as a combination of import tariff and export subsidy but this is not the case. Namely, BTA is explicitly tolerated by the General Agreement on Tariffs and Trade (GATT, see GATT Art. II:2(a) and Art VI:4) and in the Agreement on Subsidy and Countervailing Measures (SCM, see SCM Annex II).[1] In fact, BTA is applied to any domestic indirect tax, such as VAT, alcohol duties, or energy taxes.

The goods eligible for BTA include both final goods and intermediate inputs. The carbon tax levied on fuels consumed in the production process (including production processes of intermediate inputs) is also eligible according to recent judicial precedents (WTO and UNEP, 2009, p. 105). However, there are conditions under which the possibility of BTA is constrained. The two most important principles of the World Trade Organization (WTO) rules are the principles of 'most-favoured nation (MFN) treatment' and of 'national treatment.'

Under the MFN principle, a country cannot treat any trading partner (country) less favorably than any other trading partners. Therefore, it is not permitted to discriminate against trade partners according to what environmental and trade policies they have adopted. Besides this, under the principle of national treatment, imported goods cannot be treated in a less favorable manner than domestic products. Therefore, there needs to be a domestic carbon tax for the BTA to be practicable, and this should be imposed on imported goods at a rate no higher than that on domestic products, regardless of the country of origin (or regardless of their environmental policy). Additionally, the domestic carbon tax imposed on goods to be exported shall be refunded at a rate no higher than that domestically charged, regardless of the destination.

BTA, in this respect, cannot be a trigger of trade war. There is, however, a remaining question concerning the, rather practical, matter of calculating the *implicit* carbon tax per unit of final production so as to eliminate the possibility of discrimination. We think that BTA is not (and needs not be) practicable for *all* products, but could be implemented for limited categories of energy-intensive goods. So in order to apply a BTA that conforms to the national principle, there should be a list of standardized implicit carbon tax rates (like a tariff table) for designated product categories on the basis of *domestic* emission data – based on, for example, best-available technology (BAT) or the predominant method of production (PMP) – reported by *domestic* producers (see, e.g., Holzer, 2014, Chapter 8). The CO_2 emission data of foreign producers does not have to be collected except in cases where importers or foreign producers voluntarily report these for more accurate tax imposition (likely to be rather exceptional). This would be the same as the US Superfund Law, which was legitimized by the GATT Panel (WTO and UNEP, 2009, p. 102).

It would be very difficult to list the carbon contents of thousands of final product categories that often consist of many different parts. However, there is only a limited number of energy-intensive trade exposed goods (or EITE goods), such as steel and chemicals, that will be subject to heavy carbon costs (see Chapter 13). These are also commoditized sectors, and it is relatively easy to define specific CO_2 intensities for them.

In summary, BTA is commonplace in international trade, and BTA of carbon taxes can be practiced in a manner that conforms to WTO rules. It is clearly different from the three categories of discriminatory measures in Table 14.1 (and described in the following section). Every country considering a carbon tax could examine the possibility of introducing BTA, although it should be noted that one European country on its own would not be able to introduce BTA. In this regard, the US or East Asian countries (including all of China, Japan, Korea, and Taiwan) are in a better position to introduce carbon taxes together with BTA. Furthermore, Japan, Korea, and Taiwan are (quasi-)island countries, so it is easier for customs to control imported goods.

Anti-dumping and countervailing duties

Since carbon pricing usually imposes costs on domestic producers, it is, arguably, a kind of eco dumping or unfair subsidization to not cooperate with global climate initiatives. For example, Stiglitz argues that '[. . .] if some country subsidizes its firms, the playing field is not level. A subsidy means that a firm does not pay the full costs of production. Not paying the cost of damage to the environment is a subsidy . . .' (Stiglitz, 2006). Therefore, sanctions using anti-dumping or countervailing duties must be feasible. However, WTO and UNEP have expressed no positive views on this idea (WTO and UNEP, 2009, p. 101).

GATT article XX: general exceptions to the trade rules

The WTO claims that it values environmental protection. According to GATT article XX, any country can implement domestic policy measures and trade measures to achieve environmental policy goals, as long as this is not deemed disguised protectionism.

Environmental protection, in this context, can be not only domestic but also foreign or global. For example, the Shrimp–Turtle Case, the import prohibition taken by the US which banned the import of shrimp from South Asia caught in a manner that harms turtles, was deemed to conform to GATT/WTO rules (WTO and UNEP, 2009, p. 108). Such a dispute demonstrates the extent to which any trade restriction could be tolerated – on the basis of domestic environmental law – against the products of trade partners, who do not set carbon prices or do not take part in a global climate framework. In this case, no complicated practices to calculate the implicit carbon emissions are necessary.

For these measures to be tolerated, certain conditions are necessary. These include 'relevant coordination and cooperation activities undertaken by the defendant at the international level in the trade and environment area, the design of the measure, its flexibility to take into account different situations in different countries, as well as an analysis of the rationale put forward to explain the existence of a discrimination' (WTO and UNEP, 2009, p. 109).

Border adjustments in relation to an emission trading scheme

Border adjustments in relation to an emissions trading scheme (ETS) should be clearly differentiated from BTA. Border adjustments within an ETS means, for example, that importers must purchase allowances or credits to cover the emissions that occurred during the production process. The US Waxman–Markey Bill (HR. 2454) had a corresponding clause. In the case of the EU ETS, this kind of measure is supported only by some member countries, such as France, and remains a future option for mitigating leakage. The standard approach in the EU is to cope with competitiveness issues by giving free allocation of emission allowances. Unlike exemptions from, or reduced rates of, environmental taxes, free allocation does not (directly) affect the effectiveness and efficiency of an ETS given a fixed cap. It does, however, reduce the revenues available to government.

It is difficult to defend border adjustment in an ETS as a type of BTA. First of all, it is hard to treat ETS as a tax, especially when allowances to polluters are given free of charge, but even in the case when allowances are auctioned. Whereas a refund of an indirect tax on exports is allowed in the case of BTA, the refund of carbon costs in the case of ETS may be regarded as an undue subsidy that violates the SCM agreement. There are two possible reasons for this: first, allowances are often given free of charge, and second, the price in carbon markets fluctuates. For example, a steel manufacturer might be given the necessary emission allowances for the production of goods that are to be exported for free, or the manufacturer might have bought them when the allowance price was low; therefore, if the rebate for emission allowance of exported goods – assuming it is based on the current market price – is given when the allowance price is high, the 'capital gain' of the value of emission allowances will be deemed an export subsidy.[2] However, this kind of adjustment might be allowed by the General Exception of GATT Art. XX, as mentioned previously.

14.3   Literature

In the literature, there have been many studies about BTA or border adjustments as part of emissions trading. The last five years saw a strong requirement for this kind of research in the context of the strengthened energy and climate package in the EU, and many concrete legal bills for ETS in the US. In this section we focus on the modeling literature of border adjustments.

Park, Yamazaki, and Takeda (2012) analyzed the effectiveness of BTA (with the same interpretation as in this chapter) in the context of single-country implementation of ETR in the Asia-Pacific region using a static CGE model based on the GTAP 7 database. It was assumed that BTA (a tax on imports and refund for exports) is practiced by each country for *all* traded goods and is based on the calculated average direct domestic carbon emissions in the *domestic* production process per unit of the domestic final product, regardless of the climate policy or carbon tax rates of the *foreign* trading partner. By only considering direct emissions, the study did not include carbon emissions through production of intermediate goods, including electricity. The results show that BTA has a slightly positive impact on exports and slightly negative impact on imports, remedying carbon leakage, with limited macroeconomic effects.

Takeda et al. (2012) used a static CGE model based on the GTAP 7 database to analyze the effectiveness of several anti-leakage measures in the context of domestic ETS introduced only in Japan; namely, import tariffs, rebate of carbon costs for exports, and output-based allocation (OBA) – the free allocation of permits based on sectoral emission intensity and on the level of output. In a legal sense, their measures cannot claim to be BTAs. The rate of tariff and rebate are calculated based on the production sector's intensity of direct emissions (fuel input) and indirect emissions (emissions from electricity generation) without taking the indirect emissions through intermediate products into account. Interestingly, the authors analyzed both cases of import tariff on the basis of emission intensity in Japan and those of foreign countries (especially China). According to their results, import tariffs based on foreign production processes had the best result as an anti-leakage measure because the high emission intensity of China was properly taken into account. The results also showed that it is important to include export rebates as well as import taxes to protect domestic industry. Finally, the study found that OBA is inferior as an anti-leakage instrument.

Using the macro-econometric E3MG model (a predecessor to E3ME-Asia), Pollitt, Summerton, and Thoung (2012) analyzed the effectiveness of border adjustments of ETS in the context of a shift from the EU's 20 percent GHG emissions reduction target to a 30 percent target. The analysis focused on just two industrial sectors in the E3MG model, non-metallic mineral products (representing cement) and basic metals (representing iron and steel and aluminum). 'Border adjustments' in that study are referred to as the CO_2 price (border taxes) imposed on imports to the EU, with no measures on exports. Revenues from adjustments were not recycled in one scenario (i.e., were used to reduce public debt) but were recycled in another (by reducing labor costs). The border tax was designed to off-set the direct carbon costs only, meaning that emissions from electricity were not included. The impact of the border measure was to increase the price of EU imports for basic metals by 6–7 percent and non-metallic minerals by 12–14 percent, and reduce imports by 13.2–15.6 percent and 1.6–1.9 percent, respectively, depending on assumptions. As the E3MG version used in this analysis used the concept of 'pooled trade' rather than the bilateral trade used in E3ME-Asia, it is interesting to compare the results of this study with those given later in this chapter.

Overall, we can draw quite a clear message from the literature. In general, the results of border adjustment analyses are qualitatively very similar, with minor quantitative differences, which are mainly due to different trade elasticities used in the models.

14.4   The design of BTA in our model and our scenarios

In our scenarios we do not apply BTA to all commodity categories because most services are not traded, and most (non-energy-intensive) goods are not strongly affected by the carbon taxes. So a limited number of energy-intensive and trade-exposed (EITE) goods fall into the category for which BTA should be considered. Following on from Chapter 13, which analyzed the six sectors producing those goods ('Big Six'),[3] we select the following four sectors in the E3ME-Asia model (sectoral numbers in the model in brackets):

(a) Wood and paper (no. 7)
(b) Chemicals, excluding pharmaceuticals (no. 11)
(c) Non-metallic mineral products (no. 13)
(d) Basic metals (no. 14)

For the sake of analysis simplicity and transparency, we further assume that each of these sectors produce a single homogenous product.[4]

Table 14.2 summarizes the EITE sectors in each of the four East Asian countries, and shows in the upper half that the share of value added from the four sectors was higher in China (10.78 percent) than Japan (2.65 percent), Korea (6.12 percent) and Taiwan (6.30 percent) in 2012. Overall, these sectors account

Table 14.2 Characteristics of EITE sectors within the E3ME-Asia model

Macroeconomic	Share of country's value added				Share of country's employment			
%, in 2012	China	Japan	Korea	Taiwan	China	Japan	Korea	Taiwan
(a) Wood & paper (no. 7)	0.65	0.49	1.22	0.41	1.32	0.37	0.45	0.35
(b) Chemicals (no. 11)	2.90	0.88	1.59	3.52	0.80	0.46	0.63	3.78
(c) Non-metallic mineral products (no. 13)	2.46	0.41	0.83	0.47	1.26	0.50	0.46	0.39
(d) Basic metals (no. 14)	4.77	0.87	2.47	1.90	1.01	0.66	0.68	2.32
Sum of four sectors	10.78	2.65	6.11	6.30	4.39	1.99	2.22	6.84
Sectoral	Exports over total output				Imports over domestic demand			
%, in 2012	China	Japan	Korea	Taiwan	China	Japan	Korea	Taiwan
(a) Wood & paper (no. 7)	27.2	3.9	5.0	71.2	9.9	25.3	9.1	30.9
(b) Chemicals (no. 11)	7.4	44.7	43.3	35.6	13.8	24.9	39.4	35.2
(c) Non-metallic mineral products (no. 13)	2.7	14.3	5.0	76.6	2.2	8.8	20.6	30.8
(d) Basic metals (no. 14)	0.8	17.3	17.0	12.2	0.9	13.9	20.7	7.9

Source: E3ME-Asia, figures from baseline calculation in 2012.

Note: Value added is the industry value added at market prices (2005 price).

for between 2 percent and 7 percent of total employment in the East Asian countries. The lower half of the table shows the range of import and export ratios. We can see that these ratios also vary between different sectors and countries.

The table shows the aggregate features of the four EITE sectors, which are useful for interpreting the results in this chapter. However, we must bear in mind that these sectors are made up of different sub-sectors, and the characteristics of those sub-sectors may differ widely. Readers who are interested in sub-sectors are referred to Chapter 13.

In order for BTA to conform to international trade law (WTO rules), it must satisfy the principles of MFN treatment and national treatment. Therefore, we have to apply an identical implicit carbon tax rate for BTA (hereafter referred to as 'BTA rate') to the same commodity produced domestically or imported, regardless of country of origin. This means that we do not need to calculate different BTA rates for imports from different origin countries so as to differentiate the rates to reflect the level of climate policy in those countries. The BTA rate for a product will be calculated based on *domestic* emission data reported by *domestic* producers. If the practice of BTA is deemed to conform to the trade law, no trade partner can take retaliatory measures, such as countervailing duties against it (see GATT Art. IV:4 and footnote 1 of SCM Agreement).

In the model, we calculate the BTA rate for any eligible product (sector) as the increase of production costs initiated by the domestic carbon tax using the following two methods. Method 1 (direct): increase of the costs of direct fossil fuel inputs (oil, gas, and coal products). Method 2 (indirect): increase of the costs of direct fossil fuel inputs (oil, gas, and coal products), and increase of the costs of electricity on the basis of the average fossil fuel input per MWh in the domestic power sector.

We do not deal with additional costs (including ripple effects) of other intermediate inputs in this book, although it might be legally possible in practice. After calculating the BTA rates, we apply the border tax, and refund for EITE imports and exports, of course at the same rate for exports and imports, regardless of countries of origin and destination.

For the analysis in this chapter, we set the following three scenario groups:

(a) Baseline (base)
(b) Scenarios without BTA for a single-country carbon tax scenario (CNN, JNN, KNN, TNN)
(c) Scenarios with BTA per (direct) Method 1 (CBT1, JBT1, KBT1, TBT1)
(d) Scenarios with BTA per (indirect) Method 2 (CBT2, JBT2, KBT2, TBT2)

As indicated by the scenario names, the carbon taxes that we apply are consistent with those used to meet the national GHG-reduction targets in Chapter 8. Also consistent with the naming conventions for the scenarios in Chapter 8, we do not apply any revenue recycling in the analysis in this chapter.

In the presentation of our results, we focus on the impact of introducing BTAs (i.e., comparing scenarios c and d with scenario b), but we will also consider the overall impact of the whole potential package (comparing back with scenario a).

14.5   Model results and discussion

Table 14.3 presents the results for the year 2020 for the scenarios that introduced BTA, using both the direct method (c) and indirect method (d), compared to the scenario without BTA (b). When the BTAs also take into account effects of higher electricity costs (d), the impacts increase in magnitude. The overall pattern, however, is quite similar.

The table shows that, in almost all cases, the introduction of BTA leads to an increase in GDP. This increase is driven primarily by an increase in import prices and a reduction in export prices. In our scenarios, the effect of the export refund of carbon tax in BTA is assumed to be rather strong (full pass-through). Exports increase in almost all cases, but the effect on imports is ambiguous; although higher import prices reduce import volumes, imports can increase again because of higher domestic activity levels. The magnitude of the impacts varies across countries. This is due to the different price elasticities of imports and exports, the

Table 14.3 Macroeconomic summary, 2020 (% difference to scenarios without BTA)

	Method 1: direct (c versus b)				Method 2: indirect (d versus b)			
	China	Japan	Korea	Taiwan	China	Japan	Korea	Taiwan
GDP	0.03	0.24	0.01	0.03	0.07	0.37	0.04	−0.02
Imports	−0.04	0.01	0.01	0.19	−0.08	0.04	0.04	0.39
Exports	0.02	0.60	0.04	0.25	0.05	0.97	0.11	0.49
Consumer spending	0.03	0.11	0.00	−0.04	0.06	0.16	0.00	−0.20
Investment	0.01	0.10	0.02	0.06	0.03	0.16	0.04	0.16
Average import prices	0.07	0.26	0.13	0.49	0.15	0.42	0.55	1.53
Average export prices	−0.07	−0.31	−0.12	−0.77	−0.16	−0.51	−0.56	−2.16
Average consumer prices	−0.01	−0.12	0.00	0.07	−0.02	−0.17	0.01	0.33
Employment	0.01	0.06	0.01	0.04	0.01	0.10	0.03	0.10
Carbon tax rate ($/tCO$_2$)	52.44	153.70	213.37	495.44	52.44	153.70	213.37	495.44
CO$_2$ emissions	0.05	0.40	0.02	0.50	0.09	0.62	0.06	0.91
EITE share of value added	10.78	2.65	6.11	6.30	10.78	2.65	6.11	6.30

Source: Authors' calculation using E3ME-Asia.

different carbon tax rates that are imposed (i.e., higher carbon tax implies larger BTA), and the relative sizes of the energy-intensive sectors covered. In the case of China, the carbon tax is set at a relatively low rate, and therefore, the impacts of BTA on the main macroeconomic indicators are small. In Japan, BTA leads to a strong increase in exports and increased GDP levels. For Korea, a reduction in export prices does not cause a large increase in exports. In the case of Taiwan, lower export prices do lead to higher export volumes, but these attract additional imports (despite higher prices) because many of Taiwan's exports are supported by imported materials.

Employment also increases slightly in all four countries due to the competitiveness benefits enjoyed by energy-intensive firms and the slight increase in activity in the wider economy. However, overall – at macro-level – the effects of BTA are limited due to the limited size of the share of EITE sectors in the total share of value added.

One important point to note is that there is a small increase in domestic emissions in BTA scenarios because production that would have taken place abroad now occurs domestically, meaning reduced leakage. This also means that the national emission targets in Japan and Taiwan might not be met in these scenarios, and that, if the targets were to be achieved rigidly, a slightly higher carbon price would be required.

Now we compare the overall results of the domestic carbon tax with BTA (scenario d compared to baseline, or d versus a) with the effects of carbon tax without BTA (scenario b, compared to a; see Table 14.4). The gap between 'd versus a' and 'b versus a' corresponds to the results of 'd versus b' in Table 14.3. We see that, for Japan, the negative impact of carbon taxation on GDP could be reduced by almost a third (even without revenue recycling). However, the impact of BTA on overall GDP is small for the other countries. It is clear that the macroeconomic impacts of BTA are not as large as the impacts of applying revenue recycling measures (see Chapter 8).

Overall, these results suggest that a domestic carbon tax with BTA can be implemented with only small overall cost to the economy, which could be turned into a benefit if revenues were recycled in a manner that enables double dividend. Alternatively, referring back to Chapter 10, we find that a carbon tax with BTA could be a very efficient way of keeping sound fiscal balance, especially for Japan.

Finally we consider the harmonized tax scenario, in which all countries apply the same carbon tax rate.[5] In this way, we can remove the effect of different carbon tax rates across the countries. Table 14.5 presents results for this case, again using the 'indirect' BTA method (d). In this case, the effect of BTA on import and export prices becomes very similar across the four countries (although Taiwan's case is somewhat exceptional). The table, therefore, highlights some other structural differences between the countries. In particular, the response of export volumes to lower export prices is, again, stronger for Japan than for other countries. We can also see that the impact of BTA on imports is positive for Taiwan but negative for China.

Table 14.4 Macroeconomic summary, 2020 (% difference to the baseline)

	Without BTA versus baseline (b versus a)				With BTA versus baseline (d versus a)			
	China	Japan	Korea	Taiwan	China	Japan	Korea	Taiwan
GDP	−0.85	−1.25	−1.00	−2.49	−0.79	−0.88	−0.96	−2.51
Imports	0.17	−2.16	−1.94	−3.43	0.09	−2.13	−1.90	−3.05
Exports	0.04	0.00	−0.19	0.03	0.09	0.97	−0.08	0.52
Consumer spending	−1.42	−2.48	−3.28	−7.61	−1.36	−2.33	−3.28	−7.79
Investment	−0.86	−0.81	−1.42	−2.35	−0.84	−0.65	−1.38	−2.20
Average import prices	0.50	−0.05	−0.08	−1.18	0.65	0.36	0.47	0.33
Average export prices	0.09	0.01	0.04	0.06	−0.07	−0.50	−0.53	−2.09
Average consumer prices	2.96	3.72	3.87	10.01	2.94	3.54	3.89	10.37
Employment	−0.16	−0.50	−0.45	−3.17	−0.14	−0.40	−0.42	−3.07
Carbon tax rate ($/tCO$_2$)	52.44	153.70	213.37	495.44	52.44	153.70	213.37	495.44
CO$_2$ emissions	−5.34	−11.22	−30.14	−43.71	−5.25	−10.67	−30.10	−43.19
EITE share of value added	10.78	2.65	6.11	6.30	10.78	2.65	6.11	6.30
Estimated rate of carbon leakage (%)	0.7	−0.5	−0.8	−0.9	−0.3	−5.8	−1.1	−1.2

Source: Authors' calculation with E3ME-Asia.

Note: The observed negative carbon leakage can be explained by the technology spillover effect of a country's low-carbon policy through the FTT model; see Chapter 13.

As discussed in Chapter 13, low overall economic cost does not mean the absence of people who potentially lose out from ETR, that is, people who may be strongly against the reforms. Therefore, let us turn attention to the EITE sectors. In Tables 14.6 and 14.7, we consider output, export prices, import volumes, export volumes, and employment for each sector. The results are for our main scenarios (described earlier) in which the carbon tax rates are set so that the national emission reduction targets are met as in Chapter 8.

Overall, as the impact of BTA with Method 2 is stronger than Method 1, the former is preferred and, generally, produces more positive results. We can also see quite clearly that the sectoral impact of BTA is, in most cases, far greater than the overall impact at national level.

The results for sectoral export prices show how much BTA reduces the prices of these goods. Exports will also improve with BTA, showing different magnitudes

Table 14.5 Macroeconomic summary (2020), with harmonized tax rates (% difference to scenarios without BTA)

	Harmonized tax rates (d versus b)				Different tax rates (d versus b)			
	China	Japan	Korea	Taiwan	China	Japan	Korea	Taiwan
GDP	0.11	0.21	0.02	0.01	0.07	0.37	0.04	−0.02
Imports	−0.13	0.03	0.02	0.14	−0.08	0.04	0.04	0.39
Exports	0.09	0.55	0.05	0.19	0.05	0.97	0.11	0.49
Consumer spending	0.10	0.09	0.00	−0.05	0.06	0.16	0.00	−0.20
Investment	0.04	0.09	0.02	0.06	0.03	0.16	0.04	0.16
Average import prices	0.23	0.25	0.25	0.35	0.15	0.42	0.55	1.53
Average export prices	−0.27	−0.29	−0.25	−0.68	−0.16	−0.51	−0.56	−2.16
Average consumer prices	−0.04	−0.09	0.01	0.08	−0.02	−0.17	0.01	0.33
Employment	0.02	0.05	0.02	0.03	0.01	0.10	0.03	0.10
Carbon tax rate ($/tCO$_2$)	82.09	82.09	82.09	82.09	52.44	153.70	213.37	495.44
CO$_2$ emissions	0.16	0.35	0.00	0.37	0.09	0.62	0.06	0.91
EITE share of value added	10.78	2.65	6.11	6.30	10.78	2.65	6.11	6.30

Source: Authors' calculation with E3ME-Asia.

of improvement according to the price elasticity of exports. Imports will usually decrease due to higher prices but, in some cases, will increase due to higher demand for imported materials or parts that are used to produce the additional exports.

Table 14.7 compares the scenario results with the baseline. It highlights one key assumption of the analysis, in that reduced export costs of BTA are fully passed on, whereas higher export costs due to carbon prices may not be. If not all of the reduced export costs were passed on, the magnitude of impacts would be smaller but the tenor of the results would be the same.

In some sectors, the effect of BTA on sectoral output and export is remarkably positive (e.g., basic metals in Japan, or non-metal mineral products in Taiwan). For other sectors, however, the effect of BTA on sectoral output is almost negligible, and in this respect, we do not observe the same pattern across countries. Employment effects are in most cases correlated with output.

According to Table 14.7, BTA will over-compensate negative effects of the carbon taxes on industrial output in some sectors, but, in many cases, the sectors will still see a loss of output because of reduced domestic demand resulting from higher prices.

Table 14.6 Sectoral impacts of BTA, 2020 (% difference to the scenarios without BTA)

	Method 1 (direct), c versus b				Method 2 (indirect), d versus b			
Sectoral output (%)	China	Japan	Korea	Taiwan	China	Japan	Korea	Taiwan
a) Wood & paper no. 7	0.21	0.41	0.04	1.07	0.77	0.83	0.13	4.73
b) Chemicals no. 11	0.03	1.46	0.01	0.00	0.06	2.43	0.03	−0.08
c) Non-metallic mineral products no. 13	0.30	1.48	0.14	7.13	0.55	2.33	0.39	11.16
d) Basic metals no. 14	0.01	4.36	0.17	0.30	0.02	6.46	0.55	0.71
Total output of all sectors	0.02	0.33	0.02	0.06	0.05	0.51	0.05	0.06
Sectoral export price (%)	China	Japan	Korea	Taiwan	China	Japan	Korea	Taiwan
a) Wood & paper no. 7	−0.30	−1.81	−0.72	−3.76	−1.19	−4.39	−2.57	−16.38
b) Chemicals no. 11	−0.20	−1.31	−0.44	−1.68	−0.76	−2.15	−2.50	−7.21
c) Non-metallic mineral products no. 13	−6.91	−3.26	−1.50	−17.04	−12.69	−5.03	−3.95	−23.58
d) Basic metals no. 14	−1.30	−4.06	−0.69	−2.12	−1.94	−5.92	−2.15	−5.70
Sectoral import (%)	China	Japan	Korea	Taiwan	China	Japan	Korea	Taiwan
a) Wood & paper no. 7	−0.58	0.29	0.01	0.60	−2.40	0.94	0.04	2.79
b) Chemicals no. 11	0.00	−0.33	0.01	0.08	−0.11	−0.52	0.02	0.16
c) Non-metallic mineral products no. 13	−11.43	−1.03	0.01	7.13	−19.57	−1.55	0.03	11.16
d) Basic metals no. 14	−0.14	−4.10	0.07	0.19	−0.21	−5.84	0.21	0.41
Total imports of all sectors	−0.04	0.01	0.01	0.19	−0.08	0.04	0.04	0.39

(*Continued*)

Table 14.6 (Continued)

	Method 1 (direct), c versus b				Method 2 (indirect), d versus b			
Sectoral export (%)	China	Japan	Korea	Taiwan	China	Japan	Korea	Taiwan
a) Wood & paper no. 7	0.03	4.38	0.31	1.13	0.20	11.08	1.12	5.53
b) Chemicals no. 11	−0.03	1.72	0.00	0.00	−0.12	2.88	0.01	0.00
c) Non-metallic mineral products. no. 13	4.79	5.49	1.54	9.97	9.77	8.69	4.12	15.65
d) Basic metals no. 14	0.60	7.67	0.54	1.16	0.91	11.49	1.71	3.25
Total exports of all sectors	0.02	0.60	0.04	0.25	0.05	0.97	0.11	0.49
Sectoral employment (%)	China	Japan	Korea	Taiwan	China	Japan	Korea	Taiwan
a) Wood & paper no. 7	0.07	0.91	0.04	0.69	0.21	1.92	0.09	3.12
b) Chemicals no. 11	0.00	−0.14	−0.03	0.29	0.00	−0.23	−0.18	1.12
c) Non-metallic mineral products no. 13	0.20	0.55	2.07	0.00	0.39	0.88	4.79	0.01
d) Basic metals no. 14	−0.02	2.97	0.17	0.27	−0.02	4.34	0.54	0.64
Total employment of all sectors	0.01	0.06	0.01	0.04	0.01	0.10	0.03	0.10
Carbon tax rate ($/tCO$_2$)	52.44	153.70	213.37	495.44	52.44	153.70	213.37	495.44

Source: Authors' calculation with E3ME-Asia.

The most important factors that determine the sectoral differences across countries are:

- The degree of the BTA (which corresponds to the carbon tax rate)
- The ratio of trade to total output in the sector
- The price elasticities of demand and trade.

The sectoral features shown in Table 14.2 are, therefore, useful in interpreting the results in Tables 14.6 and 14.7.

Table 14.7 Sectoral impacts of BTA, 2020 (% difference to the baseline scenarios)

	Method 1 (direct), c versus a				*Method 2 (indirect), d versus a*			
Sectoral output (%)	China	Japan	Korea	Taiwan	China	Japan	Korea	Taiwan
a) Wood & paper no. 7	−1.53	−1.52	−1.93	−7.00	−0.97	−1.10	−1.84	−3.63
b) Chemicals no. 11	−0.63	0.67	−0.69	−2.90	−0.60	1.63	−0.67	−2.97
c) Non-metallic mineral products no. 13	−0.45	−0.07	−0.97	4.99	−0.20	0.77	−0.73	8.95
d) Basic metals no. 14	−0.37	0.65	−0.58	−3.69	−0.36	2.68	−0.20	−3.30
Total output of all sectors	−0.66	−2.00	−1.14	−4.00	−0.63	−1.82	−1.10	−4.00
Sectoral export price (%)	China	Japan	Korea	Taiwan	China	Japan	Korea	Taiwan
a) Wood & paper no. 7	−0.30	−1.75	6.75	−3.76	−1.18	−4.33	4.76	−16.38
b) Chemicals no. 11	−0.20	−1.31	−0.23	−1.67	−0.76	−2.15	−2.30	−7.20
c) Non-metallic mineral products no. 13	−6.99	−3.26	−1.50	−17.04	−12.77	−5.03	−3.95	−23.58
d) Basic metals no. 14	−1.27	−4.05	−0.31	−2.14	−1.91	−5.92	−1.77	−5.72
Sectoral import (%)	China	Japan	Korea	Taiwan	China	Japan	Korea	Taiwan
a) Wood & paper no. 7	−0.74	2.12	−1.30	1.47	−2.56	2.78	−1.27	3.68
b) Chemicals no. 11	0.97	−0.89	−0.76	−1.48	0.87	−1.07	−0.75	−1.40
c) Non-metallic Mineral products no. 13	13.97	5.43	−0.37	4.99	3.50	4.88	−0.35	8.95
d) Basic metals no. 14	−2.48	3.73	−0.65	−3.71	−2.54	1.84	−0.51	−3.50
Total imports of all sectors	0.13	−2.15	−1.93	−3.25	0.09	−2.13	−1.90	−3.05
Sectoral export (%)	China	Japan	Korea	Taiwan	China	Japan	Korea	Taiwan
a) Wood & paper no. 7	0.06	4.27	2.23	1.14	0.23	10.96	3.05	5.54
b) Chemicals no. 11	0.50	1.70	−0.05	0.01	0.41	2.86	−0.04	0.01
c) Non-metallic mineral products no. 13	5.16	5.56	2.59	9.89	10.15	8.77	5.20	15.57
d) Basic ,metals no. 14	0.82	7.83	0.30	1.15	1.13	11.65	1.47	3.25
Total exports of all sectors	0.06	0.60	−0.15	0.28	0.09	0.97	−0.08	0.52

(*Continued*)

Table 14.7 (Continued)

Sectoral employment (%)	Method 1 (direct), c versus a				Method 2 (indirect), d versus a			
	China	Japan	Korea	Taiwan	China	Japan	Korea	Taiwan
a) Wood & paper no. 7	−0.74	−2.14	8.92	−4.57	−0.60	−1.16	8.98	−2.27
b) Chemicals no. 11	0.00	−0.30	−0.82	−0.52	0.00	−0.39	−0.98	0.32
c) Non-metallic mineral products no. 13	1.44	1.14	−3.28	0.00	1.63	1.47	−0.70	0.01
d) Basic metals no. 14	−0.51	1.68	−0.15	−2.58	−0.52	3.03	0.22	−2.23
Total employment of all sectors	−0.15	−0.43	−0.44	−3.13	−0.14	−0.40	−0.42	−3.07

Source: Authors' calculation with E3ME-Asia.

When considering the sectoral impacts, it is important to note that the modeling is limited to this relatively aggregated sectoral classification. Within each of these sectors are sub-sectors with quite different characteristics. For example, within non-metallic mineral products, cement stands out as being a carbon-intensive sub-sector. Within basic metals, the iron and steel sub-sector is very carbon-intensive, whereas aluminum is very electricity-intensive in production. The modeling can only provide an average impact for the more aggregate sector. For a more detailed analysis we must refer back to Chapter 13.

14.6   Conclusions

In this chapter we have analyzed the effects of BTA as an anti-carbon-leakage measure that, arguably, conforms to WTO rules. The results of our analysis show that BTA very effectively reduces the export prices of EITE sectors through export rebates of the carbon tax, leading to higher export volumes (see Table 14.6). It should be noted that the effect of the export refund of carbon tax in BTA is assumed to be rather strong (full pass-through), whereas the price effect of the carbon tax on energy inputs is not so strong (partial pass-through). This, in our view, is a realistic assumption about how sectors form their prices but additional testing showed that it does not have a major impact on our results.

The impact on imports of EITE products is rather ambiguous because import volumes depend on overall activity levels as well as changes in import prices.

The effects of BTA on output and employment in the EITE sectors are also positive (see Table 14.6), but BTA may not be enough to compensate the overall negative impacts of the carbon taxes within some sectors (see Table 14.7). This is because domestic demand for energy intensive goods will inevitably be reduced by higher domestic prices, which is of course part of the purpose of the carbon tax. In order to fully 'neutralize' the negative impact of the carbon tax on EITE sectors, a sort of undesirable subsidy or regulation, which would deliberately maintain the position of the existing 'polluting industry,' would be required. Nevertheless, BTA contributes to guaranteeing a level playing field for domestic and foreign producers in the EITE sectors, addressing the carbon leakage debate.

The overall impact of BTA on the national economy is positive but small, reflecting the fact that the EITE sectors account for only a limited share of the economy in terms of value added and employment. So although we see a role for BTA in protecting certain domestic industries, the negative effects of the carbon tax on the economy as a whole would be more effectively addressed by revenue recycling, with possible double dividends.

Notes

1 According to footnote 1 of the SCM Agreement, 'The exemption of an exported product from duties or taxes borne by the like product when destined for domestic consumption, or the remission of such duties or taxes in amounts not in excess of those which have accrued, shall not be deemed to be a subsidy.'
2 GATT Art. II:2 states,

> Nothing in this Article shall prevent any contracting party from imposing at any time on the importation of any product: (a) a charge equivalent to an internal tax imposed consistently with the provisions of paragraph 2 of Article III in respect of the like domestic product or in respect of an article from which the imported product has been manufactured or produced in whole or in part.

Art. VI:4 reads,

> No product of the territory of any contracting party imported into the territory of any other contracting party shall be subject to antidumping or countervailing duty by reason of the exemption of such product from duties or taxes borne by the like product when destined for consumption in the country of origin or exportation, or by reason of the refund of such duties or taxes.

Furthermore, SCM's Annex II includes 'Guidelines on Consumption of Inputs in the Production Process' for indirect tax rebate schemes. For detailed discussion on this issue, see Holzer, 2014, pp. 233–236.

3 The Big Six in Chapter 13 comprise (1) iron and steel, (2) aluminum, (3) refining, (4) cement and lime, (5) basic inorganic chemicals, (6) pulp and paper. In the E3ME-Asia model, these sectors fit mostly within broader sectors; for example iron/steel and aluminum are part of the more aggregate basic metals sector, whereas cement and lime are part of non-metallic mineral products.
4 Clearly, making this assumption is a shortcoming of the analysis. It demonstrates the importance of combining the modeling, which assesses the links between sectors and regions, with the more detailed single-sector analysis in Chapter 13.
5 Again, see Chapter 8 for more details, but in summary, this tax rate is higher in China than the one that meets the national target. It is lower in the other three countries.

References

EurActiv (2009, September 14). 'Sarkozy renews pressure for CO_2 border tax.' http://www.euractiv.com/climate-change/sarkozy-renews-pressure-co2-bord-news-222460 (accessed June 1, 2015).

Holzer, Kateryna (2014). *Carbon-Related Border Adjustment and WTO Law*. Cheltenham: Edward Elgar.

Park, Seung-Joon (2014). 'Unilateral initiatives for carbon pricing after Copenhagen.' In Morotomi, T., and Niizawa, H. (Eds.), *Governing Low-Carbon Development and the Economy*. Tokyo, Japan: United Nations University Press.

Park, Seung-Joon, Yamazaki, Masato, and Takeda, Shiro (2012). 'Environmental tax reform: Major findings and policy implications from a multi-regional economic simulation analysis.' Background Policy Paper for *Low Carbon Green Growth Roadmap for Asia and the Pacific*, Bangkok: United Nations ESCAP.

Pollitt, Hector, Summerton, Philip, and Thoung, Chris (2012). 'Modelling the impact of policy interventions on carbon leakage, assessment with the E3MG model.' Climate Strategies Working Paper. http://climatestrategies.org/wp-content/uploads/2012/06/assessment-with-the-e3mg-model-final-120612.pdf (accessed May 17, 2015).

Reinaud, Julia (2008). *Issues Behind Competitiveness and Carbon Leakage. Focus on Heavy Industry*. Paris: International Energy Agency. http://webcom.upmf-grenoble.fr/edden/spip/IMG/pdf/Reinaud_issues-behind-competitiveness_2008.pdf.

Stiglitz, Joseph E. (2006). 'A new agenda for global warming.' *Economist's Voice*, 3(7), pp. 1–4.

Takeda, Shiro, Horie, Tetsuya, and Arimura, Toshi-Hide (2012). 'Nihon-no Kokkyo Chousei Sochi Seisaku – Tanso Leakage Boushi to Kokusai Kyousouryoku Hoji eno Kouka.' In Arimura, Thoshi-Hide, Yomogida, Morihiro, and Kawase, Tsuyoshi (Eds.), *Chikyu Ondanka Taisaku to Kokusai Boueki*. Tokyo: Tokyo University Press (pp. 87–108; in Japanese).

World Trade Organization (WTO) and United Nations Environment Program (UNEP) (2009). *Trade and Climate Change*. Geneva: WTO Publications.

Introduction to Part 3

The economic and environmental impacts of international trade in East Asia

Much of the previous analysis of environmental policy in East Asia, including most previous modeling studies, has concerned single countries; very few studies have comprehensively covered the interdependent East Asian economies. As a result, the trends and spillovers in related policy reforms in East Asia are not very well understood. But the level of economic interdependence between the countries of East Asia has increased substantially in recent years, which has also resulted in increased international competition between the corporate and industrial sectors of these countries. This trend may be accelerated by the further development of international free-trade agreements for finance and services, such as the Trans-Pacific Partnership and the Japan–China–South Korea free trade agreements, which are currently under discussion.

As we saw in Chapter 13, competition through trade has made it increasingly difficult for governments to introduce policies that might burden domestic industries, even for environmental and energy measures that have been demonstrated to be effective at the macroeconomic level. Consideration of future energy and environmental reforms in East Asia therefore requires more than a single-country framework: it requires a simultaneous and comprehensive examination that considers the effects of policy, both positive and negative, on all the economies in the region.

One significant problem that East Asian countries face is a reliance on imported resources, fossil fuels in particular, that are subject to extreme market volatility. Whether or not they are intended to address climate change, improvements to renewable energy technology and energy-use efficiency are expected to make positive economic contributions to countries in the region through a reduction in fossil fuel imports. The effects of policies and measures to promote renewables and energy efficiency can spread beyond borders through technology transfer and trade of related products.

The first two chapters (Chapters 15 and 16) focus on the ever-growing inter-linkages in global supply chains and ask the question of who is responsible for the world's CO_2 emissions from a consumption-based perspective. In Chapter 17, we then focus on another consequence of growing trade: rising emissions from maritime freight transport. Finally, in Chapters 18 and 19, we consider how possible future trade deals may affect rates of economic growth and CO_2 emissions in East Asia.

15 Measuring both production-based and consumption-based CO_2 emissions of different countries based on the multi-region input–output model

Jun Pang, Eva Alexandri, Shih-Mo Lin and Soocheol Lee

15.1 Introduction

As has been discussed throughout this book, climate change is a serious global challenge, and a successful policy response will require coordination across the world. If a global agreement is reached, the United Nations Framework Convention on Climate Change (UNFCCC) will determine the national responsibility for emissions reductions based on each country's total greenhouse gas (GHG) emissions. However, in the process of global economic integration, a country can both consume imported goods from foreign countries as well as export its own commodities.

Therefore, the production process of goods that are traded creates both direct and indirect CO_2 emissions, the indirect emissions being those that are embodied in international trade. A country's CO_2 emissions are – according to standard production-based accounting principles – those that result from domestic production, regardless of whether these goods are consumed domestically or exported. This measure does not include CO_2 emissions from goods that are produced abroad and are then imported for domestic consumption.

Owing to this method of carbon emission accounting, a country with increasing exports is also increasing its total CO_2 emissions, whereas import-oriented countries can cut their total CO_2 emissions by reducing domestic production levels. Consequently, a comprehensive assessment of a country's global environmental impact should take both production-based and consumption-based CO_2 emissions into consideration.

So far, a large number of studies that have investigated CO_2 emissions embodied in international trade came to similar conclusions, in that developed countries achieve a carbon transfer to developing countries through international trade. As a result, developed countries have been able to cut domestic energy consumption and CO_2 emissions, whereas most developing countries have become net export countries of embodied carbon (Machado, Schaeffer, and Worrell,

2001; Peters and Hertwich, 2006; Gavrilova, 2010; Li and Hewitt, 2008; Tan, Sun, and Lau, 2013; Shui and Harriss, 2006).

Input–output models are the main analytic tool for this type of analysis. Most of the publications referenced above adopted a single-region input–output model. There are also some applications of dual-region input–output models, such as by Ackerman, Ishikawa, and Suga (2007). More recently, the multi-region input–output (MRIO) model has gradually been adopted by researchers. For example, Peters and Hertwich (2008) calculated embodied CO_2 emissions for 87 countries and regions in 2001; Zhou and Kojima (2009) calculated embodied CO_2 emissions for ten countries and regions by constructing an MRIO model on the basis of the GTAP 6 database. Liu et al. (2010) discussed the impact of Sino–Japanese trade on total carbon emissions based on the Asian International Input–Output Tables (which are also applied in Chapters 16 and 17 of this book). In contrast to the single- and dual-region input–output model, the MRIO models can internalize the import and export relations of various production sectors of different countries, and then construct the input–output relations between multiple industries of different countries (or regions) so as to estimate the impact of international trade on global or regional carbon emissions more accurately. Related studies have already proved that the global MRIO model is the most suitable method to analyze embodied carbon emissions at the national level (Peters & Solli, 2010; Rodrigues, Domingos, and Marques, 2010).

In this chapter, we estimate production-based and consumption-based CO_2 emissions – including the industrial distribution of emissions – for the world's largest economies. We do this by creating a global MRIO model that is based on the GTAP 8.02 database and described in Section 15.2. The results from our analysis are presented in Section 15.3. In Section 15.4 we consider possible future trends in production- and consumption-based emissions, by linking our approach to the decarbonization scenarios that were developed in Chapter 8. The trade flows of embodied CO_2 emission are analyzed further in Chapter 16 of this book.[1]

15.2   Methodology and data source

In this chapter, we apply an example of an MRIO model. These models are different from the macroeconomic modeling approaches that were discussed in Chapters 8 and 9; they use a single base year but are able to incorporate a lot of data for that base year. Using this information, MRIO models can internalize the import and export relations of each industry in different countries on the basis of historical trade patterns and, therefore, can estimate the role of international trade by determining historical global or regional carbon emissions more accurately. Details of the equations used in this model are provided in Appendix 15.A.

Our global MRIO model was created for the years 2004 and 2007, based on the GTAP 8.02 database – the latest available. It was published in 2013 and holds data for 57 industries in 134 countries/regions.[2] For each country/region, the database provides input–output tables and also distinguishes between intermediate inputs and final consumption from domestic supply and foreign imports in each country. The database provides figures for bilateral trade and CO_2 emissions by industry and fuel type (coal, petroleum, natural gas, electricity, oil products, and coal gas).

In this chapter, we aggregate the 134 countries/regions provided by the GTAP 8.02 database into six single countries and regional groupings of countries (hereafter referred to as regions). They are China (mainland China here), the United States, the European Union, Japan, Korea, and the rest of the world (ROW). Table 15.1 provides further details on the specific aggregation.

Table 15.1 Aggregation by regions in GTAP 8.02

No.	Region	Countries (or regions) contained in this region[a]
1	China	chn
2	United States	usa
3	European Union	aut, bel, cyp, cze, dnk, est, fin, fra, deu, grc, hun, irl, ita, lva, pol, ltu, lux, mlt, nld, prt, svk, esp, svn, swe, gbr, bgr, rou, hrv
4	Japan	jpn
5	Korea	kor
6	ROW	aus, nzl, xoc;mng, khm, idn, lao, mys, phl, sgp, tha, vnm, bgd, xse, ind, npl, pak, lka, xsa, kaz, kgz, xsu, irn, arm, aze, geo, bhr;can, mex, xna, arg, bol, bra, chl, ury, col, ecu, pry, per, ven, xsm, cri, gtm, hnd, nic, pan, slv, xca, xcb;che, nor, alb, blr, rus, ukr, xee, xef, xer, isr, kwt, omn, qat, sau, tur, are, xws, egy, mar;tun, xnf, ben, bfa, cmr, civ, gha, gin, nga, sen, tgo, xwf, xcf, xac, eth, ken, mdg, mwi, mus;moz, rwa, tza, uga, zmb, zwe, xec, bwa, nam, zaf, xsc, xtw, hkg, xea, twn

a See Appendix 15.B for the explanations of each abbreviation.

We also aggregate the 57 industries provided by GTAP 8.02 into 14 industries. Table 15.2 provides further details.

Table 15.2 Aggregation of industries in GTAP 8.02

No.	Aggregate Industry	Industries contained in this aggregate industry[b]
1	Agriculture	PDR, WHT, GRO, V_F, OSD, C_B, PFB, OCR, CTL, OAP, RMK, WOL, FRS, FSH
2	Food processing	CMT, OMT, VOL, MIL, PCR, SGR, OFD, B_T
3	Energy exploitation	COA, OIL, GAS
4	Other resources	OMN
5	Petrochemicals	P_C, CRP
6	Metal smelters and production	I_S, NFM, FMP
7	Non-metallic minerals	NMM
8	Textiles and apparel	TEX, WAP, LEA
9	Equipment manufacturing	MVH, ELE, OTN, OME
10	Other manufacturing	PPP, LUM, OMF
11	Electricity, gas, and water	ELY, GDT, WTR
12	Construction	CNS
13	Transportation	ATP, WTP, OTP
14	Services	TRD, CMN, OFI, ISR, OBS, ROS, OSG, DWE

b See Appendix 15.C for explanations of each abbreviation.

15.3 Results and analysis

Production-based and consumption-based CO_2 emissions

The results shown in Table 15.3 were obtained by using the method described above. The table also provides the results calculated based on the World Input–Output Database (WIOD) for comparison. The WIOD provides time series of world input–output tables for forty countries worldwide and a model for the ROW, covering the period from 1995 to 2011 (Timmer, 2012).

The comparison of production- and consumption-based CO_2 emissions shows that there can be quite large differences in a country's CO_2 emissions, depending on whether we use the production- or consumption-based approach. We can see that production-based emissions in China and Korea are 15 percent

Table 15.3 Production-based and consumption-based CO$_2$ emissions of China, the US, the EU, Japan, and Korea in 2004 and 2007

	2004			2007		
	Production-based (mt CO$_2$)	Consumption-based (mt CO$_2$)	Production-based vs consumption-based	Production-based (mt CO$_2$)	Consumption-based (mt CO$_2$)	Production-based vs. consumption-based
China	3701.54 (3866.94)	3201.88 (3354.36)	15.61% (15.28%)	4690.97 (4923.17)	4051.27 (4098.70)	15.79% (20.12%)
USA	5937.45 (5216.96)	6289.21 (5705.40)	−5.59% (−8.56%)	5967.73 (5179.92)	6272.59 (5653.93)	−4.86% (−8.38%)
EU	4665.61 (4003.58)	4947.30 (4193.21)	−5.69% (−4.52%)	4747.97 (4183.11)	5004.41 (4438.94)	−5.12% (−5.76%)
JAPAN	1248.27 (1233.27)	1339.50 (1324.25)	−6.81% (−6.87%)	1223.59 (1219.66)	1276.46 (1281.64)	−4.14% (−4.84%)
KOREA	443.28 (498.70)	403.97 (456.88)	9.73% (9.15%)	487.64 (535.69)	462.05 (508.95)	5.54% (5.25%)

Note: Numbers in parentheses are calculated based on the WIOD.

and 5 percent higher than their consumption-based CO_2 emissions, respectively, in 2007. In contrast, production-based emissions in each of the US, the EU, and Japan are about 5 percent less than their consumption-based CO_2 emissions.

According to our GTAP results, the gap between production-based and consumption-based CO_2 emissions in China increased in the period 2004–2007 from 499.66 $mtCO_2$ to 639.70 $mtCO_2$. In the same period, the (negative) gap between production- and consumption-based CO_2 emissions in the US and the EU decreased from 351.76 $mtCO_2$ and 281.69 $mtCO_2$ to 304.86 $mtCO_2$ and 256.44 $mtCO_2$ respectively. The gap was even bigger in Japan, falling almost by half (91.22 $mtCO_2$ to 53.9 $mtCO_2$) in this three-year period.

Nevertheless, despite the gap getting smaller, the status of each country does not change. China remains a net exporter of embodied carbon, whereas the US, the EU, and Japan remain net importers.

Comparing both sets of calculated results (based on GTAP and WIOD databases) we find no obvious difference between the two and, therefore, draw the same conclusions from both.

Analysis of production-based CO_2 emissions by industry

Table 15.4 shows the production-based CO_2 emissions of each industry in China, the US, the EU, Japan, and Korea, in 2004 and 2007 (again, based on GTAP 8.02). Figure 15.1 provides the share of emissions from each industry in the national total.

From Table 15.4 and Figure 15.1, we can see that there are substantial differences in the distribution of production-based CO_2 emissions between the countries. Based on the results from GTAP 8.02, the largest contribution to production-based CO_2 emissions in China comes from the construction industry, whose share is around 28 percent. The largest shares of CO_2 emissions in the US, the EU, Japan, and Korea all come from the services sectors;[3] the share of CO_2 emissions from services is almost 50 percent in the United States.

Although total production-based CO_2 emissions in China are lower than those in the US and the EU in 2004 and 2007, China's emissions from equipment manufacturing are higher than those for the United States and the EU. Figure 15.1 shows that, in 2007, CO_2 emissions from equipment manufacturing accounted for 18.88 percent of total emissions in China, and 20.17 percent of total emissions in Korea. However, shares in the US, the EU, and Japan were only 9.65 percent, 12.7 percent, and 14.91 percent, respectively.

The electricity industry is also an important source of emissions in all countries. In the US, it is the second highest contributor to total emissions.

Table 15.4 Production-based CO_2 emissions of each industry in China, the US, the EU, Japan, and Korea (mtCO$_2$) in 2004 and 2007

	CHN		USA		EU		JAPAN		KOREA	
	2004	2007	2004	2007	2004	2007	2004	2007	2004	2007
Agriculture	136.06	150.0	43.09	36.84	52.68	47.95	11.95	10.36	6.58	6.65
Food processing	227.48	263.48	295.84	301.63	372.86	369.34	82.66	72.29	21.88	22.96
Energy exploitation	5.57	4.69	0.03	0.04	0.55	0.45	0.00	0.00	0.09	0.13
Other resources	0.05	0.03	0.26	1.49	0.71	2.24	0.00	0.00	0.00	0.00
Petrochemicals	122.51	154.54	266.73	273.49	210.34	210.13	36.18	40.05	14.57	17.32
Metal smelters and production	37.60	54.31	21.29	21.75	45.70	48.41	5.42	6.32	3.25	4.07
Non-metallic minerals	16.18	18.76	7.56	8.75	24.62	24.92	1.95	1.94	0.58	0.61
Textiles and apparel	218.39	266.46	91.48	87.77	162.28	155.85	9.29	7.49	20.32	18.17
Equipment manufacturing	656.91	885.54	579.24	575.89	576.19	603.16	181.75	182.40	88.11	98.38
Other manufacturing	8.39	110.64	148.2	144	157.18	155.67	9.73	8.92	6.14	6.28
Electricity, gas, and water	393.43	513.95	949.93	981.77	458.72	479.59	126.87	145.32	34.71	39.75
Construction	1019.90	1307.02	384.81	380.28	449.33	488.45	150.20	142.88	64.06	72.34
Transportation	91.78	117.68	367.73	371.44	528.59	554.59	103.69	97.68	39.87	40.99
Services	695.30	843.87	2781.26	2782.59	1625.85	1607.21	528.56	507.95	143.11	160.00
Total	3071.54	4690.97	5937.45	5967.73	4665.61	4747.97	1248.27	1223.59	443.28	487.64

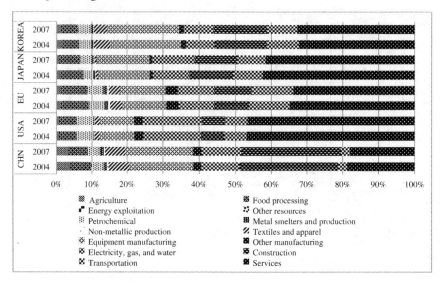

Figure 15.1 Sectoral shares of production-based CO$_2$ emissions from each industry in China, the US, the EU, Japan, and Korea in 2004 and 2007.

Analysis of consumption-based carbon emissions of each industry

Table 15.5 shows the consumption-based CO$_2$ emissions of each industry in China, the US, the EU, Japan, and Korea in 2004 and 2007. Figure 15.2 provides the share of emissions from each industry.

Table 15.5 and Figure 15.2 show that construction is the biggest source of consumption-based emissions in China, both for 2004 and 2007, with a share reaching 32 percent in 2007. In the same years, the biggest share of consumption-based CO$_2$ emissions in the US, the EU, Japan, and Korea all come from the services industry. Services in the United States contributed 44 percent to the national total consumption-based CO$_2$ emissions in 2004 and 2007.

When calculating CO$_2$ emissions on a consumption basis, emissions from the equipment manufacturing industry in China are less than from the same sector in the US and the EU. In 2007, the share of consumption-based CO$_2$ emissions attributed to the equipment manufacturing industry was 14.25 percent in China. The sector shares in emissions in the US and the EU were 11.98 percent and 13.23 percent respectively, and only 13.38 percent and 12.60 percent in Japan and Korea respectively.

When viewed from the consumption-based perspective, the electricity industry was still a significant emitter in all regions in both 2004 and 2007; it ranked second highest in the US.

Table 15.5 Consumption-based CO_2 emissions from each industry in China, the US, the EU, Japan, and Korea (mtCO_2) in 2004 and 2007

	CHN		USA		EU		JAPAN		KOREA	
	2004	2007	2004	2007	2004	2007	2004	2007	2004	2007
Agriculture	133.50	147.35	40.76	33.96	65.18	56.75	13.88	11.56	7.44	7.43
Food processing	215.35	250.64	306.67	308.62	384.39	378.52	95.14	81.61	23.33	24.86
Energy exploitation	5.37	4.62	0.00	0.00	3.28	3.02	0.26	0.20	0.69	0.75
Other resources	0.00	0.00	0.30	1.53	0.85	2.37	0.00	0.00	0.01	0.01
Petrochemicals	88.83	111.60	295.60	299.16	230.00	232.59	36.76	39.67	11.15	13.54
Metal smelters and production	29.09	39.55	27.90	26.12	49.79	52.80	6.85	6.92	2.69	3.42
Non-metallic minerals	9.14	9.76	13.13	13.37	24.61	25.38	2.46	2.28	0.50	0.63
Textiles and apparel	82.18	101.96	173.34	158.13	220.35	220.99	42.37	32.98	16.42	18.35
Equipment manufacturing	426.49	577.22	758.22	751.36	649.79	661.91	186.63	170.81	48.12	58.24
Other manufacturing	41.00	50.22	206.72	202.14	168.67	170.04	13.59	12.78	6.43	7.50
Electricity, gas, and water	388.87	508.24	955.42	991.39	471.47	511.18	129.46	148.98	35.54	41.21
Construction	1017.63	1302.96	384.65	379.24	452.45	491.32	152.00	144.65	62.98	69.73
Transportation	84.81	110.88	354.86	341.04	561.75	558.82	126.65	112.98	44.02	52.98
Services	688.62	836.25	2771.62	2766.55	1664.73	1638.73	533.47	511.04	144.65	163.41
Total	3201.88	4051.27	6289.21	6272.59	4947.30	5004.41	1339.50	1276.46	403.97	462.05

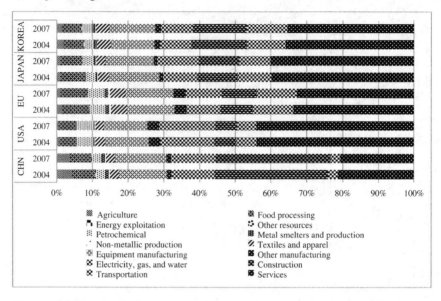

Figure 15.2 The share of consumption-based CO_2 emissions from each industry in China, the US, the EU, Japan, and Korea in 2004 and 2007.

A comparison between production-based and consumption-based CO_2 emissions of each industry

Table 15.6 gives values for both production-based and consumption-based CO_2 emissions from each industry in China, the US, the EU, Japan, and Korea in 2007, based on the GTAP 8.02 database. Figure 15.3 shows the share of each sector's production-based and consumption-based emissions in the five regions.

From Table 15.6 and Figure 15.3 we can conclude that there are quite large differences between sectoral production-based and consumption-based CO_2 emissions in China, the US, the EU, Japan, and Korea. In addition, the situation in China is substantially different from the situation in the US, the EU, and Japan.

The absolute levels of production-based CO_2 emissions of all 14 industries are higher than their consumption-based equivalents in China. In some sectors the differences are small, but the production-based CO_2 emissions of petrochemicals, metal smelters and production, non-metallic minerals, textiles and apparel, equipment manufacturing, and other manufacturing are notably higher than their consumption-based measures. However, for the US, the EU, and Japan, the situation is, with few exceptions, reversed in most industries. For example, consumption-based emissions in the textiles and apparel industry are much higher than production-based emissions. The equipment and manufacturing sector shows the same pattern for the US and the EU.

Table 15.6 Comparison of production-based and consumption-based CO_2 emissions of each industry in China, the US, the EU, Japan, and Korea in 2007

$mtCO_2$	CHN		USA		EU		JAPAN		KOREA	
	P	C	P	C	P	C	P	C	P	C
Agriculture	150.01	147.35	36.84	33.96	47.95	56.75	10.36	11.56	6.65	7.43
Food processing	263.48	250.64	301.63	308.62	369.34	378.52	72.29	81.61	22.96	24.86
Energy exploitation	4.69	4.62	0.04	0.00	0.45	3.02	0.00	0.20	0.13	0.75
Other resources	0.03	0.00	1.49	1.53	2.24	2.37	0.00	0.00	0.00	0.01
Petrochemicals	154.54	111.60	273.49	299.16	210.13	232.59	40.05	39.67	17.32	13.54
Metal smelters and production	54.31	39.55	21.75	26.12	48.41	52.80	6.32	6.92	4.07	3.42
Non-metallic minerals	18.76	9.76	8.75	13.37	24.92	25.38	1.94	2.28	0.61	0.63
Textiles and apparel	266.46	101.96	87.77	158.13	155.85	220.99	7.49	32.98	18.17	18.35
Equipment manufacturing	885.54	577.22	575.89	751.36	603.16	661.91	182.40	170.81	98.38	58.24
Other manufacturing	110.64	50.22	144	202.14	155.67	170.04	8.92	12.78	6.28	7.5
Electricity, gas, and water	513.95	508.24	981.77	991.39	479.59	511.18	145.32	148.98	39.75	41.21
Construction	1307.02	1302.96	380.28	379.24	488.45	491.32	142.88	144.65	72.34	69.73
Transportation	117.68	110.88	371.44	341.04	554.59	558.82	97.68	112.98	40.99	52.98
Services	843.87	836.25	2782.59	2766.55	1607.21	1638.73	507.95	511.04	160.00	163.41
Total	**4690.97**	**4051.27**	**5967.73**	**6272.59**	**4747.97**	**5004.41**	**1223.59**	**1276.46**	**487.64**	**462.05**

P: production-based CO_2 emissions; C: consumption-based CO_2 emissions

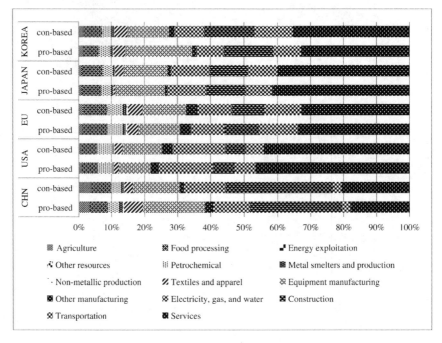

Figure 15.3 Comparison of the share of sectoral production-based and consumption-based CO$_2$ emissions in China, the US, the EU, Japan, and Korea in 2007.

In Korea, the differences between production-based CO$_2$ emissions and consumption-based CO$_2$ emissions vary by industry. For some industries, such as petrochemicals and equipment manufacturing, production-based CO$_2$ emissions are higher than consumption-based emissions. However, for other industries, such as food processing and transportation, production-based CO$_2$ emissions are less than the consumption-based emissions.

It is notable that China, Japan, and Korea all have higher CO$_2$ emissions in equipment manufacturing when measured on a production, rather than consumption, basis. This sector includes motor cars, shipbuilding, and other machinery; it has been an important driver of economic growth in East Asia and is one where there is strong global competition.

Finally, analyzing the share of CO$_2$ emissions of each industry in China, the textiles and apparel, equipment manufacturing, and other manufacturing industries all have a lower share of emissions when measured on a consumption basis. The proportion of emissions accounted for by services increases.

For the US, the EU, and Japan, the share of emissions accounted for by the textiles and apparel industry increases when measured on a consumption basis, but the proportion of services emissions declines slightly. For the US and the EU, the proportion of equipment manufacturing, and other manufacturing also increases when measured on a consumption basis. In addition, for Korea, the share of CO_2 emissions from the equipment manufacturing industry is reduced when measuring on a consumption basis, whereas other industries show only slight changes.

15.4 Lessons from Chapter 8

In Chapter 8, we assessed several different scenarios of environmental tax reform (ETR), in which three East Asian countries (China, Japan and Korea) reduce their domestic production-based emission levels to meet national targets. But would emission levels also be reduced if they were measured on a consumption basis? This question can be addressed by converting the E3ME-Asia emissions results to a consumption basis by using the model's own projections.

Table 15.7 summarizes the E3ME-Asia results for the baseline and two of the scenarios:

- ANN: a carbon tax is set such that all four countries meet their national emission reduction targets simultaneously, without revenue recycling.
- ANC: the same carbon tax is set but the revenues are used to reduce consumption taxes.

Emissions measured on a production basis are marked (P) and on a consumption basis as (C). It is important to note that the values are for the year 2020, and thus there are some discrepancies compared with the historical estimates earlier in this chapter. However, the broad patterns are similar, for example, with China being a net exporter of emissions and Japan a net importer.

It is striking that in Japan and Korea the reduction in consumption-based emissions is less than the reduction in production-based emissions. In China, consumption-based emissions decrease slightly more than production-based emissions, but the reductions are, in both cases, much less than for Japan and Korea.

Table 15.7 Changes in production-based and consumption-based CO_2 emissions under the scenarios described in Chapter 8 (2020)

	Emission levels (mtCO₂)					
	China	Japan	Korea			
Base (P)	10,965.4	1,236.1	710.1	% difference from base		
Base (C)	10,135.7	1,334.2	718.2	China	Japan	Korea
ANN (P)	10,365.1	1,099.8	486.6	−5.5	−11.0	−31.5
ANN (C)	9,547.0	1,209.4	527.5	−5.8	−9.4	−26.6
ANC (P)	10,731.9	1,100.3	488.4	−2.1	−11.0	−31.2
ANC (C)	9,902.3	1,234.3	536.5	−2.3	−7.5	−25.3

Source: E3ME-Asia model results.

For the baseline, Korea's exports and imports of embodied CO_2 emissions almost balance, but the country becomes a strong net importer of CO_2 in the policy scenarios. This is because the policies implemented in the scenarios are focused on production; which is why production-based emissions fall further. This might be a good indicator of some of the limitations of policies implemented to alter emissions levels on a consumption basis (discussed in Chapter 14).

15.5   Conclusions and discussion

In this chapter we have compared two different ways of measuring a country's (or region's; see definition in Section 15.2) CO_2 emissions. We found that the two different measures can produce quite different results, especially in countries that are very open to international trade, which includes most of the countries in East Asia. Our results show that China's and Korea's production-based CO_2 emissions were, respectively, 15 percent and 5 percent higher than their consumption-based equivalents in 2007, whereas production-based CO_2 emissions of the United States, the EU, and Japan were each about 5 percent less than their consumption-based equivalents.

Considering the industrial distribution of CO_2 emissions, construction, equipment manufacturing, and electricity are the top three CO_2-emitting industries in China, whereas services, electricity, and equipment manufacturing contributed the most CO_2 emissions in the US, the EU, and Japan. For Korea, services, equipment manufacturing, and construction were the top three sources of CO_2 emissions.

The equipment manufacturing industry is a major carbon emitter in China. When adopting the production-based accounting system, the sector's CO_2 emissions are higher than emissions from the same sector in the United States or the EU. However, if measured on a consumption basis, China's emissions are lower.

Emissions are higher for China when measured on a production rather than consumption basis in all 14 of the aggregated industries we looked at, but we see the opposite situation in these industries for the US, the EU, and Japan. For Korea, the share of CO_2 emissions from equipment manufacturing is much lower when measured on a consumption basis, whereas other industries show only slight changes.

When considering the environmental tax reform policies discussed and modeled in Chapter 8, we find that they lead to reductions in both production-based and consumption-based emissions in all countries. However, the reduction in CO_2 emissions in those countries that have implemented ETR is smaller when considered on a consumption basis. This suggests that there is a role for consumption-based policies, including the border tax adjustments that are discussed in Chapter 14.

The current production-based accounting method of CO_2 emissions has ignored the carbon transfer embodied in exported goods. As net importers of embodied carbon, many developed countries, such as the US, the EU, and Japan can avoid increasing domestic production-based emissions. However, at the same time China – as a main exporter of embodied carbon – must undertake mitigation measures to reduce CO$_2$ emissions that result from production for export. Therefore, it is necessary to take both production-based and consumption-based accounting systems into consideration when assessing CO$_2$ emissions in different countries, so as to establish a better foundation to distribute national CO$_2$ mitigation responsibilities for each country. This shows low carbon policies between developing countries(more production-based CO2 emitters) and developed countries(more consumption-based emitters) is important to reduce CO2 emission effectively.

Appendix 15.A

15.A1 Multi-region input–output table

By convention, i and j used in this and the following section represent each industry. Variables r and s represent each country (or region; see definition in Section 15.2). In GTAP 8.02, the input–output relation of domestic products of country r can be represented as:

$$x_i^r = \sum_j vdfm_{ij}^r + vdpm_i^r + vdgm_i^r + \sum_s vxmd_i^{rs} \tag{15.A1}$$

where x_i^r is the total output of industry i of country r, $vdfm_{ij}^r$ is the intermediate input demand of industry j of country r towards industry i, $vdpm_i^r$ is the personal consumption demand of country r towards the product of industry i, $vdgm_i^r$ is the government consumption demand of country r towards the product of industry i, and $vxmd_i^{rs}$ is the output demand of country s towards the product of industry i of country r.

In addition, GTAP 8.02 provides the data for intermediate inputs and final consumption in the total imports of each country, but it does not divide the total imports by importing country. Therefore, if we use GTAP 8.02 to create a global MRIO table, it is necessary to do further subdivisions of each country's intermediate inputs and final consumption of total imports by importing country. To achieve this goal, we assumed that, when country r imported product i from other countries (including country s) and used product i as intermediate inputs or final consumption, the percentage of product i that became the intermediate inputs of country r from country s, compared to the total global imports of product i of country r, equals to the percentage of product i as the final consumption of country r imported from country s compared to the total global imports of product i of country r. Both ratios were equal to the percentage of country r's imports from country s compared to country r's total global imports. Therefore,

$$z_{ij}^{sr} = z_{ij}^{*r} \times \frac{e_i^{sr}}{m_i^r} \tag{15.A2}$$

$$y_{ij}^{sr} = y_{ij}^{*r} \times \frac{e_i^{sr}}{m_i^r} \tag{15.A3}$$

Table 15.A1 The basic structure of the global MRIO tables

		Intermediate inputs				Final consumption				Total output	CO_2 emission
		A	B	...	F	A	B	...	E		
Intermediate inputs	A	Z^{AA}	Z^{AB}	...	Z^{AF}	Y^{AA}	Y^{AB}	...	Y^{AF}	X^A	C^A
	B	Z^{BA}	Z^{BB}	...	Z^{BF}	Y^{BA}	Y^{BB}	...	Y^{BF}	X^B	C^B
	...	...	...	...	...	...	...	...	...	...	...
	F	Z^{FA}	Z^{FB}		Z^{FF}	Y^{FA}	Y^{FB}		Y^{FF}	X^F	C^F
Value added		...	...	...	...						
Total input		X^A	X^B	...	X^F						

where z_{ij}^{sr} is the imports from industry i of country s as the intermediate inputs of industry j in country r, z_{ij}^{*r} is the total imports from industry i of other countries as the intermediate inputs of industry j in country r, e_i^{sr} is the imports from country s to industry i of country r, m_i^{sr} is the imports from around the world to industry i of country r, y_{ij}^{sr} is the imports from industry i of country s as the final consumption of industry j in country r, and y_{ij}^{*r} is the total imports from industry i of other countries as the final consumption of industry j in country r.

Applying the above actions yielded the MRIO table with six regions, each with 14 industries. The basic structure of the MRIO table is given in Table 15.A1.

Where $A, B, \ldots, F$ all represent the countries. The intermediate inputs Z^{AA}, Z^{AB} are 14 × 14 matrixes reflecting the input-output relations of 14 industries among or within regions. $Y^{AA}, Y^{AB}, \ldots, Y^{FF}, X^A, X^B, \ldots, X^E, C^A, C^B, \ldots, C^F$ are 14 × 1 matrixes. $Y^{AA}, Y^{AB}, \ldots, Y^{FF}$ are the final consumption of each region including domestic use and foreign output. $X^A, X^B, \ldots, X^F$ are the total output. $C^A, C^B, \ldots, C^F$ are the CO_2 emissions.

15.A2 Production-based and consumption-based CO_2 emissions accounting

On the bases of the above MRIO tables, the input–output relations of all the countries can be represented as

$$\begin{pmatrix} X^A \\ X^B \\ \vdots \\ X^F \end{pmatrix} = \begin{pmatrix} A^{AA} & A^{AB} & \cdots & A^{AF} \\ A^{BA} & A^{BB} & \cdots & A^{BF} \\ \vdots & \vdots & \ddots & \vdots \\ A^{FA} & A^{FB} & \cdots & A^{FF} \end{pmatrix} \begin{pmatrix} X^A \\ X^B \\ \vdots \\ X^F \end{pmatrix} + \begin{pmatrix} \sum_{k=A}^{E} Y^{Ak} \\ \sum_{k=A}^{E} Y^{Bk} \\ \vdots \\ \sum_{k=A}^{E} Y^{Fk} \end{pmatrix} \qquad (15.A4)$$

The column vector on the left side of the equation is the total output of each industry in each region. The first part on the right side of the equation is an 84 × 84 matrix representing the direct consumption coefficient composed by the element $a_{ij}^{sr} = {z_{ij}^{sr}}\big/{r^r}$, showing the input-output relations of the industries between different regions. A^{rr} on the diagonal of the matrix is the input-output relations of domestic industry, whereas A^{rs} on the off-diagonal of the matrix is the input-output relations of industries between country r and country s. The last column of the matrix on the right side of the equation is the final demand matrix, representing the final demands produced by each region that provided to its own region (Y^{rr}) and exported to foreign countries (Y^{rs}).

In equation 15.A4, we obtained the final consumption column vector of region r, $d^r = (Y^{Ar} Y^{Br} \cdots Y^{Fr})^T$, including the final consumption of the imports (Y^{sr}) and the domestic final consumption (Y^{rr}). We also obtained the production row vector of region r, $p^r = (Y^{rA} Y^{rB} \cdots Y^{rF})^T$, including the final consumption of the domestic production of goods (Y^{rr}) and the final consumption of domestic production of goods exported to region s (Y^{rs}). The consumption-based CO_2 emissions C_d^r and the production-based CO_2 emissions C_p^r of a region can be represented as:

$$C_d^r = E(I-A)^{-1}\hat{d}^r \tag{15.A5}$$

$$C_p^r = E(I-A)^{-1}\hat{p}^r \tag{15.A6}$$

Here, $\hat{d}^r$, $\hat{p}^r$ are diagonal matrixes. E is an 84 × 1 CO_2 direct consumption coefficient matrix composed by element $e_j^r = {c_i^r}\big/{r^r}$

Appendix 15.B

Abbr.	Country	Abbr.	Country
alb	Albania	mng	Mongolia
arg	Argentina	mar	Morocco
arm	Armenia	moz	Mozambique
aus	Australia	nam	Namibia
aut	Austria	npl	Nepal
aze	Azerbaijan	nld	Netherlands
bhr	Bahrain	nzl	New Zealand
bgd	Bangladesh	nic	Nicaragua
blr	Belarus	nga	Nigeria
bel	Belgium	nor	Norway
bol	Bolivia	omn	Oman
bwa	Botswana	pak	Pakistan
bra	Brazil	pan	Panama
bgr	Bulgaria	pry	Paraguay
khm	Cambodia	per	Peru
cmr	Cameroon	phl	Philippines
can	Canada	pol	Poland
xcb	Caribbean	prt	Portugal
xcf	Central Africa	qat	Qatar
chl	Chile	xca	Rest of Central America
chn	China	xea	Rest of East Asia
col	Colombia	xec	Rest of Eastern Africa
cri	Costa Rica	xee	Rest of Eastern Europe
civ	Cote d'lvoire	xef	Rest of EFTA
hrv	Croatia	xer	Rest of Europe
cyp	Cyprus	xsu	Rest of Former Soviet Union
cze	Czech Republic	xnf	Rest of North Africa
dnk	Denmark	xna	Rest of North America
ecu	Ecuador	xoc	Rest of Oceania

Abbr.	Country	Abbr.	Country
egy	Egypt	xsc	Rest of South African Customs
slv	El Salvador	xsm	Rest of South America
est	Estonia	xsa	Rest of South Asia
eth	Ethiopia	xse	Rest of Southeast Asia
fin	Finland	xwf	Rest of Western Africa
fra	France	xws	Rest of Western Asia
geo	Georgia	xtw	Rest of World
deu	Germany	rou	Romania
gha	Ghana	rus	Russian Federation
grc	Greece	sau	Saudi Arabia
gtm	Guatemala	sen	Senegal
hnd	Honduras	sgp	Singapore
hkg	Hong Kong	svk	Slovakia
hun	Hungary	svn	Slovenia
ind	India	zaf	South Africa
idn	Indonesia	xac	South Central Africa
irl	Ireland	esp	Spain
irn	Islamic Republic of Iran	lka	Sri Lanka
isr	Israel	swe	Sweden
ita	Italy	che	Switzerland
jpn	Japan	twn	Taiwan
kaz	Kazakhstan	tza	Tanzania
ken	Kenya	tha	Thailand
kor	Korea	tun	Tunisia
kwt	Kuwait	tur	Turkey
kgr	Kyrgyzstan	uga	Uganda
lao	Lao People's Democratic Republic	ukr	Ukraine
lva	Latvia	are	United Arab Emirates
ltu	Lithuania	gbr	United Kingdom
lux	Luxembourg	usa	United States of America
mdg	Madagascar	ury	Uruguay
mwi	Malawi	ven	Venezuela
mys	Malaysia	vnm	Viet Nam
mlt	Malta	zmb	Zambia
mus	Mauritius	zwe	Zimbabwe
mex	Mexico	ben	Benin
rwa	Rwanda	gin	Guinea
bfa	Burkina Faso	tgo	Togo

Appendix 15.C

Abbr.	Industry	Abbr.	Industry
ATP	Air transport	OFD	Food products nec
B_T	Beverages and tobacco products	OFI	Financial services nec
C_B	Sugar cane, sugar beet	OIL	Oil
CMN	Communication	OME	Machinery and equipment nec
CMT	Bovine meat products	OMF	Manufactures nec
CNS	Construction	OMN	Minerals nec
COA	Coal	OMT	Meat products nec
CRP	Chemicals, rubber, and plastic products	OSD	Oil seeds
CTL	Bovine cattle, sheep, and goats, horses	OSG	Public administration, defense, Education, health
DWE	Dwellings		
ELE	Electronic equipment	OTN	Transport equipment nec
ELY	Electricity	OTP	Transport nec
FMP	Metal products	P_C	Petroleum, coal products
FRS	Forestry	PCR	Processed rice
FSH	Fishing	PDR	Paddy rice
GAS	Gas	PFB	Plant-based fibers
GDT	Gas manufacture, distribution	PPP	Paper products, publishing
GRO	Cereal grains nec	RMK	Raw milk
I_S	Ferrous metals	ROS	Recreational and other services
ISR	Insurance	SGR	Sugar
LEA	Leather products	TEX	Textiles
LUM	Wood products	TRD	Trade
MIL	Dairy products	V_F	Vegetables, fruit, nuts

Abbr.	Industry	Abbr.	Industry
MVH	Motor vehicles and parts	VOL	Vegetable oils and fats
NFM	Metals nec	WAP	Wearing apparel
NMM	Mineral products nec	WHT	Wheat
OAP	Animal products nec	WOL	Wool, silk-worm cocoons
OBS	Business services nec	WTP	Water transport
OCR	Crops nec	WTR	Water

Notes

1 Chapter 16 addresses almost the same issue as this chapter. There are, however, some differences in the approach. For example, the concept of production-based CO_2 emissions in a country is different in the two chapters. Chapter 16 defines these as CO_2 emissions resulting from domestic production activities for both intermediate and final goods in one country, whereas Chapter 15 defines them as CO_2 emissions for the production of final goods against one country in the world. In addition, Chapter 16 is focusing on the trade of embodied CO_2 emissions between countries, whereas the main interest in Chapter 15 is the comparison of consumption-based and production-based CO_2 emissions, defined by country and by industry.
2 These 134 counties/regions are a combination of single countries and regional groupings of countries.
3 In this chapter, the services category includes eight sub-sectors: trade; communication; financial services nec; insurance; business services nec; recreational and other services; public administration, defense, education, health; dwellings.

References

Ackerman, F., Ishikawa, M., and Suga, M. (2007). 'The carbon content of Japan–US trade.' *Energy Policy*, *9*(35), pp. 4455–4462.

Gavrilova, O., Jonas, M., Erb, K., and Haberl, H. (2010). 'International trade and Austria's livestock system: Direct and hidden carbon emission flows associated with production and consumption of products.' *Ecological Economics*, *69*(4), pp. 920–929.

Li, Y., and Hewitt, C. N. (2008). 'The effect of trade between China and the UK on national and global carbon dioxide emissions .' *Energy Policy*, *6*(36), pp. 1907–1914.

Liu, X., Ishikawa, M., Wang, C., Dong, Y., and Liu, W. (2010). 'Analyses of CO_2 emissions embodied in Japan–China trade.' *Energy Policy*, *3*(38), pp. 1510–1518.

Machado, G, Schaeffer, R, and Worrell, E. (2001). 'Energy and carbon embodied in the international trade of Brazil: An input–output approach.' *Ecological Economics*, *39*(3), pp. 409–424.

Peters, G. P., and Hertwich, E. G. (2008). 'CO_2 embodied in international trade with implications for global climate policy.' *Environmental Science & Technology*, *42*(5), pp. 1401–1407.

Peters, G. P., and Hertwich, E. G. (2006). 'Pollution embodied in trade: The Norwegian case.' *Global Environmental Change*, *16*(4), pp. 379–387.

Peter, G. and Solli, C. (2010). *Global Carbon Footprints: Methods and Import/Export Corrected Results from the Nordic Countries in Global Carbon Footprint Studies.* Copenhagen: Nordic Council of Ministers.

Rodrigues, J.F.D, Domingos, T.M.D, and Marques, A.P.S. (2010). *Carbon Responsibility and Embodied Emissions: Theory and Measurement.* London: Routledge; Taylor & Francis.

Shui, B., and Harriss, R. C. (2006). 'The role of CO$_2$ embodiment in US–China trade.' *Energy Policy*, *18*(34), pp. 4063–4068.

Tan, H., Sun, A. J., and Lau, H. (2013). 'CO$_2$ embodiment in China-Australia trade: The drivers and implications.' *Energy Policy*, 61, pp. 1212–1220.

Timmer, M. P. (Ed.) (2012). 'The world input–output database (WIOD): Contents, sources and methods.' WIOD Working Paper No. 10. http://www.wiod.org/publications/papers/wiod10.pdf (accessed January 30, 2015).

Zhou, X., and Kojima, S. (2009). 'How does trade adjustment influence national inventory of open economies? Accounting embodied carbon based on multi-region input–output model.' 18th International Input–Output Conference, June 20–25, Sydney, Australia. pp. 1–20.

16 An empirical study on the interdependency of energy consumption and CO_2 emissions under the international input–output structure of the Asia-Pacific region

Kiyoshi Fujikawa and Hikari Ban

16.1 Introduction

Questions such as "Who uses energy?" or "Who emits CO_2?" are rather difficult to answer. Roughly speaking, before the 1980s (or before 'China's open door'), it was possible to categorize countries into developed countries that import primary goods and export manufactured goods, and developing countries that export primary goods and import manufactured goods. The structure of the international division of labor was rather simple. It is impossible, however, to create such a simple categorization today, because the structure of international division of labor, especially in East Asia, has changed substantially, in line with the economic development of the region, including China, since the 1980s.

Producers of final goods use a combination of intermediate inputs, capital, labor, and other factors of production. The intermediate goods form part of the product's supply chain. If the supply chain begins and ends in a single country, we can say that this country uses energy – or emits CO_2 – to both produce and consume the goods. However, as trade volumes have expanded, supply chains cross national borders more frequently, and it is rare that a good is entirely produced and consumed in one country.

As a result, not only labor but also energy use and CO_2 emissions are internationally divided. Or, to put it another way, the consumption of final goods in one country requires the production of intermediate inputs from other countries, and this production in other countries again requires the production of intermediate inputs from other countries. In short, the consumption of final goods in one country typically embodies the energy use or CO_2 emissions of other intermediate input-supplying countries. For example, Japan currently depends on China to supply a lot of its daily consumer goods. This means that Japan imports goods from China and that demand in Japan causes China to consume energy. In other words, Japan exports CO_2 to China.

As described in Chapter 15, the current standard definition of CO_2 emissions is territorial, based on the 'energy consuming place' criterion. This could also be referred to as the 'goods-producing place' criterion and emissions are measured on a production basis.

Since manufactured goods are, in general, relatively energy intensive, direct and indirect CO_2 emissions from the manufacturing sector are large. Some countries, like China, export manufactured goods and import CO_2 emissions. Other countries, including most developed countries, import manufactured goods and export (or reduce) domestic CO_2 emissions by moving manufacturing sites to foreign countries. If the definition of the location of CO_2 emissions is not the 'goods-producing place' criterion but is instead the 'goods-consuming place' criterion, the situation is considerably different. In summary, using the standard production-based measure of emissions, CO_2 emissions of a net goods importer are undervalued, and CO_2 emissions of net goods exporter are overvalued.[1]

This issue is of critical importance to international negotiations about carbon targets. Japan hosted the UNFCCC's Third Conference of the Parties (COP) in 1997 and as host nation helped to establish the Kyoto Protocol to combat global warming. Japan managed to meet its target of a 6 percent reduction in emissions compared to 1990 levels in the first promise period (from 2008 to 2012), but the country has also put off participation in the second promise period (to 2020). The use of fossil fuels in Japan has increased since the Fukushima accident and the subsequent closure of nuclear plants. Currently (2015), no country in the Asia-Pacific region has made an international promise to reduce CO_2 emissions. Nevertheless, the problem of global warming still exists, and its negative impacts have aggravated further.

As its name suggests, global warming is a global problem, and international cooperation is indispensable for easing this problem. However, there is bitter confrontation between developed and developing countries over the responsibility for sharing the burden of emissions reduction. Understanding trade patterns and the linkages between production and consumption may be an important step in bridging the gap between the two groups.

Other studies that cover this issue in the East Asian region are those by Imura and Moriguchi (1995), Na (2000), and Imura, Nakamura, and Morisugi (2005). This chapter is an extension of these studies on the basis of data from 2005. The analysis is based on a standard input–output (IO) model, which can be used to trace the path of intermediate inputs for any final product. It can, thus, be used to estimate the energy consumption and natural resources that have been used in making that product.[2]

16.2 Data and model

Data

Data sources are listed the in the references of statistical data at the end of this chapter; explanation of the content is provided here.

International input–output table

The national statistics offices of countries in the Asia-Pacific region have compiled Asian international input–output (IO) tables under a project headed by the Institute of Developing Economies (IDE) of Japan. The IO tables that have been published cover the years 1985, 1990, 1995, 2000 and 2005.[3] The ten regions covered (endogenous in our analysis) are Indonesia, Malaysia, the Philippines, Singapore, Thailand, China, Taiwan, Korea, Japan, and the US.

Table 16.1 shows the Asian international IO table published by the Institute of Developing Economies. The rows show how much of each produced good is sold to each region. Blocks of intermediate demand and final demand are listed by region in the same order as given previously (Indonesia, Malaysia [. . .], the US); the rightmost column shows the totals for domestic output. In a standard one-country table, if the specified goods cross borders between countries, they are treated as part of final demand and labeled as exports. However, in the international IO table these flows are treated as an endogenous, internal part of the system; only goods that leave the Asia-Pacific region are treated as exports.

The columns in the IO table show how much input (i.e., input to economic production, such as materials, etc.) is sourced from other regions for the production of goods. Again, the regions are listed in the same order as stated above, and value added is shown under the 10 regions. The row at the very bottom is the column sum, that is, total inputs. Since international trade costs and export insurance are difficult to identify, they are calculated separately.

Although the Asian international IO table has 24 industrial sectors, it does not correspond exactly in sectors to the energy statistics described in the next section. Therefore, in order to ensure consistency between the two data sources, we aggregated the 24 sectors into the 13 sectors shown in the appendix, Table 16.A1, based on the classification of Imura et al. (2005).

Energy and CO_2 emissions

For energy consumption, we used data from the energy balance tables (*World Energy Statistics and Balances*) published by the International Energy Agency (IEA). The set of energy balances for each country is given in tons of oil equivalent (toe).

The fuels covered are coal, petroleum, and natural gas. Crude oil and petroleum products were integrated and treated as 'petroleum' for simplification. The allotment of fuels to industries in the energy balance table is shown in Table 16.A2.

For CO_2 emissions, we use standard coefficients of units of CO_2 per unit of energy consumption. They are: coal, 4.018 tons/toe; petroleum, 3.313 tons/toe; and natural gas, 2.317 tons/toe.[4]

Model

We use input–output modelling for the analysis in this chapter. The approach is described in detail in the appendix.[5]

Table 16.1 Structure of IDE international input–output table

	Intermediate Demand (A)										Final Demand (f)										Exports (l)			Statistical Discrepancy	Total Outputs
	Indonesia	Malaysia	Philippines	Singapore	Thailand	China	Taiwan	Korea	Japan	US	US	Japan	Korea	Taiwan	China	Thailand	Singapore	Philippines	Malaysia	Indonesia	Export to Hong Kong	Export to EU	Export to ROW		
Indonesia	A_{II}	A_{IM}	A_{IP}	A_{IS}	A_{IT}	A_{IC}	A_{IN}	A_{IK}	A_{IJ}	A_{IU}	f_{IU}	f_{IJ}	f_{IK}	f_{IN}	f_{IC}	f_{IT}	f_{IS}	f_{IP}	f_{IM}	f_{II}	e_{IH}	e_{IE}	e_{IR}	q_I	x_I
Malaysia	A_{MI}	A_{MM}	A_{MP}	A_{MS}	A_{MT}	A_{MC}	A_{MN}	A_{MK}	A_{MJ}	A_{MU}	f_{MU}	f_{MJ}	f_{MK}	f_{MN}	f_{MC}	f_{MT}	f_{MS}	f_{MP}	f_{MM}	f_{MI}	e_{MH}	e_{ME}	e_{MR}	q_M	x_M
Philippines	A_{PI}	A_{PM}	A_{PP}	A_{PS}	A_{PT}	A_{PC}	A_{PN}	A_{PK}	A_{PJ}	A_{PU}	f_{PU}	f_{PJ}	f_{PK}	f_{PN}	f_{PC}	f_{PT}	f_{PS}	f_{PP}	f_{PM}	f_{PI}	e_{PH}	e_{PE}	e_{PR}	q_P	x_P
Singapore	A_{SI}	A_{SM}	A_{SP}	A_{SS}	A_{ST}	A_{SC}	A_{SN}	A_{SK}	A_{SJ}	A_{SU}	f_{SU}	f_{SJ}	f_{SK}	f_{SN}	f_{SC}	f_{ST}	f_{SS}	f_{SP}	f_{SM}	f_{SI}	e_{SH}	e_{SE}	e_{SR}	q_S	x_S
Thailand	A_{TI}	A_{TM}	A_{TP}	A_{TS}	A_{TT}	A_{TC}	A_{TN}	A_{TK}	A_{TJ}	A_{TU}	f_{TU}	f_{TJ}	f_{TK}	f_{TN}	f_{TC}	f_{TT}	f_{TS}	f_{TP}	f_{TM}	f_{TI}	e_{TH}	e_{TE}	e_{TR}	q_T	x_T
China	A_{CI}	A_{CM}	A_{CP}	A_{CS}	A_{CT}	A_{CC}	A_{CN}	A_{CK}	A_{CJ}	A_{CU}	f_{CU}	f_{CJ}	f_{CK}	f_{CN}	f_{CC}	f_{CT}	f_{CS}	f_{CP}	f_{CM}	f_{CI}	e_{CH}	e_{CE}	e_{CR}	q_C	x_C
Taiwan	A_{NI}	A_{NM}	A_{NP}	A_{NS}	A_{NT}	A_{NC}	A_{NN}	A_{NK}	A_{NJ}	A_{NU}	f_{NU}	f_{NJ}	f_{NK}	f_{NN}	f_{NC}	f_{NT}	f_{NS}	f_{NP}	f_{NM}	f_{NI}	e_{NH}	e_{NE}	e_{NR}	q_N	x_N
Korea	A_{KI}	A_{KM}	A_{KP}	A_{KS}	A_{KT}	A_{KC}	A_{KN}	A_{KK}	A_{KJ}	A_{KU}	f_{KU}	f_{KJ}	f_{KK}	f_{KN}	f_{KC}	f_{KT}	f_{KS}	f_{KP}	f_{KM}	f_{KI}	e_{KH}	e_{KE}	e_{KR}	q_K	x_K
Japan	A_{JI}	A_{JM}	A_{JP}	A_{JS}	A_{JT}	A_{JC}	A_{JN}	A_{JK}	A_{JJ}	A_{JU}	f_{JU}	f_{JJ}	f_{JK}	f_{JN}	f_{JC}	f_{JT}	f_{JS}	f_{JP}	f_{JM}	f_{JI}	e_{JH}	e_{JE}	e_{JR}	q_J	x_J
US	A_{UI}	A_{UM}	A_{UP}	A_{US}	A_{UT}	A_{UC}	A_{UN}	A_{UK}	A_{UJ}	A_{UU}	f_{UU}	f_{UJ}	f_{UK}	f_{UN}	f_{UC}	f_{UT}	f_{US}	f_{UP}	f_{UM}	f_{UI}	e_{UH}	e_{UE}	e_{UR}	q_U	x_U
Freight and Insurance	ba_I	ba_M	ba_P	ba_S	ba_T	ba_C	ba_N	ba_K	ba_J	ba_U	bf_U	bf_J	bf_K	bf_N	bf_C	bf_T	bf_S	bf_P	bf_M	bf_I					
Import from Hong Kong	A_{HI}	A_{HM}	A_{HP}	A_{HS}	A_{HT}	A_{HC}	A_{HN}	A_{HK}	A_{HJ}	A_{HU}	f_{HU}	f_{HJ}	f_{HK}	f_{HN}	f_{HC}	f_{HT}	f_{HS}	f_{HP}	f_{HM}	f_{HI}					
Import from EU	A_{EI}	A_{EM}	A_{EP}	A_{ES}	A_{ET}	A_{EC}	A_{EN}	A_{EK}	A_{EJ}	A_{EU}	f_{EU}	f_{EJ}	f_{EK}	f_{EN}	f_{EC}	f_{ET}	f_{ES}	f_{EP}	f_{EM}	f_{EI}					
Import from the ROW	A_{RI}	A_{RM}	A_{RP}	A_{RS}	A_{RT}	A_{RC}	A_{RN}	A_{RK}	A_{RJ}	A_{RU}	f_{RU}	f_{RJ}	f_{RK}	f_{RN}	f_{RC}	f_{RT}	f_{RS}	f_{RP}	f_{RM}	f_{RI}					
Duties and Import Commodity Taxes	da_I	da_M	da_P	da_S	da_T	da_C	da_N	da_K	da_J	da_U	df_U	df_J	df_K	df_N	df_C	df_T	df_S	df_P	df_M	df_I					
Value Added	v_I	v_M	v_P	v_S	v_T	v_C	v_N	v_K	v_J	v_U															
Total Inputs	x_I	x_M	x_P	x_S	x_T	x_C	x_N	x_K	x_J	x_U															

Source: Adapted from IDE (2006).

16.3   Results from the calculations

In this section, we show the calculation results of international transactions of energy and CO_2 embodied in goods and services in the Asia-Pacific region, based on the model described in the previous section, for 1985 and 2005.

Embodied energy transactions

Tables 16.2 and 16.3 show the embodied energy transactions in 1985 and 2005, respectively. The columns give the regions that generate final demands. The rows show the countries in which energy consumption is induced by the final demands of the countries shown in the columns. For example, the number 16.1 in the intersection of the column for the US and the row for Japan shows that final demand in the US induced 16.1 million toe (Mtoe) of energy consumption in Japan. However, the number 9.4 in the intersection of the column for Japan and the row for the US shows that final demand in Japan induced energy consumption of 9.4 Mtoe in the US. Combined, these numbers indicate that the US (directly and indirectly) imported energy for 16.1 Mtoe from Japan, and that Japan (directly and indirectly) imported energy for 9.4 Mtoe from the US. As a result, Japan has, in terms of energy, a 'trade surplus' of 6.7 Mtoe against the US.

The last column (Total), gives the total energy consumption of each country. The light grey cells are the diagonal elements, which are naturally large. The dark grey cells show the ten largest off-diagonal elements, indicating intra-country energy transactions. The top three largest countries by total energy consumption are marked with bold borders.

First, we consider total energy consumption in 1985. The top three countries regarding total energy consumption were the US (1.47 Gtoe), China (0.41 Gtoe), and Japan (0.29 Gtoe), respectively. Although this order does not change in 2005 (see Table 16.3), the relative increase for China was especially large (3.3 times), whereas that for the US and Japan was no more than 1.3 and 1.2 times respectively. This pattern is greatly influenced by how China's role in international trade has changed during the two decades between 1985 and 2005. It is remarkable that China's ratio of energy consumption induced by overseas final demand in other countries has surged from 10.6 percent to 24.4 percent. This is in sharp contrast to the ratio of energy consumption induced by final demand in Japan and the US, which has decreased respectively from 17.1 percent to 12.7 percent and from 8.3 percent to 4.7 percent.

Even back in 1985, China consumed a considerably large amount of energy for demand from Japan and the US (7.1 Mtoe due to Japan and 6.2 Mtoe due to the US). These amounts, however, were smaller than the energy flows between Japan and the US (16.1 Mtoe from Japan to the US and 9.4 Mtoe from the US to Japan). But the situation had changed dramatically by 2005. China's energy consumption for demand from Japan and the US in 2005 jumped to 44.6 Mtoe and 91.3 Mtoe, respectively. In comparison, demands between Japan and the US have not changed that much (13.7 Mtoe from Japan to the US and 14.5 Mtoe from the US to Japan).

Table 16.2 Embodied energy transactions in 1985 (in Mtoe)

	Importing Countries											
Exporting countries	In	Ma	Ph	Si	Th	Ch	Ta	Ko	Jp	US	ROW	Total
Indonesia	21.0	0.1	0.1	0.2	0.0	0.1	0.0	0.1	1.2	0.8	1.3	25.0
Malaysia	0.0	6.3	0.1	0.3	0.1	0.1	0.0	0.1	0.4	1.3	2.7	11.5
Philippines	0.0	0.1	6.7	0.0	0.0	0.0	0.0	0.0	0.3	0.7	1.0	8.9
Singapore	0.2	0.3	0.0	2.2	0.1	0.0	0.0	0.0	0.4	0.5	3.8	7.6
Thailand	0.0	0.1	0.0	0.0	11.2	0.1	0.0	0.0	0.3	0.4	2.6	14.7
China	0.4	0.5	0.4	1.1	0.5	367.6	0.1	0.1	7.1	6.2	27.3	411.2
Taiwan	0.1	0.1	0.0	0.1	0.1	0.3	12.1	0.1	0.9	4.9	4.0	22.8
Korea	0.1	0.1	0.1	0.1	0.1	0.0	0.1	22.3	1.3	3.6	7.0	34.6
Japan	0.8	0.5	0.1	0.5	0.6	4.0	0.8	1.4	241.4	16.1	25.0	291.2
US	0.8	0.7	0.3	0.7	0.4	2.3	1.29	2.1	9.4	1,343.9	104.1	1,466.1
Total	23.4	8.7	7.7	5.3	13.0	374.6	14.4	26.2	262.7	1,378.5	178.9	2,293.5

Note: The rows show the countries in which energy consumption is induced by the final demands of countries shown in the columns.

Source: Authors' calculations.

Table 16.3 Embodied energy transactions in 2005 (in Mtoe)

Exporting countries		In	Ma	Ph	Si	Th	Ch	Ta	Ko	Jp	US	ROW	Total
							Importing countries						
Indonesia		90.0	1.0	0.3	1.5	1.4	3.0	0.9	2.7	5.0	6.4	7.1	119.3
Malaysia		0.6	26.4	0.3	2.3	1.1	2.5	0.7	1.0	2.6	7.9	15.1	60.6
Philippines		0.1	0.2	17.0	0.1	0.2	0.8	0.3	0.4	1.2	2.9	1.5	24.6
Singapore		0.3	0.7	0.2	5.5	0.5	1.1	0.4	0.4	0.5	1.5	11.4	22.7
Thailand		0.8	1.1	0.4	0.9	59.8	3.0	0.7	0.9	4.2	6.5	8.3	86.5
China		4.0	3.7	1.3	4.8	3.7	1,030.3	5.2	14.3	44.6	91.3	160.5	1,363.7
Taiwan		0.3	0.4	0.1	0.3	0.5	5.9	40.7	0.8	2.2	5.9	22.4	79.5
Korea		0.5	0.5	0.2	0.4	0.4	6.4	0.9	99.8	3.7	6.6	11.2	130.7
Japan		0.8	0.9	0.4	1.0	1.4	6.7	2.7	3.8	332.3	13.7	17.2	380.8
USA		0.8	1.0	0.4	1.4	1.1	6.6	2.8	5.8	14.5	1,706.1	50.7	1,791.1
Total		98.1	35.9	20.6	18.2	70.2	1,066.5	55.1	129.9	410.7	1,848.7	305.6	4,059.5

Note: The rows show the countries in which energy consumption is induced by the final demands of countries shown in the columns.

Source: Authors' calculations.

Regarding Japan and the US, the characteristics can be summarized as follows. In 1985, Japan and the US induced large amounts of energy consumption in other countries, whereas large amounts of energy consumption in Japan and the US were concurrently induced by other countries. In Table 16.2, all the cells shaded dark gray are allocated to columns or rows for Japan or the US. However, as shown in Table 16.3, in 2005 Japan and the US induced much higher energy consumptions in other countries than energy consumption was induced upon them. To put it another way, in 1985 Japan and the US each were both energy-exporting and energy-importing countries, whereas in 2005 both were energy-importing countries only, while China had become an energy-exporting country.

Embodied CO$_2$ transactions

Tables 16.4 and 16.5 show the embodied CO$_2$ transactions in 1985 and 2005, respectively. Since CO$_2$ emissions are calculated by multiplying energy consumption (coal, petroleum, and natural gas) by the emission coefficients, the results would be expected to be similar to those for embodied energy transactions shown above.

Whereas the top three countries in terms of CO$_2$ emissions were the US, China, and Japan in both 1985 and 2005, the increase in CO$_2$ emissions in China was very large in the period 1985–2005; China increased its CO$_2$ emissions 3.3 times compared to 1.3 times in Japan and 1.2 times in the US.

This contrast again has a great deal to do with China's role in international trade having changed between 1985 and 2005. China's ratio of CO$_2$ emissions induced by the final demand in other countries increased from 10.6 percent to 24.4 percent in the period 1985–2005. By contrast, the ratio of CO$_2$ emissions induced by overseas final demand in Japan and the US decreased during the same period from 17.1 percent to 12.7 percent and 8.3 percent to 4.7 percent, respectively.

The findings are very similar to those for energy consumption. In 1985, Japan and the US carried CO$_2$ emissions for other countries but, at the same time, made other countries carry their own CO$_2$ emissions. By 2005, however, only one half of this situation remained: both countries made other countries carry their own CO$_2$ emissions as goods-importing countries. In other words, they shifted their position from 'producing and consuming places' to 'consuming places' of goods. By contrast, China, a quarter of whose CO$_2$ emissions are the result of exports, emerged as a 'producing place' of goods in 2005. In other words, China had become a surrogate CO$_2$ emitter by 2005.

16.4   Concluding Remarks

This chapter estimated the levels of 'embodied energy use' and 'embodied CO$_2$ emissions' in the Asia-Pacific region, based on input–output analysis using an Asian international input–output table. The main findings are as follows:

First, the US, China, and Japan ranked as the top three consumers of energy and producers of CO$_2$ emissions in the Asia-Pacific region in both 1985 and

Table 16.4 Embodied CO$_2$ transactions in 1985 (in Mt)

					Importing countries							
		In	Ma	Ph	Si	Th	Ch	Ta	Ko	Jp	US	ROW	Total
Exporting Countries	Indonesia	64.9	0.2	0.2	0.6	0.1	0.4	0.1	0.2	3.5	2.4	3.9	76.4
	Malaysia	0.1	20.0	0.3	1.0	0.2	0.2	0.1	0.3	1.4	4.1	8.2	35.9
	Philippines	0.0	0.3	22.9	0.1	0.1	0.1	0.1	0.1	1.0	2.4	3.5	30.6
	Singapore	0.6	1.0	0.0	7.3	0.5	0.1	0.1	0.1	1.3	1.8	12.5	25.3
	Thailand	0.0	0.2	0.0	0.1	35.7	0.2	0.1	0.1	0.8	1.3	8.6	47.2
	China	1.7	2.0	1.5	4.1	1.8	1,403.0	0.2	0.3	27.0	23.6	104.0	1,569.2
	Taiwan	0.4	0.3	0.1	0.4	0.3	1.2	42.3	0.4	3.1	17.2	14.0	79.6
	Korea	0.4	0.3	0.2	0.3	0.2	0.1	0.2	78.2	4.5	13.0	24.8	122.1
	Japan	2.7	1.6	0.3	1.7	2.0	14.1	2.7	4.9	810.9	55.6	85.9	982.5
	US	2.5	2.2	0.9	2.3	1.2	7.5	4.2	6.7	30.6	4,427.6	332.3	4,818.0
	Total	73.3	28.2	26.4	17.9	42.1	1,426.9	50.0	91.3	884.0	4,548.9	597.7	7,786.8

Note: The rows show the countries in which CO$_2$ emissions are induced by the final demands of countries shown in the columns.

Source: Authors' calculations.

Table 16.5 Embodied CO$_2$ transactions in 2005 (in Mt)

Exporting countries	Importing countries											
	In	Ma	Ph	Si	Tb	Ch	Ta	Ko	Jp	US	ROW	Total
Indonesia	284.0	3.0	1.0	4.7	4.2	9.6	2.7	8.1	15.6	20.2	22.2	375.1
Malaysia	1.6	76.2	0.8	6.7	3.2	7.1	2.1	3.0	7.7	22.7	44.5	175.6
Philippines	0.2	0.7	57.7	0.4	0.7	2.8	0.9	1.3	4.0	9.7	5.1	83.4
Singapore	0.9	2.2	0.6	15.9	1.7	3.6	1.1	1.2	1.7	4.6	35.8	69.2
Thailand	2.4	3.6	1.3	2.8	181.5	9.2	2.1	2.7	13.0	20.0	25.7	264.1
China	15.5	14.1	4.8	18.8	14.2	3,954.7	20.3	55.1	172.2	353.3	621.2	5,244.3
Taiwan	1.0	1.5	0.4	1.0	1.9	21.2	144.3	3.0	7.7	21.1	78.7	281.8
Korea	1.8	1.6	0.8	1.3	1.4	22.3	3.0	341.9	12.7	22.5	38.4	447.8
Japan	2.8	3.2	1.3	3.4	4.9	23.2	9.1	13.0	1,112.5	47.2	59.2	1,279.7
US	2.5	3.1	1.2	4.3	3.5	20.9	8.8	18.4	46.3	5,618.0	161.4	5,888.5
Total	312.8	109.3	70.0	59.3	217.1	4,074.5	194.4	447.6	1,393.2	6,139.1	1,092.2	14,109.6

Note: The rows show the countries in which CO$_2$ emissions are induced by the final demands of countries shown in the columns.

Source: Authors' calculations.

2005. It should be noted that China's increase has been very large during the 20 years between 1985 and 2005. In 1985, the US and Japan were production places of goods (goods-exporting countries) and consumption places of goods (goods-importing countries). In other words, they not only carried CO_2 emissions on behalf of other countries but they also made other countries carry their CO_2 emissions. However, by 2005 Japan and the US had both become consuming places of goods (countries that use other countries' energy). China, by contrast, became a 'goods-importing-and-exporting country' in place of the US and Japan over the period 1985–2005.

If we can put these findings into a single sentence, it would be that in the Asia-Pacific region during the 20 years from 1985 to 2005, there was a tendency for developed countries, such as Japan and the US, to make developing countries shoulder their CO_2 emissions.

Looking to the future, none of the large CO_2 emitters (China, the US, Japan, and India) have a target for GHG reduction for the second Kyoto commitment period (2013–2018). The developing countries insist that developed countries are responsible for current global warming because developed countries have emitted CO_2 by consuming a lot of energy in the past. But the developed countries insist that cooperation with developing countries – whose energy consumption and CO_2 emissions are rapidly increasing – is indispensable to mitigate global warming in the future. The phrase 'common but differentiated responsibilities'(UN, 1992) became famous after the Rio Earth Summit (the United Nations Conference on Environment and Development) in 1992. One example for the use of this phase is the differentiated GHG reduction targets among countries, and we now might change our view of this phrase. As we have discussed in this chapter, developing countries are supporting a share of the emissions of developed countries. It is important to acknowledge this situation in order to lessen the friction between developed countries and developing countries during future negotiations.

One idea for cooperation is the issuance of CO_2 certificates that indicate the CO_2 contents during a production process. This might provide a way to allocate the responsibility of emissions by applying the final goods consumption criterion. The goods importers must buy this CO_2 certificate when they import the goods. The price of the CO_2 certificate could be different depending on the importing country.[6] The price of CO_2 certificates for developing countries, for example, could be lower than those for developed countries or, for developing countries, could even be zero. And if the revenue from this transaction would be pooled and used for energy savings or adaptation investment in developing countries, the system of CO_2 certificates could have major benefits for developing countries.

As Na (2000) pointed out, introduction of the final goods consumption criterion could be an incentive for energy saving in developing countries. If the transaction of CO_2 started, exporting goods that embodied more CO_2 would be more expensive. The goods-exporting countries or developing countries, therefore, would try to reduce embodied CO_2 in their exports to keep them competitive in the international market. In this context, the introduction of the final goods consumption criterion is worth considering.

Appendix

CO_2 emissions from energy consumption account for the largest share of green-house gas (GHG) emissions. When defining the location of these emissions, three possible criteria can be used: 'energy production', 'energy consumption', or 'final goods consumption'. However, the energy production criterion is not widely used because it allocates all emissions to the country in which the fuel is extracted.

The Kyoto Protocol is based on the energy consumption criterion, which focuses on production processes and direct environmental load. However, here we focus on the final goods consumption criterion, or the 'direct and indirect' environmental load.[7] This section summarizes a calculation method of direct and indirect environmental load.

In the one-country IO model, the following supply-demand relationship holds between the final demand for domestic goods ($\mathbf{f}^d$) and domestic supply ($\mathbf{x}$):[8]

$$\mathbf{x} = \mathbf{A}^d \mathbf{x} + \mathbf{f}^d \tag{16.1}$$

$\mathbf{A}^d$ is the domestic input coefficient matrix, where each column shows the directly required quantity of domestically produced intermediate inputs in order to produce one unit of the corresponding output. Imports from abroad ($\mathbf{m}$) are defined as the total of intermediate demand and final demand ($\mathbf{f}^m$).

$$\mathbf{m} = \mathbf{A}^m \mathbf{x} + \mathbf{f}^m \tag{16.2}$$

$\mathbf{A}^m$ is the import input coefficient matrix, where each column shows the directly required quantity of imported intermediate inputs required to produce one unit of the corresponding output.

Solving equation 16.1 in terms of domestic output ($\mathbf{x}$), we can get the following equilibrium output equation, where the matrix $\mathbf{B}$ is known as the Leontief inverse matrix.

$$\mathbf{x} = (\mathbf{I} - \mathbf{A}^d)^{-1} \mathbf{f}^d = \mathbf{B} \mathbf{f}^d \tag{16.3}$$

Here, assuming vector $\mathbf{a}$ to be an energy input coefficient[9] and multiplying energy input coefficient ($\mathbf{a}$) and domestic output ($\mathbf{x}$), we can calculate a direct energy use vector (**ep**), which is the energy use in the energy consumption criterion.

$$ep = a\hat{x} = a \begin{bmatrix} x_1 & & \\ & \ddots & \\ & & x_n \end{bmatrix} \qquad (16.4)$$

However, to obtain energy use in the final goods consumption criterion, we calculate a direct and indirect energy use vector, or an embodied energy use vector (**ec**), as follows.

$$ec = aB\hat{f}^d = aB \begin{bmatrix} f_1^d & & \\ & \ddots & \\ & & f_n^d \end{bmatrix} \qquad (16.5)$$

As noted in the previous section, the rate of CO_2 emissions is proportional to calorie-based energy consumption. Therefore, direct CO_2 emissions – or CO_2 emissions in the energy consumption criterion by industry (**cp**) – can be calculated by multiplying the CO_2 emission coefficient (**c**) by the level of energy consumption obtained from Eq. 16.4.

$$c = 4.018 \text{ for coal, } 3.313 \text{ for oil, } 2.317 \text{ for natural gas} \qquad (16.6)$$
$$cp = c \cdot a\hat{x} \qquad (16.7)$$

The embodied CO_2 emissions, or CO_2 emissions in the final goods consumption criterion, by industry (**cc**) can be calculated by multiplying the CO_2 emission coefficient (**c**) with embodied energy consumption obtained in Eq. 16.5.

$$cc = c \cdot aB\hat{f}^d \qquad (16.8)$$

The model is so far for a single-region IO table, but this model can be extended for multi-regional IO tables. We can demonstrate this by using a bi-regional IO table. The following supply-demand relation holds for both regions 1 and 2.

$$\begin{bmatrix} x_1 \\ x_2 \end{bmatrix} = \begin{bmatrix} A_{11} & A_{12} \\ A_{21} & A_{22} \end{bmatrix} \begin{bmatrix} x_1 \\ x_2 \end{bmatrix} + \begin{bmatrix} f_{11} + f_{12} + f_{13} \\ f_{21} + f_{22} + f_{23} \end{bmatrix} \qquad (16.9)$$

Suffixes 1 and 2 identify the region. A_{ij} stands for the input coefficient; when $i = j$, it is the intra-country input coefficient; when $i \neq j$, it is the input coefficient for inputs in region i to produce goods in region j. For final demand f_{ij}, when $i = j$ it is the own country's final demand, and when $i \neq j$ it is the final demand for region i by region j. The vector f_{i3} stands for the export from region i to the rest of the world (ROW). In Table 16.1, the last column (total outputs) corresponds to the domestic output **x**, and the total of final demand (**f**) and exports (**I**) correspond to the final demands in the equations.

$$\begin{bmatrix} \mathbf{x}_1 \\ \mathbf{x}_2 \end{bmatrix} = \begin{bmatrix} \mathbf{I} - \begin{bmatrix} \mathbf{A}_{11} & \mathbf{A}_{12} \\ \mathbf{A}_{21} & \mathbf{A}_{22} \end{bmatrix} \end{bmatrix}^{-1} \begin{bmatrix} \mathbf{f}_{11} + \mathbf{f}_{12} + \mathbf{f}_{13} \\ \mathbf{f}_{21} + \mathbf{f}_{22} + \mathbf{f}_{23} \end{bmatrix} \tag{16.10}$$

Imports of region i (i = 1, 2) from the third (external) region are expressed as follows:

$$\mathbf{m}_{3i} = \mathbf{A}_{3i} \mathbf{x}_i + \mathbf{f}_{3i} \tag{16.11}$$

We calculate direct energy use (**ep**) and embodied energy use (**ec**), respectively, as follows in the framework of the international input–output table.

$$\mathbf{ep} = \begin{bmatrix} \mathbf{a}_1 & \mathbf{a}_2 \end{bmatrix} \begin{bmatrix} \hat{\mathbf{x}}_1 & 0 \\ 0 & \hat{\mathbf{x}}_2 \end{bmatrix} \tag{16.12}$$

$$\mathbf{ec} = \begin{bmatrix} \mathbf{a}_1 & \mathbf{a}_2 \end{bmatrix} \begin{bmatrix} \mathbf{B}_{11} & \mathbf{B}_{12} \\ \mathbf{B}_{21} & \mathbf{B}_{22} \end{bmatrix} \begin{bmatrix} \mathbf{f}_{11} & \mathbf{f}_{12} & \mathbf{f}_{13} \\ \mathbf{f}_{21} & \mathbf{f}_{22} & \mathbf{f}_{23} \end{bmatrix} \tag{16.13}$$

CO_2 emissions under the energy consumption (**cp**) criterion and those in the final goods consumption (**cc**) criterion are calculated, respectively, as follows.

$$\mathbf{cp} = \mathbf{c} \cdot \begin{bmatrix} \mathbf{a}_1 & \mathbf{a}_2 \end{bmatrix} \begin{bmatrix} \hat{\mathbf{x}}_1 & 0 \\ 0 & \hat{\mathbf{x}}_2 \end{bmatrix} \tag{16.14}$$

$$\mathbf{cc} = \mathbf{c} \cdot \begin{bmatrix} \mathbf{a}_1 & \mathbf{a}_2 \end{bmatrix} \begin{bmatrix} \mathbf{B}_{11} & \mathbf{B}_{12} \\ \mathbf{B}_{21} & \mathbf{B}_{22} \end{bmatrix} \begin{bmatrix} \mathbf{f}_{11} & \mathbf{f}_{12} & \mathbf{f}_{13} \\ \mathbf{f}_{21} & \mathbf{f}_{22} & \mathbf{f}_{23} \end{bmatrix} \tag{16.15}$$

Table 16.A1 Industry aggregation in this study

	Original industry classification in IDE Asian IO table		Industry classification in this study
01	Paddy	01	Primary industry
02	Other agricultural products		
03	Livestock		
04	Forestry		
05	Fishery		
06	Crude petroleum and natural gas	02	Mining
07	Other mining		

(*Continued*)

Table 16.A1 (Continued)

	Original industry classification in IDE Asian IO table		Industry classification in this study
08	Food, beverage, and tobacco	03	Food, beverage, and tobacco
09	Textiles, leather, and the products thereof	04	Textiles and leather products
10	Timber and wooden products	05	Timber and wooden products
11	Pulp, paper, and printing	06	Pulp and paper products
12	Chemical products	07	Chemical and non-metallic mineral products
13	Petroleum and petro products		
14	Rubber products		
15	Non-metallic mineral products		
16	Metal products	08	Metal products
17	Machinery	09	Machinery
18	Transport equipment		
19	Other manufacturing products		
20	Electricity, gas, and water supply	10	Electricity, gas, and water supply
21	Construction	11	Construction
22	Trade and transport	12	Transportation
23	Services	13	Other services
24	Public administration		

Source: Authors' compilation.

Table 16.A2 Energy-using industry aggregation in this study

IEA Classification	Classification in this study
Energy transfer sector	Energy transfer sector
Transfer	Neglected
Statistical discrepancy	Neglected
Electricity plants	10 Electricity, gas, and water supply
HCP plants	
Heat plants	
Gas works	
Petroleum refineries	07 Chemical and non-metallic mineral products
Coal transformation	
Liquefaction plants	
Other transformation	
Own use	
Distribution losses	

Table 16.A2 (Continued)

IEA Classification	Classification in this study
Energy consumption sector	Energy consumption sector
Iron and steel	08 Metal products
Non-ferrous metals	
Chemicals and petrochemicals	07 Chemicals and non-metallic
Non-metallic minerals	mineral products
Transport equipment	09 Machinery
Machinery	
Mining and quarrying	02 Mining
Food and tobacco	03 Food, beverage, and tobacco
Paper pulp and printing	06 Pulp and paper products
Wood and wood products	05 Timber and wooden products
Non-specified	09 Machinery
Construction	11 Construction
Textiles and leather	04 Textiles and leather products
Transport sector	12 Transportation
Agriculture	01 Primary industry
Comm. and publ. services	13 Other services
Residential	Neglected

Source: Authors' compilation.

Statistics

1 International input–output tables

Institute of Developing Economics (IDE) (2006). *The Schematic Image of the 2000 Asian International Input–Output Table.* http://www.ide.go.jp/Japanese/Publish/Books/Tokei/xls/AIO(85-00).xls (accessed May 17, 2015) .

Institute of Developing Economies (IDE) (1993). *Asian International Input–Output Table, 1985.* Statistical Data Series, No. 65.

Chen, Y, and Jin, T. (2012). 'Progress of the international interdependence in East Asia with a focus on China: Through the estimate of the Asian international input–output table of year 2005.' *Journal of Northeast Asian Studies*, 18, pp. 49–72. (In Japanese).

2 Energy consumption

Organization for Economic Co-operation and Development (OECD) and the International Energy Agency (IEA) (1990). *World Energy Statistics and Balances, 1985–1988.* Paris: Organisation for Economic Cooperation and Development.

Organization for Economic Co-operation and Development (OECD) and the International Energy Agency (IEA) (2005). *Energy Balances of OECD Countries 2005.* Paris: Organisation for Economic Cooperation and Development.

Organization for Economic Co-operation and Development (OECD) and the International Energy Agency (IEA) (2005). *Energy Balances of Non OECD Countries 2005*. Paris: Organisation for Economic Cooperation and Development.

3   *CO₂ emission coefficient*

Institute of Energy Economics, Japan (2008). *2008 EDMC Handbook of Energy & Economic Statistics in Japan*. Tokyo: Energy Conservation Center.

Notes

1 Chapter 15 discussed an issue similar to that discussed here, but the concept of production-based CO_2 emissions in a country is different between the two chapters. Our research here defines this as CO_2 emissions from domestic production activities for both intermediate and final goods in one country, whereas Chapter 15 defines it as CO_2 emissions for the production of final goods against one country in the world. Our research is focused on trade of embodied CO_2 emissions among countries, whereas Chapter 15 mainly compares consumption-based CO_2 emissions and production-based CO_2 emissions in a unique definition by country and industry.
2 The concept of 'consumption-based CO_2 emissions' is expressed in several variants. Imura, Nakamura, and Morisugi (2005, p. 11) uses 'embodied CO_2 emissions' and Na (2000, p. 311) uses 'attributed CO_2 emissions.' *Economic Systems Research*, the Journal of the International Input–Output Association, issued a special issue covering carbon-footprinting and IO analysis in 2009. The concept of carbon-footprinting is the same as that of 'consumption-based CO_2 emissions'. See Minx et al. (2009), and Nansai et al. (2009).
3 We used the Asian international IO table for 1985 and 2005. For the 1985 table, see IDE (1993). The 2005 table was published in mid-2014 by the Institute of Developing Economies (IDE) after we had started this research. We, therefore, used the preliminary estimates of the Asian international IO table for 2005 provided by Chen and Jin (2012).
4 The Institute of Energy Economics, Japan (2008)
5 This type of IO modeling is summarized in Wiebe et al. (2012).
6 This is the main difference between an international carbon tax and CO_2 certificate transaction.
7 This philosophy can be applied to land usage and water consumption when producing agricultural goods. An importer of agricultural goods indirectly uses the land of the exporter, although the exporter cultivates its own land and an importer of agricultural goods indirectly uses the water of the exporter. Ultimate water usage is referred to as 'vertical water consumption.'
8 This type of IO modeling is summarized by Wiebe et al. (2012).
9 Since this research considers three kinds of fossil energy, there also are three kinds of input coefficient for energy: coal, petroleum, and natural gas.

References

Chen, Y, and Jin, T. (2012). 'Progress of the international interdependence in East Asia with a focus on China: Through the estimate of the Asian international input–output table of year 2005.' *Journal of Northeast Asian Studies*, 18, pp. 49–72. (In Japanese).

Imura, H., and Moriguchi, Y. (1995). 'Economic interdependence and eco-balance: Accounting for the flow of environmental loads associated with trade.' In Murai, S. (Ed.), *Toward Global Planning of Sustainable Use of the Earth: Development of Global Eco-Engineering.* Amsterdam: Elsevier Science. pp. 189–208.

Imura, H., Nakamura, E., and Morisugi, M. (2005). 'International–dependence of environmental loads associate with trade among Japan, US and Asian countries.' *Journals of the Japan Society of Civil Engineers*, 790, pp. 11–23. (In Japanese).

Minx, J. C., Wiedmann, T., Wood, R., Peterse, G. P., Lenzen, M., Owen, A., Scott, K., Barrett, J., Hubacek, K., Baiocchi, G., Paul, A., Dawkins, E., Briggs, J., Guan, D., Suh, S., and Ackerman, F. (2009). 'Input–output analysis and carbon footprinting: An overview of applications.' *Economic Systems Research*, 21(3), pp. 187–216.

Na, S. I. (2000). 'Input–output analysis of CO_2 emissions for industrial sector in Korea.' *Environmental Economics and Policy Studies*, 3(3), pp. 311–333.

Nansai, K., Kagawa, S., Kondo, Y., Suh, S., Inaba, R., and Nakajima, K. (2009). 'Improving the completeness of product carbon footprints using a global link input–output model: The case of JAPAN.' *Economic Systems Research*, 21(3), pp. 267–290.

United Nations (UN) (1992). 'Rio Declaration on Environment and Development.' http://www.un.org/documents/ga/conf151/aconf15126-1annex1.htm/ (accessed May 17, 2015)

Wiebe, K. S., Bruckner, M., Giljum, S., and Lutz, C. (2012). 'Calculating energy-related CO_2 emissions embodied in international trade using a global input–output model.' *Economic Systems Research*, 24(2), pp. 113–139.

17 Emissions from international maritime transportation in East Asia

Yoshifumi Ishikawa

17.1 Introduction

East Asia is witnessing a rapid increase in international trade volume owing to globalization. In the 20 years from 1993 to 2013, Japan's total imports grew by a factor of 3.5, and those of China and Korea grew 18.8 times and 6.2 times, respectively. In tandem with this increase, greenhouse gas (GHG) emissions from fuel consumption have increased. According to the International Maritime Organization (IMO), GHG emissions resulting from international shipping accounted for 2.7 percent of global GHG emissions in 2007, a figure equivalent to Germany's total GHG emissions. In addition, the IMO predicts that, in the absence of policies, CO_2 emissions from international shipping will increase by a factor of two to three in 2050 compared with those in 2007 (IMO, 2009).

It is, therefore, very important to formulate policies in response to rising maritime GHG emissions in a progressively globalizing world. Although GHG emissions from cargo transport are steadily increasing, neither emissions from international shipping nor international aviation are subject to the limitation and reduction commitments agreed by Annex 1 Parties (i.e., developed countries) under the United Nations Framework Convention on Climate Change (UNFCCC) and the Kyoto Protocol. This is because individual countries responsible for these emissions are difficult to identify. Therefore, the environmental regulation of international shipping and aviation has been entrusted to specialized international organizations, namely the IMO and the International Civil Aviation Organization (ICAO).

The quantification principle usually followed by the Intergovernmental Panel on Climate Change (IPCC) involves identifying the economic location where emissions occur. However, due to the fragmentation of production processes and global supply chains, producers and consumers differ. For instance, even though GHG emissions increase in a developing country, this increase may be attributed to developed countries. As we have seen in Chapters 15 and 16, GHG emissions focused on producers and consumers can be analyzed by using input–output tables, but GHG emissions from international shipping and aviation are generally estimated by using fuel consumption and fuel-based emission factors. However, to identify the countries responsible for these emissions, it is essential to analyze not only the direct emissions from international transport, but the means by which intermediate and final goods are transported between producers and consumers. In this respect, conventional approaches cannot be used for such analysis. Further, since fuel consumption increases according to distance travelled and amount of goods traded, it is also necessary to analyze GHG emissions associated with international trade from these perspectives.

Because GHG emissions from ships and airplanes are determined by volume of goods and distance travelled, we must take into account transport statistics if we are to allocate responsibility for emissions. In this chapter, we analyze the structure of GHG emissions from international shipping caused by final product demands from China, Japan, and Korea in terms of distance travelled, and relationship between producers and consumers.

The structure of the chapter is as follows. In Section 17.2, we describe CO_2 emissions from international bunkers owing to international trade in East Asia, and in Section 17.3 we review previous literature on the topic. In Section 17.4, we describe methods to estimate CO_2 emissions from international shipping. Section 17.5 presents these resulting estimates for emissions required to meet demand in China and Japan. Section 17.6 provides simulation results based on a particular scenario with improvements to energy efficiency, and Section 17.7 presents our conclusions.

17.2 CO_2 emissions from international bunkers owing to international trade

The increase in international trade and the GHG emissions attributable to international cargo

In recent years, international trade volumes have been increasing rapidly due to a combination of globalization and wider economic growth. A substantial share of GHG emissions is now caused by international freight transport. According to the Organisation for Economic Co-operation and Development (OECD, 2010), carbon dioxide (CO_2) emissions from transport, including international freight transport, increased by 44 percent between 1990 and 2008, and accounted for 23 percent of global CO_2 emissions in 2008. In particular, international shipping, central to cargo transport, accounted for 580 million tons (mt) of CO_2 emissions in 2008 – an increase of 63 percent from the 1990 level, which was around 2 percent of global CO_2 emissions in 2008.

International freight volumes in East Asia, including China, Japan, and Korea, are also increasing rapidly. Between 1993 and 2013, China's total exports and imports increased by factors of 18.8 and 24 respectively; Japan's increased by factors of 3.5 and 2, while Korea's increased by factors of 6.2 and 6.8 (see Figure 17.1 and Figure 17.2).

In terms of trade partnerships, between 2003 and 2013 the value of Japan's exports to China and Korea increased respectively by 125 percent and 62 percent, and the three economies have become increasingly interdependent. China and

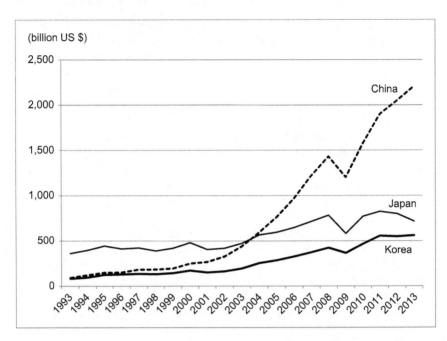

Figure 17.1 Exports from China, Japan, and Korea (billion US$, nominal values).
Source: UN(2014).

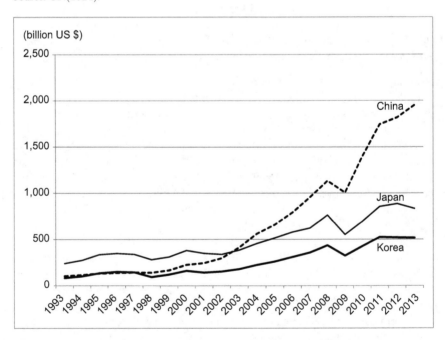

Figure 17.2 Imports to China, Japan, and Korea (billion US$, nominal values).
Source: UN (2014).

Table 17.1 Exports by China, Japan, and Korea (million US$, nominal values)

	Partner	2003	2013	Rate of increase
Japan	World	471,996	715,097	52%
Japan	China	57,415	129,401	125%
Japan	Korea	34,806	56,513	62%
Japan	USA	117,539	134,540	14%
Korea	World	193,817	559,619	189%
Korea	China	35,110	145,869	315%
Korea	Japan	17,276	34,662	101%
Korea	USA	34,369	62,327	81%
China	World	438,228	2,209,007	404%
China	Japan	59,409	150,133	153%
China	Korea	20,095	91,165	354%
China	USA	92,626	369,064	298%

Source: UN (2014).

Table 17.2 Imports by China, Japan, and Korea (million US$, nominal values)

	Partner	2003	2013	Rate of increase
Japan	World	383,452	833,166	117%
Japan	China	75,469	180,978	140%
Japan	Korea	17,903	35,822	100%
Japan	USA	59,995	71,959	20%
Korea	World	178,826	515,573	188%
Korea	China	21,909	83,051	279%
Korea	Japan	36,313	60,029	65%
Korea	USA	24,935	41,762	67%
China	World	412,760	1,949,992	372%
China	Japan	74,148	162,246	119%
China	Korea	43,128	183,073	324%
China	USA	33,944	153,395	352%

Source: UN (2014).

Korea are experiencing a similar growth in international trade and, hence, GHG emissions from international shipping are likely to increase further (see Table 17.1 and Table 17.2).

Demand for commercial marine transportation is growing rapidly and, consequently, GHG emissions are also increasing. When international emissions attributed to a country are estimated by using the UNFCCC guidelines, these estimates are based on the country's sales of international bunker fuels. However, this may misrepresent the country's contribution to international marine transportation emissions, because ships can visit ports in a country without refueling there. Thus, it is not generally possible to accurately estimate the international proportion of a country's emissions from maritime transport. In accordance with IPCC and UNFCCC guidelines, emissions from fuels used in international maritime shipping are included as part of a country's national GHG inventory, but are excluded from the national total and reported separately. These emissions are not subject to the limitations and reduction commitments of Annex 1 Parties under the UNFCCC and the Kyoto Protocol. Article 2.2 of the Protocol has set out a different method for estimating international emissions from aviation and marine shipping: 'The parties included in Annex 1 shall pursue limitation or reduction of emission of greenhouse gases not controlled by the Montreal Protocol from aviation and marine bunker fuels, working through the International Civil Aviation Organization and the International Maritime Organization, respectively' (Article 2.2 of the Kyoto Protocol to the UNFCC, 1998).

Therefore, responsibility to cut bunker emissions was not given to individual countries. Reductions by UNFCCC Annex 1 countries should instead be achieved by working through the responsible international bodies for these transport modes – the ICAO for aviation and the IMO for maritime transport.

CO_2 emissions from international shipping

GHG emissions in exhaust gases have been generally estimated by establishing fuel-based emission factors for each of the relevant components of the exhaust gas, plus a fuel consumption inventory. Fuel-based emission factors are factors that convert fuel consumption into the emissions that are derived from the combustion process. Using the fuel estimates and fuel-based emission factors, emissions of exhaust gases have been calculated by the IMO. CO_2 is the most important GHG emitted by ships in terms of quantity and global warming potential. CO_2 emissions from shipping as a whole and for international shipping from 1990 to 2007 are shown in Figure 17.3.

As shown in Figure 17.3, CO_2 emissions from total shipping and international shipping roughly doubled in the period between 1990 and 2007. Shipping is estimated to have emitted 1,046 mt CO_2 in 2007, which corresponded to around 3.3 percent of global emissions. International shipping is estimated to have emitted 870 mt CO_2, or around 2.7 percent, of global CO_2 emissions in 2007 (IMO, 2009).

IMO (2009) provides a range of possible future emissions trajectories from shipping up to the year 2050. In this report, midrange emission scenarios show that, by 2050, in the absence of mitigating policies and action, CO_2 emissions from international shipping may increase by a factor of two to three compared with 2007 levels.

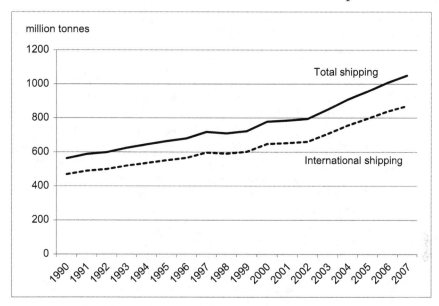

Figure 17.3 CO$_2$ emissions (mt) from shipping, 1990–2007.
Source: IMO (2009)

17.3 Literature review

There are two main ways in which international trade leads to GHG emissions: the production of trade goods, and the transportation of goods between trading countries. On the first source, a large body of literature has focused on the allocation of responsibility for the environmental consequences of international trade. In terms of the allocation criterion for GHG emissions, the IPCC and the Kyoto Protocol consider producer responsibility rather than consumer responsibility. The principle of producer responsibility means that a country is responsible for pollutant emissions from the domestic process of the production of goods, regardless of where these commodities are consumed. By contrast, the principle of consumer responsibility allocates responsibility for emissions to the final consumer of commodities (see Chapters 15 and 16). In order to discuss these principles, detailed analyses of the impact of international trade and consumption patterns on a country's GHG emissions have been conducted by using input–output tables. The earliest studies in this area used a single-country input–output table (e.g. Wyckoff and Roop, 1994; Antweiler, 1996; Kondo, Moriguchi, and Shimizu, 1998; Lenzen, 1998; Machado, Schaeffer, and Worrell, 2001; Munksgaard and Pedersen, 2001; Muradian, O'Connor, and Martinez-Alier, 2002; Ferng, 2003; Sanchez-Choliz and Duarte, 2004; Mongelli, Tassielli, and Notarnicola , 2006). In these studies, it was assumed that all countries used similar technologies and production processes in order to estimate the level of embodied emissions in imports.

More recent studies have used multi-country input–output tables (e.g. Ahmad and Wyckoff, 2003; Lenzen, Pade, and Munksgaard, 2004; Peters and Hertwich, 2008). This approach allows for the use of different technologies in different countries. However, they consider only unidirectional trade or limit the trading partners. In these studies, it is assumed that the domestic economy trades with all countries, but the other counties do not trade amongst each other; an assumption that reduces many of the feedback loops.

None of these papers explicitly deals with the emissions linked to the transport needed for international trade. Cadarso et al. (2010) proposed a methodology for estimating the impact of international freight transport on CO_2 emissions and assigning the responsibility for emissions to consumers by using an input–output methodology. However, this methodology also does not take international trade among other countries into account.

Regarding emissions linked to transport services required for international trade, the most detailed research is found in the case study based on life cycle analyses (LCA) by Sim et al. (2007) and Williams (2007). These studies assess the environmental impact of every input into the production and delivery of a product. LCA studies provide detailed calculations of transport emissions for a particular product and trade. However, they are micro in focus (i.e., related to specific products) and do not calculate the emissions for all products at once. Although there are studies that focus on the impact of international trade related to specific transport modes, such as those by Corbett and Koehler (2003), Endresen et al. (2003), and Corbett and Winebrake (2008), they do not consider the relationship with the production of trade goods that is caused by final demand.

Most recent studies have not attributed international transport emissions to origin and destination countries. However, Cristea et al. (2013) provides an extensive database on output and transport emissions associated with every origin–destination–product trade flow worldwide, and employs this database to quantify the contribution of international transport to total emissions. However, this study does not analyze all possible ripple effects from supply chains.

Hence, this chapter is proposing a method for quantifying CO_2 emissions that are linked to international transport in terms of allocation of responsibility for emissions to the final consumer of commodities. In addition, we analyze the CO_2 emissions from international shipping linked to international trade caused by final demand.

17.4   Methods to estimate CO_2 emissions from international shipping

In this chapter, we use input–output methods to estimate all greenhouse gas (GHG) emissions generated from international shipping during each step of the production process and, thereby, assess the direct and indirect impacts of final demands. As described above, one conventional approach to doing this is to use a single-country model, applying the domestic production technology assumption to account for emissions resulting from imports. Recently, researchers have used multiregional models that allow a variation of technologies across import countries of origin. However, these approaches only allow calculating the pollution generated in the last round of inputs – that is, the last stage of travel before reaching the consuming country. This approach, thus, does not take into account the pollution generated through the transport of inputs manufactured in multiple countries and, later, integrated within international production networks. In order to consider this, one must account for higher-order transportation emissions (i.e., those occurring earlier in the value chain). Therefore, we use a multilateral input–output table based on a non-competitive import model; the one most applicable to our purposes is the Asian international input–output table, which includes China, Japan, and Korea.

To calculate international maritime emissions while considering the effect of induced production, a Leontief inverse matrix is generally used. However, this considers only the effects that induce domestic production: even if emissions per unit of production are multiplied by the Leontief inverse, this process does not calculate the shipping-linked emissions that arise from induced production in each country. Multilateral input–output tables, such as the Asian international input–output tables created by the Institute of Developing Economies (IDE) can thus be used to calculate indirect effects in each country, taking into consideration the inter-regional feedback effects. However, we cannot calculate maritime emissions resulting from each stage of the production process using the Leontief inverse derived from the input–output table. Therefore, we estimate them through an iterative process, using inter-industry requirements between countries in order to obtain convergent values.

Firstly, we first obtain the inter-industry requirements from industry i in country r and input into industry j in country s by using a multiregional input–output table. The vector of total final demand of country s can, thus, be expressed in terms of the composition of goods and services that have contributed to the sectors represented in its final demand. By multiplying the input coefficients matrix by each final demand vector, we obtain the intermediate goods that have to be imported to meet the country's final demand. This shows the first round of ripple effects of final demand. Since the intermediate goods required in each country are given in monetary units, it is necessary to convert these into physical units. By multiplying these amounts by the distance between origin (i.e., the country exporting intermediate goods) and destination (i.e., the country requiring the intermediate goods), we can calculate the shipping burden in freight ton-kilometers (ton-km). Finally, the CO_2 emissions linked to this first round of international shipping can be calculated by multiplying these quantities by the relevant emission factors.

The equations in the Appendix show how the emissions due to imports from each country are estimated at the first stage. This calculation is performed for every term, and the total first-round emissions linked to imports from each country are calculated by summing all exporting-country-specific emissions amounts. In order to calculate the total emissions linked to the ripple effects of international shipping of intermediate goods, we must sum emissions across all stages. As such, the amounts of intermediate goods required in the second stage are calculated by multiplying the intermediate goods required in the first stage by the input coefficients matrix. As above, we can obtain the intermediate requirements needed to meet the final demand of a country by multiplying the divided vectors of the first-stage requirements by the input coefficients.

The CO_2 emissions linked to international shipping during the second and subsequent rounds are estimated by using analogous methods. By repeating these successive calculations, it is possible to estimate the total emissions from international shipping that are required to meet the final demand of the country in question.

To estimate total maritime GHG emissions using the above method, we must convert monetary units into physical units, and use data on the distances between origin and destination as well as on GHG emission factors. The relevant conversion coefficients and data can be obtained from UN trade statistics, an online tool for calculating distances between seaports (sea-distances.org), and emission factors used in previous research[1] (Hiraoka and Kameyama, 2005). The multiregional input–output table is obtained from IDE's 2005 Asian international input–output table.[2] While there are three types of classification in the original data, we use 76 sector classifications. The next section presents the resulting estimates for emissions that will occur if demand from China and Japan is met.

17.5   Estimation of CO_2 emissions in East Asian countries

Currently, final demand in China totals 2.1 trillion US dollars (US$), 96 percent of which is sourced from the US and East Asia (see Table 17.3). The largest volume of final goods was procured domestically (in China), totaling 1.92 trillion US$, followed by Japan, Korea, Taiwan, and the US. However, even Japan, the largest contributor to Chinese imports, supplies only 1.5 percent of total demand. CO_2 emissions from international shipping are primarily generated by the shipping of finished goods, followed by the transport of intermediate goods used to produce these finished goods. The need to transport intermediate goods internationally arises from the fragmentation of production; CO_2 is emitted as a by-product of this process according to the amount of goods, the port distance, and the emission factor. Intermediate goods used to produce the final goods consumed in China are produced in all the countries considered here. The ratio of domestic supply (i.e., from within China) is lower than the ratio for finished goods: domestic supply accounts for 88.9 percent of China's total procurement of intermediate goods when expressed in monetary values. Many intermediate goods are transported from Japan and Korea, with Japan supplying 3.9 percent of intermediate goods. Considering this breakdown on the basis of ton weight, China supplies 92.6 percent of its total intermediate goods domestically. The amount of CO_2 emitted depends on the shipping distance, and the highest share of ton-kilometers shipped is the 36.1 percent originating from the U.S. This is likely to be related to the shipping distance, which is at least 1.6 times that from Indonesia, the country

Table 17.3 Goods required to meet China's final demand – volumes, values, and associated emissions

	CO_2 emissions (ton), final goods and intermediate goods		CO_2 emissions (ton), final goods		CO_2 emissions (ton), intermediate goods	
Indonesia	546,985	12.2%	29,253	5.4%	517,733	13.1%
Malaysia	370,785	8.3%	42,438	7.9%	328,347	8.3%
Philippines	17,955	0.4%	1,038	0.2%	16,918	0.4%
Singapore	239,239	5.3%	14,653	2.7%	224,585	5.7%
Thailand	241,254	5.4%	36,966	6.9%	204,288	5.2%
China	89,495	2.0%	0	0.0%	89,495	2.3%
Taiwan	168,597	3.8%	17,936	3.3%	150,661	3.8%
Korea	226,652	5.1%	25,768	4.8%	200,884	5.1%
Japan	424,234	9.5%	85,536	15.9%	338,698	8.6%
US	2,157,566	48.1%	286,007	53.0%	1,871,559	47.5%
Total	4,482,762	100.0%	539,595	100.0%	3,943,167	100.0%

	Final demand (F) (US$1000)		UF (ton 1,000)		DUF (ton-km)		AF (US$1,000)		UAF (ton 1,000)		DUAF (ton-km)	
Indonesia	553,942	0.0%	304,009	0.1%	1,420,514,717	6.5%	8,027,056	0.3%	16,553,172	0.8%	61,166,293,686	22.0%
Malaysia	3,268,018	0.2%	417,951	0.1%	1,894,069,306	8.7%	16,441,217	0.6%	11,547,143	0.5%	20,692,488,930	7.5%
Philippines	1,303,082	0.1%	22,711	0.0%	47,446,339	0.2%	3,962,686	0.1%	1,687,292	0.1%	1,959,416,496	0.7%
Singapore	3,858,562	0.2%	173,359	0.0%	718,209,587	3.3%	11,993,947	0.4%	6,857,026	0.3%	23,143,096,104	8.3%
Thailand	2,602,023	0.1%	396,200	0.1%	1,617,208,031	7.4%	8,400,989	0.3%	5,850,035	0.3%	14,001,825,602	5.0%
China	1,924,360,178	95.8%	587,122,919	99.0%	0	0.0%	2,405,537,873	88.9%	2,010,996,406	92.6%	8,810,328,733	3.2%
Taiwan	14,427,488	0.7%	810,860	0.1%	901,027,408	4.1%	39,014,420	1.4%	21,703,461	1.0%	9,700,442,671	3.5%
Korea	14,485,049	0.7%	959,802	0.2%	874,552,751	4.0%	57,375,830	2.1%	40,427,924	1.9%	15,784,316,893	5.7%
Japan	30,473,835	1.5%	1,617,587	0.3%	2,795,028,790	12.9%	106,361,479	3.9%	34,216,560	1.6%	22,013,704,600	7.9%
US	13,203,176	0.7%	1,084,719	0.2%	11,466,562,501	52.8%	49,120,682	1.8%	22,602,968	1.0%	100,324,131,636	36.1%
Total	2,008,535,353	100.0%	592,910,117	100.0%	21,734,619,429	100.0%	2,706,236,181	100.0%	2,172,441,989	100.0%	277,596,045,351	100.0%

UF: Final Demand in physical units (ton)
DUF: The shipping burden in freight ton-kilometers (ton-km)
AF: The intermediate goods that have to be imported to meet the country's final demand in monetary units (US $)
UAF: The intermediate goods that have to be imported to meet the country's final demand in physical units (ton)
DUAF: The shipping burden of the intermediate goods that have to be imported to meet the country's final demand in freight ton-kilometers (ton-km)

that is farthest from China. CO_2 emissions linked to the production of intermediate goods in Indonesia account for 13.1 percent of total emissions from international shipping of intermediate goods. This is because crude petroleum and natural gas are produced in Indonesia and exported to other East Asian countries, including China, as raw materials. Total CO_2 emissions from international shipping that arise from China's final demand are 4.48 mt CO_2. Mirroring the aforementioned results for ton-kilometers, the emissions linked to the production of intermediate goods and final goods in the US account for the highest proportion (48.1 percent) of this total, followed by 12.2 percent for Indonesia. Although Japan is located comparatively close to China, the emissions linked to the production of intermediate goods in Japan account for 9.5 percent of total emissions, because many of the intermediate goods and final goods required to meet China's final demand are produced in Japan. International shipping linked to the production of intermediate goods and final goods in Malaysia also results in a relatively high amount of emissions.

Final demand in Japan was 4.44 trillion US$ in 2005, of which supply from the US and East Asian countries accounted for 4.36 trillion US$, or 98 percent (see Table 17.4). Like China, Japan purchases most finished goods domestically: supply within Japan accounts for 97 percent of total final demand (when expressed in value terms). China is the largest external supplier to Japan, accounting for 1.6 percent of the total. The rate of domestic supply of total intermediate goods is 88.1 percent, with the largest imported share coming from China (5.0 percent). In terms of unit weight, China accounts for 11.2 percent of the total supply of intermediate goods, followed by 4.8 percent from Indonesia and 4.3 percent from the US. The burden of total transport of intermediate goods and final goods for Japan's final demand (in ton-km) varies according to distance from Japan, and emissions linked to international shipping of intermediate goods and final goods are highest for goods from Indonesia, accounting for 1.79 mt CO_2 or 18.6 percent of the total (9.6 mt CO_2). In the case of Japan, a substantial amount of CO_2 emissions are a result of international shipping of intermediate goods produced in the US, Indonesia, China, Malaysia, and Thailand. In terms of emissions from international shipping of final goods, the emissions linked to shipping from the US, China, and Thailand are considerable.

Final demand in Korea was 821 billion US$ in 2005, of which supply from the US and East Asian countries accounted for 788 billion US$, or 96 percent (see Table 17.5). Korea also purchases most final goods domestically: procurement within Korea accounts for 96 percent of total final demand (when expressed in value terms). Japan is the largest supplier to Korea, accounting for 1.6 percent of the total. The rate of domestic supply of intermediate goods is 80.6 percent, with the largest imported share coming from Japan (6.3 percent). In terms of unit weight, China accounts for 7.4 percent of total supply for Korea's final demand, followed by 2.9 percent from Indonesia and 2.5 percent from Japan. The burden of transport of intermediate goods to Korea (in ton-km) varies according to the distance from Korea, and emissions linked to international shipping are highest for goods from the US, accounting for 1.2 mt CO_2, or 46.3 percent of the total (2.5 mt CO_2). In

Table 17.4 Goods required to meet Japan's final demand – volumes, values, and associated emissions

	CO_2 emissions (ton), final goods and intermediate goods		CO_2 emissions (ton), final goods		CO_2 emissions (ton), intermediate goods	
Indonesia	1,790,099	18.6%	56,012	3.8%	1,734,087	21.4%
Malaysia	625,063	6.5%	61,184	4.1%	563,879	6.9%
Philippines	87,527	0.9%	21,839	1.5%	65,688	0.8%
Singapore	128,014	1.3%	27,026	1.8%	100,987	1.2%
Thailand	537,987	5.6%	191,676	12.9%	346,311	4.3%
China	995,190	10.4%	251,604	16.9%	743,586	9.2%
Taiwan	141,037	1.5%	33,566	2.3%	107,471	1.3%
Korea	157,527	1.6%	27,998	1.9%	129,529	1.6%
Japan	111,389	1.2%	0	0.0%	111,389	1.4%
US	5,031,581	52.4%	814,088	54.8%	4,217,493	51.9%
Total	9,605,413	100.0%	1,484,993	100.0%	8,120,420	100.0%

	Final demand (F) (US$1,000)		UF (ton 1,000)		DUF (ton-km)		AF (US$1,000)		UAF (ton 1,000)		DUAF (ton-km)	
Indonesia	2,477,357	0.1%	410,702	0.1%	2,376,937,846	3.4%	20,625,223	0.6%	58,033,263	4.8%	286,330,230,341	38.1%
Malaysia	3,908,531	0.1%	533,175	0.1%	2,962,322,883	4.2%	18,057,686	0.6%	21,876,710	1.8%	81,482,067,399	10.9%
Philippines	3,239,856	0.1%	278,733	0.1%	858,471,089	1.2%	6,512,701	0.2%	3,959,732	0.3%	5,891,184,577	0.8%
Singapore	4,782,594	0.1%	530,229	0.1%	2,739,745,826	3.9%	11,916,252	0.4%	2,981,566	0.2%	9,934,516,137	1.3%
Thailand	7,816,312	0.2%	1,302,089	0.3%	6,843,778,005	9.8%	17,115,768	0.5%	11,089,105	0.9%	19,308,518,779	2.6%
China	68,157,281	1.6%	6,398,670	1.5%	11,056,261,048	15.8%	163,556,472	5.0%	137,121,548	11.2%	82,096,50,100	10.9%
Taiwan	5,346,494	0.1%	628,902	0.1%	1,437,293,225	2.1%	21,733,567	0.7%	9,474,385	0.8%	7,678,632,093	1.0%
Korea	6,417,555	0.1%	2,179,283	0.5%	2,235,943,985	3.2%	32,184,684	1.0%	23,537,730	1.9%	11,645,090,046	1.6%
Japan	4,230,524,240	97.1%	424,406,176	96.2%	39,577,371,674	56.5%	2,880,504,997	88.1%	899,862,128	73.7%	6,398,741,092	0.9%
US	23,234,137	0.5%	4,284,285	1.0%	0	0.0%	95,721,559	2.9%	52,659,414	4.3%	240,041,185,103	32.0%
Total	4,355,904,357	100.0%	440,952,244	100.0%	70,088,125,581	100.0%	3,267,928,909	100.0%	1,220,595,581	100.0%	750,806,215,666	100.0%

Table 17.5 Goods required to meet Korea's final demand – volumes, values, and associated emissions

	CO_2 emissions (ton), final goods and intermediate goods		CO_2 emissions (ton), final goods		CO_2 emissions (ton), intermediate goods	
Indonesia	643,007	21.9%	31,968	7.9%	611,039	24.2%
Malaysia	201,128	6.9%	21,301	5.2%	179,827	7.1%
Philippines	33,064	1.1%	10,103	2.5%	22,961	0.9%
Singapore	49,515	1.7%	17,156	4.2%	32,359	1.3%
Thailand	91,159	3.1%	21,007	5.2%	70,153	2.8%
China	350,239	11.9%	55,361	13.6%	294,879	11.7%
Taiwan	37,374	1.3%	9,006	2.2%	28,367	1.1%
Korea	11,596	0.4%	0	0.0%	11,596	0.5%
Japan	123,361	4.2%	18,696	4.6%	104,665	4.1%
US	1,393,066	47.5%	221,789	54.6%	1,171,277	46.3%
Total	2,933,510	100.0%	406,386	100.0%	2,527,124	100.0%

	Final demand (F) (US$1,000)		UF (ton 1,000)		DUF (ton-km)		AF (US$1,000)		UAF (ton 1,000)		DUAF (ton-km)	
Indonesia	389,554	0.0%	272,136	0.2%	1,430,834,077	0.2%	6,120,081	6.9%	20,429,850	0.9%	94,827,888,331	2.9%
Malaysia	610,975	0.1%	236,360	0.2%	1,187,589,807	0.2%	4,857,132	5.7%	6,539,363	0.7%	22,970,594,060	0.9%
Philippines	214,259	0.0%	172,568	0.1%	450,626,049	0.1%	1,250,912	2.2%	934,672	0.2%	1,207,585,633	0.1%
Singapore	1,732,164	0.2%	218,772	0.2%	1,014,137,366	0.2%	5,371,649	4.9%	894,183	0.8%	2,411,851,965	0.1%
Thailand	533,732	0.1%	208,994	0.2%	976,149,107	0.2%	2,303,387	4.7%	1,849,034	0.3%	4,669,317,068	0.3%
China	8,047,764	1.0%	2,984,765	2.1%	2,719,657,947	2.1%	37,228,958	13.0%	51,596,402	5.3%	30,498,017,355	7.4%
Taiwan	848,284	0.1%	329,345	0.2%	553,826,558	0.2%	4,686,594	2.7%	2,473,405	0.7%	2,216,007,588	0.4%
Korea	755,083,030	95.8%	132,513,748	95.3%	0	95.3%	568,272,784	0.0%	578,220,195	80.6%	954,263,903	83.2%
Japan	12,398,113	1.6%	879,734	0.6%	902,607,269	0.6%	44,408,496	4.3%	17,540,334	6.3%	8,392,971,482	2.5%
US	8,194,793	1.0%	1,201,415	0.9%	11,636,902,351	0.9%	30,696,914	55.8%	14,817,848	4.4%	63,277,117,679	2.1%
Total	788,052,668	100.0%	139,017,835	100.0%	20,872,330,531	100.0%	705,196,906	100.0%	695,295,286	100.0%	231,425,615,064	100.0%

the case of Korea, a substantial amount of CO_2 emissions linked to international shipping of final and intermediate goods are a result of international shipping of intermediate goods produced in the US, Indonesia, Malaysia, Japan, and China.

17.6   Simulation results

As reported by IMO (2009), demand for shipping is expected to grow in the long term. The CO_2 emissions from international shipping are forecast to increase by a factor of two to three by 2050, compared with 2007 levels. To reduce emissions from ships, a number of policies are conceivable. In principle, improving energy efficiency is one option. To increase energy efficiency (i.e., to do the same amount of work while using less energy, thereby changing the level of the emission factors), two elements can be modified: ship design and ship operation. Options categorized under design include approaches such as concept improvement, designed speed, power-generation systems, and optimization of hull form. To save energy by modifying operations, one can consider factors, such as fleet management, voyage optimization, and energy management. Since voyage optimization includes the selection of the optimal route, this change can be simulated by changing the distance travelled.[3]

Emissions from international shipping can be simulated under certain scenarios of energy efficiency improvements, including changes to ship designs. Ships are categorized by the type of cargo. In this chapter, GHG emissions were estimated in consideration of the category of ship, such as container vessels, bulk vessels, ro-ro vessels, and tanker vessels. We carried out simulations for which the emission factor was reduced by 10 percent for each type of ship.

Table 17.6 shows the estimates for emissions required to meet demand in China. For example, if the emission factor for container ships decreases by 10 percent, CO_2 emissions decrease by 7.8 percent in total. In particular, the reductions in the rates of emissions linked to container vessels travelling from the US and Malaysia are large (9.0 percent and 8.8 percent, respectively) compared to the baseline case. In terms of total CO_2 emissions, a reduction in the emission factors of tanker vessels, bulk vessels, and ro-ro vessels does not contribute much to reducing total CO_2 emissions from ships associated with final demand in China; however, within these categories, tanker vessels from Indonesia and bulk vessels from the Philippines have the largest potential emission reductions.

In the cases or China (Table 17.6), Japan (Table 17.7), and Korea (Table 17.8), reductions in the emissions factors of container vessels would have the largest impact on total CO_2 emissions from international shipping. In terms of emissions from ships required to meet final demand in Japan, a reduction of the emission factor for tanker vessels would also contribute 2 percent to the decrease of total emissions. This is mainly caused by a reduction of emissions linked to ships from Indonesia and Malaysia. In the case of demands from Korea (and also Japan), a reduction of emissions factors of tankers from Indonesia and Malaysia, and bulk vessels from China would also result in fairly large decreases in total CO_2 emissions from international shipping.

Table 17.6 CO$_2$ emissions from shipping required to meet final demand in China that assume a 10% reduction of emission factor (distinction by type of ship)

	Tanker			Bulk			Container			Ro-ro		
	CO$_2$ emissions (ton)		Reduction rate	CO$_2$ emissions (ton)		Reduction rate	CO$_2$ emissions (ton)		Reduction rate	CO$_2$ emissions (ton)		Reduction rate
Indonesia	527,316	11.9%	3.6%	537,982	12.1%	1.6%	521,073	12.6%	4.7%	546,872	12.2%	0.0%
Malaysia	367,495	8.3%	0.9%	369,521	8.3%	0.3%	338,340	8.2%	8.8%	370,704	8.3%	0.0%
Philippines	17,636	0.4%	1.8%	17,283	0.4%	3.7%	17,169	0.4%	4.4%	17,937	0.4%	0.1%
Singapore	230,031	5.2%	3.8%	239,181	5.4%	0.0%	224,635	5.4%	6.1%	239,184	5.4%	0.0%
Thailand	238,800	5.4%	1.0%	239,923	5.4%	0.6%	221,250	5.4%	8.3%	240,918	5.4%	0.1%
China	88,703	2.0%	0.9%	86,179	1.9%	3.7%	84,766	2.1%	5.3%	89,381	2.0%	0.1%
Taiwan	167,735	3.8%	0.5%	166,882	3.8%	1.0%	154,482	3.7%	8.4%	168,429	3.8%	0.1%
Korea	223,261	5.0%	1.5%	224,515	5.0%	0.9%	211,439	5.1%	6.7%	224,726	5.0%	0.8%
Japan	422,651	9.5%	0.4%	419,059	9.4%	1.2%	394,665	9.6%	7.0%	418,139	9.4%	1.4%
US	2,151,936	48.5%	0.3%	2,148,372	48.3%	0.4%	1,963,809	47.5%	9.0%	2,150,390	48.1%	0.3%
Total	4,435,565	100.0%	1.1%	4,448,897	100.0%	0.8%	4,131,629	100.0%	7.8%	4,466,680	100.0%	0.4%

Table 17.7 CO_2 emissions from shipping required to meet final demand in Japan that assume a 10% reduction of emission factor (distinction by type of ship)

	Tanker			Bulk			Container			Ro-ro		
	CO_2 emissions (ton)		Reduction rate	CO_2 emissions (ton)		Reduction rate	CO_2 emissions (ton)		Reduction rate	CO_2 emissions (ton)		Reduction rate
Indonesia	1,670,107	17.7%	6.7%	1,756,596	18.5%	1.9%	1,765,827	19.7%	1.4%	1,788,858	18.7%	0.1%
Malaysia	590,143	6.3%	5.6%	618,944	6.5%	1.0%	604,254	6.7%	3.3%	624,403	6.5%	0.1%
Philippines	87,439	0.9%	0.1%	84,951	0.9%	2.9%	81,926	0.9%	6.4%	87,039	0.9%	0.6%
Singapore	123,160	1.3%	3.8%	127,972	1.3%	0.0%	120,136	1.3%	6.2%	127,985	1.3%	0.1%
Thailand	536,440	5.7%	0.3%	535,308	5.6%	0.5%	496,906	5.5%	7.6%	529,495	5.5%	1.6%
China	990,090	10.5%	0.5%	957,414	10.1%	3.8%	941,349	10.5%	5.4%	992,389	10.4%	0.3%
Taiwan	140,345	1.5%	0.5%	139,040	1.5%	1.4%	130,739	1.5%	7.3%	139,919	1.5%	0.8%
Korea	153,989	1.6%	2.2%	155,639	1.6%	1.2%	148,097	1.6%	6.0%	156,631	1.6%	0.6%
Japan	111,262	1.2%	0.1%	109,583	1.2%	1.6%	104,369	1.2%	6.3%	109,203	1.1%	2.0%
US	5,011,092	53.2%	0.4%	5,005,004	52.7%	0.5%	4,584,888	51.1%	8.9%	5,022,179	52.4%	0.2%
Total	9,414,066	100.0%	2.0%	9,490,451	100.0%	1.2%	8,978,491	100.0%	6.5%	9,578,102	100.0%	0.3%

Table 17.8 CO$_2$ emissions from shipping required to meet final demand in Korea that assume a 10% reduction of emission factor (distinction by type of ship)

	Tanker			Bulk			Container			Ro-ro		
	CO$_2$ emissions (ton)		Reduction rate	CO$_2$ emissions (ton)		Reduction rate	CO$_2$ emissions (ton)		Reduction rate	CO$_2$ emissions (ton)		Reduction rate
Indonesia	605,549	21.0%	5.8%	630,547	21.8%	1.9%	628,632	23.0%	2.2%	643,000	21.9%	0.0%
Malaysia	192,303	6.7%	4.4%	198,824	6.9%	1.1%	192,181	7.0%	4.4%	201,090	6.9%	0.0%
Philippines	33,050	1.1%	0.0%	32,911	1.1%	0.5%	29,934	1.1%	9.5%	33,054	1.1%	0.0%
Singapore	48,670	1.7%	1.7%	49,452	1.7%	0.1%	45,631	1.7%	7.8%	49,356	1.7%	0.3%
Thailand	90,544	3.1%	0.7%	90,501	3.1%	0.7%	83,404	3.0%	8.5%	91,073	3.1%	0.1%
China	348,809	12.1%	0.4%	336,295	11.6%	4.0%	330,941	12.1%	5.5%	349,888	11.9%	0.1%
Taiwan	36,965	1.3%	1.1%	36,873	1.3%	1.3%	34,662	1.3%	7.3%	37,257	1.3%	0.3%
Korea	11,404	0.4%	1.7%	11,433	0.4%	1.4%	10,850	0.4%	6.4%	11,539	0.4%	0.5%
Japan	123,074	4.3%	0.2%	120,082	4.1%	2.7%	115,436	4.2%	6.4%	122,518	4.2%	0.7%
US	1,388,110	48.2%	0.2%	1,387,253	47.9%	0.3%	1,266,374	46.3%	5.9%	1,391,219	47.5%	0.1%
Total	2,878,477	100.0%	1.9%	2,894,172	100.0%	1.3%	2,738,046	100.0%	6.7%	2,929,993	100.0%	0.1%

17.7 Conclusion

In this chapter, we analyzed the structure of GHG emissions caused by the international shipping of China, Japan, and Korea, by using the Asian international input–output table. In particular, we estimated the amount of CO_2 emitted from international shipping in response to the final demands of these countries and simulated the impact of reductions to emission factors for each type of ship (i.e., greater efficiency), and found that CO_2 emissions from international shipping of total intermediate goods are much larger than emissions from final goods. Therefore, to identify individual countries responsible for these emissions – as analyzed in this chapter – it is necessary to estimate the direct and indirect emissions from shipping. By using the input–output technique, we were able to identify countries with high rates of CO_2 emissions due to international shipping; for example, final demand in Japan caused substantial CO_2 emissions from international shipping from the US, Indonesia, and China. Furthermore, measures to improve energy efficiency of tanker vessels from Indonesia and the US would help to reduce emissions from shipping.

Appendix

We obtain the inter-industry requirements (A), output from industry i in country r, and then input into industry j in country s using a multilateral input–output table, given by:

$$A = (a_{ij}^{rs}) = \begin{bmatrix} A^{11} & A^{12} & A^{13} & \cdots & A^{1m} \\ A^{21} & A^{22} & A^{23} & & A^{2m} \\ A^{31} & A^{32} & A^{33} & & A^{3m} \\ \vdots & & & \ddots & \vdots \\ A^{m1} & A^{m2} & A^{m3} & \cdots & A^{mm} \end{bmatrix} \qquad (17.\text{A}1), \text{ where}$$

r denotes the country supplying the goods/services;
s denotes the country demanding the goods/services;
i denotes a given industry in country r, with $1 \leq i \leq n$; and
j denotes a given industry in country s, with $1 \leq j \leq n$.

The vector of total final demand (F) of country s can thus be expressed in terms of the composition of goods and services that have contributed to the sectors represented in its final demand. This is given by:

$$\begin{bmatrix} F^{11} \\ F^{21} \\ F^{31} \\ \vdots \\ F^{m1} \end{bmatrix} = \begin{bmatrix} F^{11} \\ 0 \\ 0 \\ \vdots \\ 0 \end{bmatrix} + \begin{bmatrix} 0 \\ F^{21} \\ 0 \\ \vdots \\ 0 \end{bmatrix} + \cdots + \begin{bmatrix} 0 \\ 0 \\ 0 \\ \\ F^{m1} \end{bmatrix} \qquad (17.\text{A}2)$$

By multiplying the input coefficient matrix by each final demand vector, we obtain the intermediate goods that have to be imported (X) in order to meet the country's final demand. This is depicted in the following relationship where, superscript (1) shows the first round of ripple effects of final demand, and the second term on the right side of the equation relates to the intermediate goods required as imports from country 2 in order to meet the final demand of country 1.

$$
\begin{bmatrix} X^{11(1)} \\ X^{21(1)} \\ X^{31(1)} \\ \vdots \\ X^{m1(1)} \end{bmatrix} = \begin{bmatrix} A^{11} & A^{12} & A^{13} & \cdots & A^{1m} \\ A^{21} & A^{22} & A^{23} & & A^{2m} \\ A^{31} & A^{32} & A^{33} & & A^{3m} \\ \vdots & & & \ddots & \vdots \\ A^{m1} & A^{m2} & A^{m3} & \cdots & A^{mm} \end{bmatrix} \begin{bmatrix} F^{11} \\ 0 \\ 0 \\ \vdots \\ 0 \end{bmatrix} + \begin{bmatrix} A^{11} & A^{12} & A^{13} & \cdots & A^{1m} \\ A^{21} & A^{22} & A^{23} & & A^{2m} \\ A^{31} & A^{32} & A^{33} & & A^{3m} \\ \vdots & & & \ddots & \vdots \\ A^{m1} & A^{m2} & A^{m3} & \cdots & A^{mm} \end{bmatrix} \begin{bmatrix} 0 \\ F^{21} \\ 0 \\ \vdots \\ 0 \end{bmatrix}
$$

$$
+ \cdots + \begin{bmatrix} A^{11} & A^{12} & A^{13} & \cdots & A^{1m} \\ A^{21} & A^{22} & A^{23} & & A^{2m} \\ A^{31} & A^{32} & A^{33} & & A^{3m} \\ \vdots & & & \ddots & \vdots \\ A^{m1} & A^{m2} & A^{m3} & \cdots & A^{mm} \end{bmatrix} \begin{bmatrix} 0 \\ 0 \\ 0 \\ \vdots \\ F^{m1} \end{bmatrix} \tag{17.A3}
$$

$$
\begin{bmatrix} X^{11(1)} \\ X^{21(1)} \\ X^{31(1)} \\ \vdots \\ X^{m1(1)} \end{bmatrix} = \begin{bmatrix} A^{11}F^{11} \\ A^{21}F^{11} \\ A^{31}F^{11} \\ \vdots \\ A^{m1}F^{11} \end{bmatrix} + \begin{bmatrix} A^{12}F^{21} \\ A^{22}F^{21} \\ A^{32}F^{21} \\ \vdots \\ A^{m2}F^{21} \end{bmatrix} + \cdots + \begin{bmatrix} A^{1m}F^{m1} \\ A^{2m}F^{m1} \\ A^{3m}F^{m1} \\ \vdots \\ A^{mm}F^{m1} \end{bmatrix} \tag{17.A4}
$$

Since the intermediate goods required in each country are given in monetary units, it is necessary to convert these into physical units. By multiplying these amounts by the distance between origin (i.e., the country exporting intermediate goods) and destination (i.e., the country requiring the intermediate goods), we can calculate the shipping burdens in freight ton-km. Finally, the CO_2 emissions linked to this first round of international shipping can be calculated by multiplying these quantities by the relevant emission factors. The following expression shows the emissions due to imports from each country to country 1 in the first stage.

$$
\begin{bmatrix} E^{11(1)} \\ E^{21(1)} \\ E^{31(1)} \\ \vdots \\ E^{m1(1)} \end{bmatrix} = \begin{bmatrix} E^{11} & 0 & 0 & \cdots & 0 \\ 0 & E^{22} & 0 & & 0 \\ 0 & 0 & E^{33} & & 0 \\ \vdots & & & \ddots & \vdots \\ 0 & 0 & 0 & \cdots & E^{mm} \end{bmatrix} \begin{bmatrix} 0 & 0 & 0 & \cdots & 0 \\ 0 & D^{22} & 0 & & 0 \\ 0 & 0 & D^{33} & & 0 \\ \vdots & & & \ddots & \vdots \\ 0 & 0 & 0 & \cdots & D^{mm} \end{bmatrix}
$$

$$
\begin{bmatrix} U^{11} & 0 & 0 & \cdots & 0 \\ 0 & U^{21} & 0 & & 0 \\ 0 & 0 & U^{31} & & 0 \\ \vdots & & & \ddots & \vdots \\ 0 & 0 & 0 & \cdots & U^{m1} \end{bmatrix} \begin{bmatrix} A^{11}F^{11} \\ A^{21}F^{11} \\ 0 \\ \vdots \\ A^{m1}F^{11} \end{bmatrix} \tag{17.A5}
$$

This calculation is performed for every term in Eq. 17.A4, and the total first-round emissions linked to imports from each country are calculated by summing all exporting-country-specific emissions amounts. In order to calculate the total emissions linked to the ripple effects of international shipping of intermediate goods, we must sum emissions across all stages. As such, the amounts of intermediate goods required in the second stage are calculated by multiplying the intermediate goods required in the first stage by the inter-industry requirements.

$$
\begin{bmatrix} X^{11(2)} \\ X^{21(2)} \\ X^{31(2)} \\ \vdots \\ X^{m1(2)} \end{bmatrix} = \begin{bmatrix} A^{11}F^{11} + A^{12}F^{21} + A^{13}F^{31} + \cdots + A^{1m}F^{m1} \\ A^{21}F^{11} + A^{22}F^{21} + A^{23}F^{31} + \cdots + A^{2m}F^{m1} \\ A^{31}F^{11} + A^{32}F^{21} + A^{33}F^{31} + \cdots + A^{3m}F^{m1} \\ \vdots \\ A^{m1}F^{11} + A^{m1}F^{21} + A^{m3}F^{31} + \cdots + A^{mm}F^{m1} \end{bmatrix} \tag{17.A6}
$$

As above, we can obtain the intermediate requirements that are needed to meet the final demand of country 1, by multiplying the divided vectors of the first-stage requirements by the input coefficients.

$$
\begin{bmatrix} X^{11(2)} \\ X^{21(2)} \\ X^{31(2)} \\ \vdots \\ X^{m1(2)} \end{bmatrix} = \begin{bmatrix} A^{11} & A^{12} & A^{13} & \cdots & A^{1m} \\ A^{21} & A^{22} & A^{23} & & A^{2m} \\ A^{31} & A^{32} & A^{33} & & A^{3m} \\ \vdots & & & \ddots & \vdots \\ A^{m1} & A^{m2} & A^{m3} & \cdots & A^{mm} \end{bmatrix} \begin{bmatrix} A^{11}F^{11} + A^{12}F^{21} + \cdots + A^{1m}F^{m1} \\ 0 \\ 0 \\ \vdots \\ 0 \end{bmatrix}
$$

$$
+ \begin{bmatrix} A^{11} & A^{12} & A^{13} & \cdots & A^{1m} \\ A^{21} & A^{22} & A^{23} & & A^{2m} \\ A^{31} & A^{32} & A^{33} & & A^{3m} \\ \vdots & & & \ddots & \vdots \\ A^{m1} & A^{m2} & A^{m3} & \cdots & A^{mm} \end{bmatrix} \begin{bmatrix} 0 \\ A^{21}F^{11} + A^{22}F^{21} + \cdots + A^{2m}F^{m1} \\ 0 \\ \vdots \\ 0 \end{bmatrix} \tag{17.A7}
$$

$$
+ \cdots + \begin{bmatrix} A^{11} & A^{12} & A^{13} & \cdots & A^{1m} \\ A^{21} & \cdot A^{22} & A^{23} & & A^{2m} \\ A^{31} & A^{32} & A^{33} & & A^{3m} \\ \vdots & & & \ddots & \vdots \\ A^{m1} & A^{m2} & A^{m3} & \cdots & A^{mm} \end{bmatrix} \begin{bmatrix} 0 \\ 0 \\ 0 \\ 0 \\ A^{m1}F^{11} + A^{m1}F^{21} + \cdots + A^{mm}F^{m1} \end{bmatrix}
$$

The CO_2 emissions linked to international shipping during the second and subsequent rounds are estimated by using analogous methods. By repeating these successive calculations, we can estimate the total emissions from international shipping that are needed to meet the final demand of the country in question, as follows:

$$
\begin{bmatrix} E^{11} \\ E^{21} \\ \vdots \\ E^{m1} \end{bmatrix} = \begin{bmatrix} E^{(1)} \\ E^{(1)} \\ \vdots \\ E^{(1)} \end{bmatrix} + \begin{bmatrix} E^{(2)} \\ E^{(2)} \\ \vdots \\ E^{(2)} \end{bmatrix} + \begin{bmatrix} E^{(3)} \\ E^{(3)} \\ E^{(3)} \end{bmatrix} + \cdots \tag{17.A8}
$$

Notes

1 In this chapter, emission factors are analyzed by type of ship; and the type of ship is linked to the goods.
2 The Asian International Input–Output Table is designed to depict the industrial network extended over ten countries: China, Indonesia, Korea, Malaysia, Taiwan, the Philippines, Singapore, Thailand, Japan, and the United States.
3 Policy options for reductions of GHG are shown in IMO (2009).

References

Ahmad, N., and Wyckoff, A. (2003). 'Carbon dioxide emissions embodied in international trade of goods.' OECD Science, Technology and Industry Working Paper No. 15.

Antweiler, W. (1996). 'The pollution terms of trade.' *Economic System Research*, 8(4), pp. 361–365.

Cadarso, M. A., Lopez, L. A., Gomez, N., and Tobarra, M. A. (2010). 'CO_2 emissions of international freight transport and offshoring: Measurement and allocation.' *Ecological Economics*, 69, pp. 1682–1694.

Corbett, J. J., and Winebrake, J. J. (2008). 'International trade and the global shipping.' In: Gallagher, K. P. (Ed.), *Handbook on Trade and the Environment*. Chentelham, UK: Edward Elgar. Pp. 33–48.

Corbett, J. J., and Koehler., H. W. (2003). 'Updated emissions form ocean shipping.' *Journal of Geophysical Research – Atmospheres*, 108, pp. 4650–4666.

Cristea, A., Hummels, D., Puzzello, L., and Avetisyan, M. (2013). 'Trade and the greenhouse gas emissions from international freight transport.' *Journal of Environmental Economics and Management*, 65, pp. 153–173.

Endresen, O., Sorgard, E., Sundet, J. K., Dalsoren, S. B., Isaksen, I.S.A., Berglen, T. F., and Gravir, G. (2003). 'Emission from international sea transportation and environmental impact.' *Journal of Geographical Research*, 108(D17), http://onlinelibrary.wiley.com/doi/10.1029/2002JD002898/full (accessed June 2, 2015).

Ferng, J. J. (2003). 'Allocating the responsibility of CO_2 over-emissions from the perspectives of benefit principle and ecological deficit.' *Ecological Economics*, 46, pp. 121–141.

Hiraoka, K., and Kameyama, M. (2005). 'Emission factors of gaseous exhaust emissions based on analysis of actual voyage logs of oceangoing cargo ships for life cycle assessment of seaborne transportation.' *Journal of the National Maritime Research Institute*, 5(3), pp. 25–90 (in Japanese).

International Maritime Organization (IMO) (2009). *Second IMO GHG Study 2009*. http://www.imo.org/OurWork/Environment/PollutionPrevention/AirPollution/Pages/Second-IMO-GHG-Study-2009.aspx (accessed June 2, 2015).

Kondo, Y., Moriguchi, Y., and Shimizu, H. (1998). 'CO_2 emissions in Japan: Influences of imports and exports.' *Applied Energy*, 59(2–3), pp. 163–174.

Lenzen, M. (1998). 'Primary energy and greenhouse gases embodied in Australian final consumption: An input–output analysis.' *Energy Policy*, 26, pp. 495–506.

Lenzen, M., Pade, L. L., and Munksgaard, J. (2004). 'CO_2 multipliers in multi-region input–output models.' *Economic System Research*, 16(4), pp. 391–412.

Machado, G., Schaeffer, R., and Worrell, E. (2001). 'Energy and carbon embodied in the international trade of Brazil: An input–output approach.' *Ecological Economics*, 39, pp. 409–424.

Mongelli, I., Tassielli, G., and Notarnicola, B. (2006). 'Global warming agreements, international trade and energy/carbon embodiments: An input–output approach to the Italian case.' *Energy Policy, 34*(1), pp. 88–100.

Munksgaard, J., and Pedersen, K. A.(2001). 'CO_2 accounts for open economies: Producer or consumer responsibility?' *Energy Policy*, 29, pp. 327–334.

Muradian, R., O'Connor, M., and Martinez-Alier, J. (2002). 'Embodied pollution in trade: Estimating the "environmental load displacement" of industrialised countries.' *Ecological Economics, 41*(1), pp. 51–67.

Organization for Economic Co-operation and Development (OECD) (2010). *Transport Greenhouse Gas Emissions Country Data 2010.* http://www.internationaltrans portforum.org/pub/pdf/10GHGCountry.pdf.

Peters, G. P., and Hertwich, E. G. (2008). 'CO_2 embodied in international trade with implications for global climate policy.' *Environmental Science and Technology, 42*(5), pp. 1401–1407.

Sanchez-Choliz, J., and Duarte, R. (2004). 'CO_2 emissions embodied in international trade: Evidence for Spain.' *Energy Policy*, 32, pp. 1999–2005.

Sim, S., Barry, M., Clift, R., and Cowell, S. (2007). 'The relative importance of transport in determining an appropriate sustainability strategy for food sourcing: A case study of fresh produce supply chains.' *International Journal of Life Cycle Assessment*, 12, pp. 422–431.

United Nations (UN) (2014). UN Comtrade Database. http://comtrade.un.org (accessed June 2, 2015). United Nations Framework Convention on Climate Change (UNFCCC) (2005a). 'Information on greenhouse gas emissions from international aviation and maritime transport.' FCCC/SBSTA/2005/INF.2. United Nations Framework Convention on Climate Change.

United Nations Framework Convention on Climate Change (UNFCCC) (1998). 'Kyoto Protocol to the United Nations Framework Convention on Climate Change.' http://unfccc.int/resource/docs/convkp/kpeng.pdf (accessed June 2, 2015).

United Nations Framework Convention on Climate Change (UNFCCC) (2005b). 'Methodological issues relating to emissions from fuel used for international aviation and maritime transport.' FCCC/SBSTA/2005/MISC.6. United Nations Framework Convention on Climate Change.

Williams, A. (2007). 'Comparative study of cut roses for the British market produced in Kenya and the Netherlands.' Precis Report for World Flowers, February.

Wyckoff, A. W., and Roop, J. M. (1994). 'The embodiment of carbon in imports of manufactured products: Implications for international agreements on greenhouse gas emissions.' *Energy Policy*, 22, pp. 187–194.

18 An environmental assessment of free trade agreements in East Asian regions using the CGE modeling approach

Hikari Ban and Kiyoshi Fujikawa

18.1 Introduction

Amid ongoing economic globalization, the relationship between trade and the environment has become a controversial topic, as symbolized by the tuna–dolphin case.[1] With rising awareness of environmental issues, the importance of ensuring that trade and environmental policies are mutually supportive was affirmed at the Rio Earth Summit in 1992. In addition, a negotiation on trade and environment was part of the Doha Round of the World Trade Organization (WTO), launched in 2001. Issues such as the relationship between WTO rules and multilateral environmental agreements (MEAs), the collaboration between the WTO's and MEAs' secretariats, and the elimination of barriers on environmental goods and services are now included in negotiations.

The assessment of environmental impact was encouraged as a tool to identify the relationship between trade and the environment at a national level at the Johannesburg summit in 2002. Talks on the environmental assessment of free trade agreements (FTAs) were given by international organizations like the Organisation for Economic Co-operation and Development (OECD), and by industrialized countries, such as the United States, Canada, EU member states, and Japan. The environmental impacts of FTAs are assessed within several categories, including atmosphere, water, land, biodiversity, natural resources, control of hazardous substances, and management of waste. The assessments use both quantitative and qualitative methods.

In this chapter, we analyze the environmental load of FTAs in the East Asia region by measuring CO_2 emissions. As East Asia is an important part of the global supply chain, and because China – the world's largest energy consumer and CO_2 emitter – is one of the main trade partners, it is important to investigate the relationship between trade and the environment in the region. In our analysis we discuss two ways in which FTAs have an effect on total CO_2 emissions in the region. The first is by changing industry output or industrial structure, and the second is by changing the relative prices of input factors, including energy. As to the first, CO_2 emissions per unit of GDP in the FTA region will decrease (or increase) if production of energy-intensive goods moves to more energy-efficient (or energy-inefficient) countries. As to the second, CO_2 emissions per unit of

GDP in the FTA region will decrease (or increase) when demand for energy decreases (or increases) because of changes in relative prices. Additionally, changes to the relative prices of different energy carriers are also important, because the energy carriers have different carbon contents. The change of environmental loads because of FTAs should, therefore, be assessed comprehensively by taking all these factors into account.

To assess the environmental impacts of FTAs, in this chapter we use an energy-environment version on the Global Trade Analysis Project (GTAP-E) model and GTAP database version 8.1, matching the 2007 baseline.[2] The GTAP-E model is a static, multi-regional computable general equilibrium (CGE) model that links economic activity with energy and the environment, allowing us to evaluate environmental loads due to FTAs from both the demand and supply sides of goods and services, including fossil-fuel-based energy.

We assess the following seven simulations: China–Korea FTA, Japan–Korea FTA, China–Japan–Korea FTA, TPP members' FTA, TPP plus China–Korea FTA, TPP plus Japan–Korea FTA, and TPP plus China–Japan–Korea FTA. In most cases, the same scenarios are assessed using the E3ME-Asia model described in Chapter 19. We can, therefore, make a comparison of the model results (see Chapter 19).

18.2   GTAP-E model

We start with a brief description of the GTAP-E model structure.[3] The model is composed of market equilibrium conditions for the factors of production (i.e., inputs to economic production, such as labor, capital, or land) and goods – and also considers a zero-profit condition[4] – similar to the standard CGE model with perfect competition and constant returns. The model addresses all relevant production factors, from regional households to firms. The regional household in the GTAP-E model has a role in both the private household and government. The regional household divides income into consumption, government expenditure and saving.

The GTAP-E model assumes two distinct global sectors. The first is a global banking sector, which assembles savings and distributes investment to each region. Regional investment is distributed so that the rate of change in the expected rate of return on capital equalizes across regions. The second is a global transport sector that purchases transport services from regions and supplies international transport services.

Figure 18.1 depicts the production function in the GTAP-E model. The model has a Leontief structure with zero elasticity of substitution at the top level, and a constant elasticity of substitution (CES) structure at the lower level. One feature of the GTAP-E production function is that the energy composite is combined with capital, and incorporated into the value-added nest to consider energy-capital adjustments in response to their relative price changes. The substitution elasticity within the capital-energy composite (σ_{KE}) is 0.50 for all industries and countries, except coal, oil, gas, and petroleum and coal products ($\sigma_{KE} = 0.00$).

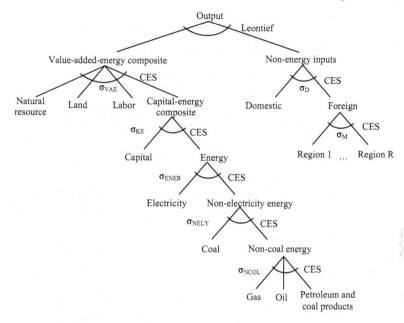

Figure 18.1 Production structure in the GTAP-E model.

Source: Based on Burniaux and Truong (2002).

Note: For electricity, coal, gas, oil, and petroleum and coal products, a graphical description of substitutability between domestic and imported goods is omitted in the figure.

The substitution elasticity within the value-added-energy composite (σ_{VAE}) differs among industries and regions. For example, the value of Japan's σ_{VAE} ranges from 0.00 (gas) to 4.00 (coal).

Energy commodities are incorporated into the energy composite at three levels of nested substitution: (1) substitution between the non-electricity energy composite and electricity σ_{ENER}, (2) substitution between the non-coal energy composite and coal σ_{NELY}, and (3) substitution among non-coal products σ_{NCOL}.[5] We use the following parameters.

Coal, oil, gas, and the petroleum and coal products industries: σ_{ENER} = 0.00, σ_{NELY} = 0.00, σ_{NCOL} = 0.00

Electricity industry: σ_{ENER} = 0.00, σ_{NELY} = 0.50, σ_{NCOL} = 1.00

Other industries: σ_{ENER} = 1.00, σ_{NELY} = 0.50, σ_{NCOL} = 1.00

The model is based on the Armington assumption that products are differentiated by country of origin.[6] Firms first determine the source of their imports and then compare the prices of domestic goods with the optimal mix of imports. The Armington parameters for regional allocation of imports (σ_M) and domestic or imported allocation (σ_D) are different among industries but the same among regions. The value of σ_M ranges from 1.80 (mining) to 30.29 (gas). The value of σ_D ranges from 0.90 (mining) to 10.96 (gas).

The GTAP-E model originated from Burniaux and Truong (2002), and the two latest versions of the GTAP-E model, Truong (2007) and McDougall and Golub (2007) are now available. We use the McDougall and Golub version.

18.3   Simulation data and the scenarios

We use the GTAP 8.1 database, which corresponds to the global economy of 2007, with 134 countries/regions and 57 industries. The database contains regional input–output tables, macro data, bilateral trade data, and protection data. In addition, energy volume data and CO_2 emission data are available. We combine these data into 22 regions and 24 industries.[7]

Seven simulations were implemented to evaluate the economic and environmental impacts of the FTAs. In this study, FTA means the complete abolition of any *ad valorem* import tariffs.

(1) The CK scenario: FTA between China and Korea
(2) The JK scenario: FTA between Japan and Korea
(3) The CJK scenario: FTA between China, Japan, and Korea
(4) The TPP scenario: FTA between TPP members (Australia, New Zealand, Japan, Malaysia, Singapore, Vietnam, Canada, the US, Mexico, Chile, and Peru)
(5) The TPPCK scenario: FTA between TPP members, and FTA between China and Korea
(6) The TPPJK scenario: FTA between TPP members, and FTA between Japan and Korea
(7) The TPPCJK scenario: FTA between TPP members, and FTA between China, Japan, and Korea.

The FTA simulation results depend substantially on the initial tariff rates. Some features of the initial tariff rates on energy-intensive products within FTA countries are described below.[8] The tariff rates charged on Japanese exports are provided in parentheses:

(1) The tariff rate on petroleum and coal products is remarkably high in Vietnam (18.5 percent), followed by Mexico, China, Chile, and Korea (ranging from approximately 7.2 percent to 5.0 percent).
(2) In New Zealand, Japan, Korea, Singapore, Canada, and the US, tariff rates on paper products are near zero. However, they are substantially higher in Vietnam, Peru, Malaysia, and Mexico (ranging from approximately 17.7 percent to 9.8 percent).
(3) Vietnam, Mexico, Malaysia, and Peru impose noticeably high tariff rates on chemical products (ranging from approximately 11.6 percent to 7.9 percent).
(4) Regarding mineral products, Vietnam, Mexico, China, Peru, Malaysia, and Korea impose relatively high tariff rates (ranging from approximately 13.7 percent to 7.1 percent).

(5) The tariff rate on ferrous metals is the highest in Malaysia (33.7 percent), whereas rates are considerably lower in Japan, Canada, and the US, and zero in Singapore. Other FTA countries impose tariff rates of several percent.

Even if the tariff rates on disaggregated imported products are the same across countries, the tariff rates on aggregated imported products are not, because the composition of these products in aggregated imported products differs across countries. For example, Japan imposes a tariff rate of 0.1 percent on chemical products imported from China, and of 2.0 percent on products from Korea. However, the above description is useful for obtaining a rough indication of the main tariff rates on energy-intensive goods.

18.4   The economic impacts of FTA

Before discussing the environmental effects of FTA in Section 18.5, we discuss their economic effects. Table 18.1 shows the change in GDP in the base year for each scenario. Generally, within FTA countries GDP increases slightly, whereas outside the FTA area it either stays almost the same or it decreases slightly. The results indicate that the effects of FTA on GDP do not appear to be significant.

Table 18.2 shows that equivalent variation (EV) tends to increase in FTA countries but decreases outside the FTA area.[9] Japan is likely to experience the largest EV. The US also shows positive EV under the TPP scenario, even though GDP is unchanged. However, some FTA countries show negative EV, for example Korea

Table 18.1 Percentage change in GDP from base

	CK	JK	CJK	TPP	TPPCK	TPPJK	TPPCJK
Australia	−0.00	−0.00	−0.01	0.01	0.01	0.01	0.01
New Zealand	−0.00	−0.00	−0.01	0.06	0.06	0.06	0.05
China	−0.01	−0.00	0.01	−0.03	−0.04	−0.03	−0.00
Japan	−0.00	0.02	0.11	0.08	0.08	0.10	0.17
Korea	0.19	0.03	0.20	−0.03	0.16	−0.00	0.17
Malaysia	−0.01	−0.01	−0.03	0.17	0.16	0.17	0.15
Singapore	−0.00	−0.00	−0.01	0.01	0.01	0.01	0.01
Vietnam	−0.03	−0.01	−0.11	1.18	1.15	1.18	1.08
Canada	−0.00	−0.00	−0.00	0.06	0.06	0.06	0.06
US	−0.00	−0.00	−0.00	0.00	−0.00	−0.00	−0.00
Mexico	−0.00	−0.00	−0.01	0.05	0.04	0.05	0.04
Chile	−0.00	−0.00	−0.01	0.02	0.01	0.01	0.01
Peru	−0.00	−0.00	−0.00	0.00	0.00	0.00	0.00
World	0.00	0.00	0.01	0.01	0.01	0.01	0.02

Source: Authors' calculations based on the GTAP 8.1 database.

Table 18.2 Equivalent variation (million US$)

	CK	JK	CJK	TPP	TPPCK	TPPJK	TPPCJK
Australia	−186	−87	−557	1,298	1,114	1,212	768
New Zealand	−33	−16	−100	631	598	616	535
China	11	−500	−153	−3,131	−3,153	−3,595	−3,191
Japan	−1,061	3,095	13,251	6,682	5,644	9,564	19,488
Korea	5,795	−270	4,174	−981	4,846	−1,280	3,250
Malaysia	−104	−58	−418	906	806	847	491
Singapore	−67	−26	−208	238	169	212	31
Vietnam	−96	−30	−246	1,941	1,852	1,914	1,686
Canada	−63	−20	−212	134	67	117	−47
US	−1,092	−658	−3,250	2,293	1,161	1,679	−1,275
Mexico	−88	3	−128	−201	−288	−196	−286
Chile	−67	−24	−164	87	19	62	−75
Peru	−11	−4	−30	64	53	60	36

Source: Authors' calculations based on the GTAP 8.1 database.

Table 18.3 Percentage change in exports from base

	CK	JK	CJK	TPP	TPPCK	TPPJK	TPPCJK
Australia	−0.0	0.0	0.1	0.8	0.8	0.9	0.9
New Zealand	0.0	0.0	0.1	0.7	0.7	0.7	0.8
China	1.0	−0.0	2.5	−0.1	0.8	−0.2	2.3
Japan	0.0	0.2	1.5	2.0	2.0	2.1	3.1
Korea	2.1	1.5	3.1	0.0	2.1	1.4	3.1
Malaysia	−0.0	−0.0	−0.2	1.3	1.3	1.3	1.2
Singapore	−0.1	−0.0	−0.2	0.6	0.6	0.6	0.5
Vietnam	−0.0	0.0	−0.0	10.0	10.0	10.0	9.9
Canada	0.0	0.0	0.1	1.2	1.2	1.3	1.4
US	−0.0	0.0	0.0	0.8	0.8	0.8	0.8
Mexico	0.0	0.0	0.1	0.9	1.0	0.9	1.0
Chile	0.0	0.0	0.1	0.1	0.2	0.2	0.2
Peru	−0.0	0.0	0.0	2.9	2.9	2.9	2.9

Source: Authors' calculations based on the GTAP 8.1 database.

in the JK scenario, China in the CJK scenario and Mexico in the TPP scenario. In these cases, the main explanation for negative EVs is the terms of trade.

The effects of FTA on exports and imports are relatively large compared with the effects on GDP (Tables 18.3 and 18.4). All FTA countries show increasing

Table 18.4 Percentage change in imports from base

	CK	JK	CJK	TPP	TPPCK	TPPJK	TPPCJK
Australia	−0.2	−0.1	−0.4	2.6	2.4	2.5	2.1
New Zealand	−0.1	−0.1	−0.3	3.2	3.1	3.1	2.8
China	1.3	−0.1	3.2	−0.4	1.0	−0.4	2.8
Japan	−0.3	0.8	4.3	3.2	2.9	4.0	7.1
Korea	4.3	1.8	5.2	−0.3	4.0	1.5	4.9
Malaysia	−0.1	−0.0	−0.5	2.9	2.8	2.8	2.4
Singapore	−0.2	−0.0	−0.4	0.9	0.7	0.8	0.5
Vietnam	−0.2	−0.0	−0.5	14.5	14.4	14.4	13.9
Canada	−0.0	0.0	−0.0	1.1	1.1	1.2	1.1
US	−0.1	−0.1	−0.3	0.6	0.5	0.6	0.3
Mexico	−0.0	0.0	−0.0	0.9	0.9	0.9	0.9
Chile	−0.1	−0.0	−0.2	0.3	0.2	0.3	0.1
Peru	−0.1	−0.0	−0.2	5.8	5.8	5.8	5.6

Source: Authors' calculations based on the GTAP 8.1 database.

rates of both exports and imports. For exports, the largest change is expected for Vietnam, followed by Korea, Japan, Peru, and China. Imports also change by the largest amount in Vietnam, followed by Japan, Peru, Korea, and China. Most FTA countries show larger changes in imports than in exports, except Canada, the US, and Mexico under the TPP scenario.

Table 18.5 shows the changes in nominal factor prices for each scenario. Wage and capital rental rates are likely to rise in most FTA member countries. Because full use of all production factors is assumed, and there are no unused factors in the model, an increase in factor demand will lead to a rise in factor prices. Significant increases in factor prices can be observed in Vietnam. In the TPP scenario Canada, the US, Mexico, and Chile have zero or negative changes. However, real wage and rental rates tend to rise even in these countries.

Table 18.6 shows changes in the output of energy-intensive industries in China, Japan, Korea, Vietnam, and the US.[10] We begin by looking at the results of the CK and JK scenarios. For paper products, ferrous metals, and transport services, output decreases in FTA countries. Possible reasons for this outcome are relatively low initial tariffs on these products and the low volume of trade between the two countries.[11] Under these conditions, both countries are likely to lose international competitiveness due to increases in factor prices. For the CK scenario, output of mineral products increases in China but decreases in Korea. Output of other energy-intensive products decreases in China but increases in Korea. For the JK scenario, output of energy-intensive products – except paper products, ferrous metals, and

Table 18.5 Percentage change from base in nominal factor prices

	CK		JK		CJK		TPP	
	Labor	Capital	Labor	Capital	Labor	Capital	Labor	Capital
Australia	-0.1	-0.1	-0.1	-0.1	-0.4	-0.4	0.9	0.9
New Zealand	-0.1	-0.1	-0.1	-0.1	-0.4	-0.4	1.9	1.8
China	0.2	0.2	-0.1	-0.1	0.3	0.1	-0.2	-0.2
Japan	-0.2	-0.2	0.4	0.4	1.5	1.6	0.7	0.7
Korea	2.3	2.5	0.3	0.3	2.1	2.3	-0.2	-0.2
Malaysia	-0.1	-0.1	-0.0	-0.0	-0.4	-0.4	1.5	1.7
Singapore	-0.1	-0.1	-0.0	-0.0	-0.2	-0.3	0.3	0.2
Vietnam	-0.3	-0.3	-0.1	-0.1	-0.7	-0.8	11.4	13.2
Canada	-0.1	-0.1	-0.0	-0.0	-0.2	-0.2	-0.2	-0.1
US	-0.1	-0.1	-0.0	-0.0	-0.2	-0.2	0.0	0.1
Mexico	-0.1	-0.1	-0.0	-0.0	-0.2	-0.2	-0.0	-0.0
Chile	-0.1	-0.1	-0.1	-0.1	-0.4	-0.4	0.0	0.1
Peru	-0.1	-0.1	-0.0	-0.0	-0.2	-0.2	0.4	0.6

Source: Authors' calculations based on the GTAP 8.1 database.

Table 18.6 Percentage change from base in output of the energy-intensive industries

	Petroleum & coal products	Electricity	Paper products	Chemical product	Mineral products	Ferrous metals	Transport services	Share
China								(26.28)
CK	-0.16	-0.09	-0.17	-0.47	0.09	-0.24	-0.04	26.25
JK	-0.00	-0.01	0.02	-0.03	-0.05	0.05	0.02	26.28
CJK	-0.35	-0.24	-0.40	-1.28	-0.25	-0.74	-0.06	26.17
TPP	-0.09	0.01	0.09	0.15	0.05	0.02	0.13	26.30
Japan								(18.86)
CK	-0.10	-0.01	0.04	-0.10	-0.17	0.15	0.07	18.86
JK	0.31	0.06	-0.07	0.36	0.55	-0.35	-0.06	18.87
CJK	1.27	0.38	0.05	1.02	1.03	-0.07	-0.20	18.92
TPP	0.60	0.22	-0.03	0.65	0.36	1.77	-0.08	18.92
Korea								(24.20)
CK	2.49	0.71	-0.53	3.62	-0.72	-1.18	-0.74	24.43
JK	0.02	0.01	-0.15	-0.20	-1.14	-0.32	-0.13	24.15
CJK	2.32	0.63	-0.42	3.18	-1.59	-1.04	-0.52	24.39
TPP	-0.17	-0.10	0.06	-0.03	0.16	-0.08	0.27	24.21
Vietnam								(17.80)
TPP	-14.80	-2.10	-7.07	-9.22	-1.08	-29.25	11.59	16.59
US								(13.69)
TPP	0.03	-0.03	0.06	-0.10	-0.06	-0.47	0.01	13.69

Source: Authors' calculations based on the GTAP 8.1 database.

transport services – increases in Japan, whereas output of chemical and mineral products decreases in Korea.

The trend of output in paper products, ferrous metals, and transport services under the CK and JK scenarios is almost the same as under the CJK scenario, except for Japan's paper products. For ferrous metals, Japan and Korea increase exports to China because initial Chinese tariff rates are relatively high, but exports to other countries (and output) decrease. Japan and Korea increase output in other energy-intensive industries, except for mineral products in Korea. China decreases output of all energy-intensive products. It is notable that the ferrous metals industry in Vietnam increases output by 2.7 percent under the CJK scenario. This result is attributed to the high export dependency of Vietnam's ferrous metals industry (97.4 percent) as well as the relative fall in factor prices.

Under the TPP scenario, Japanese ferrous metal output increases. This result is due to the initial high tariff rate on Japanese ferrous metals in Malaysia. Abolition of tariffs yields Japan a large increase in exports to Malaysia (189.9 percent, US$2,273 million) followed by an increase in output (1.8 percent, US$4,463 million). In Vietnam, output from energy-intensive industries, except transportation services, decreases. Because Vietnamese initial tariff rates on almost all products are highest among the FTA countries in the TPP scenario, output of many industries decreases with the presence of FTA. Transport services output increases remarkably in Vietnam due to a fall in prices of petroleum and coal products (–6.4 percent) and its relatively high export dependency (40.3 percent), as well as the initial zero tariff rate on it. Most US industries also decrease output under the TPP scenario. Output increases only in petroleum and coal products, food (1.5 percent), and paper product industries.

The last column in Table 18.6 indicates the share of output accounted for by energy-intensive industries. Initial shares are the values given in parentheses.[12] From these ratios, we can estimate the possible environmental outcomes: regarding a change in industrial structure, Japan is likely to worsen its environmental load by taking part in the FTA, whereas China and Vietnam can improve theirs. Korea is likely to worsen its environmental burden under the CK and CJK scenarios.

18.5   The environmental impacts of FTA

In this section we discuss the impacts on the environment, measured by the CO_2 load, for each scenario. Table 18.7 provides the CO_2 impact for each scenario. Most FTA countries are likely to increase CO_2 emissions, although there are some exceptions. China shows a decrease in CO_2 emissions under the CK, CJK, and TPPCJK scenarios. Australia, Mexico, and Peru show decreases under the TPP, TPPCK, TPPJK, and TPPCJK scenarios.

There are some notable points. First, Vietnam's CO_2 emissions increase by around 5 percent under the four scenarios that comprise TPP members. Emissions in Japan and Korea increase by around 1 percent when they set up an FTA with China. Second, the increase in CO_2 emissions in Japan is much lower under the

Table 18.7 Percentage change from base in CO_2 emissions

	CK	JK	CJK	TPP	TPPCK	TPPJK	TPPCJK
Australia	−0.02	−0.00	−0.04	−0.16	−0.17	−0.16	−0.18
New Zealand	−0.00	0.00	0.01	0.13	0.13	0.14	0.14
China	−0.01	−0.01	−0.09	0.03	0.02	0.02	−0.05
Japan	−0.07	0.25	1.01	0.42	0.36	0.66	1.40
Korea	1.18	0.07	1.11	−0.14	1.04	−0.07	0.97
Malaysia	−0.04	−0.01	−0.07	0.66	0.62	0.64	0.59
Singapore	0.00	0.03	0.09	0.97	0.97	0.99	1.03
Vietnam	−0.09	−0.01	−0.12	5.06	4.98	5.04	4.94
South Asia	−0.01	−0.00	−0.01	0.13	0.12	0.13	0.12
Canada	0.00	−0.00	−0.00	0.02	0.03	0.02	0.02
US	−0.01	−0.00	−0.02	0.03	0.02	0.03	0.00
Mexico	−0.00	0.00	0.00	−0.05	−0.05	−0.05	−0.05
Chile	−0.01	−0.00	−0.01	0.28	0.27	0.27	0.26
Peru	0.00	0.00	0.01	−0.29	−0.29	−0.29	−0.28
World	0.01	0.01	0.03	0.04	0.04	0.05	0.07

Source: Authors' calculations based on the GTAP 8.1 database.

TPP scenario than under the CJK scenario. Third, in most cases, CO_2 emissions tend to decrease in the non-FTA regions. However, China shows increases of CO_2 emission rates under the TPP, TPPCK, and TPPJK scenarios.

Combining with the results for GDP (Table 18.1), we can see that a decline in CO_2 emissions per US$ of real GDP is observed in some FTA countries. The change in GDP is larger than the change in CO_2 emissions for Australia, Mexico, and Peru under the TPP scenario, and in China under the CJK scenario. Possible reasons for this are changes in industrial structure, as seen in the previous section, and changes in energy substitution (see the following).

The bar charts in Figure 18.2 illustrate the change in CO_2 emissions in each scenario. Japan shows significant increases in CO_2 emissions in all scenarios except the CK scenario. Korea and TPP members in East Asia show large increases under FTAs that include China and TPP members, respectively. More than 70 percent of the increase in emissions in TPP members in East Asia is attributable to Vietnam.[13] China's decrease in CO_2 emissions is relatively large under the CJK and TPPCJK scenarios. The lines in Figure 18.2 illustrate that the dominant cause in global CO_2 emission change is East Asia.

In our discussion of changes in CO_2 emissions by industry, we focus on China, Japan, Korea, Vietnam, and the US. Table 18.8 lists CO_2 changes by sector for the CK, JK, CJK, and TPP scenarios. Overall, the electricity industry is important in determining the change in CO_2 emissions. In cases where total industrial CO_2

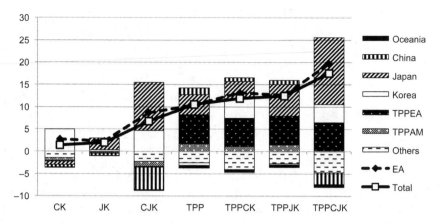

Figure 18.2 Change in CO_2 emissions from base (million tons).

Source: Authors' calculations based on the GTAP 8.1 database.

Note: Oceania: Australia and New Zealand; TPPEA: Malaysia, Singapore, and Vietnam; TPPAM: Canada, US, Mexico, Chile, and Peru; EA: China, Japan, Korea, Taiwan, Rest of ASEAN, and TPPEA.

Table 18.8 CO_2 change from base by sector (million tons)

	Petroleum & coal products	Electricity	Paper products	Chemical products	Mineral products	Ferrous metals	Transport services	Total
China								
CK	−0.13	−1.97	−0.02	−0.61	0.68	−0.37	0.53	−0.47
JK	−0.00	−0.26	0.01	−0.07	−0.20	0.12	0.04	−0.49
CJK	−0.28	−4.86	−0.07	−1.83	−0.21	−1.57	0.99	−4.64
TPP	−0.06	1.77	0.02	0.21	0.15	−0.09	0.14	1.70
Japan								
CK	−0.03	−0.18	−0.01	−0.09	−0.06	0.03	−0.06	−0.54
JK	0.09	0.85	0.03	0.30	0.21	−0.06	0.35	2.21
CJK	0.39	3.99	0.14	0.97	0.53	0.42	1.39	9.13
TPP	0.18	1.46	0.04	0.50	0.17	1.06	0.60	3.99
Korea								
CK	0.41	2.66	0.02	0.39	0.10	0.02	0.32	4.23
JK	0.01	0.23	0.00	−0.00	−0.17	−0.02	0.08	0.26
CJK	0.39	2.51	0.02	0.35	−0.06	0.03	0.51	4.09
TPP	−0.03	−0.39	−0.00	−0.01	−0.01	−0.04	0.11	−0.47
Vietnam								
TPP	−0.00	0.06	0.02	−0.06	0.38	−0.33	2.29	3.89
US								
TPP	0.05	−0.51	0.04	−0.09	−0.03	−0.17	0.31	1.41

Source: Authors' calculations using the GTAP 8.1 database.

Note: Total: The total change in industrial CO_2 emissions.

emissions grow, the electricity industry is the most important industry. However, the Vietnamese transportation service industry and the US food industry (0.99 million tons) show the largest increases in CO_2 emissions under the TPP scenario.

Almost all electricity is consumed domestically, but there are some exceptions. Vietnam imports electricity from China, and electricity trade between the US and Canada is important as well. Under the TPP scenario, the electricity price in China declines by 0.1 percent, whereas in Vietnam it increases by 8.0 percent. This results in increased exports of electricity from China to Vietnam by US$33.2 million, followed by an increase in industrial output by US$20.3 million. Under the same scenario, the electricity price declines by 0.13 percent in Canada, whereas it increases by 0.03 percent in the US. This causes an increase in electricity exports from Canada to the US by US$10.8 million and a decrease in exports from the US to Canada by US$4.2 million.

Table 18.9 Change in input demand made by the electricity industry (%)

	Labor	Capital	Coal	Oil	Gas	Petroleum & coal products	Electricity	VAE composite	Energy composite
China									
CK	−0.20	−0.10	−0.06	−0.07	−0.01	0.04	−0.04	−0.09	−0.04
JK	0.00	−0.01	−0.01	−0.02	−0.01	−0.02	−0.01	−0.01	−0.01
CJK	−0.50	−0.23	−0.15	−0.17	−0.08	−0.01	−0.13	−0.24	−0.13
TPP	0.09	0.02	−0.03	−0.04	−0.08	−0.05	−0.04	0.01	−0.04
Japan									
CK	0.05	0.01	−0.04	−0.08	−0.03	−0.07	−0.05	−0.01	−0.05
JK	−0.15	−0.02	0.19	0.19	0.20	0.16	0.18	0.06	0.18
CJK	−0.47	0.06	0.92	0.86	0.96	0.72	0.84	0.38	0.84
TPP	−0.13	0.12	0.25	0.44	0.42	0.37	0.38	0.22	0.38
Korea									
CK	−0.64	0.16	1.37	0.77	1.42	1.27	1.34	0.71	1.34
JK	−0.23	−0.07	0.11	0.04	0.10	0.13	0.12	0.01	0.12
CJK	−0.70	0.09	1.29	0.65	1.31	1.20	1.25	0.63	1.25
TPP	0.09	−0.04	−0.22	−0.13	−0.15	−0.16	−0.17	−0.10	−0.17
Vietnam									
TPP	−4.06	−3.12	0.36	13.66	−2.67	11.28	1.39	−2.10	1.39
US									
TPP	−0.02	−0.05	−0.02	−0.03	−0.02	−0.01	−0.02	−0.03	−0.02

Source: Authors' calculations based on the GTAP 8.1 database.

Sectoral output increases in Canada (US$26.7 million) and decreases in the US (US$115.2 million).[14]

We also examine the factors of change in industrial CO_2 emissions from the viewpoint of energy substitution. Table 18.9 shows changes of input demand by the electricity sector for the CK, JK, CJK, and TPP scenarios. The last two columns show changes in the aggregates. A change of demand for the value-added-energy (VAE) composite is the same as a change of output due to a Leontief structure at the top level. The table shows that the replacement of production factors with energy is likely to happen in Japan under the JK, CJK, and TPP scenarios, in Korea under the CK, JK, and CJK scenarios, and in Vietnam under the TPP scenario, because the change in demand for the energy composite is larger than the change in demand for labor and capital. Replacement of other production factors with energy is also expected in the US for the TPP scenario and in China for the CJK scenario.

A change in energy composition also affects the environmental load. For example, an increase in the coal share leads to a rise in CO_2 emissions per unit of output (CO_2 emission coefficient), whereas an increase in the gas share leads to a fall in the coefficient. China shows relatively small decreases in gas and relatively large decreases in coal under the CJK scenario, which may lower its CO_2 emission coefficient. Vietnam shows high and increased use of oil, and petroleum and coal products, and decreased use of gas. This could lead to a rise in Vietnam's CO_2 emission coefficient. A similar trend is observed for other industries.[15]

18.6 Concluding remarks

In this chapter, we examined the economic and environmental impacts of FTAs using a static CGE model.[16] We found that FTAs can cause a relatively large change in sectoral output and trade but only small changes in GDP. Accordingly, the environmental effects of FTAs differ across regions, and the reasons are diverse and region specific. However, we can draw several general conclusions.

First, an FTA with China is important in determining the industrial structure in Japan and Korea. By taking part in an FTA with China, output of many energy-intensive industries is likely to increase in Japan and Korea, whereas it decreases in China. Second, energy substitution also has important roles for CO_2 emissions in two ways. Both labor and capital are likely to be replaced by energy in the FTA regions because FTAs tend to increase wages and the cost of capital compared with energy prices. These relative price changes will affect CO_2 emission coefficients, as will changes in relative prices among energy carriers. For example, many industries in Vietnam show high rates and increasing demand for oil and petroleum and coal products, and a decreasing demand for gas. This pattern could lead to an increase in the CO_2 emission coefficient. And in Vietnam, although output from many energy-intensive industries decreases due to FTA, CO_2 emissions can increase significantly.

As for political implications, our simulation shows that environmental assessments of FTAs are important, especially for East Asia. Even under the TPP scenario, most of the environmental changes are likely to occur in East Asia. In addition, since the environmental burden caused by FTAs is not negligible, it is necessary to adopt a vision of a mutually supportive relationship between the environment and trade. Finally, our results show Japan's responsibility and role in FTAs. Domestically, it is necessary to develop and promote energy conservation technology and conversion to cleaner energy. Internationally, foreign direct investment – with technology transfer to East Asia and open labor markets to increase Japan's production without replacement of labor with energy – may be expected.

Appendix

Table 18.A1 Country/region aggregation

Aggregated country/region	*GTAP country/region*
Australia	Australia
New Zealand	New Zealand
China	China, Hong Kong
Japan	Japan
Korea	Korea
Taiwan	Taiwan
Rest of ASEAN	Cambodia, Indonesia, Lao People's Democratic Republic, Philippines, Thailand, Rest of Southeast Asia
Malaysia	Malaysia
Singapore	Singapore
Vietnam	Vietnam
South of Asia	Bangladesh, India, Nepal, Pakistan, Sri Lanka, Rest of South Asia
Canada	Canada
US	United States of America
Mexico	Mexico
Latin America	Argentina, Bolivia, Brazil, Colombia, Ecuador, Paraguay, Uruguay, Venezuela, Rest of South America, Costa Rica, Guatemala, Honduras, Nicaragua, Panama, El Salvador, Rest of Central America, Caribbean
Chile	Chile
Peru	Peru
EU	Austria, Belgium, Cyprus, Czech Republic, Denmark, Estonia, Finland, France, Germany, Greece, Hungary, Ireland, Italy, Latvia, Lithuania, Luxembourg, Malta, Netherlands, Poland, Portugal, Slovakia, Slovenia, Spain, Sweden, United Kingdom, Bulgaria, Romania

(Continued)

Table 18.A1 (Continued)

Aggregated country/region	GTAP country/region
East Europe and Former Soviet Union	Albania, Belarus, Croatia, Russian Federation, Ukraine, Rest of Eastern Europe, Kazakhstan, Kyrgyzstan, Rest of Former Soviet Union, Armenia, Azerbaijan, Georgia
Middle East and North Africa	Bahrain, Islamic Republic of Iran, Israel, Kuwait, Oman, Qatar, Saudi Arabia, Turkey, United Arab Emirates, Rest of Western Asia, Egypt, Morocco, Tunisia, Rest of North Africa
Sab-Sahara Africa	Benin, Burkina Faso, Cameroon, Cote d'Ivoire, Ghana, Guinea, Nigeria, Senegal, Togo, Rest of Western Africa, Central Africa, South Central Africa, Ethiopia, Kenya, Madagascar, Malawi, Mauritius, Mozambique, Rwanda, Tanzania, Uganda, Zambia, Zimbabwe, Rest of Eastern Africa, Botswana, Namibia, South Africa, Rest of South African Customs
Rest of the World	Rest of Oceania, Mongolia, Rest of East Asia, Rest of North America, Switzerland, Norway, Rest of EFTA, Rest of Europe, Rest of the World

Source: GTAP 8.1 database.

Table 18.A2 Industry aggregation

Aggregated sector	GTAP sector
Paddy rice	Paddy rice
Other agriculture	Wheat, cereal grains, vegetables/fruit/nuts, oil seeds, sugar cane/sugar beet, plant-based fibers, crops
Livestock	Cattle/sheep/goats/horses, animal products, raw milk, wool/silk-worm cocoons
Forestry	Forestry
Fishing	Fishing
Coal	Coal
Oil	Oil
Gas	Gas, gas manufacture/distribution
Petroleum & coal products	Petroleum & coal products
Electricity	Electricity
Mining	Other minerals
Food	Meat, meat products, vegetable oils & fats, dairy products, processed rice, sugar, food products, beverages and tobacco products
Textiles	Textiles, wearing apparel
Paper products	Paper products & publishing

Aggregated sector	GTAP sector
Chemical products	Chemical, rubber, plastic products
Mineral products	Other mineral products
Ferrous metals	Ferrous metals
Motor vehicles & parts	Motor vehicles & parts
Transport equipment	Transport equipment
Electronic equipment	Electronic equipment
Machinery	Machinery and equipment
Other manufacture	Leather products, wood products, metals, metal products, other manufactures
Transportation services	Sea transportation, air transportation, other transportation
Services	Water, construction, trade, communication, financial services, insurance, business services, recreation and other services, pubic administration/defense/health/education, dwellings

Source: The GTAP 8.1 database.

Notes

1 The United States banned imports of Mexican tuna harvested using purse-seine fishing methods that have resulted in the killings of dolphins in excess of the US standard. Mexico complained against the US tuna embargo to the General Agreement on Tariffs and Trade (GATT) in 1991.
2 Mukhopadhyay and Thomassin (2010) study economic and environmental impacts of East Asian FTA using the GTAP model.
3 See Hertel (1997), and Burniaux and Truong (2002).
4 The zero-profit condition implies that the value of output is equal to the value of all inputs. Firms cannot reap any excess profits. Value added is fully distributed between labor, capital, land, and natural resources in the GTAP-E model.
5 The GTAP-E model does not consider renewable energy and nuclear power. The CGE model used in Chapter 7, however, does consider them.
6 See Armington (1969).
7 See Appendices 18.A1 and 18.A2.
8 In this chapter, energy-intensive products mean petroleum and coal products, electricity, paper products, chemical products, mineral products, and ferrous metals. In Chapter 13, electricity and transport services are not included as energy intensive products because the focus is on the trade of industrial products.
9 The GTAP-E model computes EV as a measure of welfare change. EV is equal to the difference between the income required to obtain the new level (post-simulation) of utility at initial prices and the initial income. See Huff and Hertel (2000) on decomposing welfare changes in the GTAP model.
10 Except for energy-intensive industries, relatively large output change rates are seen in the paddy rice, food, and textiles industries. For example, paddy rice: 13.9 percent (China) and –44.7 percent (Japan) under the CJK scenario, 74.2 percent (US) and –24.1 percent (Japan) under the TPP scenario; food: 46.0 percent

(Singapore), 8.2 percent (Australia), 6.1 percent (New Zealand) under the TPP scenario; textiles: 76.7 percent (Vietnam), 33.5 percent (Malaysia), 13.6 percent (Peru) under the TPP scenario.

11 The tariff rate on transport services is zero for any country in the GTAP database.

12 These estimates are higher than the share for the East Asian countries given in Chapter 13 because they include electricity and transportation services, and because they are for 2007 rather than 2012.

13 CO_2 emission changes under the TPP scenario are as follows (million tons): Malaysia, 1.2; Singapore, 0.6; Vietnam, 4.6.

14 Although electricity is a commoditized product, the GTAP-E model adopts the Armington assumption. The Armington parameter for domestic/imported allocation-relating electricity is 2.8. It may overestimate a decrease in demand for domestic electricity when the share of imported electricity is low. That is because one unit of domestic electricity can be substituted by less than one unit of imported electricity in this model. This is still an important and unsolved problem in this study.

15 In the GTAP-E model, the fuel mix for power generation is determined by relative prices and fixed elasticities. Chapters 3 and 4 describe energy system modeling and policies designed specifically for the electricity sector.

16 We should note that we used 2007 data, which does not reflect the effects of the financial crisis and the Great East Japan Earthquake. Although there is no alternative but to wait for a data update, we may guess that the direction of our results would not change much as long as the initial tariff rates are similar to the 2007 data.

References

Armington, P. S. (1969). 'A theory of demand for products distinguished by place of production.' *International Monetary Fund Staff Papers*, XVI, pp. 159–178.

Burniaux, J. M., and Truong T. P. (2002). 'GTAP-E: An energy-environmental version of the GTAP model.' GTAP Technical Paper, No.16, Center for Global Trade Analysis, Department of Agricultural Economics, Purdue University, West Lafayette, IN.

Hertel, T. W. (Ed.) (1997). *Global Trade Analysis: Modeling and Applications.* Cambridge, UK: Cambridge University Press.

Huff, K. M., and Hertel, T. W. (2000). 'Decomposing welfare changes in the GTAP model.' GTAP Technical Paper, No. 5, Center for Global Trade Analysis, Department of Agricultural Economics, Purdue University, West Lafayette, IN.

McDougall, R., and Golub, A. (2007). 'GTAP-E: Revised energy-environmental version of the GTAP model.' GTAP Research Memorandum, No.15, Center for Global Trade Analysis, Department of Agricultural Economics, Purdue University, West Lafayette, IN.

Mukhopadhyay, K., and Thomassin, P. J. (2010). *Economic and Environmental Impact of Free Trade in East and South East Asia.* Dordrecht; Heidelberg; London; New York: Springer.

Truong, T. P. (2007). 'GTAP-E: An energy-environmental version of the GTAP model with emission trading – USER'S GUIDE.' GTAP Resource, No.2509, https://www.gtap.agecon.purdue.edu/resources/download/3552.pdf (accessed May 16, 2015).

19 An environmental assessment of East Asian trade agreements using E3ME-Asia

Unnada Chewpreecha, Hector Pollitt, Soocheol Lee, Yuri Sadoi, and Hiroshi Yoshida

19.1 Introduction

As we have seen in previous chapters, free trade and climate change have a closely intertwined relationship that has come under increasing scrutiny from both economists and environmentalists. This final chapter returns to the framework offered by the E3ME-Asia model in order to assess the economic and environmental impacts of a series of proposed trade deals that affect the East Asian economies.

Analysis using previous versions of the E3ME-Asia model has defined the net impact of free trade on an economy's emissions as the sum of the changes in three areas:

- The level of economic activity, known as the scale effect
- The relative shares of the goods produced, known as the composition effect
- The production methods, known as the technique effect

Standard trade theory suggests that, typically, the scale effect is positive. However, the direction of the latter two changes cannot be generalized as they depend upon the trading countries' specific characteristics, such as relative income, level of development, policy, and factor endowment. Hence, the composition effect is determined by the comparative advantage of the particular country relative to those of its trading partner(s), whereas the technique effect (production methods) rests upon the degree of knowledge transfer, and consumer and political pressure that originate from its trading partner(s).

A widely recognized tool for conducting such an analysis of trade policy is the Global Trade Analysis Project's (GTAP) comparative, static, multi-regional CGE model, which is described in Chapter 18 of this book. The approach adopted in E3ME-Asia is quite similar but, as we have seen throughout this book, has some important differences. As in the previous chapter, we use the model's built-in E3 linkages to assess the relationship between trade and CO_2 emissions.

In the next section, we describe E3ME-Asia's approach to modeling trade. We then recap the scenarios and present a summary of the anticipated impacts. Finally, we compare the results against those from Chapter 18 and draw some initial policy conclusions from the analysis.

19.2   Modeling environmental impacts of trade deals in E3ME-Asia

Bilateral trade modeling

As outlined in the model manual (Cambridge Econometrics, 2014), the original specification of the trade equations in E3ME-Asia was based around the proposed method described by Ragot (1994). It drew on the variety hypothesis (Barker, 1977) and its incorporation in a UK multisectoral model (Barker and Peterson, 1987). Trade was treated as if it took place through a 'pool,' that is, a transport and distribution network, with the export and import volume equations representing each country's exports into and imports from this pool. Previous versions of the E3ME model have been applied in tandem with a CGE model (that is based on the GTAP database) to assess the environmental impacts of proposed trade deals between the EU and Canada (Kirkpatrick et al., 2011) and between the EU and the US.

The current version of the E3ME-Asia model has been expanded to make use of bilateral time-series trade data that have recently become available. E3ME-Asia now fully follows a bilateral approach to modeling international trade, similar in method to a two-tier Armington model (Armington, 1969). The E3ME-Asia method is summarized as follows:

- Solve the model equations for total imports in each sector (split within and external to trading zones)
- Solve the model equations for bilateral imports
- Scale the bilateral trade results for consistency with the aggregate results
- Derive the total exports as the sum and the inverse of bilateral imports

The first stage is similar to previous model versions, in which changes in import volumes are determined by changes in economic activity, prices, and technology. In the E3ME-Asia equations, economic activity is represented by sales to the domestic market, while the following three price effects are included: import prices, the price of sales to the domestic market, and the relative price of the currency (i.e. the exchange rate). Aside from the restrictions on sign and significance, 'price homogeneity' is imposed between the price of imports and the price of sales to the domestic market in the long run. This restriction has the effect of making the price relative, removing the long-term effect of the exchange rate variable. Finally, the technical progress measures are included to allow for the effects of innovations on trade performance.

The bilateral trade data are defined at the 43-sector level. The other dimensions in the data are origin (53 regions), destination (53 regions), and year (1995–2012). The equation specification allows the bilateral import share to be determined by export prices of the exporting region and technology in the exporting region. As the time series grow in length, additional explanatory factors (e.g., to take into account scale effects) will be added to future versions of the equations.

The model results for exports (either bilaterally or as a region's total) are relatively straightforward to derive; bilateral flows are reversed and aggregated to give regional totals. However, it is necessary to make a further adjustment to account for discrepancies in trade data, in particular the well-known inconsistency between global exports and global imports.

Further information about the model's specification of the trade equations is given in the model manual (Cambridge Econometrics, 2014).

Modeling trade agreements in E3ME-Asia

In this chapter we assume that the trade agreements lead to a complete abolition of the import tariffs between participating countries, resulting in changes in bilateral trade prices. When the analysis was carried out, the extent of removal of non-tariff barriers was not clear and they were therefore not included in the analysis.

Figure 19.1 provides an overview on how trade agreements are modeled in E3ME-Asia. Existing bilateral import tariffs at the sectoral level are removed under a trade agreement. This results in an increase in trade between countries participating in the deal. Expected impacts on the economy include lower prices,

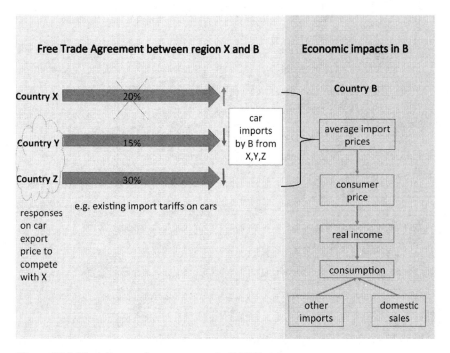

Figure 19.1 Modeling trade agreements in E3ME-Asia.

which lead to higher disposable income and consumption. It should be noted that in E3ME-Asia, export prices for non-participating regions will also respond to other regions' competing export prices. This relationship is empirically estimated at sectoral and region-specific level.

Trade and environmental impacts in E3ME-Asia

Figure 19.2 summarizes how the trade deals affect energy demand and emissions in the modeling. First, the change in prices affects trade volumes, and these changes, in turn, affect levels of economic production. In order to produce a unit of output, industries buy units of input from other industries as well as units of energy and labor, which lead to further rounds of indirect effects (other industries) and induced effects (employment, income, and consumption) in the economy.

The link between economic activity and physical energy demand comes through the estimated energy demand equations. The model is as described in Chapter 2; energy demand (in physical units) is a function of real economic output, energy prices, and measures of the capital stock's efficiency. This feeds back to the economy through the performance of the energy sectors, represented in the modeling by input–output coefficients and consumers' final demands.

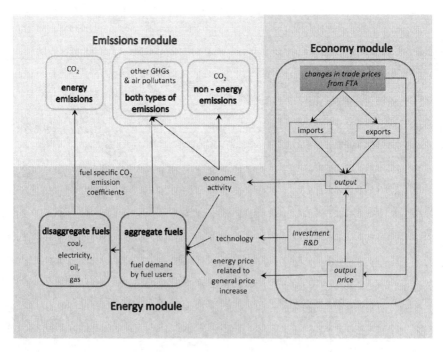

Figure 19.2 Trade and environmental impacts in E3ME-Asia.

Also as in other chapters, emissions are estimated through fixed emission factors. These are determined by taking the ratio of emissions to activity in the last year of data and maintaining this relationship thereafter. Usually the measure of activity is energy consumption (spread across different fuel types), so, for example, a 10 percent increase in consumption of coal leads to a 10 percent increase in CO_2 emissions from coal. Changes in economic activity also determine the level of emissions from non-CO_2 gases and non-energy-related CO_2 emissions in E3ME-Asia.

Scale, composition and technique effects in E3ME-Asia

The emissions results from the E3ME-Asia model capture scale, composition, and technique effects. However, it is not possible to separate out these effects since the model solves all equations simultaneously in a given year. The overall impact of trade deals on emissions will depend on the magnitude or strength of the three effects. The following explains how the scale, composition, and technique effects are captured in the model.

- The 'scale' effect is captured in E3ME-Asia through the change in emissions that results from changes in economic activity from the trade agreements between regions. A positive correlation is expected between economic activity levels and emissions (other things being equal), as an increase in economic activity results in higher energy demand and a higher level of emissions.
- The 'composition' effect is captured in E3ME-Asia through changes in emissions as a result of changes in sectoral composition from the trade deals. The detailed sectoral coverage in E3ME-Asia provides insights about sectoral comparative advantage between regions. The effects on emission levels will depend on those sectors in which a country has a comparative advantage. For example, if energy-intensive sectors expand because of a trade deal, the result is likely to be higher levels of emissions. However, the global net impact on emissions from the trade deal could still be lower if the country with the comparative advantage uses a relatively cleaner method of production than its partners. For this reason, a composition effect can either be positive or negative, depending on the nature of the trade agreement, sector compositions, input–output structure, and production methods of countries that participate in the deal.
- The 'technique' effect, according to the World Trade Organization (WTO),[1] can come about in two ways. First, through the increase in availability and the lower cost of environmentally friendly goods, services, and technologies. Second, the increases in income due to trade could lead society to demand better environmental quality. The E3ME-Asia model captures the first effect through increasing trade of environmental goods and services but also through technological spillover between regions. The model does not very well capture the behavioral changes that might result in demand to protect the environment.

In Chapter 13, we saw an important aspect of the technique effect in the E3ME-Asia modeling in which the development of power sector technologies led to increased rates of uptake across East Asia. Multi-national companies will play a key role in this type of technology transfer, but it is noted that, in some cases, protecting the development of new technologies in local firms might be justified.

The empirical approach that is used in E3ME-Asia captures these effects at the level of disaggregation that the model covers. However, as discussed below and in Chapter 13, the level of detail outside the power sector is limited by the available data. The results should be considered in the context of this limitation – that is, positive sectoral results do not imply that every firm in that sector will benefit from the measures. Linking specific environmental technologies to more aggregate economic data remains an ongoing area of research.

Criticisms of the E3ME-Asia approach

The environmental impacts of trade go further than the three effects described in the above section. The impacts of increasing demand on international transport and distribution networks as a result of trade agreements are not very well captured in E3ME-Asia. According to the WTO and the International Maritime Organization, most of the goods traded between regions are transported by sea, which accounts for less than 10 percent of total emissions in the transport sector. Nonetheless, CO_2 emissions from marine bunkers have more than doubled over the period 1985–2010, reflecting increasing trends in international trade. Some of these effects are described in Chapter 17.

Another criticism of the approach used in macroeconomic models (including both the CGE modeling approach and E3ME-Asia) is the limited sectoral disaggregation. The maximum number of sectors in a macroeconomic model is typically determined by the level of detail in the input–output tables and the national accounts economic data; both of these are usually much less detailed than published trade statistics. This leads to two potential shortcomings:

- Macroeconomic models are not generally able to assess the environmental goods and services sectors in any great level of detail. They could thus potentially miss some of the more positive effects of trade deals if they focus on these sectors (as was proposed to the WTO in 2014).
- It is possible that there is aggregation bias in model parameters. In most sectors this is not a concern, but in some specific circumstances, when an aggregate sector includes a mixture of differentiated goods and commoditized goods, the Armington assumption is violated. This can lead to a bias in estimation and is described further in McDaniel and Balistreri (2003).

Scenario description

The scenarios in this chapter are the same as those in Chapter 18, therefore allowing a direct comparison of results. There are five scenarios where various countries

Table 19.1 Trade scenario descriptions

Scenario	Description
Reference	E3ME-Asia baseline
JK	Complete abolition of ad valorem import tariffs between Japan and Korea
CJK	Complete abolition of ad valorem import tariffs between China, Japan and Korea
TPP	Complete abolition of ad valorem import tariffs between TPP members*
TPPJK	Complete abolition of ad valorem import tariffs between TPP members, Japan and Korea
TPPCJK	Complete abolition of ad valorem import tariffs between TPP members, China, Japan and Korea
	Australia, New Zealand, Japan, the rest of ASEAN, Canada, the US, Mexico, the rest of Latin America (Chile, Peru)

*TPP members(Trans-Pacific Partnership)

(inside and outside East Asia) form trade agreements. Table 19.1 summarizes the trade scenarios.

The scenarios assume a complete abolition of existing bilateral import tariffs between participating countries from 2015 onwards. The information on tariffs is taken from the GTAP database – and consistent with Chapter 18 – and the tariffs are defined as ad valorem rates on imports and disaggregated by product, source, and destination. Figure 19.3 summarizes the existing tariff rates between Japan, Korea, and China. For the TPP scenarios, similar bilateral import tariffs were modeled between TPP members, Korea, and China.[2]

It should be remembered that modeling of the TPP in this chapter only relates to the removal of import tariffs and does not include other non-tariff elements such as intellectual property rights, investment rules, and environmental and health regulations.

19.3 E3ME-Asia results

Macroeconomic impacts

Table 19.2 summarizes the macroeconomic impacts of the trade agreements in E3ME-Asia. Overall, the trade deals almost always produce positive GDP outcomes for their members through lower trade prices and subsequent increases in real rates of activity. The one exception is the TPPCJK case in China, where exports do not increase due to other changes in trade patterns. As Table 19.2 shows, countries outside the trade deals may also lose out due to changes in trading patterns.

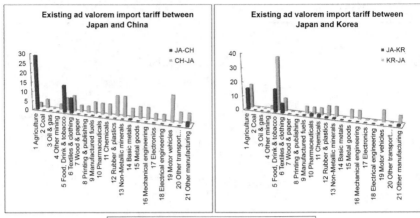

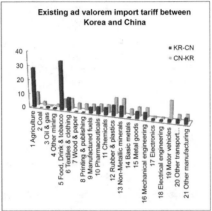

Figure 19.3 Existing import tariffs between participating regions.
Source: GTAP.

The scale of the impact on GDP in each region depends on sectoral competitiveness after existing bilateral import tariffs are removed. The net employment effects are small at regional level but usually follow the impact on GDP. Employment impacts are more distinguished at sectoral level.

The trade effects are largely as expected from scenarios where the costs of international trade are reduced. The largest impacts are in Japan, where imports increase by up to 1.6 percent and exports by up to 1.1 percent. In China and Korea the effects are much smaller, and the modeling results suggest that Chinese exports may even decrease as China's reductions in tariffs are smaller than those for the other countries.

Sectoral impacts

The sectoral results from E3ME-Asia (see Figure 19.4) provide some insights as to how the trade agreements affect member countries differently. In Japan

Table 19.2 Macroeconomic and CO_2 impacts of trade scenarios, 2030

	JK	CJK	TPP	TPPJK	TPPCJK
GDP in 2030 (% difference to baseline)					
China	0.0	0.1	-0.2	-0.2	-0.1
Japan	0.1	0.4	0.5	0.8	1.1
Korea	0.0	0.1	-0.1	0.2	0.4
TPP – excluding Japan	0.0	0.0	0.0	0.0	0.0
Employment in 2030 (% difference to baseline)					
China	0.0	0.0	0.0	0.0	-0.1
Japan	0.0	0.2	0.2	0.3	0.4
Korea	0.1	0.1	0.0	0.3	0.4
TPP – excluding Japan	0.0	0.0	0.0	0.0	0.0
Total imports in 2030 (% difference to baseline)					
China	-0.1	0.4	-0.2	-0.3	0.3
Japan	0.2	0.6	0.6	1.1	1.6
Korea	0.0	0.1	-0.2	0.0	0.2
TPP – excluding Japan	0.0	-0.1	0.1	0.1	0.1
Total exports in 2030 (% difference to baseline)					
China	0.0	0.1	-0.2	-0.2	-0.1
Japan	0.1	0.4	0.5	0.8	1.1
Korea	0.0	0.1	-0.1	0.2	0.4
TPP – excluding Japan	0.0	-0.1	0.0	0.0	-0.1

Source: E3ME-Asia (Cambridge Econometrics, 2014).

and Korea, the sectors that most benefit include engineering, motor vehicles, and some basic manufacturing sectors. Some of these sectors are energy-intensive whereas others are less so. In China, the E3ME-Asia results suggest that 'other manufacturing' (which includes furniture, games, and toys) benefits most from the trade agreements that include China. Other sectors in China see either decreases or smaller increases in their output because existing bilateral import tariffs on Chinese goods are relatively low in participating countries.

It should be noted that, whereas the manufacturing sectors benefit directly from the trade agreements, there are also secondary impacts due to lower prices, which lead to an increase in consumers' real spending power. As a result, consumer-related sectors such as retailing and hotels/catering can also benefit in the scenarios.

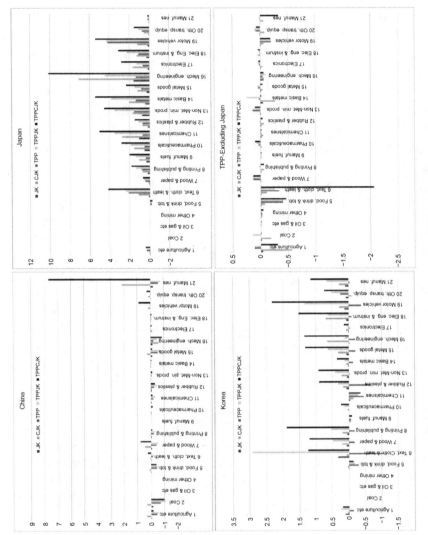

Figure 19.4 Economic output impacts by sector, 2030 (% difference from baseline).

Employment results at the sectoral level generally follow sectoral output, albeit at smaller magnitudes. There are also some changes in prices that can affect relative wage costs, leading to shifts in factor inputs. Overall, however, smaller increases in employment compared to increases in output at the sectoral level suggest an increase in labor productivity in the trade agreement scenarios.

Detailed CO_2 impacts

A summary of CO_2 impacts from the trade agreements is given in Table 19.3. Overall, CO_2 changes are in line with economic activity, although by a lower percentage. The differences represent a combination of the scale, composition and, to some extent, the technique impacts that are captured in the model's parameter coefficients. So although there is an increase in production by energy-intensive sectors, production increases less in the economy as a whole.

With the exception of the Chinese transportation sector, the changes in emissions tend to be quite evenly split between the power sector, industry, and transportation. One might expect industrial emissions to increase the most because energy-intensive sectors are covered explicitly by the trade deals, but the results suggest that the increases in emissions are the result of higher GDP growth rather than impacts on a particular sector.

Figure 19.5 shows the net impacts on CO_2 emissions in the different trade scenarios in absolute terms. As expected, higher trade activities from trade agreements lead to higher energy demand and higher emissions. However, the chart shows that the location of the economic activity is also important. The modeling results show that any agreements that divert production away from China toward other East Asian countries may result in a reduction in CO_2 emissions. This trend is particularly obvious in the TPP scenarios that do not include China, because a large share of global production (i.e., the US, Japan, and other countries) is affected. The model results suggest that emission reductions from the Chinese transport sector lead to overall reductions in CO_2 emissions in the East Asia region.

Table 19.3 CO_2 impacts of trade scenarios, 2030

	JK	CJK	TPP	TPPJK	TPPCJK
CO_2 in 2030 (% difference to baseline)					
China	0.0	0.1	−0.1	−0.1	0.0
Japan	0.1	0.2	0.3	0.5	0.7
Korea	0.0	0.0	−0.1	0.0	0.0
TPP – excluding Japan	0.0	0.0	0.0	0.0	0.0

Source: E3ME-Asia (Cambridge Econometrics, 2014).

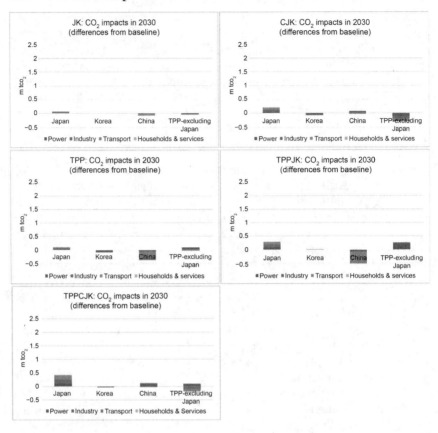

Figure 19.5 CO$_2$ absolute impacts from different trade scenarios, 2030 (m tCO$_2$ difference from baseline).

Source: E3ME-Asia (Cambridge Econometrics, 2014).

Once China is included in the trade agreements, however, the model results show an increase in overall levels of emissions. Carbon intensity still falls across the East Asia region because of scale effects, but not enough to offset the higher GDP levels.

In summary, the model results are showing the environmental impacts of both an increase in total production and a relocation of production. Both effects are important. Japan increases output and emissions in all the scenarios – with larger increases where trade agreements cover more and larger partner countries. Output and emission levels in the other countries depend on whether they are included in the trade agreements or not.

At a global level, the net impact on emissions can be quite dependent on whether the shift in production leads to an increase or decrease in carbon intensity.

China and some of the TPP members (e.g., the US, Australia) have relatively high carbon intensities, so increases in production in these countries are more likely to lead to higher net emissions.

Finally, we should also note that international transport emissions are not fully captured in the modeling approach. If transport emissions were included, we would expect to see slightly higher emission levels in the trade scenarios.

19.4 Comparison of the E3ME-Asia and GTAP-E results

Comparison of economic results

The scenarios that were assessed in Chapter 18 are the same as the scenarios described in this chapter. Theoretically at least, this set-up should allow us to make a direct comparison between the two sets of model results.

One potential difference between the results reported is the dimension of time. The GTAP-E results reported in Chapter 18 are long-term impacts that allow time for the economies covered by the trade deals to move back to an equilibrium position. Although it is never clear exactly how much time is required, we have assumed this to be roughly comparable to the E3ME-Asia results for 2030 that have been reported above.

Table 19.4 summarizes the GDP impacts in the three countries that are covered explicitly by the trade deals.

In most cases, the general pattern of result is the same in the two models, although the magnitude of the effects is typically bigger in E3ME-Asia. This is despite the fact that the impacts on trade are bigger in GTAP-E (see Table 19.5 for a comparison of the most comprehensive scenario).

Table 19.4 GDP impacts in the two models

	JK	CJK	TPP	TPPJK	TPPCJK
GTAP-E results					
China	0.0	0.0	0.0	0.0	0.0
Japan	0.0	0.1	0.1	0.1	0.2
Korea	0.0	0.2	0.0	0.0	0.2
E3ME-Asia results					
China	0.0	0.1	−0.2	−0.2	−0.1
Japan	0.1	0.4	0.5	0.8	1.1
Korea	0.0	0.1	−0.1	0.2	0.4

Table 19.5 Trade impacts in the two models, TPPCJK scenario

	GTAP-E results		E3ME-Asia results	
	Exports	Imports	Exports	Imports
China	2.3	2.8	–0.1	0.3
Japan	3.1	7.1	1.1	1.6
Korea	3.1	4.9	0.4	0.2

A closer inspection of Table 19.5 shows that both models predict a larger increase in imports than in exports in China and Japan, so it is clearly price effects rather than trade volume effects that are driving the increase in GDP. But the two tables raise two important questions in the comparison:

- Why are the trade effects larger in GTAP-E than in E3ME-Asia?
- Why, despite this, are the GDP impacts larger in E3ME-Asia than in GTAP-E?

The answer to the first of these questions lies with the models' parameterization, rather than their structure or underlying assumptions. Analyses of results from previous studies have shown that, in E3ME-Asia, the econometric estimates of trade price elasticity tend to be rather low. Furthermore, if no significant relationship is found, an elasticity of zero is applied. In the GTAP-E model used in Chapter 18, the import substitution parameters range from 0.9 to 10.96. The upper boundary of 10.96 is for a commoditized sector (gas) that E3ME-Asia does not attempt to model, so a direct comparison is not possible. However, the average long-term substitution parameters estimated are around 0.2 for China, Japan, and Taiwan, and less than 0.1 for Korea. Hence, it is not surprising that the E3ME-Asia results suggest that removing tariff barriers will have a much smaller effect on trade compared with that suggested in the GTAP-E model.

One possible answer to the second question relates to the timing of the effects. Whereas GTAP-E bases results on the base year 2007, the E3ME-Asia results in this chapter are for 2030; as trade grows faster than GDP in the baseline, one would expect changes in trade to have a greater influence on GDP in 2030. This is partly true; although we have noted above that changes in trade volumes cannot be driving the model results, a larger trade share does mean that price effects are amplified as well. This difference in approach may, therefore, explain part of the difference in results, but it is likely to be only part.

Readers of previous chapters in this book will probably have already guessed the main reason for the differences in results. Whereas the higher GDP in GTAP-E is the result of a more efficient allocation of economic resources, the impacts in E3ME-Asia are the result of both a more efficient allocation of resources and *an increased utilization of unused resources*. Or, to put it differently, in the E3ME-Asia model the initial stimulus from cheaper imports leads to domestic multiplier effects. There is, thus, scope for producers in each country to benefit, even if they do not produce export goods.

Comparison of the environmental results

Regarding CO_2 emission levels, the broad trends are the same in the two models for China and Japan. Both models suggest that emission levels in China can either increase or decrease slightly, depending on the scenario, but overall will remain roughly unchanged. In Japan, both models predict an increase in CO_2 emissions that grows as the coverage of the trade deals grows. The models differ, however, in their results for Korea. In the GTAP-E results emissions in Korea increase by up to 1 percent, whereas in the E3ME-Asia results they remain unchanged.

A further difference between the two sets of model results is the magnitude of the differences in emissions. The E3ME-Asia results show that as GDP increases, emissions of CO_2 increase less, meaning that, overall, carbon intensity falls. However, this is not what the GTAP-E results show, and there are two main reasons for the discrepancy.

The first reason is the composition effect and the changes in sectoral output that themselves are a result of the changing trade patterns. The results from GTAP-E suggest much larger changes in the manufacturing sectors that are affected directly by the trade agreements, including the energy-intensive sectors. CO_2 emissions can, therefore, increase by more than GDP. In the E3ME-Asia results, however, the economic benefits are spread across East Asia's economies, and this pattern is much less clear.

The second reason relates to the upscaling of production. E3ME-Asia does not assume constant returns to scale, so it is possible to increase production levels without increasing fuel inputs by the same proportion. In this way, carbon intensity can be lowered.

Conclusions from the comparison

This comparison exercise leads to two important conclusions for modelers and the users of model results. The first relates to the parameterization of the macroeconomic models. It would be very useful for researchers to obtain a better understanding of the different sets of price substitution elasticities that are used in the models, under what conditions they are determined, and how they relate to the available data. An assessment of how the models and their parameters deal with issues such as aggregation bias and non-significant relationships, would also be welcome.

The second conclusion relates to the way that assessments of trade deals are carried out. To date, the analysis has been heavily dominated by CGE modeling approaches and has not taken into account possible effects from domestic stimuli, such as a reduction in unemployment. There therefore seems to be an important lesson for policy makers in interpreting the modeling results from trade assessments.

19.5   Conclusions

The results from the E3ME-Asia model suggest that phasing out import tariffs will lead to slightly higher rates of economic growth in East Asia. This finding matches that from the CGE model in Chapter 18, although – as described in the previous section – there are important differences in approach and the expected magnitude of impacts.

Whereas an increase in GDP supports the trade negotiations, both models find that higher trade comes at the expense of a small increase in CO_2 emissions. This apparent trade-off brings us back to one of the key issues of this book: how to support economic development in East Asia while simultaneously reducing greenhouse gas emissions.

The modeling results in this chapter point tentatively to one possible policy. Reducing import tariffs on fossil fuels will lead to higher emissions, but this could be countered, at least partially, by reducing tariffs on renewable-energy and energy-efficient equipment. Unfortunately, as we saw in 2012 with responses to the alleged subsidies provided to solar panel production in China, this may be easier said than done. However, at the time of publication of this book, there were ongoing negotiations within the WTO on a trade deal on environmental goods and services.

Linking these findings back to earlier chapters, we can see some important policy interactions. A reduction in the barriers to trade may boost economic growth, but it also increases the exposure of national industries to international competition (see Chapter 13), which could make the introduction of environmental tax reform politically infeasible.

There are, however, some possible policy responses that may mitigate the negative outcomes from the policies. If trade barriers are removed selectively, the environmental outcomes could be more favorable. For example, technological cooperation between trading partners could support local production by favoring efficiency measures that help firms to compete. An example of this kind of support is that which has been provided to automobile producers, since the Economic Partnership Agreement between Japan and Malaysia was signed.

However one of the following two policy outcomes will probably be required in the longer term:

- A harmonization of carbon taxes across the East Asian countries and, preferably, other countries.
- The introduction of border tax adjustments, as described in Chapter 14.

The main conclusion of this chapter is, thus, that there are small potential economic benefits from reducing the barriers to trade. However, in order to mitigate the possible environmental consequences, reductions in trade barriers must be viewed in the wider policy context.

Notes

1 http://www.wto.org/english/tratop_e/envir_e/climate_impact_e.htm.
2 This has not been presented due to the number of dimensions involved and the amount of space required.

References

Armington, P. (1969). 'A theory of demand for products distinguished by place of production.' *IMF Staff Papers*, XVI, pp. 159–178.

Barker, T. S. (1977). 'International trade and economic growth: an alternative to the neoclassical approach.' *Cambridge Journal of Economics*, 1(2), pp. 153–172.

Barker, T. S., and Peterson, A.W.A. (1987). *The Cambridge Multisectoral Dynamic Model of the British Economy*. Cambridge: Cambridge University Press.

Cambridge Econometrics (2014). *E3ME Manual, Version 6.0.* http://www.e3me.com (accessed May 17, 2015).

Kirkpatrick, C., Raihan, S., Bleser, A., Prudhomme, D., Mayrand, K., Morin, J. F., Pollitt, H., Hinojosa, L., and Williams, M. (2011). *Trade Sustainability Impact Assessment (SIA) on the Comprehensive Economic and Trade Agreement (CETA) between the EU and Canada: Final Report*. http://trade.ec.europa.eu/doclib/docs/2011/march/tradoc_147755.pdf (accessed May 17, 2015).

McDaniel, C. A., and Balistreri, E. J. (2003). 'A review of Armington trade substitution elasticities.' *Integration and Trade*, 7(18), pp. 161–173.

Ragot, L. (1994). 'Le commerce extérieur dans MEGEVE. Rapport d'etape 1: les séries disponibles dans CRONOS Sec 2.' ERASME.

Conclusions from the analysis

The goal of this book is to improve public understanding of the policy challenges that must be overcome in order to realize a sustainable, low-carbon society throughout the East Asian region. Our analysis has focused on China, Japan, Korea, and Taiwan, and covered three key research topics, which form the three parts of this book:

- How should East Asia choose its energy and power sources?
- How could East Asia design energy/carbon taxes or other carbon-pricing instruments?
- How should East Asia choose and coordinate low-carbon policies in the tide of free trade?

In addressing these questions we employed a combination of modeling techniques, including input–output analysis, the new E3ME-Asia macro-econometric model, and CGE modeling. The models were used to conduct quantitative analyses of selected policy scenarios so as to obtain objective and scientific answers for the three questions above. Based on our findings, we summarize the results from the perspective of policy makers and researchers in East Asia.

How should we choose our energy and power sources?

In Part 1, we conducted several model analyses to assess how regulations on the energy sector affect the choice of power sources, the economy, and the environment in East Asia. We considered restrictions on the share of nuclear power plants, restrictions on the share of coal combustion power plants, and simultaneous restrictions on the share of nuclear power plants and coal combustion power plants. We demonstrated that, by only restricting nuclear power, CO_2 emissions might see a large rise as cheap coal-fired energy generation is increased. However, restricting the use of coal (either with or without a restriction on nuclear power) could substantially reduce CO_2 emissions. The message is quite clear: if East Asia is to reduce the generation of nuclear power while also reducing CO_2 emissions, policies on both nuclear and coal power are required.

The macroeconomic impacts of the assessed 'energy shifts' were found to be only slightly negative or, in some cases, positive in the long run. Favorable results were observed under scenarios with international policy coordination. The conclusion from the analysis is that concerns regarding economic performance, at least at macro level, need not stand in the way of reforms to the energy sector.

Finally, in the first part of the book we considered the often neglected role of energy efficiency. Although East Asian countries are actively implementing energy-efficiency measures, additional low-cost options remain available (e.g., insulation of buildings, energy-efficient appliances, fuel-efficient vehicles) in order to reduce energy consumption and CO_2 emissions. Our analysis shows that these measures can have economic benefits, but the challenge is for policy makers to ensure that they are implemented.

How should we design our energy/carbon taxes?

As noted in the introduction, countries in East Asia have already implemented a variety of 'market-based instruments' to reduce CO_2 emissions, but these instruments are either partial in coverage or set with rates that are too low to have significant impact. In Part 2 of the book, we proposed several forms of environmental tax reform (ETR) that could allow East Asian countries (and East Asia as a whole) to meet their respective emission reduction targets.

We found that environmental tax reform, which has been successfully practiced in some European countries, could be effective also in East Asia. Results from the E3ME-Asia model showed that a strong 'double dividend' (reducing CO_2 emissions while at the same time increasing a country's GDP) is possible if the revenues from carbon taxes are used to offset other taxes. Although many similar analyses using CGE models failed to show a strong double dividend, the economic cost of ETRs was found to be very small overall. We explained how key features of models, in particular those relating to assumptions about optimization, affect the outcome of simulations, showing a real prospect for double dividends from some revenue-recycling methods when spare economic capacity is available.

We also considered some designs of ETR that have not previously been assessed, either in East Asia or elsewhere. Using the E3ME-Asia model, we analyzed scenarios in which the revenues from carbon taxes were used to fund investment in human capital (education and training), or were transferred to low-income households through raising social benefits. Both approaches potentially address the perceived and real problem of regressive energy taxation. Our results show that it is possible to design ETRs that increase labor productivity and/or reduce income inequality, while at the same time showing favorable outcomes for the main macroeconomic indicators.

We also analyzed another approach of implementing carbon taxes in East Asia. We have seen that, in Japan, increases in the consumption tax were highly controversial, and a carbon tax could provide an alternative tool for raising revenues to cover the public debt. As they develop further, other East Asian countries may also look for new revenue-raising instruments to fund increased social protection. Our analysis with the E3ME-Asia model showed that, across the East Asian region, carbon taxes offer a favorable way of raising these revenues, typically costing less in terms of GDP and employment than the alternative options.

Most researchers now accept that a carbon price is a necessary (if not sufficient) requirement to meet targets for decarbonization. We have found that ETR would be effective in East Asia, and could contribute to realizing a sustainable low-carbon economy.

How should we choose and coordinate low-carbon policies in the tide of free trade?

In Part 3, we studied the relationship between free trade and a sustainable low-carbon economy. In recent decades, free trade has been a strong driver of growth in East Asia, and it is expected that the East Asian economies will continue to become more mutually interdependent, for example because of the trend toward elimination of tariffs (c.f. TPP, China-Korea FTA, China-Japan-Korea FTA, etc.).

We assessed quantitatively the macroeconomic and environmental effects of various free trade agreements (eliminating tariffs) between the East Asian countries by using the E3ME-Asia and GTAP-E models. The results of the two models show that free trade can modestly improve the macroeconomic situation (GDP and employment), but higher production levels will also lead to higher CO_2 emissions.

These models, however, do not fully account for transport emissions. In a separate analysis, we found that emissions from maritime transportation have reached a non-negligible level and are likely to continue growing in line with international trade.

Furthermore, as free trade opens up domestic economies to greater levels of competition, higher trade volumes might make it more difficult to enact future environmental policy due to stronger competitiveness effects and risks of 'carbon leakage.' So overall, we see the clear message that deepening trade relationships could inhibit the development of a sustainable low-carbon economy in East Asia unless further environmental protection measures are implemented.

Fortunately, the tools to address this issue are available. For example, if the trade deals allow for the transfer of low-carbon technology (e.g., from Japan and Korea to China), then it could be possible to have higher production levels and lower emission levels at the same time. The FTT:Power model, in tandem with the E3ME-Asia model, showed that this could be possible in the power sector.

Transport emissions could be addressed through regional cooperation agreements, but in Part 2 of the book we also assessed one possible measure that could enable a single country to implement low-carbon policies without facing a high risk of carbon leakage. Our modeling results for border tax adjustments showed that they could offer protection to the most energy-intensive sectors, enhancing the possible benefits of ETR.

On a related issue, deepening trade relationships are also now pressing for a new understanding of the national responsibility of CO_2 emissions, which is an important concept in the context of the ongoing international negotiations. Two chapters of this book gave us an entirely different view on how to account for regional CO_2 emissions by shifting the 'responsibility' of emissions from the producing to the consuming countries. The continuing growth of international trade in the region is likely to make this distinction, which already accounts for 15 percent of China's emissions, increasingly important in the future.

Overall conclusions

From the many results and discussions in this book, we see three broad policy conclusions emerging on how to bring about the transition to a low-carbon economy:

1   The implementation of a sustainable mix of energy and power sources based on restriction of nuclear power and fossil fuels, with a range of support measures for renewables and energy efficiency.
2   The promotion of carbon taxation with the revenues used to either reduce existing taxes or to improve education or social welfare.
3   The development of a low-carbon partnership in East Asia that will enable policy coordination in climate and energy issues.

The results of our model simulations show that it will take time to achieve a sustainable low-carbon economy. The transition requires a fundamental trans-formation of the energy system and substantial institutional reforms. Thus, it is crucial to build a consensus that is based on easily understandable academic evidence, and which shows the challenges and the opportunities that will arise from the necessary changes. Understanding the modeling approaches that are used to demonstrate the costs and benefits of climate policy is a critical part of this process, and we have attempted to explain some of the key assumptions that are used in the models.

But there is a much wider role for providing information to policy makers, to researchers, and to the public at large. How well are the risks associated with nuclear power understood? What are the limits of the fossil-fuel-based economy? What are the costs and benefits of implementing environmental tax reform? In all three examples, it can be guaranteed that there will be powerful interest groups presenting their own case for future policy, so there is a clear role for academic and political leadership that is not influenced by interest groups or by short-term economic situations, and that can play a leading role in producing and disseminating this knowledge.

Finally, we must always acknowledge that our analysis has its own challenges and limitations. The world of macroeconomic modeling is constrained by the data available, a fact that has restricted us to analyzing four countries in East Asia at most, sometimes fewer. China has been treated as a single region, rather than a set of provinces. There remain many topics, such as agricultural emissions or other environmental indicators (e.g., water and exhaustible resource consumption, transboundary pollutants and dematerialization) that we have not touched on. There will always be new challenges, there will always be more policy ideas, and we will continue to grapple with them.

On the behalf of authors of this book
September 2015
Hector Pollitt, Soocheol Lee, Park Seung-Joon,
and Tae-Yeoun Lee

Index